AN ACCOUNT
OF THE
INTERIOR OF CEYLON

AN ACCOUNT
OF THE
INTERIOR OF CEYLON

AND OF

ITS INHABITANTS

WITH

TRAVELS IN THAT ISLAND

JOHN DAVY

ISBN : 978-93-5324-587-0 (HB)

First Published, 1821

Published, 2020

Published by

Facsimile Publisher
12 Pragati Market
Ashok Vihar, Ph-2
Delhi-110052
E-mail: books@facsimilepublisher.com

Printed at: G. Print Process, Delhi.

An Account of the Interior of Ceylon

Author: John Davy

AN ACCOUNT

OF THE

INTERIOR OF CEYLON,

AND OF

ITS INHABITANTS.

WITH

TRAVELS IN THAT ISLAND.

BY

JOHN DAVY, M.D. F.R.S.

LONDON:

PRINTED FOR LONGMAN, HURST, REES, ORME, AND BROWN,

PATERNOSTER-ROW.

1821.

TO

GENERAL

SIR ROBERT BROWNRIGG, BART. G.C.B.

&c. &c. &c.

THE FIRST GOVERNOR OF THE WHOLE ISLAND OF CEYLON;

THIS WORK

ON THE KANDYAN PROVINCES,

WHICH HE RESCUED FROM OPPRESSION, AND,

WITH THE CONSENT OF THE PEOPLE,

MADE AN INTEGRAL PART OF THE BRITISH DOMINIONS,

IS DEDICATED,

WITH GREAT RESPECT,

BY HIS OBLIGED

AND OBEDIENT HUMBLE SERVANT,

THE AUTHOR.

PREFACE.

This work is formed from original materials, which I collected in Ceylon, during a residence on that station, on the Medical Staff of the Army, from August, 1816, to February, 1820.

The substance of the three first chapters, on the physical state of the Island in general, and on some particular branches of natural history, is the result of my own enquiries, enriched by the contributions of some medical friends.

The information contained in the fourth, fifth, and sixth chapters, on the Political Condition of the Interior, and on its Old Form of Government, was obtained from native sources; principally from Kandyan chiefs high in office, and conversant with business, and who were constantly in attendance at the court of the dethroned monarch.

The account of the Religion of the Singalese, and of the Boodhaical System, which forms the seventh chapter, was collected chiefly in Kandy, in conversations held with the most enlightened and learned of the priests, and after a good deal of laborious enquiry to ascertain the truth and avoid error, on a subject particularly liable to misconception.

The information contained in the eighth chapter, on the Literature and Arts of the Singalese, was also drawn from the fountainhead: what relates to the former, from the most intelligent natives; and what to the latter, from the artists themselves, and the inspection of their operations.

In writing the ninth chapter, on the Domestic Manners and Habits, and the Character of the Natives, I strived to lay aside prejudice, turn a deaf ear to idle stories, and do justice to a race hitherto under-rated, perhaps, and certainly often calumniated; bearing in mind what a great philosopher said of his brethren and their doctrines,—"Non ex singulis vocibus spectandi sunt, sed ex perpetuitate atque constantiâ."

The historical sketch which forms the Tenth chapter, and concludes the First Part of the work, was drawn up chiefly from information which I was so fortunate as to extract from the late Dissave of Welassey, Malawa, an old man of shrewd intellect, a poet, historian, and astrologer, and generally allowed by his countrymen to be the most able and learned of all the Kandyan chiefs. Part of the information which he communicated was given from a very retentive memory, and part was drawn from an old chronicle, or rather historical romance of Ceylon, which he had by him, and to which he referred when his memory failed him. As this chief's interest was closely connected with that of the late King, of whom he was a favourite, and in several instances the agent of his nefarious designs, the particulars given of this monstrous reign, were collected in general from more unbiassed authorities.

The other parts of this work, from their nature, do not require to be noticed very particularly in a preface. It is sufficient to mention, that the narrative of Travels, which constitutes the Second Part, is introduced with the design of illustrating the preceding topics, and for the purpose of describing the scenery of the country; and that the medical sketch relative to the climate and its diseases, and the preservation of health, which concludes the work, is not offered to the professional so much as to the general reader.

It is with great pleasure that I avail myself of this opportunity to express my grateful acknowledgments to Governor General Sir Robert Brownrigg, and to Lady Brownrigg, for many favours conferred on me during my residence in Ceylon. I have to return thanks in particular for the kind manner in which the Governor encouraged and promoted my pursuits, afforded me every facility of obtaining information, and allowed me the use of many curious documents. To him I am indebted for the views of the palace in Kandy, and of the scenery of Ouva, from the pencils of Lieuts. Lyttleton and Auber; and also for the materials from which, with a little alteration, the new map attached to this work has been formed, and which, without hesitation, may be pronounced the best that has ever yet appeared of Ceylon.

My thanks are due to many other individuals with whom it was my good fortune to come in contact in Ceylon; and, more especially, to my friends, Dr. Farrell, Deputy Inspector of Hospitals, and Lieut. Colonel Hardy, Deputy Quartermaster General, for the aid and information which, on every occasion, each most willingly gave in his respective department.

I should be ungrateful were I to conceal the obligations I am under to my friend, Mr. De Saram, (the second Maha Modeliar,) a native of a cultivated and enlightened mind, equally conversant with English and Singalese, and perfectly qualified to act as an interpreter on any subject of enquiry, — an office in which at all times, he kindly volunteered, and gave me his assistance merely from the desire of obliging and being useful.

To conclude this preface, I beg leave to remark, that the only book that has preceded this, expressly on the same subject, and written from personal knowledge, is "The History of Ceylon," by Captain Robert Knox, published a hundred and forty years ago, which I have read with great pleasure, though I am not aware that I have borrowed from it. Knox's history has ever been popular, and must be so always, from its simplicity of style and narrative, and the good sense and good feelings of the author; and, it may still be consulted with advantage for information on ordinary matters, that came within the sphere of his own observation.

PART I.

AN ACCOUNT OF THE INTERIOR OF CEYLON, AND OF ITS INHABITANTS.

CHAPTER I.

NAME. — GEOGRAPHICAL OUTLINE. — ROCKS. — MINERALS. — SOILS. — SPRINGS.

Few subjects are more obscure than the names of countries and of people; and, for the obvious reason that they are generally given in remote times and in barbarous ages, before the period of authentic history has commenced or even its dawn appeared. I do not offer this remark prefatory to any disquisition relative to the name of the island of which I am about to write, but rather as a reason for not engaging in it. I may merely mention, that the name 'Ceylon,' familiar to us, but unknown in the languages of the East, is derived, probably, from *Sinhala,* the ancient appellation, for which *Lakka* and in Pali *Lanka,* is now substituted by the natives and commonly used.

As this work is expressly on the Interior of Ceylon, the geographical notices of the island in general, may be very concise. It is only necessary to remind the reader, that the island is in the tropic of Cancer, situated nearly between the parallel of 6°

and 10° north latitude, and between 80° and 82° east longitude; that it is at the western entrance of the bay of Bengal, and off the coast of Coromandel, from which its nearest point is separated by the gulf of Manar, only about thirty miles wide; that in figure, it is nearly heart-shaped, with the island of Jaffnapatam, of a very irregular form, appended to its northern and narrowest extremity; that it is almost two-thirds the size of Ireland, containing altogether a surface of about twenty thousand seven hundred and seventy square miles; and lastly, that the coast of the island in general, including the whole of our old possessions, the maritime provinces, are, with the exception chiefly of parts of the broad southern extremity, low and almost flat country.

The Interior of Ceylon, the old kingdom of Kandy, now called the Kandyan provinces, require more minute description. They extend from about latitude 6° 20′ to 8° 45′ north, and lie between about 80° 8′ and 81° 45′ east longitude. As an approximation, their superficial contents may be stated at twelve thousand three hundred and sixty square miles. They occupy the whole middle of the island, and a great portion of its southern extremity; and are bounded by a belt of maritime district, irregularly varying in width, from eight to thirty miles, and at the northern extremity amounting nearly to eighty miles.

The character of the Interior, in relation to surface, greatly varies. Nowhere is the distinction of high land and low land more obvious. With tolerable precision, it may be divided into flat country, hilly, and mountainous. The mountainous division is skirted by the hilly; and, the latter is generally bounded by flat country. Dividing the island into two equal parts, by an imaginary line across, from west to east, the mountainous region will occupy the middle of the southern half. The centre of this region is about 7° north and 80° 46′ east. Its greatest length is about sixty-seven miles, and its greatest width, about fifty-three. It is not easy to describe with accuracy the boundaries and extent of the hilly division. Perhaps, on an average, it extends beyond the mountains to the distance of ten or twenty miles. The flat country forms the circumference of the Kandyan provinces, with the exception of a small portion of the western boundary, which is hilly. The greatest extent of this country is to the north and north-east of the mountains; in the former direction, it reaches at least sixty miles.

The features of each of the three divisions of the Interior are necessarily peculiar: grandeur is the characteristic of the mountainous, — beauty of the hilly, and sameness of the lowland country, which, a covering of luxuriant vegetation, with few exceptions spread over the whole, does not tend to diminish.

The mountainous district, in perpendicular elevation above the sea, varies from eight hundred to three thousand and even to four and five thousand feet. In general, it does not exceed one or two thousand feet. The regions of greater elevation are in extent very inconsiderable. The most extensive I am acquainted with reaching four thousand feet, is that portion of country which lies between Maturatta and Fort M'Donald, the very heart and centre of the mountainous division; and it does not exceed twelve miles in length, nor is it more, perhaps, than two or three miles wide. The only region, deserving the name, amounting to five thousand feet, is that tract of wild country called the Neura Ellya, not far distant from the preceding, and the circumference of which can hardly exceed fifteen or twenty miles. It may be right to state distinctly, that the summits of mountains are not here alluded to, but mountainous regions, or masses of continuous surface, approaching, more or less, to table-land. Many of the mountain-summits are elevated considerably above any of the heights assigned. Adam's Peak, the *Samennella* of the Singalese, the most lofty mountain of Ceylon, is about six thousand one hundred and fifty-two feet perpendicular height; and, Namana Cooli Kandy, which, there is reason to infer, is the next loftiest, is about five thousand five hundred and forty-eight feet high.*

In few countries do mountains exhibit greater variety of forms and directions. They most frequently occur connected in chains and terminating in rounded or peaked summits. I do not recollect a single instance of a solitary, insulated mountain. Their sides are always steep, and occasionally precipitous and rocky. In some parts, the chains of mountains observe a parallelism in their course; in other parts, even neighbouring mountains do not correspond with any regularity in their direction. An instance of the former, occurs in the province of Doombera, where the mountain-ridges generally run N. N. E. and S. S. W. The provinces of Ouva affords an example of the latter, of the very various directions of the mountain-chains. By some inquirers it is supposed, that a correspondence may be traced between the proportional heights of the mountains and the depths of the adjoining valleys. As a general rule, such a supposition is not applicable to Ceylon. The curious circumstance of there being no lakes, not even a single stagnant pool among the mountains, is alone almost sufficient to show the fallacy of the preceding conclu-

* The data, from which these heights are assigned, will be given in an after-part of the work.

sion. In the Highlands of Scotland, where the loftiest mountain is two thousand feet lower than Adam's Peak, there are many lakes exceeding in depth six hundred feet; and, it is hardly credible to suppose, that lakes of proportional depth ever existed in Ceylon, that have since been filled up by the detritus of rocks, little, if at all, more liable to decay and be disintegrated than the rocks of the mountains of Scotland.

Since there are no lakes in the interior, it is unnecessary to add, that every valley has an outlet; and, that the descent of every valley is gradual, though irregular, from the mountain to the plain. The forms and directions of the valleys are not less various than those of the mountains by which they are constituted. In general, their width is a very small proportion of their length; often, they are extremely narrow. The deepest valleys are in the heart of the mountains. In relation to depth, I am not acquainted with any valley that exceeds that of Maturatta. This valley, in many parts, is between three and four thousand feet deep, and from one boundary-mountain to the other, not, perhaps, half a mile wide.

The hilly division of the interior, in elevation above the sea, may vary from one to five hundred feet; and the hills themselves may vary in perpendicular height from two hundred to one thousand feet. The hills, like the mountains, are, more or less, connected in chains, generally of little length. Their outlines are rounded and gentle; their sides seldom steep, and their appearance comparatively tame. In the valleys formed by the hills, there is nothing peculiar that requires notice.

The level division of the Interior may vary in elevation, from fifty to two hundred feet. It exhibits extensive plains, either quite level to the eye, or very gently undulating; in some districts, entirely without hill; in others, interrupted by chains of low hills; and in some places dotted, as it were, with solitary hills from one hundred to five hundred feet high above the plain, and these in general are immense masses of rock.

These geographical notices of the Interior have not that precision which the subject requires, but of which, at present, it does not admit. Till very lately, the Kandyan provinces have been almost a *terra incognita.* It is only since we have had possession of the country that it has been in our power to investigate its geography. And though much has been done in this important enquiry during the last three years, still much remains to be done, to afford materials either for minute description, or for the formation of a perfectly accurate map. In a cursory manner the subject will be resumed in the progress of this work, and particularly in the narrative of travels, one of the principal objects of which will be the description of country, and the illustration of scenery.

The geology and mineralogy of Ceylon have not yet received that degree of attention which their importance deserves. The statements that have been made on these subjects by former authors, have been far from correct, and often very delusive, — tending to inspire hopes of subterranean riches never to be realised, and to encourage enterprises in which it would be madness to engage. As these remarks relate to the maritime as well as the Kandyan provinces, no apology is required for giving a sketch of the geology and mineralogy of the island in general. It may be premised, that a summary of part of the information I have to offer has been already presented to the Geological Society of London, and has been honoured with a place in their Transactions. Since that brief account was written, I have enjoyed opportunities for more extended observation, in consequence of which, much will appear in the following sketch, of which no notice is to be found in that paper.

In Ceylon, nothing is to be observed of that order and succession of rocks that occurs in Saxony and in England and in many other parts of Europe. Uniformity of formation is the most remarkable feature in the geological character of the island. As far as my information extends, the whole of Ceylon, with very few exceptions, consists of primitive rock. And the exceptions exist so very partially, presenting themselves only at Jaffnapatam and the contiguous islets, and here and there along the shores about high-water mark, that they need not interfere with the comprehensive idea, that the mass of the island is primitive, and unconnected with any other class of rocks, exclusive of those of very recent formation, to which the exceptions alluded to belong.

Another remarkable geological circumstance is, that though the varieties of primitive rock are extremely numerous and indeed almost infinite, the species are very few, and seldom well defined. The most prevailing species is granite, or gneiss; the more limited are quartz-rock, hornblende-rock and dolomite-rock, and a few others, which may be considered, perhaps, with advantage under the head of imbedded minerals.

The varieties of granite and gneiss are innumerable, passing often from one into another, and occasionally changing their character altogether, and assuming appearances, for which, in small masses, it would be extremely difficult to find appropriate names. These changes and endless varieties depend chiefly on composition, — on the proportions of the elements, — on the excess or deficiency of one or more, — or on the addition of new ingredients, — not to mention mechanical structure, variation of which, though obscure in relation to causes, has a manifest effect in modifying appearances. Regular granite is not of very common occurrence. One of the best instances I know of it, is in the neighbourhood of Point de Galle, where it is of a grey colour and fine-grained. Graphic granite is still rarer. The only good example of it, with which I am acquainted, is at Trincomalee, where it occurs of a beautiful quality, on the sea-shore about half a mile beyond Chapel Point, imbedded in a granitic rock. The quartz, in this instance, is black or grey rock crystal, and the felspar highly crystalline and of a bright flesh colour. The quartz envelopes the felspar in very thin hexagonal or triagonal cases, so that nothing can be more different in appearance than the longitudinal and transverse fracture of the rock. Neither is sienite common. I have found it in several places in the neighbourhood of Atgalle and Meddamahaneura and in some other parts of the Kandyan provinces. It occurs, rather forming a part of rocks of a different kind, than in great mountain masses. Well formed gneiss is more abundant than granite. Its peculiar structure may be seen in many places, but no where more beautiful than at Amanapoora in the Kandyan provinces, where it consists of white felspar and quartz in a finely crystalline state, with layers of black mica, containing disseminated through it, numerous crystals of a light coloured garnet.

Both the granite and gneiss are very much modified, it has been remarked, by an excess or deficiency of one or other of the ingredients. When quartz abounds in a fine-granular state, the rock often looks very like sandstone: of this there is an instance in the neighbourhood of Kandy. When felspar, or adularia abound, the rock acquires a new external character. This variety is common. In a few places the rock contains so much of these minerals, that it may with propriety be called adularia or felspar-rock. When mica prevails in gneiss, which in Ceylon is very rare, it acquires not only the appearance but very much the structure of mica-slate: I had an instance of this in a very wild and unfrequented part of the interior, amongst the mountains of Kotmale at the ford of the Poondool oya. The instances of change of appearance of the granitic varieties from the presence of unusual ingredients, are neither few in number, or of unusual occcurrence. The discussion of them may be engaged in, in the mineralogical part of the work.

The more limited varieties of primitive rock, as quartz, hornblende, and dolomite rock, seldom occur in the form of mountain masses.

Quartz in large veins and imbedded masses is abundant in the granitic rocks; and in some places to such an extent as even to rival mountain masses: Of this description is the quartz-rock at Trincomalie, where a low hill is entirely composed of it, extending from Chapel Point to the opposite point on which Fort Osthenburgh is built; a distance, perhaps, of two miles. This quartz-rock near the sea has a very singular and picturesque aspect. Quite bare, it stands erect like denuded veins. It is very precipitous, and exhibits the appearance of buildings in ruins; a circumstance from whence the name of Chapel Point is derived, which is applied to the termination of the ridge in question. The quartz is in general milk white, translucent, full of rents, and so very friable as to remind one of unannealed glass. Besides Trincomalee, other places might be mentioned, especially in the interior, in which this rock occurs in considerable quantities.

Pure hornblende-rock and primitive greenstone are far from uncommon. They constitute no entire mountain, or hill, that I am aware of; but they form a part of many, particularly of Adam's Peak and of the hills and mountains adjoining Kandy.

Dolomite-rock, I believe, is entirely confined to the interior, where it exists in very many places in veins and imbedded; and where it occasionally appears constituting low hills. In the first form, its localities are so numerous that it would be tedious to enumerate them: I may merely mention, that it is very abundant in the neighbourhood of Kandy and Badulla, and that it occurs in many parts of the districts of Doombera, Matele, Saffragam, and Ouva. Constituting hills, it is of rare occurrence; indeed, I am not aware that any hills of this rock exist, excepting in the lower parts of Matele, and near Hangranketty. The old military post of Nalandi in Matele was situated on a hill of this kind; and judging from the forms of many of the hills of this district, I suspect they are of the same nature; but I could not, when travelling, ascertain the fact, — that part of the country being uninhabited, — very generally covered with thick wood, — the hills not very near the road and of very difficult access, (if accessible,) and my time limited. The varieties of dolomite-rock are almost as numerous as those of granite. When purest, it is snow-white; generally crystalline; often highly crystalline, composed of rhombs that are easily separated by a smart blow, but rarely finely granular. I found a specimen of the highly crystalline kind, of sp. grav. 1.93, composed of

56.0	carbonat of magnesia
36.9	carbonat of lime
4.1	alumina
1.0	silica
2.0	water
100.0	

A very fine granular kind, of a beautiful whiteness, well adapted for statuary purposes, is found in the neighbourhood of Fort Macdonald. A specimen of it, that I tried, was of sp. gr. 2.74, and contained only a very small proportion of carbonat of magnesia. A proof of its being uncommon is, that before we had possession of the country, it was appropriated entirely to the king's use, and no native could venture to employ it. The great variety of this rock arises both from the proportions of carbonat of lime and of magnesia, being seldom the same, and from the admixture of various minerals. The varieties of most importance are mixtures of dolomite with felspar and mica, and even quartz. It is in rocks of this kind that the nitre caves of the interior are found, which will be described hereafter. It is from the purer kinds of dolomite rock that all the lime, employed in building in the interior, is procured. The presence of magnesia injures its quality as a cement; but though inferior, in this respect, to the lime from shell and coral, it answers sufficiently well for ordinary purposes.

In external character and general structure, the varieties of primitive rock exhibit fewer marked differences than might be expected, *à priori*. The masses, that are exposed, are generally rounded, seldom rising to craggy points, or showing any grotesque shapes. The nature of the rock, from its external appearance, may often be conjectured; but in most instances it can be determined with precision, only by an examination of a freshly fractured surface. In structure, the granitic varieties most commonly exhibit an appearance of stratification. It is not easy to decide with certainty whether this appearance is to be attributed to the mass being composed of strata, or of large laminæ or layers. I must confess I am more disposed to adopt the latter notion. I have found some great masses of rock decidedly of this structure;—masses almost insulated, quite bare, several hundred feet high, in which the same layer might be observed spreading over the rock, like the coat of an onion;—and which, if only partially exposed, might be considered a strong instance of stratification;—and, if examined in different places, on the top and at each side, might be considered an extraordinary instance of the dip of the strata in opposite directions. With this hypothesis of the structure of the rocks, the appearance of stratification in all the granitic varieties may be easily reconciled. I am aware that the question of the stratification of granite is a mysterious one: I can bring forward nothing new and satisfactory to elucidate the subject; and I am not willing to engage in useless casuistry.

The recent formation, both as a partial exception to the comprehensive idea that the whole island is composed of primitive rock, and on account of its own interesting nature, is highly deserving of investigation. The rock, that occurs in this formation, is of two kinds, limestone and sandstone.

The limestone, to the best of my knowledge, is confined to the province of Jaffnapatam, the most northern, the most productive and the most populous district of Ceylon. I have not visited it myself; for the specimens of its rocks, which I have examined, and for the little local information respecting it, that I have obtained, I am indebted to my intelligent friend Mr. Finlayson. This limestone contains numerous shells; it is generally grey or light-brown, very fine-grained and compact, and breaks with a conchoidal fracture. The specimens I have tried, have been very nearly pure carbonat of lime, exhibiting slight traces of the presence of vegetable or animal matter, and containing a little water. It is not confined to the island of Jaffnapatam; it occurs in the district on the mainland, and has been observed by Mr. Finlayson as far as Palwerayenkatte, where he found it with coral rock, in a salt-water lake, at a little distance from the sea, with which the lake communicates in the rainy season. Where it occurs, the whole of the country is similar; level, without hills or even hillocks, and elevated a very few feet only above the surface of the sea, by which, at no very remote period, there is good reason to suppose, it was once covered. The retiring of the sea from this district does not admit of a doubt. It is evident within the memory of man; many individuals recollect the waves breaking where their spray now seldom reaches: Nor is it less evident, perhaps, from the nature of the land as described, and from the circumstance of coral rock being found mixed with the limestone rock several miles from the sea. It is always more easy to observe the phenomena of nature, than to point out their causes, especially in geological changes, such as the present, which are not watched in the act, and are noticed only when completely accomplished. Minute enquiry on the spot, it is very likely, might afford a clue to an explanation of the formation of this rock, which, in all probability, is still going on in the shallows of the adjoining seas, and along the shores of Jaffnapatam. Its formation, it may be conjectured, may be connected with coral which abounds greatly in the narrow sea, between Ceylon and the continent of India, to such an extent, indeed, that most, if not all the islets in that sea, are composed of it. The difficulty is to find the cause of the solution of calcareous matter in some places, and its precipitation in others adjoining. Perhaps, in the deeper, cooler water it is dissolved, and in the warmer, shallow water it is precipitated. The solution is aided, perhaps, by the presence of a little carbonic acid, and the precipitation is assisted or produced by the escape of the acid gas. This is mere conjecture, but of that kind that it admits of being tried by the test of experiment.

Sandstone, the other rock belonging to the recent formation, is of pretty general occurrence along the shore of the island. I have seen it, in several different places between Negombo and Tangalle; I have had specimens of it from Batticaloa, and have learnt from authority to be confided in, that it appears, and not unfrequently, between Negombo and Jaffnapatam; and Mr. Orr, between Batticalo and Tangalle, met with "a ledge of freestone, lying in a horizontal stratum*," that may be justly admitted to be the rock in question. Thus, the whole island may be considered, as surrounded by an interrupted chain of this rock. Wherever I have seen it, or have heard of it, it has exhibited the same general character, and has presented itself under the same circumstances, viz. in horizontal beds along the shore, chiefly between high and low water mark, which in Ceylon, where the tides rise only about three feet in perpendicular height, is a very limited extent. In shallow water, it may extend, perhaps, further in the sea. Towards the land, I have never known it ex-

* Cordiner, ii. 125.

tend beyond the beach. The most remarkable and striking instance of this rock, that I am acquainted with, is between Colombo and Negombo, which, as an example, may be described. It commences about three quarters of a mile on the Negombo side of the mouth of the Calany river, and extends along the beach, two or three miles, indeed as far as the eye can reach, and perhaps, further. In width, the bed varies from a few feet to fifty, or even a hundred feet. Towards the sea, it presents a bold face, about twelve feet deep, perpendicular like a wall, over which the waves break, and which, when the sea runs high, as it does on this shore a great part of the year, is completely under water. On the other side, towards the land, the rock commonly terminates in sand, the beach generally rising above it. This bed, in most places, is distinctly stratified; and where the strata are not deranged by fractures and subsidences, they are quite horizontal. The appearance of the rock, when minutely examined, is not very uniform. Its principal varieties are three in number, viz. a yellowish-grey sandstone, a sandstone almost black, and a sandstone of the former kind, containing nodules of the latter. These varieties occur in the same stratum, and a vertical section often exhibits successive layers of the two first kinds. They all consist of sand, agglutinated by carbonat of lime, which, from its texture, appears to have been deposited from water. According with this assertion, the stone crumbles to pieces and is reduced to sand, when heated before the blow-pipe, or when immersed in an acid. The proportion of carbonat of lime is variable, from 26.5, to 11 per cent. The larger the proportion, the harder is the sandstone: thus, that which contained only 11 per cent. was soft; it was taken from a depth, and appeared to be in the incipient stage of its formation: Whilst that containing 26.5 per cent. taken from the surface and completely formed, was extremely hard. Independent of the proportion of carbonat of lime, the sand of which the stone is formed, is of different kinds. The sand of the light coloured variety is chiefly silicious, consisting of fine water-worn particles of quartz, like the sand in general of the shore; and like it, it occasionally contains shells and pebbles. Two specimens of it that I tried, were of sp. gr. 2.62 and 2.64. The sand of the variety nearly black, is a mixture of silicious particles, and of particles of iron glance, becoming magnetic by roasting. A specimen of this kind, which contained 22 per cent. only of carbonat of lime, was of sp. grav. 4.08. It was extremely hard, the iron no doubt acting the part of a cement, as well as the carbonat of lime. The question of the formation of the sandstone is involved in much the same difficulties as that of the limestone of Jaffnapatam; and the same conjectures may be offered respecting the probable cause of the deposition of the calcareous cement. Did this rock, in a completely unbroken, instead of a chain of which a few of the links only are to be seen, surround the island, the conjecture would amount almost to certainty.

This instance of the formation of rock, from the dissolved and disintegrated materials of old rocks, is not peculiar to Ceylon. Examples of it are almost as common as those of decomposition. They give rise to many poetical ideas, and agreeable views of the powers of nature, and of the durability of our globe. But till they are more investigated, and better understood, speculations respecting their bearings and effect cannot be too cautiously indulged in.

Both the limestone and sandstone of this recent formation, may become very useful. Very good lime may be made of the former, and serviceable mill-stones, may, perhaps, be made of the latter, if it can be found, as is very probable, of a coarse quality. For architectural purposes both stones are well adapted, — particularly the sandstone, for great public works, as it may be wrought at little expense, and when the wind blows off the land, may be removed with great facility.

The mineralogy of Ceylon is, in certain respects, singular and curious. The island is remarkable for its richness in gems, and its poverty in the useful metals. It is remarkable too,. for the number of rare minerals that it affords, and for the small variety of the ordinary species: thus, in its mineralogical character, quite oriental, better fitted for show than utility — for pomp than profit.

Its mineral productions may be considered under two heads, namely, those that belong to granitic rock, and those that belong to dolomite rock. Of the former, first, which consitute the majority of the minerals of the island.

The only metallic ores, hitherto found in Ceylon, are of iron and manganese. Iron, in different forms, is pretty generally diffused and tolerably abundant. I have met with the following species, — Iron pyrites, magnetic iron ore, specular iron ore, red hematite, bog-iron ore and earthy blue phosphat of iron. Red hematite and bog-iron ore are more common than the other species. It is from these ores that the natives extract the metal. Under the head of the Arts of the Country, the simple method of reduction employed in the Interior will be described. It will be sufficient to mention the localities of iron pyrites, magnetic iron stone, and the blue phosphat, the other kinds occurring so frequently in granitic rock, or the detritus of this rock, as not to require particular notice. Iron pyrites is rare : it is to be met with at Ratnapoora, in Saffragam, disseminated through a grey felspar rock ; and in veins of quartz, at Mount Lavinia, on the sea-shore.

Magnetic iron ore, I have found in masses, imbedded in gneiss, in the neighbourhood of Kandy, and in a granitic rock at Katabowa in Welassey, and disseminated through a similar rock at Trincomalie. The earthy blue phosphat of iron has been procured from a marshy ground, in the neighbourhood of Colombo, and from a bed of bog-iron ore, near Atgalle, not far from Kandy. It is said to be used by the natives as a pigment. It is worthy of notice, that no great bed, and that no vein of iron ore, has yet been found in Ceylon. I have been asked, could a foundery on an extensive scale, be established in the interior, with a prospect of success? To such a question, the preceding remark is a sufficient reply. To the natives, it may be worth while to collect scattered masses of ore, for their little furnaces; but, unless an extensive bed or vein of ore be found, the attempt to establish a foundery would be idle in the extreme. Only one ore of manganese, viz. grey manganese, or the black oxide, is yet known in Ceylon. I first discovered it, about two years ago, in several parts of Saffragam and of Upper Ouva. Like most of the ores of iron, it occurs finely disseminated, and imbedded in small masses in granitic rock; some specimens of it are pretty pure, and in one or two places, particularly in the Dodanata Kapella Mountain, there would be little difficulty in collecting a considerable quantity of it. Hitherto it has been applied to no useful purpose; one cannot anticipate the time, when the arts will require it in Ceylon, — and it occurs too far inland and too much scattered, to be collected with profit for exportation.

From the nature of the rock, it might be expected, that other metals would be found in Ceylon. It may be remarked, it is not for want of search, that they have not been discovered. Wherever I have been amongst the mountains, I have sought more particularly for tin and copper, but in vain, having never observed the slightest traces of either, or of lead. It has been asserted in some publications, that gold and mercury occur native in Ceylon. The result of the inquiries I have made, satisfy me that the assertion is unfounded, and that neither metal, in any state, has yet been met with in the island. Did any of the common metals, and more especially did either of the precious metals, occur in Ceylon, it would have been well known long ago; for the natives are inquisitive and curious, and being in the habit of searching for gems, and of collecting every thing that glitters, or that is in the least likely to sell, even bits of iron pyrites, and ores of iron, it would be very extraordinary, were they to pass unnoticed, substances more attractive, and with the value of which they are well acquainted.

Most of the gems, for which Ceylon is celebrated, occur, I believe, in granitic rock. I say, *believe*, because these precious stones being seldom found in their native rock, but in alluvial ground and the beds of rivers, it cannot be said with positive certainty, whence they are derived, — their source can only be conjectured from the nature of the surrounding rocks, and the quality of the sand and alluvion in which they are found. The minerals which I have discovered in granitic rock, or, believe to have been contained in this rock, are the following: —

1. Belonging to the quartz-family, may be enumerated quartz, iron-flint, chalcedony and hyalite. Ceylon affords all the varieties of quartz; as rock-crystal, amethyst, rose-quartz, cat's-eye, and prase. Rock-crystal occurs in abundance, both massive and crystallized, of various colours, good quality, and in large masses. Its localities do not require to be noticed. The natives use it instead of glass for the lenses of spectacles; they employ it, too,

for ornamental purposes and in statuary. In the chief Temple in Kandy, there is a small well-executed figure of Boodhoo, in this stone. Amethyst, also, is pretty abundant; very beautiful specimens of this mineral are found in the alluvion, derived from the decomposition of gneiss and granitic rock, in Saffragam and the Seven Korles. I have seen a large crystal of it, lately found near Ruanwelle, containing apparently two distinct drops of water. Rose-quartz, which is pretty common, is often found in the same place as amethyst. Ceylon produces the finest Cat's-eyes in the world, — indeed the only kind that is highly esteemed, and that brings a high price. The best specimens of this singular mineral, that I have seen, have been found in the granitic alluvion of Saffragam and Matura. Prase is a variety of quartz that is of rare occurrence in the island: I have met with it only amongst the pebbles on the shore of Trincomalie. The second species, iron-flint, is not uncommon in the Kandyan country; I have found rolled pieces of it in the bed of the Mahawelle ganga, and I have seen it *in situ*, forming a part of a granitic rock in Saffragam and Lower Ouva. Some varieties of it much resemble hornstone. The third species, chalcedony, there is strong reason to suppose, exists in the mountains of the Interior. During the late rebellion in the Kandyan provinces, in several firelocks that were taken from the natives of Doombera, I saw small fragments of it used as a substitute for iron-flint, which is more commonly employed. The fourth species, hyalite, is extremely rare; I have met with it only in a nitre cave in Doombera, partially encrusting a granitic rock.

2. Belonging to the schorl-family, I am acquainted with two species only that undoubtedly occur in Ceylon, which are topaz and schorl. The topaz commonly passes under the name of the

"white or water sapphire." It is generally white, or bluish or yellowish white; it is commonly much water-worn, and perfect crystals of it are very rare. It occurs in many places in the alluvion of granitic rock. Schorl I have not found in that abundance I expected: common schorl indeed is not uncommon; it is to be seen in many places in the granitic rocks; and in one spot in Lower Ouva, between Passera and Alipoota, mixed with quartz and felspar, it constitutes a rock of considerable magnitude. Tourmaline is rare; the few specimens of it I have seen of the green, honey-yellow and red varieties, were of bad quality, and I could not ascertain their locality. It is the opinion of some writers that both the emerald and beryl are found in Ceylon. The former certainly is not found, and it is even doubtful if the latter is. It is allowed by the dealers, that most of the beryls that they offer for sale, are imported; and it may be suspected, when they maintain a particular specimen has been found in the country, that they merely do it to enhance its value, — stones of the island being in greater estimation than those of the continent, which are contemptuously called "*coast stones.*"

3. Of the garnet-family three species occur in gneiss or granitic rock, viz. the garnet, pyrope, and cinnamon-stone. The common garnet is very abundantly disseminated through gneiss in almost every part of the country; its crystals are in general indistinct, small, contain a large proportion of iron, and are very apt to decompose. The best and most perfect crystals of this mineral that I have met with, have been at Trincomalie in quartz rock. The precious garnet occurs but in few places, and I have not seen it yet of good quality; at Trincomalie it is contained in hornblende-rock. Cinnamon-stone, though an abundant mineral in this island, to which it is confined, is found only in a few

places, and chiefly in the Matura district. The best specimens of it are procured in the neighbourhood of Matura and of Belligam. It occurs in granitic alluvion, in small irregularly shaped pieçes, and in large masses of several pounds weight. Near Belligam, a large detached rock is partly composed of this mineral; the other ingredients of the rock are felspar, tablespar, quartz, hornblende and graphite. The thick jungle round the spot where this interesting rock stands, prevents a minute examination of the neighbouring country; from what I saw, I was led to believe that this rock had been detached from a vein or bed included in gneiss or granitic rock in the hill above. It may be mentioned, that a mineral of a doubtful nature, disseminated in small masses, occurs in many places, as at Colombo, Mount Lavinia, &c. It is semi-transparent, and never crystallized, and has the fracture and lustre of cinnamon-stone: it certainly belongs to the garnet family, and probably is merely a variety of cinnamon-stone, from which it appears to differ chiefly in being of a redder hue, and in this respect approaches pyrope.

4. The zircon-family is richer in Ceylon than in any other part of the world. As far as my knowledge extends, it is confined to the districts of Matura and Saffragam; and, that it is most abundant in the former, seems to be indicated by the popular name, "Matura-diamond," which is applied to its finest varieties by the dealers in gems. Besides the two well-established species, common zircon and hyacinth, I have met with a third, massive, opaque, and uncrystallized, and of a dark brown colour; I have specimens of it weighing two or three ounces, from Saffragam. The natives, it scarcely requires to be observed, are completely ignorant of the true nature of zircon. The yellow varieties are sold by them as a peculiar kind of topaz; the green

as tourmalines; the hyacinth red, as inferior rubies, and the very light grey, as imperfect diamonds. All the varieties that are brought into the market are found in the beds of rivers, or in alluvial ground, which, both in Saffragam and Matura, is of the same kind, and derived from the decomposition of gneiss or granitic rock. The only places, where I have discovered zircon, *in situ*, are a small island in Belligam Bay in the district of Matura, and a few miles from Belligam on the way to Galle. On the former spot, it is sparingly disseminated through a rock consisting chiefly of quartz and schorl; at the latter, it occurs abundantly in a rock composed of quartz and felspar, and containing besides, zircon, tablespar, and graphite. The zircon in some parts of the mass is in so large a proportion as almost to entitle the rock, to be called zircon-rock. The mineral, in this instance, is crystalline, and most commonly green or brown; the rock is remarkable for its heaviness and for the resinous lustre of its fracture.

5. For the ruby-family, Ceylon has been long celebrated. Four species of it, viz. spinell, sapphire, corundum and chrysoberyll, occur, I believe, in gneiss or granitic rock. Spinell is comparatively rare: I have got small and very beautiful crystals of it, which were brought, it was said, from the Interior, and I have found it in specimens of clay-iron ore, from a part of the Kandyan country, where gneiss is the prevailing rock. Sapphire is much more common; it occurs in considerable abundance in the granitic alluvion of Matura and Saffragam, and in the neighbourhood of Avisavelli, and on the Neuraellyia patan. I have often searched for it in the rocks adjoining the places where it is found, but never with success, as indeed might be expected considering how widely it must in general be scattered through the

mass. In the places just mentioned, the principal varieties of sapphire are found in perfection; as the blue, purple, red, yellow, white, and star-stone, and occasionally of great size. I have seen fragments of a blue sapphire, not indeed of good quality, found and broken by an ignorant person, that was as large as a goose's egg. The purple variety, or the oriental amethyst, is rare; I have seen two specimens only of it. A green variety is still rarer; the only green sapphire that I have seen, appeared to owe its colour to a blending of blue and yellow, two colours of frequent occurrence in the same stone. The black sapphire, too, is rare; I have only met with two or three small crystals of it. It is not uncommon to find some other mineral included in the substance of the sapphire; I had two transparent specimens of the blue sapphire, in both of which were contained crystals apparently of iron glance, and in one, in addition, minute crystals apparently of the blue sapphire itself; and I have a light-coloured sapphire, nearly white, in which there appears to be a small mass of crystallized mica, of a silver white colour. Corundum is less frequently met with than the sapphire: I know of one place only where it abounds, and I am not aware that it has been found any where else in the island. The place alluded to, I have visited; it is called Battagammana, and is in the midst of an extremely unwholesome and almost desert country, in the Mahaweddharatta of Ouva, about twelve miles from Alipoota. The mineral is found in the bed and in the banks of a small stream, called the Agiri Kandura; I hoped to detect it in the adjoining rocks, which are different varieties of granite and gneiss, with some hornblende rock, but I was disappointed. The sand, gravel, and pebbles, amongst which the corundum occurs, in their nature correspond completely with the rocks just mentioned. The corundum of

Battagammana is frequently found in large six-sided prisms; it is commonly of a brown colour, whence it is called by the natives "Curundu galle" cinnamon-stone; occasionally it is to be met with partially or entirely covered with a black crust, which, I believe, is merely the stone, with an unusual proportion of iron. A bright brown prism, entirely free from this crust, was of sp. grav. 3.92, and another crystal, perfectly enveloped in it, was of sp. grav. 3.97. The corundum and sapphire are so very closely allied, that even the natives of Ceylon have not failed to observe the connexion. The two minerals are linked together by the coarse and opaque varieties of the latter, which are pretty common in Saffragam. Chrysoberyl is of very rare occurrence. During the whole time I was in Ceylon, I met with two or three specimens only of it, which the dealers assured me were brought from Saffragam. The more perfect crystals, of all the varieties of ruby, sapphire, corundum, and chrysoberyl, exhibiting in every direction, smooth facets, like the garnet, the diamond, and so many other minerals, seem to show that they are contemporaneous in their formation with the rock from which they are derived; that they have crystallized in its substance; and, that they are not detached till it undergoes disintegration or decomposition, when they are washed by the heavy rains and torrents, with the detritus of the parent rock, to lower ground, to reward the perseverance of the patient Indian, who might look for them in vain in the mountain mass. The method followed by the natives in searching for precious stones, will be described hereafter. Corundum is the only species of this family that is not esteemed as a gem, and the only one that is applied to any purpose of utility. In the state of fine powder it is largely employed by the lapidary in cutting and polishing stones, and by the armourer in polishing arms. It enters too into the composition of an excellent hone, made by the natives, consisting chiefly of this mineral, in very fine powder, and of kapitia, a peculiar kind of resin.

6. Of the felspar-family, it is highly probable, that several species exist in the island. Tablespar has been mentioned already, as associated in the same rock with cinnamon-stone and with zircon. I have met with all the sub-species of felspar, viz. adularia (including glassy felspar), Labrador-stone, common felspar and compact felspar. These minerals are common in gneiss and granitic rock, with the exception of Labrador-stone, which I have seen at Trincomalie only, in a bed of graphic granite. Adularia is very abundant in some parts of the Interior, particularly in the neighbourhood of Kandy, where it is occasionally the predominating ingredient of the rock.

7. Of the hornblende-family I am acquainted with two species only that occur in Ceylon, viz. common hornblende, the constituent of the rock of this name, and glassy tremolite, which I have observed at Trincomalie, in a narrow vein of quartz in gneiss.

8. Pitchstone is the only mineral of the family of this name, that I have ever found in Ceylon. Near Trincomalie I discovered a small vein of it in granite; and I have met with it no where else.

9. Mica, as a constituent part of granite and gneiss, is abundant; besides, it often occurs in large plates, imbedded in these rocks. It is collected by the natives, who use it for purposes of ordinary decoration. Common chlorite is to be met with occasionally both at Trincomalie and Galle; at both which places I have seen it disseminated through quartz. Green earth is more rare; I am acquainted with one place only where it occurs, which

is in the neighbourhood of Alipoota, in Lower Ouva, where it is pretty abundant in small veins, and included masses in clay, derived from the decomposition of a granitic rock. This mineral is of an unusually light colour, varying from green to light apple-green.

10. Magnesian minerals are far from abundant in Ceylon. The only minerals of this kind that I met with, were dolomite, carbonat of magnesia, and talc. The very rare mineral, native carbonat of magnesia, I discovered in a nitre-cave in the valley of Maturatta, accompanied with dolomite, and encrusting and included in gneiss. The best specimens of it were of a pure snow-white, earthy texture, rather harsh to the feel, destitute of smell when breathed on, and not adhering to the moist tongue. It varied in sp. grav. from 2.32 to 2.70, according to its compactness. One specimen of it that I examined was composed of

86	carbonat of magnesia
5	water
9	silica, with slight traces of carbonat of lime
100	

I believe this mineral to be contemporary with the rock in which it occurs, and not deposited subsequently from water. It has been long used by the natives of the adjoining country in white-washing their temples. Talc is very rare in Ceylon; I have met with it only in a nitre cave in Doombera, where, with calc-spar, felspar, and quartz, it entered into the composition of a very highly crystalline rock.

11. Calc-spar, anhydrous gypsum, and calc-sinter, are the only pure calcareous minerals that I have observed in Ceylon. The two former, well crystallized, I have met with in the nitre-cave

already alluded to, and of which a description will be given in another part of this work; they occur in the compound rock just mentioned when speaking of talc. Calc-sinter is not uncommon; encrusting rocks of dolomite and gneiss it abounds in Matele beyond Nalandi, and is plentiful in Lower Ouva, and in very many places in the neighbourhood of dolomite-rock, from which, in all probability, it is derived.

12. Belonging to the inflammable class of minerals, I know of two only that occur in Ceylon, viz. graphite and sulphur. Graphite in minute scales is very commonly disseminated through gneiss, and it occasionally occurs imbedded in this rock in small masses. In the latter form, it is pretty abundant in the neighbourhood of Ballangoddé, in the upper part of Saffragam. It is highly probable, it may be found in sufficient quantity to be collected and exported with profit. Sulphur is extremely rare in Ceylon; indeed its occurrence is not yet demonstrated in a manner perfectly satisfactory. Till about three weeks before I left the island, I had no suspicion of its existence, having ascertained that most of the sulphur used by the natives was brought from the continent and introduced clandestinely, by pilgrims proceeding to Adam's Peak. At the time mentioned, a specimen of rock was shown to me by the Honourable the Resident in the Kandyan provinces, John Doyley, Esq. which he had picked up in Doombera, near Memoora, and which he suspected contained sulphur. I was favoured with a fragment of it for examination. The specimen was of sp. gr. 2.9; it contained a considerable portion of sulphur, with a little sulphat of iron, and slight traces of alum. The stone itself was composed chiefly of quartz, felspar, and oxide of iron, and of some grey crystalline grains, the nature of which, I did not ascertain. Had the specimen been broken from a rock,

there would have been little room for doubt: even now, though the stone was detached, and found in a path, I am more disposed to consider it a specimen of native sulphur, than an artificial, accidental impregnation, which, in that wild and little frequented region, it would be very difficult to account for.

The mineral productions occurring in the dolomite-rock, are of two kinds,—those peculiar to it, and hitherto found in no other rock in Ceylon,—and, those common to it, and to granitic rock. Belonging to the latter, the following minerals may be enumerated; Iron pyrites, mica, white clay, probably derived from the decomposition of felspar, and graphite. With the exception of mica, none of these minerals are common or abundant in dolomite. The mica is generally of a light brown or straw-colour, translucent and crystallized in small six-sided prisms. The minerals peculiar to dolomite, as far as my experience extends, are three in number, viz. Ceylanite, apatite, and a bright-yellow mineral, which I believe to be a variety of cinnamon-stone. Ceylanite is pretty abundant in this rock and very generally disseminated through it. It occurs crystallized and amorphous, and exhibits a variety of colours, as bright azure-blue resembling the blue sapphire, violet. pink-red, grey and white. Its crystals are generally very small. The fine sapphire-blue Ceylanite, I have found at Nalandi and nowhere else. Of the pink-red, the only good specimens I have met with, were from a vein of dolomite in Saffragam, at a place called Viranea-gody, on the bank of a large stream that flows into the Kalu-ganga, about six miles below Ratna-poora.* Ceylanite of the other colours is common, particularly in the dolomite-rock, in the neighbourhood of Kandy and Badulla; where it generally occurs amorphous, or very indistinctly crystallized.

* By many mineralogists these specimens would be called examples of spinell.

Apatite, of a bright sapphire-blue colour, is frequently to be seen in dolomite, disseminated in very minute particles. The only place I know of, where it occurs well crystallized in six-sided prisms of a tolerable size, is in the neighbourhood of Fort M'Donald. For intelligence of this fact, and for a beautiful specimen of the mineral, I am indebted to Lieut. Auber. The bright-yellow mineral, which I believe to be a variety of cinnamon-stone, as it resembles cinnamon-stone in its general properties, and has never been seen crystallized, is not uncommon in dolomite, particularly in the neighbourhood of Kandy. In consequence of the small particles in which it occurs I have not been able to collect sufficient to examine it with tolerable accuracy. To conclude this part of my subject, it may be remarked, that though the number of minerals hitherto found in dolomite rock is small, it is highly probable that many more than have yet been found exist in it, the discovery of which may reward the mineralogist, who will avail himself of the ample opportunities that offer in the Interior, of inspecting this rock in the quarries where it is broke, for the purpose of making lime, and of giving it that minute and continued examination, which it deserves.

The saline productions of Ceylon are far from numerous. The only salts, the existence of which I have ascertained in a satisfactory manner, are the following; viz. nitre, nitrat of lime, sulphat of magnesia, alum, and common salt. These salts, with the exception of common salt, have been found hitherto in the Interior only, and in certain caves, where, not being liable to be washed away by the heavy tropical rains, they admit of being detected.

Nitre and nitrat of lime are of frequent occurrence. The names of twenty-two places may be enumerated, in which saltpetre is produced, and in which it has been manufactured; and no doubt, besides these, there are many other spots that yield this salt, known to the natives, whose policy it is not to make us acquainted with them.*

Judging from four nitre caves that I have visited, and from the specimens of rocks of several more that I have examined, I believe that they are all very similar; and, that the rock in which they occur, in every instance contains at least felspar and carbonat of lime; from the decomposition of the former of which, the alkaline base of the salt is generally derived, and by the peculiar influence of the latter, (yet not at all understood,) on the oxygen and azote of the atmosphere, the acid principle is generated. In confirmation of this statement, it may be remarked, that I have never been able to detect saltpetre, excepting superficially, where air could have access; never unaccompanied by nitrat of lime, or magnesia; in no rock, not containing lime and felspar; that the richness of the rock, in general, has been proportional to the

* The following list of nitre-caves is formed on the best authorities I had the means of consulting, and I believe it will be found pretty correct, as far as it extends. —In the district of the Seven Korles; 1. Werengodde; 2. Medellenewa; 3. Paremakande; all three in the Demoole-pattoo: 4. Giribawah in the Mahamedde-pattoo; 5. Maha-kelle; 6. Galgiriawah; 7. Kadooroo-wuva; all three in the Hatilispahay korle: 8. Kaddigaway, in the Magoole korle; and 9. Ressiroowey, in the Naganpahay korle. In the district of Neurrakalava; 10. Wadingapallama. In the district of Matele; 11. Agalawatte; 12. Kaloodawella; 13. Oonaweroowa; and 14. Nalandi. In the district of Doombera; 15. Memoora; and 16. Rajahvilla. In the district of Ouva; 17. near Wellaway. In the district of Hewahette; 18. Maturatta. In the district of the four Korles; 19. Kodigomoowa; 20. Doonoogama. In the district of Saffragam; 21. Meddegama. In the district of Welassey; 22. Hapola-cadavette. These names, it may be remarked, are not those of the caves themselves, which are generally nameless, but of the nearest inhabited places, which are in many instances several miles remote, most of the caves, being situated in the wildest and most deserted parts of the country.

abundance and intimate mixture of these two ingredients; and, that the results of experiments which I have made on a variety of specimens of saltpetre-earth from Bengal, for which I am indebted to the kindness of Mr. Brown of Calcutta, were similar to those just mentioned, and tended to the same conclusions. Besides the essential circumstances of the presence of atmospheric air, lime and an alkaline mineral, there are other circumstances which, if my observations be correct, greatly aid in the operation of forming the salt. I shall mention the most remarkable only, which appear to me to be slight humidity and the presence of a little animal matter. Perhaps, humidity is absolutely necessary; certainly, I have seen spots in a nitre cave, without any impregnation of saltpetre, which, excepting their great dryness, seemed to possess every requisite for the production of the salt. Animal matter, by those ignorant of chemistry, is considered of itself the chief source of nitre. Persuaded of this, my countrymen in Ceylon, with whom I conversed on the subject, generally attributed the saltpetre of the caves in question to the dung of bats, with which the caves are more or less infested. It is easy to refute such a notion; and to show, that the dung of these animals, like any animal matter, is not an essential, merely an assistant circumstance. For this purpose, it will be sufficient to remark, that in the nitre-cave near Memoora in Doombera, in a very compounded rock consisting of calcspar, felspar, quartz, mica, and talc, in a humid state, exposed to the air, and slowly decomposing, I have found a rich impregnation of saltpetre, though quite free from the dung of bats, or any other animal matter; and conversely, that I have not been able to detect any traces of this salt in the dung of bats, that had accumulated in great quantity in an old forsaken pagodah. A description of the nitre-caves which I have visited, will be found in another part of this work, and an account of the method employed by the natives, both in the manufacture of saltpetre and of gunpowder. I may here give the results of some analyses that I have made, which will shew the composition, of the most productive nitre-rock of Doombera, of the most productive nitre-earth of Ouva, and of the richest nitre-earth of Bengal. The nitre-rock of Doombera, was from the Memora cave, the same as that before mentioned, as free from animal matter; 100 parts of this very compounded rock were found to consist of

2.4	nitrat of potash
0.7	nitrat of magnesia
0.2	sulphat of magnesia
9.4	water
26.5	carbonat of lime
60.7	earthy matter, insoluble in dilute nitric acid
100.0	

100 parts of the nitre-earth, from the great cave in Lower Ouva, near Wellaway, were found to consist of

3.3	nitrat of potash, with traces of common salt and sulphat of lime
3.5	nitrat of lime
15.3	water
25.7	animal matter of difficult solubility
1.0	animal matter, easily soluble in water
51.2	carbonat of lime and earthy matter
100.0	

100 parts of nitre earth, from Bengal, from the district of Tirhoot, were found to consist of

8.3	nitrat of potash
3.7	nitrat of lime
0.8	sulphat of lime, with a trace of iron
0.2	common salt
35.0	carbonat of lime, with a trace of magnesia
40.0	earthy matter, insoluble in water and nitric acid
12.0	water, with a trace of vegetable matter.
100.0	

Nitrat of lime I have never met with, excepting in combination with nitre. Sulphat of magnesia I have found in one place only, viz. the nitre-cave of Memoora, in Doombera. In the same cave, and no where else, I discovered alum, in minute quantity. I suspect, that the acid of both these salts is derived from decomposing pyrites, and that the magnesia of the sulphat is afforded by decomposing talc. This sulphat forms with the nitre, and crystallizes with it. It is carefully picked out, and rejected by the native workmen who prepare the saltpetre, being ignorant of its value. A considerable quantity of it, equal to the best Epsom's salt, might be procured in this cave; and I know no reason why it should not be collected.

Common salt forms in great quantities in certain lakes on the sea-shore; but is of rare occurrence indeed, in the Interior, excepting in very minute quantity, dissolved in water. The only instance that I have found it in a solid form, was in the nitre-cave at Maturatta, where, mixed with silica and carbonat of magnesia, it formed a white crust on a small portion of rock consisting of dolomite, decomposing felspar and mica. For the occurrence of salt, in this instance, I do not know any adequate reason that can be assigned. Of the salt that forms in the lakes on the sea-shore, it is easy to give a pretty satisfactory account. The principal salt-lakes, and the only ones that I have visited, are situated on the southern side of the island, in the wild, low, and unwholesome district of the Megam-pattoo. They are collections of water, in the natural hollows of the country, confined by a high sand-bank, thrown up along the shore by a tempestuous sea. According to the best information I could get on the spot, the lakes from which salt is ever actually obtained, are seven in number, viz. the Conakatee-leway, the Sitricale-leway, the Maha-leway, the Colancale-leway, the Boondle-leway, the Durava-calapoo, and the Palatapane-leway. Besides which, there are other lakes in the same district similarly situated, the waters of which are brackish, but never sufficiently concentrated to yield salt. The seven lakes enumerated vary in extent, from nine miles in circumference to a mile and a half. They are all very shallow; the deepest, when its water is highest, not exceeding six feet. In the rainy months of January and February they frequently overflow, and break the bar of sand; and, at this season their diluted water is only brackish. In the dry season, particularly in the hot months of June and July, when a strong parching south-west wind blows, and evaporation is rapid, their waters are more or less concentrated to the state of brine, and often dried up entirely, when the bottoms of the lakes are covered with a crust of salt, which in different instances varies from one inch or less to a foot in thickness. The question of the source and formation of this salt has been involved in unnecessary mystery. It would be waste of time to detail the various speculations I have heard on the subject, indulged in by those either not competent to form a correct opinion, or not furnished with data for the purpose. From all the observations I made on the spot, and from all the information I could collect, it appears to me, that the sea, which is close at hand, is decidedly the source from which the salt is derived, and, that evaporation is the cause of its production or forming. In support of this proposition, a variety of facts that appear to me conclusive, may be adduced: in the soil there is nothing peculiar; it resembles that of the country in general, resulting from the decomposition of granitic rock: the encrustation of salt that forms is merely superficial; an excavation being made, the deeper it is sunk the less saline the ground becomes: in the immediate neighbourhood of more than one of the salt-lakes, there are collections of perfectly fresh water: the more rain there is in the wet season, the less salt is obtained; and, occasionally, no salt has formed when the year has been unusually rainy: the more boisterous the sea, the greater the probability is of a plentiful production of salt: lastly, to mention the most convincing circumstances, the saline contents of the lakes are similar to those of the sea, of which common salt is only the chief ingredient; and, all the lakes receive salt either from the sea directly, by the waves breaking over the bar, or by salt water, percolating through the sand, or in one instance, in which perhaps, from the unusual width of the bar, the salt is supplied in neither of these ways, the lake in the rainy season communicates with another that is so supplied. This appears to me to be a correct view of the subject, and the only one to be kept constantly in sight in any attempts to improve the salt-lakes, and make them more productive, and less liable to failure and fluctuation. The conclusions I have come to have no pretensions to novelty; others may have adopted them before me; certainly the enlightened collector of the district, with whom I had some conversation on the topic, had not merely adopted them, but had acted on them in some experiments he had made to accelerate and insure the formation of salt, by cutting the bars early, and diminishing rapidly the quantity of brackish water. The importance of the subject is greater than it may appear to a casual reader; the monopoly of the salt of the Megam-pattoo yielding government a revenue of at least £10,000 a-year, and the whole island being almost entirely dependent on this district for the supply of this necessary of life. It may be remarked further, that the importance of these lakes has not reached its maximum, and that their value is yet but partially understood. Were they scientifically managed, they might be made to yield, not only any quantity of salt, sufficient to supply all India, but almost any quantity of magnesia might be extracted from the residual brine. And, in procuring wood-ash, which this preparation would require, it would be necessary to burn the jungle with which great part of the country is over-run; — an operation that, in all probability, would be of infinite service, both in diminishing the unwholesomeness of the air so fatal to population, and in checking the increase of wild animals, so hostile to the agriculture of the district.

The soils of Ceylon, as far as my inquiries have extended, have certain points of general resemblance, as might be expected from considering the geological conformation of the island. Without any exception that I am acquainted with, they are all derived from the decomposition of gneiss, of granitic rock, or of clay iron stone; of all of them, the principal ingredients are quartz, in the form of sand or gravel, and decomposed felspar in the state of clay, with more or less oxide of iron. Quartz, in most instances, is the ingredient that predominates; and, in very many instances, it constitutes more than nine-tenths of the whole. Carbonat of lime is rarely to be detected in the soil; and in no one instance, have I discovered phosphat of lime. In several instances, I have not found carbonat of lime or of magnesia even in the soil lying incumbent on dolomite-rock, as at Nalandi; or, on limestone rock, as at Jaffnapatam. It is commonly supposed, that in tropical countries in which vegetation is so luxuriant, and wood almost universal, the soil must abound in vegetable matter. This is not the case in Ceylon: with one exception, all the natural soils I have examined, have contained between three and one per cent. only of vegetable matter. The exception alluded to is that of soil, from an elevation of between four and five thousand feet above the level of the sea, where the temperature is comparatively low, and the ground very damp. In a situation of this kind amongst the mountains of Upper Ouva, the soil was black, and contained between 7 and 10 per cent. of vegetable matter, in a state analagous to that of peat. The small proportion of vegetable matter that usually occurs, may rationally be referred to the high temperature of the climate, producing rapid decomposition, and to the heavy rains, which will not allow vegetable matter to accumulate. To this latter cause also, in all probability, may be assigned the great scarcity of calcareous matter. The best and most productive soils of Ceylon, are a brown loam resulting from the decomposition of gneiss or granitic rock, abounding in felspar, or a reddish loam, resulting from the decomposition of clay-iron stone, called in Ceylon, Kabook-stone. The worst soils, are those which abound most in quartz, derived from the disintegration of quartz-rock, or of granite or gneiss, containing a very large proportion of this mineral. For greater precision, examples may be given, of a few varieties of soil I have examined. The soil of the cinnamon-garden in the neighbourhood of Colombo, is a remarkable instance of the silicious kind. The surface of the ground in many places, where the cinnamon-plant flourishes, is white as snow: this is pure quartz-sand. Below the surface a few inches, where the roots penetrate, the sand is of a grey colour. A specimen of this, dried thoroughly, was found to consist of

98.5	silicious sand
1.0	vegetable matter
0.5	water
100.0	

It may appear surprising that the cinnamon-plant should succeed best in so poor a soil; but other circumstances considered, it admits of explanation. The garden is nearly on a level with the lake of Colombo, its situation is sheltered, the climate is remarkably damp, showers are frequent, the temperature is high, and uncommonly equable: These are the principal peculiarities to which the excellence of the cinnamon, and the luxuriant growth of this valuable shrub, in a soil apparently so unpromising, may be justly attributed.

One of the best examples of a ferruginous clay-soil, derived from the decomposition of clay-iron stone, occurs about two miles and a half from Colombo, in that beautiful part of the country, through which the Negombo road passes, decorated and shaded by the finest foliage in the world. This soil is reddish-brown; a specimen of it, well dried, was found to consist of

83.5	ferruginous clay
16.5	water, with traces of vegetable matter
100.0	

The power this soil possesses of retaining water in an eminent degree, is an excellent quality in such a climate, and to it, probably, is owing its marked fertility.

The most striking instance to be adduced, of soil destitute of calcareous matter, and incumbent on a bed of coral, is the common soil of the coral island Delft, off the coast of Jaffnapatam, celebrated for its excellent pasturage. It is a dirty-yellow, very fine sand, slightly cohering, which consists, in its dried state, of

95.0	silicious sand coloured by iron, with perhaps a very little alumine
2.5	vegetable matter
2.5	water
100.0	

Nor hardly less remarkable are some of the soils of Jaffnapatam, for which, as well as those of Delft, I am indebted to my friend, Mr. Finlayson. Two instances may be mentioned, — one of a soil of a tobacco field, which is manured by means of sheep, like turnip-ground in England; the other of rice-ground, which receives no manure, but is carefully irrigated. The tobacco soil, of a reddish-brown colour, collected when, perhaps, partially exhausted, the crop not having been long taken off the ground, consisted of

95.5 silicious sand, coloured by iron, with a few particles of calcareous matter
2.0 vegetable matter
2.5 water

100.0

The rice-soil, of a light grey colour, containing a good deal of straw in a finely divided state, consisted of

95.5 silicious sand, with traces of iron, carbonat of lime and alumine
2.5 vegetable matter
2.0 water

100.0

It seems extraordinary that in islands, the foundations of which are calcareous, there should be so little calcareous matter, and so large a proportion of silicious matter, in the soil. It is a subject deserving of minute inquiry on the spot: perhaps, the fine silicious sand is drifted there by strong winds from a distance*; and perhaps, as already hinted, the calcareous matter is washed out

* There are very many instances of sand being carried to a great distance by the wind. On our voyage from India, approaching Table Bay, at the Cape of Good Hope, the S. E. wind blowing strongly off land, was so impregnated with a subtle sand, like that of Delft, that it proved very troublesome, even three and four miles off the shore.

in process of long time, by the action of the heavy periodical rains.

The preceding observations on the soils of Ceylon, are equally applicable to the Kandyan and to the maritime provinces. In relation to agricultural improvement, the subject is highly important ; and, no where is it more deserving of attention and investigation than in Ceylon, where the ground is in its original state, and where (unless Jaffnapatam be an exception) no attempt has been made by man, either to correct the faults or to increase the productiveness of the soil, by the use of manure.

Ceylon abounds in rivers and springs, but not in mineral or medicinal waters. The former circumstance may be attributed to the mountainous nature of the interior ; the latter, perhaps, to the peculiar geological structure of the island. The springs and rivers, in general, are remarkable for the purity of their waters. Amongst the mountains, those which I have examined, have only differed from rain-water, in containing slight traces of common salt, and of vegetable matter, and occasionally of carbonat of lime and suspened clay ; and, the difference of the waters of the lowlands has consisted chiefly, in their containing, with the exception of suspended clay, larger proportions of the above substances, particularly of vegetable matter. The only springs that I am acquainted with, that require particular notice, are those which are of a temperature unusually high, and those which are supposed to be of a chalybeate or medicinal nature. Of the former several occur: besides the hot springs of Cannea, in the neighbourhood of Trincomalie, well known to Europeans, I have ascertained, in a satisfactory manner, the existence of similar springs, in two places in the Kandyan country, and of two warm springs in the province of Ouva. The springs of Cannea are situated in low ground, abounding in quartz, surrounded by low jungle, in an unhealthy country, about seven miles from Trincomalie. The following ground plan, taken on the spot, with the subjoined notices, will give a pretty correct idea of them.

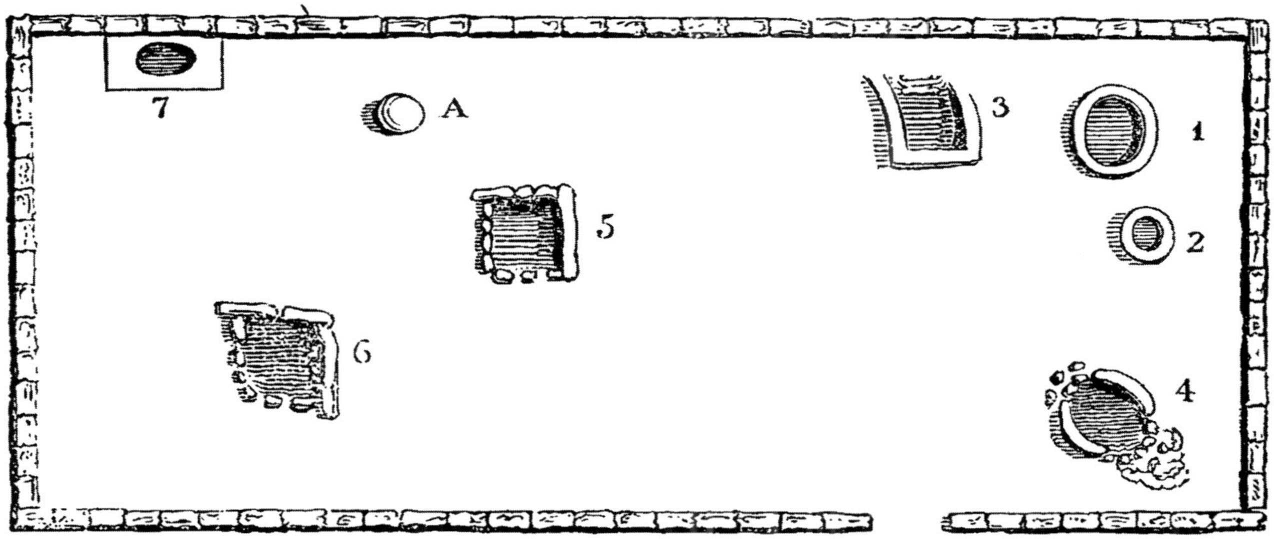

The enclosure in which the wells are situated, is about 36 feet long and 16 broad, formed by a wall of brick six feet high. Each well is protected by a little embankment about a foot and a half high. The well marked No. 1, is about three feet deep and two in diameter. On the morning I visited Cannea, (Oct. 19th, 1817, in company with my friend, the Rev. George Bisset) this well was quite clear and still, and discharging very little water; at seven A. M. when the air was 77°, its temperature was 101 of Fahrenheit. The well No. 2, is about four feet deep and one and a half wide. It was clear and still, and discharged a little more water than the first: its temperature was 101.5. The well, No. 3, is about five feet and half deep and two feet wide. It was clear, and generally still, but if watched some time, a current of air-bubbles, now and then, might be seen rising from the bottom. It discharged a good deal of water, and more than any of the other wells: its temperature was 107°. The well, No. 4, is about one foot deep and about three feet wide. It was still and slightly turbid, from a little clay suspended in it; the discharge of water from it was only just perceptible: its temperature was 88.5. The well, No. 5, is about one foot deep, and about three feet by two in dimensions. Its water is still, slightly turbid, and of temperature 86°. Whether this is a true spring I am undecided; it may be a pit merely, filled with water from the overflowing of the adjoining wells. The well, No. 6, is about three feet deep and two and a half wide. It was clear, there was no apparent flow of water from it, but a constant disengagement of air, which issued from crevices in the gravelly bottom, and ascended in large quantity: the temperature of this well was 105.75. The well, No. 7, is about one foot deep, and about two feet by one in dimensions. Its water was still, slightly turbid, not apparently flowing, and of temp. 91°; there were two or three small fish in it. The bottoms of all the wells were formed of quartz-sand and gravel, without encrustation, and clean, excepting in the instances in which the water was not quite clear, and in these there was a little mud. The water of all the different wells had no smell or peculiar taste; a bottle of water of the well, No. 3, which I took with me to Kandy, and examined about two months after, had acquired a smell of sulphuretted hydrogen, but this I suspect was owing to a common cork having been used to stop it. This water was of the same sp. grav. as distilled water; and, I could detect in it nothing but the slightest trace of common salt, and a little carbonic acid gas, and azote. The probability is, that all the wells are supplied with water from the same source. The circumstances of their temperatures being different, at first view, appears to be in opposition to this idea; but it may be easily reconciled by taking into account the quantity of water discharged, which is greatest in the hottest springs, excepting in one instance (that of No. 6.) in which the air disengaged, in the operation of raising the temperature, may be considered as a substitute for the water. To ascertain the nature of this air, I had a quantity of it collected, which I examined a few hours after at Trincomalie, and found it to consist of azotic gas, nearly pure, only adulterated with a very minute quantity of carbonic acid gas, and common air. The temperature of the wells, I believe, is liable to fluctuation; the hottest has been observed as high as 110°, and even before we left the place, three hours only having elapsed, the temperatures of all of them had undergone a change; No. 3, from 107 was reduced to 103°, and No.6, from 105.75 to 102°, whilst the temperature of the air was raised from 77° to 80°. I have been thus minute in the description of these wells on account of their very singular nature: — the purity of their water, — their high temperature, — their temperature fluctuating, — the quantity of azotic gas so nearly pure disengaged, — are circumstances highly deserving of the attention of the philosopher who directs his mind to the interior of our globe, and to the causes of the most mysterious and awful of natural phenomena. That these wells are in repute amongst the natives, is indicated by their being enclosed and put under the protection of Ganesa (the god of wisdom of the Hindoos), to whom, close by, a small temple is erected, containing his image rudely sculptured in stone. The wells are resorted to merely as warm baths, and are used chiefly in cases of rheumatism and cutaneous disease. The water is generally applied by affusion; the patient standing on a round stone (marked A in the plan), has pots of water poured on him by an assistant.

Of the hot springs in the Interior, never having visited them, I regret it is not in my power to give any very minute information. According to the best intelligence I could collect, there are, close together, two very hot springs in the Veddah-ratte of Bintenny, and one in Welassey. The former are situated in the midst of an immense jungle, in an extremely unwholesome country, inhabited only by wild animals, and by Veddahs almost as wild, about two days' journey from Aleutneura, towards Batticaloa. The temperature of their water is too high to be borne by man, and sufficiently high to dress meat and vegetables, —a use to which it is applied by the savage Veddahs; there is in both springs a constant bubbling. The hot spring in Welassey is about fifteen miles from Kotabowa, near the Patapalar river; its water is clear, too hot for the hand to bear, and constantly emitting air-bubbles. Through the kindness of Captain Ritchie of the 73d regt. and of H. Wright, Esq., I was furnished with a bottle of water of the springs of both places; I found them very similar, and very like the water of the hot springs of Cannea. The specimen from Bintenny was of sp. grav. 10011, that from Welassey was of sp. grav. 10005. I could detect in them only very slight traces of common salt, vegetable matter, and carbonic acid; and, it is not improbable that the two latter may have been produced by the action of the water on the cork.

Of the two warm springs in the province of Ouva, one is at Badulla, in Upper Ouva, about 1861 feet above the level of the sea, where the mean annual temperature, there is reason to believe, is about 69°; the other is about a mile and a half from Alipoota, in Lower Ouva, near the path on the way to Kotabowa, about 1061 feet above the level of the sea, where the mean annual temperature is probably about 76°. The Badulla spring is a very fine one, that supplies the inhabitants with abundance of excellent water; the well is about five feet deep, and eight or nine in circumference; it discharges a stream of transparent water that rising rapidly through the sand in the bottom, produces considerable commotion, which is occasionally increased by the disengagement of air. When I visited the spring on the 17th March, 1819, at seven A.M. its temperature was 76°, the air being 66°. The water was of sp. grav. 10008, and did not apparently differ from distilled water, excepting in containing slight traces of common salt. I had not the means of ascertaining the nature of the air disengaged. The spring in the neighbourhood of Alipoota I examined in a very hurried manner, only in passing; it is situated in a rice-field, and is quite neglected; it attracted my attention by its copiousness and clearness; it had no peculiar taste or smell, and like the Badulla spring, air-bubbles now and then appeared in it. On the 4th April, 1819, at 8h. 30m. A. M. when the air was 75°, the temperature of this spring was 80.5. The resemblance of the warm and hot springs is too near to be casual; it is highly probable, that be the source or cause of their heat, what it may, it is the same in each instance. The subject naturally excites conjecture and speculation, amusing to indulge in but useless to publish, at least, not fit for a work intended to be a collection of observations and facts, rather than of opinions.

It is stated by some writers that volcanic appearances are not uncommon in Ceylon; indeed it is even asserted that Adam's Peak itself is a volcanic mountain.* It is far more easy to point out such errors than explain them. Excepting the springs just de-

* Gisborne's Nat. Theolog. p. 108.

scribed, and the great depth of the harbour of Trincomalie (in some places not far from shore unfathomable), and the occurrence of ores of iron occasionally, bearing a slight resemblance to lava, I know no one circumstance that could suggest even the idea of volcanic action in Ceylon, — and much less prove that such an action has taken place, and that the highest mountain in the island is the result of its operation.

In many parts of the country, particularly in the Interior, there are appearances of chalybeate springs; the water is often seen covered with an ochreous crust, and its channel marked by a similar deposit. This crust I have found to be a mixture of hydrat of alumine, and of red oxide of iron, with a little vegetable matter. The water itself that I have examined, immediately as it issued from the earth, gave no indications of iron, when freed by filtration from a few ferruginous particles suspended in it; whence, it seems very probable, that these springs are not genuine chalybeate, and that they are not discoloured by iron, dissolved by means of an acid, but only by the peroxide in a state of mechanical suspension washed out of the ground where it had probably formed.

With the existence of any true medicinal spring in the island, I am not acquainted; nor have I ever heard of any spring of much reputation amongst the natives for its medicinal virtues. In the Seven Korles the water of Yapahoue is said to effect cures in certain diseases; but a specimen of this water, for which I was indebted to the Rev. G. Bisset, did not contain any thing in its composition to confirm such a character.

CHAPTER II.

MONSOONS. — RAINS. — RIVERS. — TEMPERATURE. — METEORS. — MIASMATA.

It would be highly desirable to have a minute and correct account of the climate of Ceylon, and of the various circumstances by which it is influenced and modified. The sketch I am about to offer is of humble pretensions: it is a sketch merely of the subject, — formed partly from my own, and partly from the observations of others. To attain the desideratum just mentioned, very much remains to be done; greatly more than can be expected soon, in an island so remote, where there are very few who take an interest in such enquiries, and where it is extremely difficult to procure and keep in order the delicate instruments the investigation requires.

Situated as Ceylon is between the parallels of 6° and 10° N. winter is unknown to it; that succession of seasons is there never witnessed, with which the year is varied in the temperate zone; and, excepting by change of wind, the difference of a few degrees of temperature, and the transition of weather from dry to rainy, and from rainy to dry, — the perennial summer which it experiences (I cannot say enjoys) is never diversified.

Over most of the island, particularly the maritime provinces, the wind blows a certain period of the year from the south-west, and a certain period, from the north-east, with some variations.

These winds, called monsoons, considerably modified by local circumstances, prevail over a great part of the continent of India, and over the whole of the Indian ocean, with a regularity surprising to those who are acquainted only with the element proverbially inconstant in our unsteady climate. The period of the south-west monsoon is whilst the sun is north of the line, and the temperature of the great continent of India is higher than that of the ocean, from May to September; it beginning generally in the latter end of April, and ceasing about the beginning of November. The period of the north-east monsoon is whilst the sun is south of the line, and the temperature of the ocean and of Southern Africa above that of Asia. As the difference of temperature is less in this instance than in the former, so is the duration of the north-east monsoon shorter, being comprised between November and March, — it beginning generally in the former month and concluding in the latter. The south-west wind is felt more generally all over the island, and prevails more steadily than the north-east: thus, in the instance of Colombo and Trincomalie, on the opposite shores, the south-west wind almost constantly blows for five months in succession; but the north-east hardly half the time at the former that it does at the latter place; at Colombo it being confined chiefly to December and January, but at Trincomalie extending to the month before and the month after. In consequence, on the Colombo side of the island, the period of variable winds is longer than on the Trincomalie side. In the one instance being about five months, comprehending February, March, April, October, and November, during which time the wind is from the sea, generally, during the day, and from the land during the night; in the other instance, being limited to the three middle months, and observing nearly the same diurnal change. On the state of the winds in the Interior, little is known, and little can be offered but conjecturally. Over the level parts of the country, there is reason to believe, that the winds do not differ very materially from what they are on the sea-coast. But amongst the mountains it is otherwise; there, varying greatly according to the features of the country, particularly the direction of the valleys and of the mountain-ridges, — and according to central situation or proximity to one or other side of the island; the country on the western side partaking more of the peculiarities of wind of Colombo, that on the eastern of Trincomalie, and that nearly central amongst the mountains, or not far removed from their base, having peculiarities of its own: thus, at Badulla, in Upper Ouva, the highest and most central district of the Interior, the wind, three-fourths of the year, is from the north-east, and in the months, June, July, and August, is variable: thus, at Kotabowa, in Welassey, only about thirty miles in a straight line from Badulla, at the foot nearly of the mountains of Ouva, from June to October, 1818, the wind blew almost invariably from the north-west; from the middle of the latter month to the 7th of January, 1819, it blew by day from the south-west, and by night from the north-east; and, from the 9th of January to the 20th of March, from the north-east both day and night. No doubt many other peculiarities might be pointed out, were the direction of the wind studied and ascertained in every part of the country.

As might be expected from its inter-tropical situation, the proportion of rain that falls in Ceylon is great, — exceeding what falls in England perhaps three or four times. The parts of the country in which the largest quantity of rain occurs, are the mountainous and the maritime provinces that are most exposed to the force of the monsoons. The parts where there is least rain are those not very near the mountains, and so situated as to render both monsoons land-winds. Tangalle, in the Megam-pattoo, to the eastward of the most southern point of the island, is thus situated; and, there a drought has been known to last more than twelve months at a time, uninterrupted by the fall of a single drop of rain. The rains in Ceylon, in comparison with those in England, as they are less frequent so they are vastly more heavy,—commonly resembling the heaviest summer thunder-showers. In illustration and proof of this assertion, it may be remarked, that it is not unusual for two or three inches to fall in a day; and once, at Colombo, in the short space of twelve hours, I witnessed the fall of 3.2 inches of rain. All over the island the rains are more or less periodical. At the northern extremity, and in the northern lowland division, and on the eastern shore, the rainy season commences about the time of the setting-in of the north-east monsoon. It lasts about two months, with great violence, flooding all the low parts of the country, and some districts almost entirely. During the other ten months of the year, the weather is the opposite extreme, nearly perpetually dry, showers very rarely refreshing the parched soil, excepting about the period of the beginning of the south-west monsoon. On the western side of the island, most rain falls about the time of the setting-in of the south-west monsoon. But it is not confined to this period,—nor is it so violent or so continued as on the opposite side. A whole day of constant rain is extremely uncommon; all the year round showers are frequent, so that it is very unusual for a month to elapse without them. It is in consequence of this happy peculiarity that the western coast of Ceylon is seldom parched, and that its aspect is almost perpetually delightfully fresh and green, exciting the admiration of strangers from less favoured parts of India. It is worth remarking, that even the showers that so frequently occur on this coast (and the observation may be extended to the mountainous district) are not irregular, but happen commonly in sequence day after day, — if the comparison may be allowed, like aguish fits, the recurrence of which may be calculated — the following being generally half an hour or an hour later or earlier than the preceding, and gradually increasing and gradually diminishing in strength. Amongst the mountains, as in respect to wind, so in a still more striking manner in respect to rain, the climate of different districts resembles, according to proximity, that of the opposite shores of the island. Amongst the eastern and northern barriers of the mountainous division, much less rain falls and less frequently than amongst the western; in several instances, especially in the district of Doombera, the transition is quite sudden from the climate of one shore of the island to that of the other, — a lofty mountain-ridge merely constituting the line of demarcation; so that, whilst one side of the mountain is covered with clouds and mist, and drenched with rain, the other is parched with drought, and scorched by an unclouded sun. It would be very desirable to know the precise quantities of rain that fall in different parts of the island in the course of the year. For four months that I observed a rain-gauge at Colombo, from the beginning of March to the end of June, 1817, 24.11 inches of rain fell; — which is at the rate of about seventy-five inches a year. During twelve months that a rain-gauge was observed by the medical officers in the General

Military Hospital at Kandy, from the first of January to the 31st December, 1819, the quantities that fell each month, were the following:—

Months	Jan.	Feb.	March.	April.	May.	June.	July.	Aug.	Sept.	Oct.	Nov.	Dec.
Rain in Inches.	1.0	0.4	8.1	11.7	6.6	2.3	10.7	3.5	8.2	7.1	7.1	18.6

making a total of 84.3 inches.* The probability is that the quantity of rain that falls at Colombo is about the average of what falls on the sea-coast of the island in general, and on the low districts; whilst the quantity at Kandy, may be about the average of the mountainous district, — Kandy being pretty central, and in respect to its rain, between the maximum and minimum of that of the western and eastern mountains. The neighbourhood of Adam's Peak receives, without doubt, the maximum quantity of rain of the mountain-region, and the neighbourhood of Namina-cooli Kandy, perhaps, the minimum. The quantity that falls annually in the former situation must be enormous; in all probability exceeding 100 inches.

Owing to the frequency of rains amongst the mountains the Interior is uncommonly well watered; —not a valley is without a stream, that is almost always perennial. To the same region the island in general is indebted for all its rivers. On account of the peculiarities mentioned, rivers are more numerous on the western than on the eastern side, and less uncommon at the southern extremity than at the northern. It would be tedious to enumerate all the rivers and rivulets that flow from the Interior to the coast of the island. The principal are eight

* From the Ceylon Gazette, 8th Jan. 1820.

in number, viz. — the Mahawellé ganga *, the Kalany ganga, the Kalu ganga, the Walleway ganga, the Maha oya, the Didroo oya, the Parapa oya, and the Navil aar. By the first four rivers, the whole of the mountainous district is drained; and by the latter four, most of the hilly and a considerable portion of the low country. The first four, which are dignified with the name *ganga* (river), are by the natives said to have their rise in Adam's Peak, which is not quite correct.

The Mahawellé ganga, by far the largest river in the island, drains two thirds, perhaps, of the mountainous district; its principal branch takes its rise from the Neuraellyia mountains, and flowing through the valley of Kotmale, under the name of the Kotmale ganga, joins at Passbage, a smaller branch that has its source in Adam's Peak, and, as far as it can be traced, is honoured with the name of the main river. The Mahawellé ganga, flows by the town of Kandy, from whence to the plains of Bintenney, a distance not exceeding 30 miles, it hurries down a descent of rather more than 1000 perpendicular feet, receiving by the way a great accession of waters. At Bintenney, at the foot of the mountains, it may be considered of its greatest magnitude; there, when of a medium height, when its water at the ford is about five feet deep, the river from bank to bank is 540 feet wide.† In its slow and tedious course, from Bintenney to the sea, through a country almost level, and a great part of the year excessively dry, it must lose by evaporation and other exhausting causes, a con-

* This river is called by us the Maha-villa ganga, which I understand is erronious; the natives pronouncing it *wellé*. *Villa* in Singalese signifies field, *wellé*, sand; the name being given, according to a learned native, because the shores of the river are very sandy.

† I state this on the authority of Capt. Sweeting, R. A. who measured it carefully.

siderable portion of its water. Like most large rivers that approach the sea, through a flat country, it divides into branches which are liable to change. Its principal branch, little more than 150 years ago, there is reason to believe, was that which enters the sea by the Cottiaar, which is now said to be very much obstructed. Now, it empties itself chiefly by the Virgal branch, between Trincomalie and Batticaloa; where it is no longer known by its inland name, but by that of the Virgal ganga. It is the opinion of some, that the Mahawellé ganga, is navigable at present, as far as Bintenney *; and, of some, that it is capable of being rendered navigable, even to Kandy. It would be fortunate for the country, were these notions correct, — could the abundant waters of this fine stream, which now run idle and waste, be made subservient to the important purpose of inland navigation. Unhappily, in the low country, the channel of the river is obstructed by sand-banks; and below Kandy, by rocks and a succession of rapids, — so that all the way, that it is supposed to be navigable, its passage is impracticable, even for boats; and where, it is conceived, it may be rendered navigable, an invincible obstacle presents itself in the great difference of level already mentioned.

The Kalany ganga, of the same name as a celebrated temple by which it flows, is next in magnitude to the Mahawellé ganga, and in importance, perhaps, surpasses it. It takes its rise amongst the group of mountains, of which Adam's Peak is the centre, draining their western side by two considerable streams, the Kehelgamua ganga and the Maskelli ganga, which joining at Weralooella, about forty miles from the sea, and about eighty-seven feet

* Vide Mr. Bertolacci's work on Ceylon, Introd. p. 37.

above its level, constitutes the river in question, which, from this place to the ocean, retains the same name. The size of this river, little, if at all, inferior to that of the Tay, is remarkably great, considering the shortness of its course, hardly amounting to sixty miles. As it is fed chiefly by mountain-streams, its water, in general, is beautifully transparent: owing to the situation of its sources, where showers are so frequently falling, its dimensions are much less liable to extreme changes, than those of most tropical rivers. Partly on this account, and partly on account of its low level, it is navigable for boats, at least three-fourths of its course, as far as Talygommua, above which its bed is rocky and its character that of a great mountain-torrent. At its mouth, about three miles to the northward of Colombo, a great bank of sand has been thrown up by the waves, which impeding the exit of its waters, the river has here expanded, and has very much the appearance of a lake. Already, much use is made of this river for inland-carriage, and the probability is, that in this respect, it will hereafter be turned to much more account than it is at present. It has often occurred to me, that a communication, by means of a good road, might be made without much difficulty, and at no great expense, between the navigable part of this river, and that of the Mahawellé ganga, about fourteen miles above Kandy, which would be of incalculable use to the country in general, and of very great consequence to the capital of the Kandyan provinces. This idea I venture to offer, as a suggestion to those in Ceylon, interested in the welfare of the island, and intent on improving the Interior. It may appear wild at first view, but the more it is examined, I am pretty confident the more feasible it will appear. A road of eight or ten miles, I conceive, would accomplish the communication. The intervening mountain is indeed high, (perhaps three or four thousand feet,) which must be crossed; but is not the object to be attained worthy the labour that may be required to overcome this difficulty?*

The Kalu ganga, (the black river,) deriving its name from the sombre hue of its waters, occasioned by the shade of its luxuriantly wooded banks, is little inferior in magnitude and utility, to the Kalany ganga, which in many respects it greatly resembles. It rises on the southern side of Adam's Peak, and is formed by the confluence of very many streams from the adjoining mountains, which takes place near Ratnapoora, between 30 and 40 miles from the sea, and about 50 feet above its level. It is navigable for boats, from its junction with the sea at Caltura, to a little above Ratnapoora. Like the two other great rivers, and the mountain-streams of Ceylon in general, it is liable, after heavy rains, to be flooded in an extraordinary manner; thus, in the short space of six hours, it has been known to rise at Ratnapoora, to the perpendicular height of 21 feet.

The Welleway ganga, in size, is considerably inferior to the preceding; and, it is of little importance, as it flows through a country, the greater part of which is uncultivated and uninhabited. From the desire, perhaps, of assigning it a sacred source, it is erroneously said by the natives to rise in Adam's Peak. The truth, I believe is, that it has its origin farther to the eastward, amongst the boundary-mountains of Ouva and Saffragam. Its mouth, situated between Tangalle and Hambantotte, in the Megampattoo, is often completely stopped by a barrier of sand, thrown up by the violent sea that breaks on that shore, occasioning the flooding of the adjoining country; — an accident to which most

* The Mahawellé ganga is already navigable for boats between Kandy and Gompola, and, with little difficulty and expense, it might be rendered navigable even up to Ambagammué.

of the other rivers of Ceylon, especially those of lesser magnitude, are equally liable.

The other four rivers, the names of which have been given, are in respect to size of second rate, a circumstance indicated by the term *oya* attached to them. They are of little consequence comparatively, and do not require particular description. In a cursory manner, I may throw out the hint of leading the Didroo oya, by means of a canal through the middle of the province of the Seven Korles, into the Maha oya, near its confluence with the sea. The level of the former river is considerably above that of the latter; for instance, the one near Kandeloya, the other at Girioulle, the intermediate country is nearly plain, and the distance only about five-and-twenty or thirty miles. The Seven Korles being the most fertile district in the island, and the most productive of rice, it is unnecessary to add, that the advantages of such a canal and junction of rivers, would be immense.

In respect to heat or temperature, no tropical country, perhaps, is more favoured than Ceylon; its hottest weather, being temperate in comparison with the summer-heats of most parts of the continent of India. This is owing to its insular situation, and to the greater part of it lying exposed to ventilation from both monsoons: owing to the same circumstances, the average temperature all the year round is high, excepting on the mountains; the medium range of the thermometer is inconsiderable, and the extreme range is not great. Of the coast of the island in general, I believe, it would not be far from the truth to state the mean annual temperature at between 79° and 81°; the extreme range of the thermometer, between 68° and 90°, and the medium range, between 75° and 85°.

Peculiarities of temperature deserving of notice, are exhibited by different parts of the island; that part of the coast, immediately exposed to the south-west monsoon, is remarkable for equality of temperature, and humidity of air; that, to which the same wind passes over land, is remarkable for a higher temperature, and a drier atmosphere; and the mountainous districts of the Interior, according to their elevation, are remarkable for variety of temperature and dryness.

Colombo may be taken as an instance, to illustrate the first kind of climate. The following table of its annual temperature, is formed from observations, made in the public library in the Fort, during the year 1815:—

Months.	Mean monthly Temperature.				Maximum difference.
	7. A. M.	Noon.	3 P. M.	8 P. M.	
January	75.8	80.1	82.6	79.0	6.8
February	78.8	81.4	82.0	79.5	3.2
March	81.0	83.0	83.75	81.4	2.75
April	83.0	84.86	85.66	83.9	2.66
May	83.3	84.0	84.3	82.8	1.5
June	81.1	81.8	82.3	80.6	1.7
July	79.8	80.8	80.8	79.8	1.0
August	80.2	80.75	81.0	80.0	1.0
September	79.8	80.6	80.66	79.2	1.4
October	78.0	80.3	80.8	79.3	2.8
November	77.6	79.9	79.9	78.2	2.3
December	77.0	78.8	78.7	77.2	1.8
Mean	78.5	81.3	81.8	80.6	

This table does not give as accurate a view of the temperature of Colombo, as could be wished, owing partly to the times of observing the thermometer, and partly to the place of the instrument against the inner wall of a large room, (well ventilated indeed,) which tends to equalize the diurnal changes of temperature. Still, though the equality of temperature is not quite so great as represented in the table, it exceeds, perhaps, that of any other part of the world, with the exception of a few small islands, at a great distance from land, such as St. Helena and Ascension; and even by these, perhaps, it is not exceeded, during the south-west monsoon. That wind, travelling over an immense tract of inter-tropical ocean, the temperature of the surface of which is between 80° and 83°, is as warm nearly by night as by day; and as long as it lasts, the climate of Colombo differs very little from that experienced at sea, in the same latitude. According to the preceding table, the mean annual temperature of Colombo, is 80.5, which I believe, is rather too high; judging from observations on the temperature of wells, (which there is no reason to consider as springs,) the mean does not exceed 78° or 79°. It is owing to the same wind that produces the great equality of temperature, that the climate, a great part of the year, is excessively moist. No one who has been at Colombo, or Galle, can help being struck with this peculiarity, in consequence of which, unless books and clothes are frequently exposed to the sun, they soon become covered with mildew and rapidly decay. From the observations which I have made with an hygrometer, the average dryness of the air during this monsoon, I have reason to believe, does not exceed 5 or 6 degrees.*

During the prevalence of the north-east monsoon, the climate is different both in temperature and dryness. This wind, coming from a colder quarter, and over mountains not more than thirty miles distant, its temperature is lower and its dryness

* The hygrometer, I made use of in Ceylon, was a delicate common thermometer, with a projecting bulb, covered with moist muslin. It was exposed to the wind; or, when calm, moved quickly to and fro; the difference of temperature between it and a dry thermometer, indicated the degree of dryness. I had recourse to it, as a substitute for Professor Leslie's very delicate and ingenious instrument.

greater: the former at Colombo, at dawn of day, I have seen as low as 68°; and the latter, at noon, equal to 14 degrees. During the period of the variable winds, which are generally from the sea through the day, and from the land by night, the climate partakes of the nature of the two opposite seasons, being cooler by night than during the south-west monsoon, and warmer by day, and more liable to calms, in consequence of which these periods are generally the hottest.

To illustrate the second kind of climate, a very good example offers in Trincomalie, which the south-west wind reaches, after having crossed the mountains of the Interior, and passed over a considerable extent of low country. For the following table of the temperature of that place, I am indebted to Mr. Marshall, Surgeon to the Forces. The observations from which it was formed, were made in Fort Frederick, in the years 1808 and 1809.

Months.	Mean temperature.			Highest monthly temperature.	Lowest monthly temperature.	Greatest daily variety.	Mean monthly temp.
	6 A.M.	3 P.M.	9 P.M.				
December	76	79⅓	77¼	82	74	7	77½
January	75½	77½	76	81	73	4	76½
February	75⅔	79½	71	82	74	5	78
March	77	83	79⅔	86	75	8	80
April	79½	85⅔	82	90	78	9	82
May	79⅔	88	82	90	77	10	82⅔
June	79½	89⅓	82⅓	90½	75	10	84⅔
July	79	88	81	90	75	10	82⅓
August	78½	87	81	90	76	11	83
September	78½	87⅓	80	90	76	11	82
October	76½	83	78⅓	90	74	12	79⅓
November	75⅜	80½	78	84	73	9	78

According to this table, the mean temperature of the coolest months at Trincomalie, when the north-east monsoon prevails, is 77.5; the mean of the hottest, when the land-wind blows, 82.8, and the mean annual temperature 80.4; which, from observations I have made with the thermometer on wells, at that place, I believe to be pretty correct. The comparatively low temperature of the air, when the north-east wind blows in the winter months of higher northern latitudes, stands in need of no comment. The circumstance of the south-west wind, having its temperature increased by the time it arrives at Trincomalie, is not so obvious to reason, and requires some elucidation, which will serve for a variety of similar cases, and to account for the seeming paradox of the northern extremity of the island being hotter than the southern. On leaving the mountains, from which it descends with considerable force, this wind is cool, almost cold, as I have experienced on the confines of Doombera, towards Bintenney. It is in passing over the low-wooded country, intermediate between the mountains and the sea, that its temperature becomes elevated; an effect, not to be expected, perhaps, from the nature of the surface over which it flows, of perennial verdure and of cooling tendency, but which the following circumstances will serve to account for. The soil of the low country is generally sandy; and, during the season of the south-west monsoon, is dry even where most densely shaded: no rain falling at this period, water is uncommonly scarce, the ground parched, and the rivers dried up. Low and rocky hills, which must radiate and reflect a good deal of heat, are not uncommon. The foliage of the forest, with which the greater part of the country is over-run, is peculiar; the leaves are small, well varnished, and dry, not subject to much perspiration, like the leaves of succulent plants, growing in a well-watered soil; and consequently, their temperature is more elevated by day, by the action of the sun's rays, than it is depressed by night, by the very inconsiderable evaporation that takes place from their surface.* These circumstances considered — these pe-

* That there is very little evaporation from the surface of these leaves; that their temperature is elevated in the sunshine, above that of the air; that the temperature

culiarities of ground and vegetation duly weighed, — one is not astonished, that the temperature of the wind exposed to them, is a very few degrees higher than that of the same wind fresh from the ocean: one is rather surprised, it is not very much higher and insupportably hot; equal to, or surpassing, that of the deserts of Africa. Were the intermediate country, like these deserts, covered with barren sand, no doubt, its heating effect would be similar. Happily, by the annual supply of rain, that is so general all over the island, a preventive cause is maintained in the perennial foliage of the immense forests, that spread from the mountains to the shore, which, though it does not cool the wind, at least moderates its temperature, and renders its heat supportable. In the most northern district of the island, that of Jaffnapatam, where the climate is very similar to that of Trincomalie, there is reason to believe that the mean annual temperature is a little higher than in any other part of Ceylon, and merely because it has not equally the advantage of the moderating circumstance just mentioned; great part of the district being free from wood, cleared and cultivated, and the land-wind, instead of coming over a green surface of shaded forest, passes along the sandy beach, and the low sandy tract, of the western coast of the island. The south-west wind, when it becomes a land-wind, is no less remarkable for its dryness and its strength, than for its higher temperature; properties which it naturally acquires, in passing into a warmer and rarer atmosphere, and in travelling over a parched country.

---

of those in the shade is not lower, in general, than that of the air, and that at night, the depression of their temperature is very inconsiderable, — are facts, of the correctness of which, I convinced myself by actual experiments made when travelling through the country in question, in September, 1817.

The third kind of climate is that of the mountainous districts of the Interior, where elevation of ground, from 1000 to 6000 feet, produces a considerable variety of temperatures, which, from complication of circumstances, cannot be calculated, I believe, with any precision, and can be ascertained only by actual experiment. Generally, the temperature of the mountains is cooler than might be expected, and their vicissitudes of temperature greater. The mean annual temperature of heights, between 1500 feet and 6000, vary, perhaps, from 73° to 50°. To illustrate the climate of the former height, in relation to temperature and dryness, Kandy, situated about 1467 feet above the level of the sea, in lat 7° 17′ north, surrounded by wooded hills, is a very good example, particularly, since it is the only station in the Interior, where very precise observations have been made on the weather. The following table formed from observations, made by the medical officers at the General Military Hospital of the Garrison, in 1819, may be considered tolerably correct. The morning observations contained in it, were made, I believe, between six and seven A. M. and the night observations, between nine and eleven P.M.

Months.	Mean morn. temp.	Mean mid-day temp.	Mean night temp.	Highest temp. in each month.	Lowest in each.	Greatest variation in 24 hours.	Mean monthly temp.
January	64⅓	76	69⅓	80	53	19	70
February	65⅔	78	70⅓	84	57	22	71⅓
March	68	80½	72⅓	87	53	17	73½
April	68⅔	80½	72½	87	63	18	74
May	69⅔	79	72	84	67	15	73⅔
June	69½	78	72	83	68	15	73
July	70½	77	72	81	68	12	73
August	71	78⅔	72	84	68	15	74
September	70	78	71½	84	68	15	73
October	69½	79	72	83	65	15	73
November	67½	82	71	82	61	20	73
December	68½	76⅔	70	82	64	17	72 *

* From the Ceylon Gazette, 8th Jan. 1820.

According to this table, the mean annual temperature of Kandy was, for the year 1819, 72.75; which, from observations on the temperature of wells, at different seasons, I am inclined to think as a general mean, a little too low, and that 73.5 is nearer the true average. During the months of January and February, when the wind is steady from the north-east, and the heavy rains attending the setting in of the monsoon are over, the weather, as might be expected, is cooler than at any other time of the year, and generally extremely clear and dry; the hygrometer exposed to the wind, has been observed to fall 14 degrees. In these months, and indeed whenever the wind is from the north-east, dense clouds are to be observed hanging on the eastern mountains. During the period that the wind blows from the opposite side of the island, from about June to October, the air is less dry and clear, and its temperature is higher and more equable. The sky is now generally clear over the eastern mountains, and obscured with clouds over the western. During the months that the winds are most variable, and calms most common, as in March and April, the air is commonly damp, the days are often extremely hot, and the nights cold. As general observations, it may be stated, that in rainy weather, in Kandy, the thermometer is seldom below 70°, and as seldom above 72°; that in dry weather, when the wind blows fresh, it is almost always below 70° at dawn, and never below 60°, and that at noon when hottest, it seldom exceeds 85°, and rarely falls below 78°; that the coolest nights as well as the hottest days, are those which are clearest and most calm, and that it is only in such weather, the thermometer sinks below 65°, or rises above 80°; and lastly, that the air is never very dry, excepting the wind blows strongly from the north or the south, or from some intermediate easterly point.

Respecting the temperature of altitudes exceeding that of Kandy, I have little but conjectures to offer, founded chiefly on the temperature of water on some of the principal heights, which it may be fairly inferred is more likely to lead to truth on the subject of mean temperature than any partial observations on so fluctuating a medium as that of the air. I shall detail a few of the observations that appear to be most deserving of confidence.

In April, 1817, at 1 h. P. M. I found the temperature of a stream, called the Setagongola, 58.75, when the air was 74°. This is a fine mountain-torrent, the principal branch of the Kalu ganga. It is about 4243 feet above the level of the sea, about three miles from the summit of Adam's Peak, and descends with great rapidity over a rocky bed, well shaded by luxuriant wood.

In April, 1819, at 8 h. 30 m. A. M., I found the temperature of a small stream flowing through a wood between Fort Macdonald and Maturatta 59.5, when the air was 62°. This stream is about 4735 feet high, and not more than five or six hundred feet below the summit of the mountain ridge.

In August, 1819, at 8 h. A. M., I found the temperature of the Wilehit oya 55.5, when the air was 60°. This is a considerable rivulet on the confines of Kotmale towards Ouva, at the height of about 5132 feet, and well shaded.

In March, 1819, on the top of Namina Cooli Kandy, about 5548 feet high, at 8 h. A. M., I found the temperature of a pit, about six feet deep, half full of rain-water, 53°, when the air was 57°.

I cannot but place some little confidence in these results, as in more than one instance I have observed the temperature of mountain-streams not to vary quite a degree in two different seasons of the year. Considered merely as approximations, they lead to the inference, that the average annual temperature of heights in the Interior between four and five thousand feet above the level of the sea, may be between 60° and 55°, and that of heights from five to six thousand feet may be between 55° and 50°, which latter, probably, is about the mean of the highest point of the island.

Respecting the extremes of temperature of the mountains, I have still less to offer than respecting their mean. Probably, they are occasionally great, for instance, in calm clear weather; and as the thermometer, in such a state of the atmosphere, has been observed at Badulla, at break of day, as low as 48°, it is very likely, that, on the top of Adam's Peak, about 4291 feet higher. it may fall below the freezing point.

In a practical point of view, the preceding inferences are not void of interest, indeed, it is in relation to such views that they are most important. It is of consequence to know, that, by ascending the mountains of the Interior, according to the degree of elevation, you may find the average temperature of every latitude between Ceylon and England; and enjoy, amongst the finest scenery of nature, the purest and most refreshing atmosphere. It is too sanguine, perhaps, but I cannot help anticipating it, that a time will arrive, when the mountain-tracts of Ceylon, many of them of surpassing beauty in their wildness, now merely charming deserts, will be inhabited and cultivated by Europeans, and made the nurseries not only of our plants, but, which is infinitely more important, of our religion and virtues, our arts and sciences.

Of the minor meteorological phenomena, as of dews, mists, clouds, thunder and lightning, &c. brief notices will suffice, the subjects not being of sufficient general interest to warrant their minute discussion.

Dew is not of very common occurrence in Ceylon, excepting in the Interior, where it is more abundant in the low valleys and plains than on the mountains. In general, agreeable to the admirable observations of the late Dr. Wells, I never remarked the formation of dew to take place with a clouded sky; or with a breeze, excepting of the gentlest kind; or when the air was dry, occasioning a fall of the moist thermometer exceeding two or three degrees; or when the air at night was not cooler by ten degrees than by day. It is commonly supposed, that the ground is moistened, and that plants are refreshed with dew, and more particularly in a tropical climate. That plants on which it *forms* (I do not venture to make use of the popular but erroneous term, *falls*) are refreshed by it, I have no doubt; but I cannot give the same unhesitating assent to the first supposition. Invert a glass on a garden-bed when dew is forming, and you will find its inside covered with moisture in the morning. I have taken a portion of mould from a small spot of such a bed; have exposed the former in a thin vessel of horn to the air in a dewy night; have covered the latter with an inverted glass, and, on examination in the morning, I have found the portion of soil exposed to the air and dew drier than that which was covered, notwithstanding the inside of the glass was copiously bedewed. Reflecting on these and some other circumstances, I am almost induced to think, that, if the ground ever gains moisture by dew, it loses much more than it gains, by the insensible perspiration which is always taking place from its warmer surface.

Mists, like dews, are much more common in the Interior, than on the coast of the island; and in the deep moist valleys amongst the mountains, than in any other situation. Very often, in such situations, they form of astonishing density, and resemble an expanse of water so much, that, to a spectator in the clear cool air on a mountain above, were he ignorant of the features of the country, they would appear to be genuine lakes. The beauty which these mists give to mountain-scenery, is greater than can be well imagined. Occasionally, after sun-rise, the mists that have formed in the higher mountain-hollows, are displaced by the wind, and poured in immense volumes down into the warmer valleys, producing a sudden chillness and extreme humidity of the air that is very disagreeable, and a sudden reduction of several degrees of temperature. The valley of Kandy is particularly liable to accidents of this kind.

Mountains are always the regions of clouds ;—nor are the Kandyan mountains an exception. Hardly a day together are the loftier mountains free from clouds ; and during the whole of the south-west monsoon, Adam's Peak is concealed by them.

By poets, it is generally represented, and it is as generally believed, that the beauties of a tropical sky are as splendid as they are fugitive. This is far from correct. Night, within the tropics, does not follow almost instantly the setting of the sun, nor does the sun rise or set in greater magnificence than in higher latitudes. The twilight is indeed short in comparison with ours, seldom exceeding half an hour, and never less, except in the most gloomy weather. The sun-risings and the sun-settings which I have seen in the torrid zone, in point of beauty or splendour of effect, excepting amongst the mountains, have always disappointed me, and have appeared very inferior to the same phenomena in this country in summer and autumn. The clouds of evening and morning, in a tropical sky, want often richness of colouring, and always variety ; and always those soft, and gradual, and insensible changes of tint and shade, that decorate the heavens in our long twilights. Yet, there are features in a tropical sky worthy of admiration ; as the general clearness of the air, brightness of light, pure blue of the heavens, and the great beams of yellow light that are often to be seen shooting up towards the zenith, from the place of the rising or setting sun.

There is a peculiar phenomenon, occasionally seen in the heavens in the Interior, that is deserving of notice. In January 1820, it was witnessed in Kandy, and by European gentlemen as well as by natives. One of the former, a most respectable individual, in whose account I could put the firmest reliance, described it to me as an appearance of rays or beams of light in motion, intersecting one another, faintly resembling the northern lights. It occurred when the atmosphere was clear, in the middle of the day, " in mid-air, beneath the vault of the sky," unattended by any unusual circumstance of weather that might lead to conjecture respecting its cause and nature. The natives call it Boodhoo rais (Boodhoo-rays), and consider it ominous ; boding ill in general, and auspicious only when it appears in the month of May. They imagine that it is never witnessed, excepting over a temple of Boodhoo, from whence, as the name they have given the phenomenon implies, they suppose it to emanate.

Thunder-storms are of very frequent occurrence in Ceylon, particularly along the coast most exposed to the south-west wind, and amongst the mountains, especially the western. They are not confined to any season, but they are most common in the variable weather, and most violent at the change of the monsoon, when indeed they are sometimes tremendous. Judging from the apparent course of the clouds, these storms seem to be generally connected with the mixing of currents of air flowing in different directions. As these storms seldom do mischief, are always attended with rain, and have the effect of cooling and refreshing the air, they are very acceptable, and not only to man, but animals. At Kandy, the birds never sing so sweetly as during a thunder-storm. I have often heard their notes between the loudest peals of thunder, and when it has been raining in torrents, as if to express their gratitude for a benefit conferred on them; reminding one of what Park, I believe, says of the inhabitants of some of the deserts he travelled over,—that when they see sheet-lightning, they hail it with acclamations, as a certain indication of their being about to be blessed with rain.

Few islands, particularly inter-tropical islands, suffer less from violent storms and hurricanes than Ceylon. In the course of nearly four years, only one storm occurred deserving the name, that did much mischief to shipping. Of hurricanes, I heard of two instances only that I recollect, during the time I was in the island. Both happened at Alipoota, in Lower Ouva, near the foot of the mountains, through the ravines of which they seemed to have rushed. One occurred in July, and the other in August, 1819, attended with violent thunder, and vivid lightning, and heavy rain and hail. Describing the latter hurricane, Mr. Assistant-Surgeon Hoatson, who was on the spot, in a letter on the subject, remarks,—"A dreadful clap of thunder was instantly followed by a tremendous gust of wind, rain and hail, such as I never witnessed before. The whole went in an instant, unroofing our houses, and levelling many of the huts of the soldiers with the ground. Large trees were literally torn up by the roots, and trees which we have since measured, and found fourteen feet in circumference, were broke in two. The hail fell in such quantities, that it might be gathered in handfuls."

Hail is a very uncommon phenomenon in the low parts of Ceylon, particularly in the maritime provinces, where perhaps it is not seen once in a century. It is less rare in the mountain-valleys; and, on the higher mountains it has been observed by Major Fraser to occur frequently.

In relation to climate, the last subject that requires consideration, is its salubrity. * In an island of the extent of Ceylon, the local circumstances of different parts of which vary so greatly, it would be unreasonable to expect that one uniform character of wholesomeness or unwholesomeness of air should be generally applicable. Were a scale, to express different degrees of salubrity of air, constructed, almost the whole of it might be exemplified in Ceylon. Nearly the extreme degrees of atmospheric salubrity are enjoyed on the south-west coast, and on the loftier grounds of the Interior: nearly the extremes of insalubrity are felt in the low wooded country, between the mountains and the sea, in all directions, excepting towards the south-west coast; and the middle degrees are experienced in the lower mountainous and hilly districts of the Interior, and on the northern and eastern shores of the island. This division is the result of some experience, and is pretty accurate. To account for each peculiarity in a satisfactory manner, in the present state of our knowledge, is hardly possible, and yet it is right to attempt it. It is not surprising that the south-west shore of the island, and the loftier mountainous districts, should be the most wholesome parts of

* I use this term in its popular sense, and chiefly in relation to absence of miasmata, or the causes of endemic fever.

Ceylon. That shore, great part of the year, is ventilated by the south-west wind, fresh and pure from the ocean; and it is refreshed by the frequent fall of showers. Along its whole extent, it is more or less cultivated, and agreeably shaded by magnificent cocoa-nut groves, and various fruit-trees. These, perhaps, are the chief circumstances that conduce to its salubrity. Respecting the good effect of the wind from the sea, there can be no doubt; and, almost as little can be entertained respecting the ameliorating effect of cultivation, and the benefit derived from the shade of cultivated trees. Unfortunate would it be for the island, were the notions of a noble traveller on this subject correct, or were his suggestions, founded on these notions, carried into execution, who, supposing cocoa-nut trees to be injurious to the air, has recommended the destruction of those fine groves in the neighbourhood of Galle, with the idea of improving the wholesomeness of a place already remarkably wholesome. It was from notions similar to this, not long after we had possession of Trincomalie, that the majority of the cocoa-nut trees at that place were cut down, to the great detriment of the inhabitants, and to the deterioration rather than the improvement of the air. It is well established, and ought never to be forgotten, that it is not shade that is prejudicial in a hot climate; that it is not vigorous, healthy vegetation that is noxious; but the accumulation of dead vegetable matter and its putrefaction; and, that whilst every means are taken to prevent the latter, too much encouragement cannot be given to promote the former. A variety of circumstances conduces to the salubrity of the mountainous districts; the principal circumstances in Ceylon seem to be the frequent occurrence of showers, tending to wash the decaying remains of vegetables to lower levels; the cooler air, that at the same time invigorates the animal frame, and retards vegetable putrefaction, and the frequent thunder-storms, which, while they agitate, seem to purify the atmosphere. The *precise cause* of the extreme unhealthiness of the low wooded parts of the country, that have not the benefit of a sea-breeze and of cultivation, is still obscure. Whatever it may be in Ceylon, it appears to be contained in the air or wind from low uncultivated country covered with wood. It appears too, to be connected with great dryness of the air *, being most active during the longest droughts, and generally disappearing with the commencement of the rainy season; and this so regularly and generally, that, knowing the season that is sickly in any part of the low country, you need not enquire if it be dry, or *vice versâ*. The probability is, that the cause in question is some effluvia produced by the decomposition of vegetable matter, but of what nature yet remains to be investigated. I have examined the air disengaged from stagnant pools in the Interior, and from the mud of rice-fields under water, in a state of preparation to receive the grain: I have found them both alike, and similar to the air of our marshes,—a mixture of carburetted hydrogen, a little carbonic acid, and a little common air. To suppose carburetted hydrogen to be the cause of unwholesomeness of air, is far from probable, and indeed is highly improbable, when we reflect, that it is breathed

* Though this state of the air may retard the decay of vegetable matter on the surface of the ground, it may have a contrary effect on that beneath the surface; and that it will occasion an increased exhalation there can be no doubt. The quantity of exhalation that takes place from the low flat grounds during the dry season must be immense. The foliage in general continuing green during the longest droughts is a satisfactory proof that there must be a stock of moisture below equal to the great demand on it.

occasionally with impunity in our laboratories, in quantities much less minute, than it can be imagined to exist in the atmosphere of the most unhealthy climate. Generally speaking, the lower mountainous and hilly districts, and the eastern and northern shores of the island, that experience the middle degrees of salubrity of air, are so situated as to participate, at different seasons, of the circumstances conducive to the extremes of healthiness and unhealthiness, which alone will serve to account tolerably for their peculiarities: Thus Trincomalie, (and very many other places might be mentioned,) is never very sickly whilst the north-east monsoon prevails; is never so, till the south-west wind reaches it from the opposite shore of the island, after having passed over a great extent of low, wooded, and very unwholesome country. But, there are instances of occasional insalubrity of air, that cannot be thus explained; and instances too, unfortunately of common occurrence, especially in the Kandyan country. Particular spots and districts, that have been remarkably healthy for years, have suddenly changed their character, and passed from the extreme of salubrity to that of insalubrity. They have remained some time in this state, and have gradually returned to their former condition. These changes of climate in Ceylon often take place, like similar changes did take place in this country, in the time of Sydenham, without any cause being apparent. I have known a little district of the Interior, that for years was the envy of the adjoining country, on account of its healthiness, suddenly desolated by endemic fever, whilst the weather, season, and every other appreciable circumstance seemed to promise a continuance of that healthiness that had unaccountably disappeared. Though we may never be able to account for these changes, it is of high importance, that they are known and studied, and their character investigated. It may be found, that they have regular periods of return; — circumstances may be observed to indicate their return. Any discovery of this kind (not to allude to others that probably may be made) would be of incalculable benefit; allowing time to prepare to resist the attack of disease; or, what would be more prudent, to avoid the danger by removal to a healthy district.

CHAPTER III.

SNAKES — EXPERIMENTS ON THEIR POISON. — CEYLON LEECH.

It is not my intention, in this work, to give an account of any of the plants of Ceylon; and, of its animals I propose to treat very briefly, restricting myself to such notices as appear to me new, or promise to be useful.

It is natural to enquire, do the same animals occur in Ceylon as on the adjoining continent of India?—In respect to the mammalia, I am not aware that any species unknown on the continent is to be found in Ceylon, though there are several unknown in the latter, that are common on the continent; for instance, the royal tiger, the wolf, and different species of antelope. From the absence of these animals, it has been argued by some, that Ceylon was never an integral part of India. But the circumstance of the majority of the mammalia of the continent and of the island being the same, is a better reason to suppose, that they were once united and that the narrow and shallow strait which now separates them, was formed at a period not very remote in the history of our globe. Indeed, no one who looks at a map, and sees the little distance between the nearest points of the island and continent, and how, by the chain of rocks and sand-banks, commonly called Adam's Bridge, they are still imperfectly connected, can entertain much doubt, that the connection was once perfect.* This enquiry is rather curious than useful. It would be much more useful, to endeavour to complete that which nature has begun, and make the channel, which is now so obstructed and dangerous, clear and safe, and fit for the purposes of coast-navigation. The accomplishment of this is said to be impossible. It may be so; yet I cannot help thinking, that the decision has been rather hasty and premature, and made from imperfect information. An object surely of such importance should not be relinquished, till its impracticability is demonstrated; and I believe no very minute survey has been made of the channel to warrant any decided opinion on the subject.

Whilst I was in Ceylon, my professional pursuits led me to pay particular attention to the snakes of the Island, especially to those whose bite is poisonous. I intend to give here the results of my inquiries relative to these animals, though in a very unfinished state.

It is commonly supposed that Ceylon abounds in snakes; that they are very dangerous, and that they cannot be too carefully avoided. All this is greatly exaggerated. Where the fears are much concerned, the reason is generally weak; and snakes, from time immemorial, —indeed in all ages and all countries, have been objects of aversion and dread, and subjects for superstition and fable. Snakes are neither numerous in Ceylon, nor much to be apprehended. Those who have most experience, have the greatest confi-

* If on examination sandstone and coral-rock should be found constituting part of Adam's Bridge, instead of primitive rock, one necessary inference is, that the channel, at whatever period formed, was once deeper and more open than it is at present; and another inference is, that in process of time it will be closed up, and Ceylon again joined to the continent.

dence; the old sportsman, in pursuit of game, plunges into the wildest jungle, without dread or apprehension, whilst the newly arrived European, does not cross a lawn but with fear, almost amounting to trembling, of snakes in the grass. The latter is terrified by his imagination — the former is fearless from the knowledge of his security: one of the best and keenest sportsmen in the island, who has lived several years in the Megam-pattoo, a district almost deserted by man, and extremely infested with wild animals, has assured me, that in all his rambles and excursions, he has never met with a poisonous snake. My object in making these remarks, is to endeavour to remove senseless horrors, which apprehension of snakes in Ceylon too often gives rise to; and which, if not opposed and subdued, detract more from the comfort and happiness of life, than can well be imagined, excepting by those, on whose minds is still impressed the memory of the miseries produced in childhood, by the dread of hobgoblins.

Though snakes are not abundant in Ceylon, there are several different species in the island. I have procured, through the kindness of friends, and by employing men to collect for me, twenty different kinds: of these, sixteen were harmless, though the majority had the character of being venomous, and were called "bad snakes" by the natives; and four only were really poisonous. Of the sixteen former, there was not a single boa; nor have I met with any snake of this genus in Ceylon: — one was a species of python; thirteen were species of coluber, and two of anguis. The four poisonous snakes were all of the coluber kind.

For those who are not conversant with natural history, and may not have it in their power to refer to works on the subject, at a moment, when they might wish to determine whether a snake

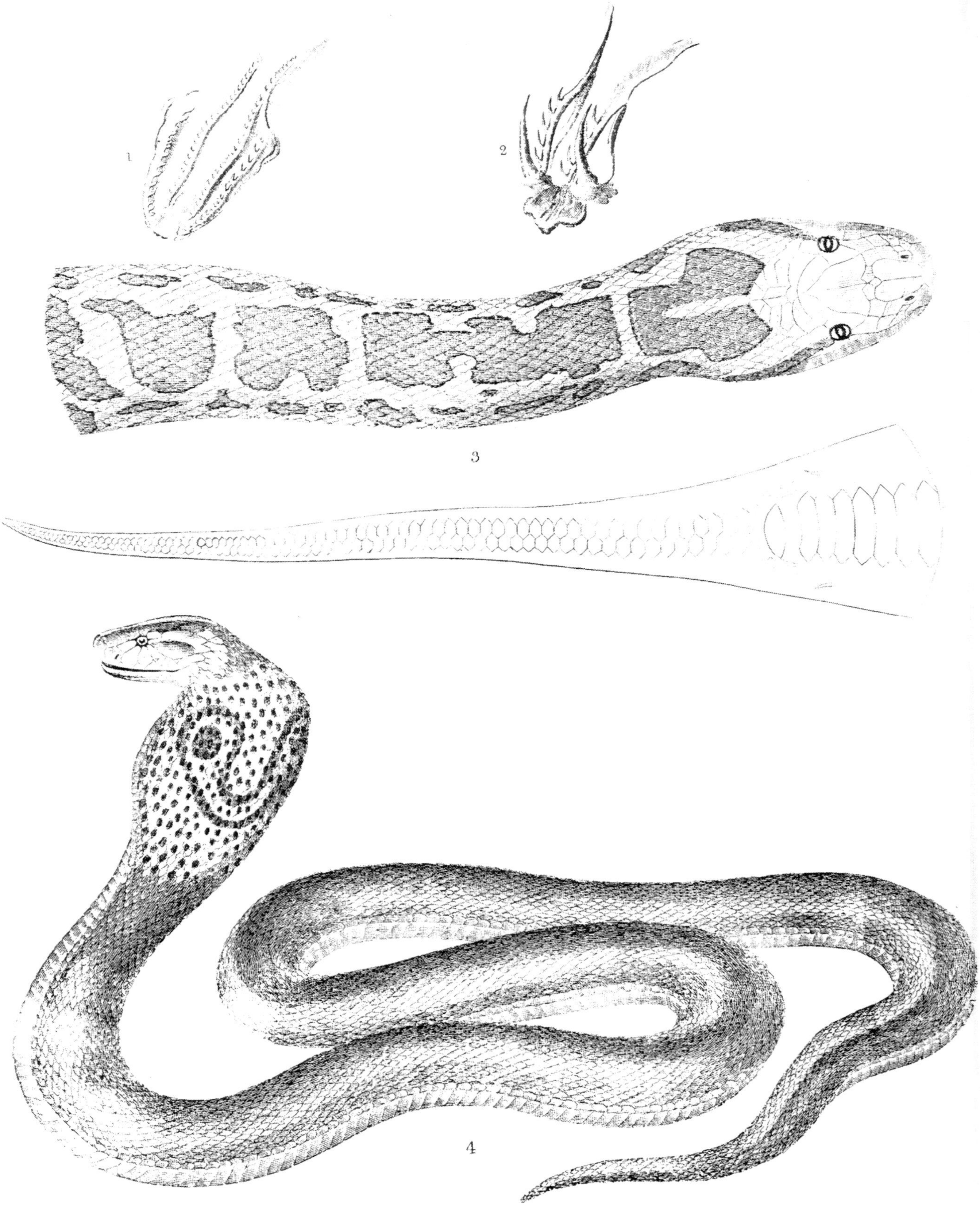
1
2
3
4

be poisonous or harmless, (which, independent of gratifying curiosity, may sometimes be extremely useful,) it may not be amiss to point out the discriminative marks, with the help of figures.

Figure 1. Plate I. represents the skeleton of the head of a harmless snake inverted, with the lower jaw detached; and fig. 2. a similar view of the head of a poisonous snake. They differ essentially, in the one being provided with a double row of teeth; and the other with a single row and two fangs, each of which is perforated with a canal: that at the base of the tooth communicates with the poison-duct from the poison-gland, and terminates in a longitudinal opening, just below the point of the fang, which is solid.

The only snakes I shall describe and give drawings of, are the species of Python, and those that are poisonous; — the harmless snakes being of little interest, except to the professed naturalist.

The Pimberah, (fig. 3. Plate I.) as this snake is called by the natives, or the rock-snake, as it is sometimes called by the English, belongs to the new genus python, of M. Cuvier. It is characterised by its great size, and by a couple of horny processes in form and curvature not unlike the spurs of the common fowl, penetrating the skin and projecting a little anterior to the anus.* By these peculiarities the pimbera is separated from

* These horny spurs are perhaps useful to the animal in climbing trees and holding fast its prey. They seem to afford a remarkable instance, of what Blumenbach calls the *nisus formativus* (*a*) to produce articulated hind-extremities, — the base of the spur being attached to a small bone with a minute head, which is received into the glenoid cavity of a thin long bone that terminates in a tapering cartilaginous process. Small muscles are attached to these bones; the cartilaginous extremity is only slightly connected with the surrounding cellular membrane.

(*a*) **Blumenbachi de Nisu formativo et generationis negotio nuperæ observat.—Gotting. 1787.**

the genus Coluber, to which it is allied by similarity of abdominal scuta, and subcaudal squamæ or scutella.

This snake is the largest species in Ceylon; and indeed is the only one that grows to a great size. I have seen a specimen of it about seventeen feet long, and proportionably thick.* It is said by the natives to attain a much greater magnitude, and to be found occasionally twenty-five and thirty feet long, and of the thickness of a common-sized man. The colour of different specimens that I have seen has varied a little; it is generally a mixture of brown and yellow; the back and sides are strongly and rather handsomely marked with irregular patches of dark brown with very dark margins. The jaws are powerful, and capable of great dilatation; and they are armed with large strong sharp teeth, reclining backwards. As the muscular strength of this snake is immense, and its activity and courage considerable, it may be credited that it will occasionally attack man;, there can be no doubt that it overpowers deer, and swallows them entire.

The natives have many ridiculous stories respecting this snake. They say, that when young it is a polonga, and provided with poisonous fangs; and that when of a certain age and size it loses these fangs, acquires spurs, and becomes a pimberah. They suppose its spurs are poisonous, and that the animal uses them in striking and killing its prey. They imagine that parturition is always fatal to the female, owing to the abdomen bursting on the

* This animal belonged to Dr. Farrell, who was so obliging as to allow me to examine it, when it was killed after having been four months in confinement without eating, though frequently tried with fowls, frogs, &c. The inner reticulated surface of the lung of this snake was composed of fibres that appeared to be muscular, and which were certainly irritable and contractile. I have observed the same in the lungs of other snakes, but never before in so decided a manner.

occasion; and, that the males, aware of this circumstance, out of regard for the females of their species, avoid them, and choose for their mates, female noyas.

The cobra de capello of the Portuguese, the hooded snake of the English, the noya of the natives, the coluber naja of Linnæus, is too well known to require description. (Fig. 4. Plate I.) It is the most common of the poisonous snakes of Ceylon. The largest I ever saw in the island was nearly six feet long; its general length is between two and four feet. It varies much in colour; those of a light colour are called high-cast snakes by the natives, and those of a dark colour, low-cast.

The natives in general rather venerate this snake, than dread it. They conceive that it belongs to another world, and that when it appears in this, it is merely as a visitor; they imagine that it possesses great power, that it is somewhat akin to the gods, and greatly superior to man. In consequence, they superstitiously refrain from killing it, and always avoid it, if possible; even when they find one in their house they will not kill it, but putting it into a bag, throw it into water. They believe that this snake has a good and generous disposition, and that it will do no harm to man, unless provoked.

Frequent exhibitions are made of this snake in Ceylon as well as on the continent of India, by men called snake-charmers. The exhibition is rather a curious one, and not a little amusing to those who can calmly contemplate it. The charmer irritates the snake by striking it, and by rapid threatening motions of his hand; and appeases it by his voice, by gentle circular movements of his hand, and by stroking it gently. He avoids with great agility the attacks of the animal when enraged, and plays with it and handles it only when pacified, when he will bring the mouth of the animal in contact with his forehead, and draw it over his face. The ignorant vulgar believe that these men really possess a charm by which they thus play without dread, and with impunity, with danger. The more enlightened, laughing at this idea, consider the men impostors, and that in playing their tricks, there is no danger to be avoided, it being removed by the extraction of the poison-fangs. The enlightened in this instance are mistaken, and the vulgar are nearer the truth in their opinion. I have examined the snakes I have seen exhibited, and have found their poison-fangs in, and uninjured. These men do possess a charm, though not a supernatural one, viz. that of confidence and courage: acquainted with the habits and disposition of the snake, they know how averse it is to use the fatal weapon nature has given it for its defence in extreme danger, and that it never bites without much preparatory threatening. Any one possessing the confidence and agility of these men may imitate them, and I have made the trial more than once. They will play their tricks with any hooded snake, whether just taken or long in confinement, but with no other kind of poisonous snake.

The snake, called by the natives Carawilla, next to the hooded snake, is the most common of the poisonous kind in Ceylon. (Fig. 1. Plate II.) Its average length is about a foot. Its back is of a dull reddish-brown colour; its belly nearly silver-white, and towards the tail greyish. On each side, between the ridge of the back, and the boundary-line between the back and the belly, there are two rows of black velvety spots; and of these, there are three in the tail. The head is nearly triangular and compressed; it is of a darker colour than the body, and is free from spots. Its

1
2
3
4

jaws are very dilatable. Its fang-teeth are very long, slender and sharp. It lies coiled up, its head projecting at right angles nearly to its body. When provoked, it hisses, darts its head with great rapidity at the irritating object, and wounds almost to a certainty. It is active, and when frightened and anxious to escape, it moves, *per saltim*, with considerable rapidity.

The snake, called by the natives the Tic-polonga, is difficult to be procured. (fig. 2. Plate II.) It is considered, and I believe justly, the most dangerous snake in the island. When full grown, it is from four to five feet long; and, in proportion to its length, it is very thick. Its head is small, and nearly triangular; its tail is tapering, round and short. The colour of its upper surface is a dark, dull, brownish grey; of its under surface, light yellow. Its belly is not spotted, but its back is marked very regularly. In some specimens, the marks are oval; in some, they are more pointed and rather trapezoidal. In some, they are surrounded with a white margin; and, in others, the spots are lightest in the middle. This snake is rather indolent and inactive. It is averse to attack; it lies coiled up, very like the carawilla; and, when irritated much, it hisses dreadfully, and darts forward, and strikes very much in the manner of the snake just mentioned.

A snake, which appears to me to be the same, as the Bodroo Pam of Dr. Russell*, is extremely rare in Ceylon (fig. 3. Plate II.) The natives have no name for it, that I am aware; and, the only place that I know of, where it has been met with, is Fort King, where two were found, for one of which, I was indebted to the kindness of Captain King, then commanding at that post.

* Russell on Indian Serpents, vol. i. p. 60.

The specimen, from which the figure was taken *, appeared to be full grown. It was about two feet two inches long; its head was large and irregularly heart-shaped; its neck was small; its body thin, its sides compressed, and its tail rather abrupt and tapering. It had two large cavities, one on each side, between the eye and nostril, the diameter of each of which rather exceeded one-tenth of an inch. Its lower surface was yellow, variegated with green; its upper, bright apple-green. This colour was confined to the scales; the cutis beneath was black, consequently, where the scales were very close, (as they were in patches along the back,) black was excluded; and, where they did not over-lap completely, the green appeared to be shaded with black. A line of black scales may be mentioned, as occurring above the upper jaw, and a few of the same colour appeared along the ridge of the back.

Of the four poisonous snakes, I have tried the effects of three on animals. I shall relate the experiments in detail, not certainly to amuse the general reader, but with the better hope of being useful, and affording some little help towards the elucidation of an important and most mysterious subject.

Experiments on the Poison of the Hooded Snake.

Experiment 1. The snake used in this experiment was found in a bag floating down the Kalany ganga. It was about five feet long, and its broadest part about six inches in circumference. It appeared to be active and in good health. On the 30th of November, 1816, at Colombo, a full-grown hen was brought near it. After much threatening the snake darted on the hen, and fixed

* The figures of the other snakes are copied, on a reduced scale, with some slight alterations, from Dr. Russell's splendid work on Indian Serpents.

its fangs in the skin, covering the lower part of the left pectoral muscle. It kept its hold about two or three seconds, when I succeeded in shaking it off.

Immediately, the hen appeared to be but little affected; she seemed rather uneasy and restless, and was every now and then pecking the part bitten. Some corn being thrown on the ground, she ate only a very little. In two hours she was worse, but even now, the action of the poison was not apparent from any remarkakble symptom, merely from a certain degree of debility and languor produced, indicated by her being easily caught, and by her couching when not disturbed. There was no swelling or inflammation round the punctured wound. Her temperature, ascertained before the experiment, and now, by a thermometer placed in the rectum, was found to have fallen from 109° to 108°. In four hours she was much worse; her breathing had become quick and laborious; venous blood seemed to predominate in the circulation; the comb being bluish and turgid. There was great prostration of strength, so that she was unable to stand; the sensorial functions were not apparently deranged; the pupil was rather dilated than contracted; there were no convulsions and no rigors. Several liquid dejections occurred, and some watery fluid was thrown up: her temperature was now reduced to 106°. I was obliged to leave the house, and just before my return she expired, eight hours having elapsed from the time she was bitten.

I examined the fowl the next morning, ten hours after death. Externally, there was no appearance of swelling, or of inflammation, or of any kind of change, not even immediately on the spot wounded. Beneath the skin, where the fangs had penetrated, there was much cellular membrane, and a layer of fat, sufficient to have prevented the teeth reaching the muscle. The cellular membrane under the wound, exhibited slight indistinct traces of inflammation. On the mucous membrane of the intestines, there were a few red spots. With this exception, the abdominal viscera, in general, had no unusual appearance; the brain exhibited no marks of disease. Both ventricles of the heart were empty, contracted, and hard; the auricles contained coagulated blood. The lungs were unusually red, and the air-cells were full of serum, which, on pressure, flowed out copiously.

Experiment 2. Three days after, I exposed to the same snake, a large powerful cock. The snake fastened on his comb, and kept its hold with its fangs, for one or two seconds. A little blood flowed from the wound.

During the first four hours, the bird did not appear in the least unwell, walking about and eating as usual. After the fourth hour, he began to droop and lose his strength: in eight hours, he appeared very weak, could scarcely walk, his feathers were ruffled, his eyes nearly closed, his breathing laborious. In this state, he continued about twenty-four hours, without eating; he voided much greenish excrement. His temperature was reduced from 109.75, which it was before he was bitten, to 106. About the twenty-eighth hour, he appeared a little better, but still refused to eat: this was in the evening; the next morning (he was in my bed-room in a basket) I was awoke by his loud and vigorous crowing. He now appeared recovered; he had regained his appetite, and his temperature had risen to 108°.

Experiment 3. The day following, I tried the same snake on two puppies, both of whom it bit. In neither instance, was the health deranged; nor had its bite, sixteen days after, any effect on a small dog.

Experiment 4. The snake used in this experiment was of the same size nearly as the last. It was recently taken, and was active and vigorous.

On the 13th of February, 1817, a young cock, about half-grown, was bitten by it on the breast; the wound was so very slight, that it was only just perceptible. During the first hour, the bird walked about and ate, as if nothing ailed him. Then he gradually sickened, his feathers became ruffled, he ate very little, and remained stationary in one place. For a day and a half, he continued growing slowly worse; on the morning of the second day, he was found lying down, breathing very quick, and apparently insensible. He expired without convulsions, about the forty-third hour from the time he was bitten. On dissection, no diseased appearances could be detected, excepting, perhaps, in the lungs, which were a little redder than natural.

Experiment 5. A few minutes after the last fowl was bitten, another young cock, of the same age nearly and size as the preceding, was exposed to the snake. The snake fastened on his thigh, and inflicted rather a severe wound, from which some blood flowed. The cock became instantly lame, and in less than a minute was unable to stand. In about five minutes, his respiration became hurried and rather laborious; some alvine dejections took place. In about ten minutes, he appeared to be in a comatose state, and for about five minutes he continued in this state,—his respiration gradually becoming more feeble and laboured. In seventeen minutes, when his breathing was hardly perceptible, he was seized with a convulsive fit, which in the course of the next minute, returned four or five times, each less violent than the former; and, the last proved fatal. The heart was immediately exposed, and the auricles were found still acting. The lungs were redder than usual, and were turgid with blood and serum. The brain carefully examined, displayed no morbid appearance. The thigh bitten was slightly swelled; the skin surrounding the wound, and the subjacent muscle, were livid.

From these experiments, it appears, — that the bite of the hooded-snake is not necessarily fatal to fowls; that the effect of the bite varies a good deal, according to circumstances, which it is not very easy to calculate; that the poison is capable of being soon exhausted; that the symptoms produced by the poison, though not uniformly the same, pretty generally correspond; and that, in conjunction with the appearances on dissection, they seem to indicate, that the lungs are the *principal* seat of the diseased action.

Experiments on the Poison of the Carawilla.

Experiment 1. The snake used in this experiment, and the following, was about a foot long, just taken, and very active. At Colombo, in December, 1816, it bit a puppy about two months old, in two places, — the side of the face, and the foot of one of the hind legs. Immediately, judging from his howling, the animal seemed to suffer much pain: he ran away, when liberated, on three legs, making no use of the wounded leg. A drop of blood came from each wound.

In less than two minutes, the parts wounded began to swell and to discharge a thin reddish-brown ichor. In an hour, the swellings were very considerable; and the puppy was very unwell, crying piteously, lying down, and when roused, hardly able to stand. In about twenty-four hours, the swelling had extended to the parts adjoining the wounds, having nearly subsided where it first appeared. The wounds still discharged an ichorous fluid, and appeared slightly livid. The health of the dog was improved; he was able to eat, and move about on three legs. In about forty-eight hours, the swelling had nearly disappeared, and the animal seemed to have recovered its health. The wounds had sphacelated extensively and deeply, and a purulent discharge had commenced. In twenty-four hours more, a slough had separated from the wounds, which were now large, deep ulcers, of a healthy appearance, promising to heal readily by the common process of nature.

Experiment 2. On the same day, another puppy was bitten by the snake in the fore-foot. The part immediately swelled and discharged an ichorous fluid. From the foot, the swelling extended to the shoulder, and from the shoulder to the integuments of the chest; subsiding where it first appeared as it spread beyond. The health of the dog was much deranged; for two days, it could stand with difficulty, and ate very little. It had frequent small bloody stools, as if its bowels were inflamed. At the end of three days the dog was considerably better, a great part of the skin of the leg bitten was now livid, and on the fourth day sloughed off, exposing an extensive healthy ulcerating surface. On the fifth day, the animal was still sickly; the ulcer healed slowly, and the dog gradually recovered its health.

Experiment 3. On the day following that on which the two preceding experiments had been made, a half-grown fowl was bit by the snake just above the left eye. The eye immediately closed; a watery fluid, like tears flowed from it, and there was a similar discharge from the nostrils. When the eye-lid was forced open, the pupil contracted readily on the admission of stronger light. The opposite side of the face soon became considerably swoln. The fowl drooped, but never lost the use of its legs. It refused to eat and was much purged; what it voided had a chalky appearance. On the third day, it seemed to recover a little, and ate a small quantity of grain. On the morning of the fourth day, I found it dead.

Under the skin of the part bitten there was some coagulated blood, and the cellular membrane was discoloured. On the external surface of the heart, there was a covering of coagulable lymph of a reticulated appearance, strongly indicating recent inflammation of the organ. The lungs were rather redder than natural. The gall-bladder was distended with green bile. The intestines were not inflamed, and the other viscera had a healthy appearance.

Experiment 4. On the day following, another fowl half-grown, was bitten by the snake, in the comb, which bled pretty freely. The comb and the skin of the head swelled slightly. For twelve hours, the fowl was sickly and ate very little. The next day the swelling had disappeared, and the fowl was well.

Experiment 5. After a month's confinement, during which time the snake had ate nothing, it appeared to be as active and as fierce as when first taken. It bit a fowl half grown on the side of the face, about a quarter of an inch only below the eye. The surrounding skin immediately began to swell, and the eye to discharge a copious watery fluid. In a few hours, the eye was greatly swelled and distended with effused coagulated blood. During the first twelve hours, the fowl seemed sickly, drooped, and ate nothing. It had numerous white alvine evacuations. In about twenty-four hours, its appetite returned, and it seemed pretty well, notwithstanding the diseased state of the eye, the sight of which it had lost from ulceration.

Experiment 6. After another fortnight, spent fasting and without apparent diminution of activity, the snake bit a bull-frog on the head. The skin bitten swelled slightly, and discharged a bloody sanies. The swelling extended from the head to the trunk. The animal died in about five hours.

From these experiments it appears, that the bite of the carawilla is rarely fatal to small animals; that its poison is not easily exhausted; that the symptoms it produces are pretty uniform; that they are different from those produced by the poison of the hooded snake, — the diseased action being more local, and much more inflammatory, commencing in the part bitten, spreading progressively, losing its force as it extends, and probably, never proving fatal, except it reach a vital organ.

Experiments on the Poison of the Tic-polonga.

Experiment 1. This and the following experiments were made with a tic-polonga, about four feet and a half long, and very thick. It was just taken, and in full vigour.

In February 1816, at Colombo, the same fowl was exposed to this snake, that had lost an eye from the bite of the carawilla. It seemed desirous to avoid the fowl, retiring and hissing with extraordinary shrillness and loudness; after being irritated very much, it darted at the fowl and struck it, but did not appear to have wounded it, though it really had, in the slightest manner possible, near the insertion of the great pectoral muscle.

In about a minute, the fowl was seized with violent convulsions, which in two or three seconds terminated in death. The pupil was rather dilated, and did not contract on the admission of strong light.

The chest was immediately opened. The two auricles and the right ventricle, and the great veins and arteries, were distended with coagulated blood. When first exposed, the heart was motionless; after the removal of the pericardium, the auricles exhibited, for a few seconds, a slight tremulous action. In the brain, lungs and other viscera, no diseased appearances could be detected. The vessels generally were distended with coagulated blood. The muscles were very flaccid, and could not be stimulated to the feeblest contraction, immediately after death; even the pectoral muscles, when divided, showed no signs of irritability, nor did the intestines. Where the wound had been inflicted, the skin, and the muscle under it, were a little darker than natural, as if from a minute portion of extravasated blood. The muscular fibre was extremely soft and weak; slight pressure on the muscle occasioned the exudation of a little watery fluid and some minute globules of air. There was not the slightest swelling of thepart, or appearance of local inflammation.

Experiment 2. About half an hour after the preceding experiment, a full-grown fowl was exposed to the snake. Even more provocation was required in this instance than in the first, to excite the snake to act; at length he bit the fowl on the wing; and the fangs, penetrating the loose skin, drew a little blood.

Immediately, the fowl did not appear to suffer any pain. In about a quarter of a minute by a second-watch, its breathing had become accelerated, the eyes nearly closed, and the pupils a little contracted. In a minute, the fowl was seized with convulsions of a very severe kind; the head was bent down, and fixed on the breast, the legs were drawn up; in brief, every muscle appeared to be in violent action and spasmodically contracted. The convulsions lasted about half a minute, when the fowl expired.

The appearances on dissection were the same as in the preceding instance. There was no discolouration, or apparent change in the parts surrounding the wound.

Experiment 3. Six days after, the snake bit a young dog, nearly full-grown, in the hind-leg. A good deal of blood flowed from the wound. The dog immediately ran away howling, with the foot bitten drawn up.

During the first *ten* minutes, he was very restless; his movements were rather convulsive, particularly the motions of the hind-leg that was not bitten; sometimes be would lie down, and appear a little composed, and as suddenly start up, and re-commence a piteous howling.

In about *fifteen* minutes his breathing became hurried; his muscles became spasmodically affected, and violently so, particularly those concerned in respiration; copious evacuations took place *sursum et deorsum*. His strength was now much diminished; he lay on the ground breathing rapidly, and crying shrilly; every now and then, starting up, as if from pain, and almost instantly falling again, as if from inability to support himself. In about *twenty* minutes, he was apparently almost exhausted; his breathing was short and spasmodic, as it were by jerks, and amazingly rapid,—about ninety in a minute; each expiration was accompanied with a shrill sound, and now and then there was a full inspiration and a deep groan. Even now, the sensorial powers, seemed to be little affected; the poor animal was conscious of what was passing, and when patted on the head seemed to be soothed.

In about *twenty-six* minutes he became insensible, and apparently comatose, not to be roused by any excitement. The pupils were rather contracted; respiration was quick, but not so quick as before, and more full: now and then it was more hurried, — now and then there was a deep inspiration and a moan: his extremities were nearly cold.

In about *fifty-one* minutes his respiration became spasmodic; the head pulled down at each inspiration. The respiration became slower and slower, and gradually more feeble, till at the *fifty-eighth* minute it ceased entirely. The pupil was dilated; just before death there was a slight convulsive motion of the whole body.

The body of the dog was immediately examined. A good deal of serum was found effused on the surface of the brain, in its ventricles, and at its base: the surface of the brain was perhaps redder than usual; there were air-bubbles under the tunica arachnoidea, and in the larger veins. The liver was very red and gorged with blood. The lungs were rather red, condensed, and contained little air; the ventricles of the heart were distended with blood, the right ventricle especially; the right auricle was less distended, and the left auricle was empty. The blood in the heart and veins was liquid, and did not coagulate on exposure to the air. There were red spots on the villous coat of the stomach. The other viscera exhibited nothing unusual. The foot bitten was very slightly swelled, owing to the effusion of a little serum and blood; the muscle under the wound was nearly black, and there were air-bubbles in the adjoining cellular membrane, but no bad smell: the body was still warm.

Experiment 4. Thirty-four days after the last experiment, during which time the snake would eat nothing, it bit a rat. The animal immediately lay down motionless; its respiration became quick and convulsive, and after two or three slight convulsions of the body in general, it expired.

The body was immediately opened; the heart had ceased to contract, nor did the auricles even contract when punctured. The surface of the heart was unusually red and vascular, as if inflamed. Its cavities were distended with blood; the lungs were rather redder than natural; the muscular fibre in general had entirely lost its irritability. There were no marks of disease amongst the abdominal viscera.

The first experiment with this snake was made on the day it was brought to me, the 3d of February; the last, which I have now to describe, on the 27th and 28th of June, the interval being 146 days, which it had passed fasting. It had refused different kinds of food that were offered to it, and yet it looked now as well as ever, and appeared as active as ever; and from the result of the following experiments its poison seemed to be not exhausted or weakened, but concentrated and more terribly active. As I was obliged to leave Colombo at this time, I do not know how much longer the snake lived without eating.

Experiment 5. On the 27th June the snake bit a full-grown fowl in the face. The wound was inflicted in an instant, and the fangs were immediately disengaged. In a few seconds the fowl was convulsed; every muscle seemed to be thrown into violent spasmodic action; the head was drawn down on the breast;

the legs were extended, and the animal, lying on its belly, was moved about rapidly and irregularly by a quick succession of these involuntary spasmodic actions of its muscles, till it expired, which it did in rather less than a minute from the instant it was wounded. During this time it uttered no cries, and judging from appearances, seemed to be insensible.

The body was immediately opened. The muscles divided by the knife did not show the slightest signs of irritability, nor did the intestines; the heart contracted very irregularly, and so very feebly that it had no effect in propelling its contents. The auricles were gorged with blood, particularly the right; the left ventricle was empty, and the right contained only a small quantity of blood; the arteries and veins were full of blood, which had coagulated firmly, even in the minute branches. There was no unusual appearance in the brain, or in any of the other viscera, excepting the distended state of their blood-vessels. A reddish sanies oozed from the wound; the skin round it was discoloured without swelling; the muscle underneath the skin was blackish and tender, as if severely bruised, and the adjoining cellular membrane was slightly emphysematous.

Experiment 6. On the following day the snake wounded another full-grown fowl, inflicting with its fang, on the side of the face, a puncture only just perceptible. During the first minute and half the fowl did not appear to suffer in the least, when it was seized with violent convulsions that proved fatal in about fifteen seconds. The appearances on dissection, which was commenced immediately, were very similar to the last. The action of the heart was perhaps a little less feeble; the vermicular motion of the intestines had not entirely ceased, and the blood was not quite so firmly coagulated.

All the cavities of the heart were empty, with the exception of the right auricle, which was distended with blood.

From these experiments it may be inferred, that the bite of the tic-polonga greatly exceeds in fatality that of either of the preceding snakes; and that the action of its poison is different and peculiar. Judging from the symptoms and the appearances on dissection, its poison seems to exert its influence primarily and principally on the blood and muscular system, tending to coagulate the former, and convulse and paralyze the latter. All the experiments seem to point directly to this conclusion; not excepting even the third, the peculiarities of which may be referred to the re-action which it may be conceived took place, the animal being pretty large and strong, and not overpowered by the immediate effect of the poison.

From the whole of the preceding experiments and from those of Dr. Russell on the poison of the Bodroo Pam *, it may be inferred, reasoning from analogy, that there are only two snakes in Ceylon (at least yet known) whose bite is likely to prove fatal to man, — the hooded snake, and the tic-polonga; and that the danger from the latter is much greater than from the former. The result of the enquiries which I made amongst the natives, though not very satisfactory, tended to confirm this conclusion; I found them generally of opinion that the bite of the tic-polonga is unavoidably fatal, but that of the hooded snake only occasionally so. Perhaps they exaggerated a little in maintaining the first part of this statement; the latter part of which I believe to be quite correct, for I have seen several men who have recovered from the bite of the hooded snake, and I have heard of two or three only to whom it has proved fatal.

* Russell on Indian Serpents, vol. i. p. 60.

I regret that I have nothing original to offer, respecting the medical treatment of the bites of these snakes. It was my intention to have made a series of experiments on the subject; indeed, the experiments that I have detailed, were merely preliminary to that enquiry, being instituted to smooth the way, to determine, if possible, the mode of action of each poison, and furnish data for inferring what are the pure effects of the poison, what of the *vis medicatrix naturæ* opposing its effects, and what those of the medicine administered. In no subject is more discrimination required than in this mysterious one; and, in no one perhaps has there been less used. It has often been taken for granted that the poison of all snakes is similar,—not differing in its kind, but only in its intensity of action; and, agreeably to this assumption, that the medicine useful in one instance must be serviceable in all. And, too often, medicines have got into repute as antidotes, from being given in slight cases, that would have recovered without medical treatment,—referring to the medicine, beneficial changes that were due merely to the preservative powers of the constitution. The reputation that many Indian medicines, and especially that snake-stones have acquired, afford striking proof of the preceding remarks. Of the three different kinds of these stones, that I have examined, one was composed of partially burnt bone, another of chalk, and the third resembled a bezoar, consisting chiefly of vegetable matter; all of them (excepting the first, possessed of a slight absorbent power) were quite inert, and incapable of having any effect, exclusive of that on the imagination of the patient. *

* It is the opinion of the natives, that these stones are found in the brain of snakes. From Sir Alexander Johnston, to whom I was indebted for the specimens I examined, I learnt that those of the first kind are manufactured by the monks at Manilla, who carry on a lucrative trade in these snake-stones with the merchants of India.

The probability is, that the poison of each different kind of snake is peculiar; and that, when fully investigated, the effects of each will be found to require a peculiar mode of treatment, the nature of which can only be ascertained by actual experiment. Fortunately for man, in this great obscurity, the immediate treatment of all poisoned wounds is simple and very similar. The obvious indications are, to extract the poison as much and as speedily as possible; and endeavour to prevent, its entering the circulation. The first indication is best accomplished by cutting out the part bitten, and scarifying the surrounding flesh. If the person bitten want courage to do this, he should suck the wound well, and apply caustic, if at hand. The second indication, may be tolerably fulfilled, (if the part admit of the application of a ligature,) by tying a handkerchief very tightly just above the wound. Respecting the employment of oil, arsenic, and eau de luce, having no experience of their effects, I shall offer no decided opinion. Oil seems to have been useful, both applied externally, and taken internally, in many instances of the bite of the viper; and arsenic seems to have done good, in some instances of the bite of the hooded snake. Eau de luce does not appear to have deserved the high character that was first given to it, and I am not aware of any satisfactory proof, of its ever having been beneficial.

The other poisonous animals of Ceylon, as scorpions, centipeds, and two or three different species of spider, attracted my attention very little, — less, perhaps, than they deserved. The horror, commonly entertained of them, like that of snakes, suggested by fear, is much greater than reason, or the effects of their sting, warrant. Their poison, I believe, is very little, if at all, more active than that of the wasp or bee; and their sting seldom requires medical treatment. In two or three instances, that I tried the sting of the large black scorpion on fowls, it appeared to have no effect.

There is another animal in Ceylon, less dreaded, indeed, than any of the preceding, but much more troublesome, and the cause of the loss of more lives, than all the rest. I allude to the Ceylon Leech, (fig. 4. Plate II.)

This animal varies much in its dimensions ; the largest are seldom more than half an inch long, in a state of rest ; the smallest are minute indeed. It is broadest behind, and tapers towards the forepart ; above, it is roundish ; below, flat. Its colour varies from brown to light-brown ; it is more generally the latter, and rarely dark-brown. It is marked with three longitudinal light-yellow lines, extending from one extremity to the other ; one dorsal and central ; the two others, lateral. The substance of the animal is nearly semi-transparent, and in consequence, its internal structure may be seen pretty distinctly. A canal appears to extend centrically the whole length of the body, arising from a crucial mouth, at the smaller extremity, and terminating in a small circular anus, at the broader extremity, on each side of which are two light spots.

This leech is a very active animal : it moves with considerable rapidity ; and it is said, occasionally to spring. Its powers of contraction and extension are very great ; when fully extended, it is like a fine chord, and its point is so sharp, that it readily makes its way through very small openings. It is supposed to have an acute sense of smelling, for no sooner does a person stop where leeches abound, than they appear to crowd eagerly to the spot from all quarters.

This animal is peculiar to those parts of Ceylon, which are subject to frequent showers; and consequently it is unknown in those districts, that have a long dry season. It is most abundant amongst the mountains, — not on the highest ranges where the temperature appears to be too low for it, but on those, not exceeding two or three thousand feet above the level of the sea. It delights in shady damp places, and is to be seen on moist leaves and stones, more frequently than in water. In dry weather, it retires into the close damp jungle, and only in rainy weather quits its cover, and infests the pathways and roads, and open parts of of the country.

Whether it is found in any other country than Ceylon, is not quite certain; perhaps the leech of the mountainous parts of Sumatra, noticed in Mr. Marsden's history of that island, is similar to it; and it is not unlikely, that it occurs amongst the damp and wooded hills of the South of India. Those who have had no experience of these animals, — of their immense numbers in their favourite haunts, — of their activity, keen appetite, and love of blood, can have no idea of the kind and extent of annoyance they are to travellers in the Interior, of which they may be truly said to be the plague. In rainy weather, it is almost shocking to see the legs of men on a long march, thickly beset with them gorged with blood, and the blood trickling down in streams. It might be supposed, that there would be little difficulty in keeping them off; this is a very mistaken notion; for they crowd to the attack and fasten on, quicker than they can be removed. I do not exaggerate when I say, that I have occasionally seen at least fifty on a person at a time.

Their bites too are much more troublesome than could be imagined, being very apt to fester and become sores; and, in persons of a bad habit of body, to degenerate into extensive ulcers, that in too many instances have occasioned the loss of limb, and even of life.

The instant the leech fastens on, an acute pain is generally felt, like that produced by the bite of the medicinal leech. A few hours after the bite, the surrounding skin becomes slightly inflamed, and itching of a very tormenting kind commonly occurs, producing such a desire to scratch, that few have resolution enough to resist, though well aware of its aggravating effect. This itching may continue several days, till either the wound has healed or ulcerated. The former termination is most common, if only common precautions be taken, and provided the habit of body be pretty good. The latter termination may always be traced either to great neglect, or to a deranged state of the system or a bad habit of body, which was very common amongst the troops serving in the Interior during the late rebellion, especially amongst the Madras auxiliary Sepoys.

It may be worth while to mention the means found by experience best adapted to guard off the attacks, or prevent bad effects, from the bites of these mischievous and troublesome animals. The only way to defend the skin from them entirely, is to wear a particular kind of dress. Half-boots and tight pantaloons, or short boots and long loose trowsers tucked into the boot, or trowsers and stockings of a piece;— either of these answers pretty well. It was natural to suppose that the same end might be attained by the use of applications to the skin disagreeable to the leech. Trial has been made of a great variety; those which seemed to have the best effect were oil, particularly castor-oil, the infusion of tobacco, lime-juice, and the infusion of any astringent bark, of which there are several kinds in the woods of the Interior. One or other of these has often been employed with advantage;

but, unfortunately, none of them are tolerably effectual when their aid is most required; as on long marches, in rainy weather, through a country abounding in streams, without bridges, and covered with jungle penetrated merely by pathways: under such circumstances even oily applications are soon rubbed and washed off, and the limbs left defenceless. The treatment of leech-bites that is most successful in preventing bad consequences, is simple and easily practised; the limbs, immediately on arriving at the end of a march or journey, should be bathed in hot water, and the bathing should be repeated twice a-day till the wounds are healed. To prevent the troublesome itching, and expedite the healing, bits of common sticking-plaster may be applied with advantage to the bites; or they may be touched with a solution of corrosive sublimate, or of nitrat of silver. These solutions generally answer when the sticking-plaster does not agree with the skin, as happens to some individuals. When, from neglect, or bad habit of body, the bites ulcerate, surgical treatment is required, in which the stimulating plan is found to succeed much better than the emollient.

CHAPTER IV.

POPULATION. — CASTES.

In such a country as the Interior of Ceylon, where no statistical enquiries have yet been instituted, where the population is not concentrated in cities or towns, but scattered through sequestered valleys, — it would be unreasonable to expect a precise estimate of the number of the inhabitants; and one must be satisfied, for the present, with any approximation to the truth, however remote.

That the whole island of Ceylon is but thinly inhabited, is obvious to any one who has any knowledge of the country: nor it is less obvious to those who have had opportunities of judging, and of drawing a comparison between the maritime and the Kandyan provinces, that the population of the latter is considerably smaller than that of the former. Supposing then, a tolerably correct knowledge of the one, it will be less difficult to form some definite opinion respecting the other; and by help of what is ascertained, try and appreciate that which is merely conjectured.

According to the census made by the collectors of districts in 1814, by order of government, the whole population of our old possessions, the maritime provinces, amounted only to about

476,000 souls of both sexes and of all ages.* The conjectures of the best-informed natives, respecting the population of the Interior, differ most widely; it being the opinion of some that it may amount to a million, and of others that it does not exceed three hundred thousand. Now, when it is considered how prone the mind is to exaggerate; — when it is further considered how small the proportion of the inhabited is to the uninhabited parts of the Interior, and when one compares the former with the inhabited parts of the maritime districts, — one is disposed to adopt the smallest number as the most probable approximation, and admit that the population of the whole island does

* The following are the general results of the returns of population that were made of all the districts:

Above the age of puberty.		Below that age.	
Males.	Females.	Males.	Females.
156,447	142,453	95,091	81,892

Forming a grand total of 475,883; and an excess of the number of males over the females of 27,193. This excess appears to be in a large proportion: perhaps the census is not quite correct; perhaps the disproportion of the sexes is above the truth; yet from examining the particular returns, and from considering the manner in which they were made out, I cannot help thinking that the census is not much below the truth, and that the number of males is greater than that of the females. The disproportion appears to be greatest in the poorest parts of the country, where the population is thinnest, and it is most difficult to support life; and smallest, where there is least want. Indeed, in some of the fishing-villages, where there is abundance of food, the number of females rather exceeds that of the males. May it not be a wise provision of provident Nature to promote, by *extreme poverty*, the generation of males rather than of females?

not exceed eight hundred thousand souls, which is in the proportion of about thirty-eight only to the square mile. It would not be difficult to point out the leading causes of this thin population in an island which, at first view, it might be imagined, would be teeming with inhabitants: many of these causes, moral and physical, will develope themselves as we proceed.

The inhabitants of Ceylon may be divided into two great classes:—the aborigines of the country, and foreigners naturalized. The former are the Singalese, the almost exclusive inhabitants of the Interior, and of the south-west parts of the island. The latter are chiefly Malabars and Moors;—the one, confined principally to the northern and eastern maritime provinces; the other, the Moors, confined to no particular district, but living scattered amongst the people of the country, like the Jews in Europe, whom, in some other respects, they resemble.

Three hundred years ago, there is good reason to believe that the Singalese were one people, without any points of difference, excepting such trifling ones as might result from the peculiarities of climate, and of other physical circumstances of the lowlands and highlands. But since that period,—since the maritime provinces have been in the possession of Europeans, a change has been taking place in the lowland Singalese, which, though very slow, gradual, and imperceptible in progress, is now obvious in effect, and easily discernible in certain alterations and innovations in their language, manners and customs—varying in degree of change, more or less, according to proximity to our settlements.

During the period alluded to, no corresponding change, that we know of, has occurred amongst the highland Singalese. The probability is, that they are much the same now that they were three hundred years ago, and that they were then very similar to what they were in ages preceding. Supposing this view to be correct, no small interest is imparted to the studying of such a people, by the consideration that they are the living examples of a remote antiquity, and that they are almost as fresh and original to us, as the inhabitants of the coasts of the island were to their early invaders; and this feeling of interest is surely not diminished by the reflection, that this people, for ages the same, are, in their turn, arrived at an eventful period of change, so that the next generation probably will no longer be the exact likeness of the past, and a good deal of that which is still in practice, or fresh in remembrance, in a few years will be altered or forgotten, and if not recorded now, lost perhaps for ever.

The pure Singalese of the Interior, whom alone I shall describe, are completely Indians in person, language, manners, customs, religion, and government.

Like Indians in general, the Singalese differ from Europeans less in features, than in the more trifling circumstances of colour, size, and form. The colour of their skin varies from light-brown to black. The colour, too, of their hair and eyes varies, but not so often as that of the skin; black hair and eyes are most common; hazel eyes are less uncommon than brown hair; grey eyes and red hair are still more uncommon; and the light flaxen hair, and the light-blue or red eye of the Albino, are the most uncommon of all. In size, though they generally exceed the lowland Singalese, and most of the natives of the coast of Coromandel and Malabar, they are inferior to Europeans. Their average height may be about five feet four or five inches. They are clean-made, with neat muscle and small bone. For Indians, they are stout, and generally have capacious chests and broad shoulders, particularly the inhabitants of the mountainous districts, who, like highlanders in general, have rather short, but strong and very muscular thighs and legs. Their hands and feet are commonly very small, indeed, so much smaller than ours, that they appear out of proportion. The form of their head is generally good, perhaps longer than the European, a peculiarity, according to Dr. Spurzheim, of the Asiatic.* Their features are commonly neat, and often handsome; their countenances are intelligent and animated. Nature has given them a liberal supply of hair, which they universally allow to grow on their face, as well as head, to a considerable length, being of opinion that the beard does not deform, but improve the face; and, certainly, in many instances, I have seen it have the effect of giving to the countenance an air of dignity that would have disappeared with the use of the razor.

The Singalese women are generally well made and well looking, and often handsome. Their countrymen, who are great connoisseurs of the charms of the sex, and who have books on the subject, and rules to aid the judgment, would not allow a woman to be a perfect belle, unless of the following character, the particulars of which I shall give in detail as they were enumerated to me by a Kandyan courtier, well versed and deeply read in such matters:—"Her hair should be voluminous, like the tail of the peacock; long, reaching to the knees, and terminating in graceful curls; her eyebrows should resemble the rainbow; her eyes, the blue sapphire and the petals of the blue manilla-flower. Her nose should be like the bill of the hawk; her lips should be bright and red, like coral on the young

* The cranium represented in Plate III. belonged to a Singalese Chief of a secluded part of the Interior, and is a faithful figure.

Pl. III

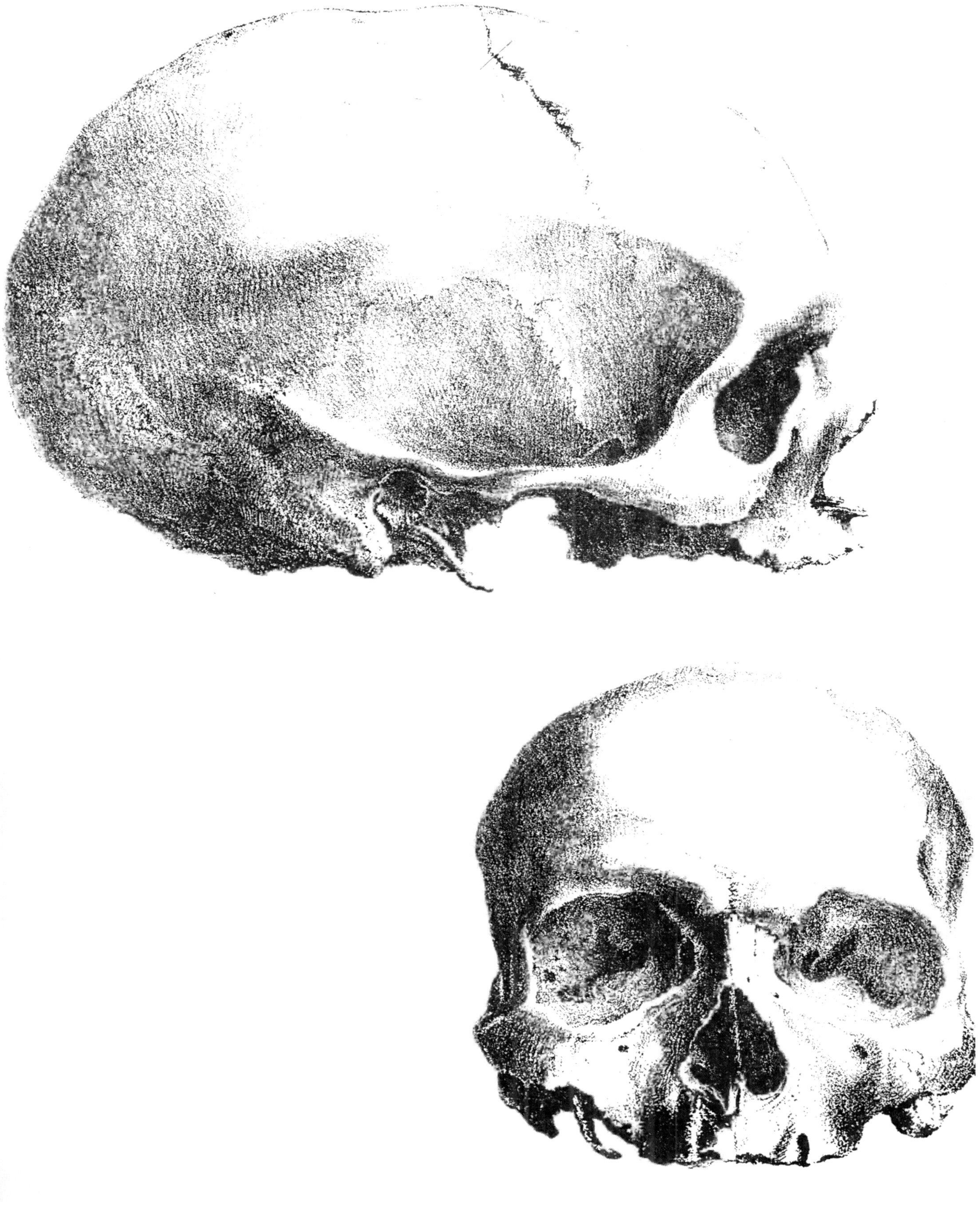

leaf of the iron-tree. Her teeth should be small, regular, and closely set, and like jessamine buds. Her neck should be large and round, resembling the berrigodea. Her chest should be capacious; her breasts, firm and conical, like the yellow cocoa-nut, and her waist small—almost small enough to be clasped by the hand. Her hips should be wide; her limbs tapering; the soles of her feet, without any hollow, and the surface of her body in general, soft, delicate, smooth, and rounded, without the asperities of projecting bones and sinews."

The preceding is the most general external character that can be given of the Singalese. It may be added, that corresponding to their conformation of body, they are rather remarkable for agility and flexibility than for strength of limb; and that they are capable rather of long continued, than of great exertion. Their moral character will be best considered, after those subjects have passed in review which have the greatest influence in forming it.

That remarkable feature of Indian society, distinction of caste, prevails amongst the Singalese, as well as the Hindoos, though to a less extent, and with less effect on the minds of the people. Both acknowledge the existence of four principal castes, which in each system, differ little but in name and arrangement. According to the best authorities I could consult, the four great castes admitted by the Singalese are the following:—1. Ekshastria wansè, or royal caste: 2. Brachmina wansè, or cast of Brahmens: 3. Wiessia wansè, composed of three subdivisions, viz. merchants, cultivators of the earth, and shepherds: 4. Kshoodra wansè, subdivided into sixty low castes—Kshoodra signifying small and mean.

Fortunately, in repect to caste, the population of the country is more useful than honourable, being composed of the two lower castes, almost to the complete exclusion of the regal and brahminical, those two prolific sources of mental and political despotism. The following scheme will give an idea of the subdivisions of the two principal castes, preparatory to a description of each.

I. *Wiessia wansè.*

1.	Goewansè,	-	Cultivators.
2.	Nillemakareya,	-	Shepherds.

II. *Kshoodra wansè.*

1.	Carawè,	-	Fishermen.
2.	Chandos,	-	Toddy-drawers.
3.	Achari,	-	Smiths, &c.
4.	Hannawli,	-	Taylors.
5.	Badda hela badda,	-	Potters.
6.	Ambattea people,	-	Barbers.
7.	Rada badda,	-	Washermen.
8.	Hālee,	-	Chalias.
9.	Hakooro,	-	Jaggery-makers.
10.	Hunu baddè,	-	Chunam or Lime burners.
11.	Paṇnayo,	-	Grass-cutters.
12.	Villedurai.		
13.	Dodda weddahs.		
14.	Paduas		Paduas. Iron-smelters. Executioners.
15.	Baṛrawa baddè, or Maha baddè,		Tom-tom beaters.
16.	Handee.		
17.	Pallarōo.		

18. Olee.
19. Radayo.
20. Palee.
21. Kinnera baddè.

Out-castes.

Gattaroo.
Rhodees.

Of no caste, but attached

The Singalese Christians to the Goewanse.
The Marakkala, or Moormen, to the Carawè.

This list, though made with a good deal of trouble, and after much enquiry, is not perhaps quite complete, or thoroughly accurate. There may be some low sub-castes omitted, such as are confined to certain parts of the country, and are hardly known out of the districts in which they live; and, the arrangement, in some instances, may be faulty, as the relative rank of the lower castes is of little consequence, — not determined with the precision of court precedency, and differently adjusted in different provinces.

1. The Goewansè, or, as named in the low country, Wellales, constitute by far the largest caste of the Singalese. Agriculture, their original employ, is not now their sole occupation. They are a privileged people, and monopolize all the honours of church and state, and possess all the hereditary rank in the country.

The common dress of these people, and which may be considered the national dress, is extremely simple, and not unbecoming. The dress of the men consists of a handkerchief about the head, wrapped like a turban, leaving the top of the head exposed; and of a long cloth of two breadths, called *topetty*, wrapped about the loins, and reaching as low as the ankles. The material of the women's dress is very similar; they leave the head uncovered, and wear a long cloth, of a single breadth, called *hala*, wrapped round their loins, and thrown over their left shoulder. On occasions of ceremony, when full dressed, the men cover the body with a short jacket *; and those who have the privilege, lay aside the handkerchief for a cap, and decorate themselves with gold chains and girdles. The women, when full dressed, use a jacket, with a kind of ruff, hanging from the neck over the shoulders. The ornaments they wear, besides rings, are silver or crystal bangles, and ear-rings. Like the men, the favoured few only are entitled to decorate their persons with gold, — those only who have been honoured with presents of the kind from the hands of royalty, to whom, according to their sumptuary laws, this precious metal is peculiarly confined. The rank and wealth of individuals are marked, not so much by the fashion of their apparel, as by their rich quality and large quantity. A man of rank and of fortune will appear in the finest embroidered muslin, swelled out by a number of topetties, sometimes amounting to six or eight, put on one over the other in succession, with his shoulders as unnaturally widened in appearance, by a jacket stuffed and puffed out to correspond to the bulk of the hips. (Plate IV.)

Raised by caste above the rest of the people, the Goewansè cannot intermarry with the Kshoodra wansè, without being degraded. He may connect himself by marriage with a Nillema-

* An exception may be mentioned; — they invariably bare their shoulders, when they enter a temple; conceiving that the offender, who should do otherwise, would, in another life, draw on himself the punishment of boils and cutaneous diseases.

No. 1 & 2. A Singalese Man and Woman in plain dress.

No. 3. A Mohottala.

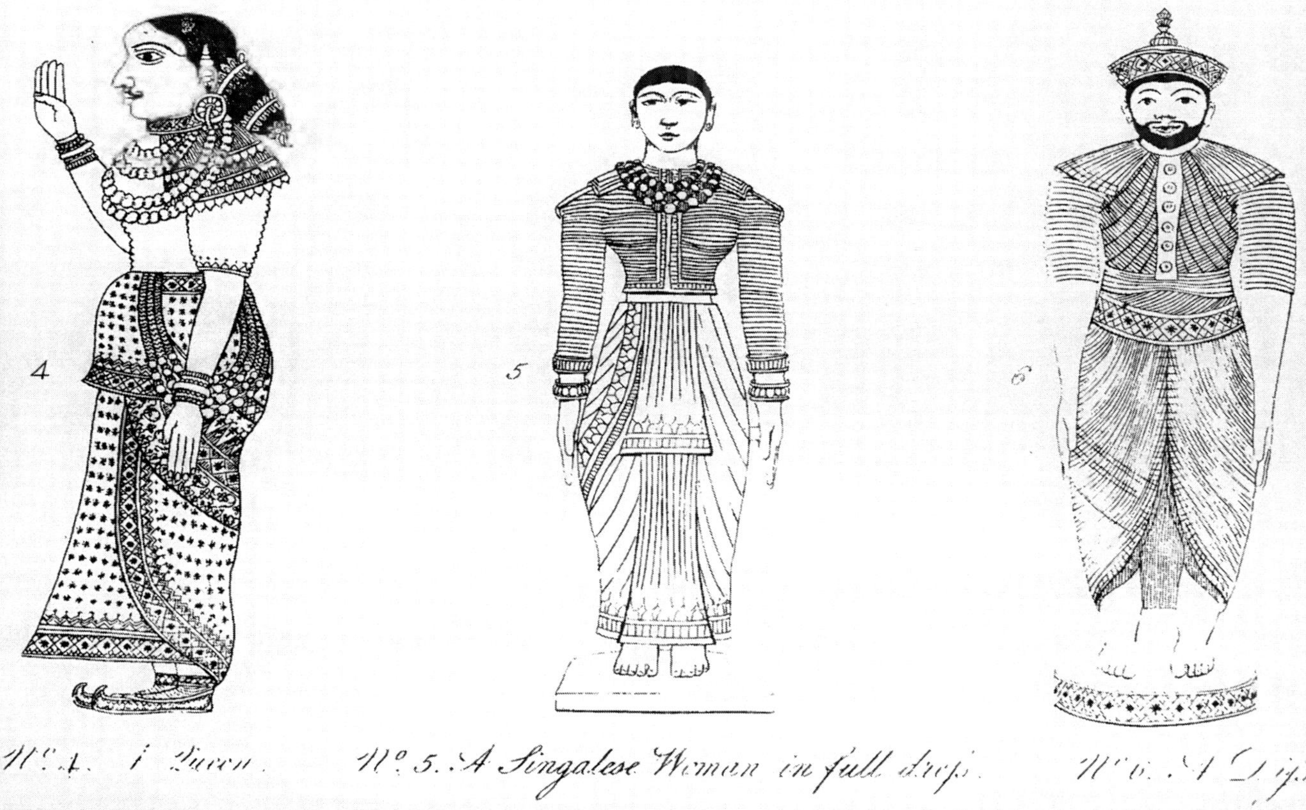

No. 4. A Queen.

No. 5. A Singalese Woman in full dress.

No. 6. A Dissar

kareyea woman; but a man of the latter sub-caste is not allowed to take a wife from the former, though it is occasionally done and winked at. The prohibitory decree of caste extends to the board as well as the bed, — and indeed to all forms of social intercourse.

The duties and services that this people owed to government, or (to be more precise) to the king, were of a fixed and definite kind. They formerly constituted the militia of the country, and were required to appear in arms as often as summoned by the king to repel an enemy. Each man was expected to take the field, with a musket of his own, (the king providing ammunition), and he was obliged to continue on service, either till the enemy was repulsed, or till he obtained leave to return home. They were liable to be called on to labour at certain public works, as in making roads, levelling hills, and excavating tanks; and, according to the extent of their land-tenures, they might be employed annually in such services, from fifteen to thirty days. Farther, the presence of all, or of certain classes of them, was required on the four great festivals held annually in the capital; and, on all public occasions of moment, as the choosing of a king, a royal marriage, or burial. What taxes they had to pay, before we had possession of the country, has not been determined in a satisfactory manner, notwithstanding all the enquiry that has been made to discover the truth. According to the best information I could collect, they had to pay an annual quit-rent to the king, as lord of the soil, of one-twentieth of the rice it produced, and six challies, or about a halfpenny each, for their high ground.

To this caste belong that singular and savage people the Weddahs, who inhabit the extensive forests on the south-eastern side of the island, between the mountains and the sea, confined chiefly to the wild and unwholesome tracts called the Weddahrattè of Bintenney and the Mahaveddahrattè of Ouva, which they consider exclusively their own territory. They may, with propriety, be divided into the village Weddahs and the forest Weddahs; the one, having a fixed abode and living in society; the other, having no fixed habitation, being rather solitary animals than social, and resembling more beasts of prey, in their habits, than men.

Such of the village Weddahs that I have seen, were in general small men, between five feet three and five feet five inches high, slender, muscular, and well made; in colour, form, and features resembling the Singalese. Their appearance was wild in the extreme, and completely savage. They wore no clothes, only a scrap of cloth for the sake of decency, hanging in front, fastened by a string tied round the loins, to which was attached a small bag. Their hair was quite emblematic of their forests: it seemed never to have been cut, or combed, or cleaned; and was long, bushy, and matted, hanging about their shoulders, and shading their face in a very luxuriant and disgusting manner; nor were their beards less neglected. Their language appeared to be a dialect of the Singalese, and was intelligible to those who understood the latter, with the exception of a few words.

According to their own account, they are perfectly distinct from the wild Weddahs, with whom they have no intercourse, and whom they both fear and hate. Their dwellings are huts made of the bark of trees; their food, the flesh of deer, elk, the wild hog, and the inguana*, with a little Indian corn, and corican

* The "Tala gowa" of the natives; "Le Monitor Terrestre d'Egypte" of M. Cuvier.

of their own growing, the wild yam, and the roots of some water-lillies. They use, besides, honey and wax; and, in times of scarcity, decayed wood, which, mixed with honey, and made into cakes, they eat, not so much for nourishment, as to distend the empty stomach, and to allay the distressing feelings of emptiness and the pains of hunger. They have dogs, but they do not employ them in hunting, excepting the Talagowa. They lie in wait for their game, or steal upon it when feeding, and kill it with their arrows.

Few traces of even incipient civilisation can be observed amongst them. Though living together, they seem to be ignorant of all social rites, and strangers to almost every circumstance that ennobles man and distinguishes him from the brute. To procure a wife, the Weddah does not commence a process of courtship; but goes immediately to the parents, asks their consent to have their single daughter, and, if the first to ask, is never refused. They appear to be without names. A Weddah interrogated on the subject, said, "I am called a man: when young, I was called the little man: and when old, I shall be called the old man." It could hardly be expected that such a people would have any burial rites: they do not even bury their dead; but, as soon as the body has expired, throw it into the jungle. They appear to be ignorant of every art, excepting such as hardly deserve the name, and without which they could not exist, such as making a bow, an arrow, a cord from tough fibrous plants, scratching the ground, and sowing a few seeds, and so forth. The bit of cloth they wear, and the iron heads of their arrows, they obtain by barter, receiving them in exchange for their dried venison, the skins of deer, or for honey and wax.

They have hardly any knowledge of numbers, and cannot count above five; they have no knowledge of medicinal plants, and only the grossest and simplest superstitious notions. They believe in the existence of evil demons, and make offerings to them when labouring under sickness, or any great misfortune. They have no idea of a supreme and beneficent God, or of a state of future existence, or of a system of rewards and punishments; and, in consequence, they are of opinion that it signifies little whether they do good or evil.

Attached by habit to their free, but miserable mode of life, any other more refined would be intolerable to them. They consider themselves at the height of happiness, when they have ate to repletion. Their only other enjoyments, that I have heard of, consist in what cannot very properly be called dancing and singing. On one occasion that I witnessed an exhibition of their performance, they began jumping about with their feet together; as they became warm from exercise, their hands, which were at first inactive, were employed in patting their bellies; and gradually becoming more animated, they clapped their hands as they jumped, and nodded their heads, throwing their long entangled fore-locks from behind, over their face. This strange dancing was accompanied by a rude kind of song.

Of the forest Weddahs, I have been able to collect very little information to be relied on. They appear to be the same race as the preceding, only more wild, supporting themselves entirely by the chace, living in pairs, and only occasionally assembling in greater numbers. Like the preceding, they have their chiefs, who are generally Singalese of the adjoining country, of Weddah extraction, who now and then assemble them to renew their acquaintance and retain their influence, which, in a country liable to political storms, like the Interior of Ceylon was, is of more value than it may at first appear.

The received account of the origin of these people, and that which is generally believed by the Singalese, is truly an Oriental tale, with no other claim to be recorded, but the wildness of its fiction, and the strange circumstance of its being credited by those who relate it. The story is, that Pandoowassa, the seventh king of Ceylon, was visited by "the tiger disease," a complicated malady of cough, asthma, fever, and diabetes, in consequence of Wijeya, the first king, having killed his old benefactor and discarded mistress, Koowanè, when, in the shape of a tiger, she endeavoured to revenge her slighted charms. The gods taking pity on Pandoowassa, consulted by what means he might be restored to health, and found that it could not be effected without the aid of one not born of woman. The difficulty was to find such a person: Iswera volunteered his services. Whilst he changed himself into a monster like a Brachmea, Rahoo, the mischievous king of the Assooriahs became a Bingooroo, (a kind of beetle,) went under ground, and bit Iswera in the sole of the foot till it bled, which the gods observing, laughed, and asked him if he were fit for the enterprise, who could not take care of his own feet. Rahoo being preferred and sent on the service, discovered Malaya-rajah, King of Malla-wadaise, the son of Visnu, sprung from a flower. Rahoo, changing himself into an immense boar, laid waste the royal gardens, to the great consternation of the gardeners, who fled to the palace and told what was passing. The King, who was a keen sportsman, hastened to the spot with his huntsmen, whom he ordered to drive the boar towards him. The boar when pressed, at one bound flew over the head of the King, who shot an arrow through him in passing, but without effect, the animal continuing his flight. The King, irritated, instantly gave pursuit with his attendants in the direction that the beast had taken, and landed in Ceylon at Oorastotta, (Hog-ferry,) near Jaffna: the boar alighted near Attapittia. A piece of sweet potatoe that he brought from the garden in his mouth, and which he here dropt, was immediately changed, it is said, into a rock, that still preserves its original form, and is still called Battalegallè, or sweet-potatoe rock.* The King came up with the beast on the hill Hantana, near Kandy, instantly attacked him sword in hand, and with the first blow inflicted a deep gash. On receiving this wound, the boar became transformed into a rock, which is now called Ooragallè, is very like a hog, and is said to retain the mark of the wound. The King, whilst surprised, and unable to comprehend the meaning of the marvels he had just witnessed, received a visit from Sacrea, Visnu, and other gods, who explained the mystery that perplexed him, and the object in view in drawing him to Ceylon,—he alone, not being born of woman, having it in his power to break the charm under which Pandoowassa laboured. Malay-rajah, complying with the wishes of the gods, ordered the Cohomba-yakoo dance to be performed, which, it is said, drove the sickness out of the King into a rock to the northward of Kandy, which is still called "The Rock of the Tiger Sickness." The King returned to Malla-wadaise, and left most of his attendants in Ceylon at the desire of the grateful Pandoowassa, who allotted them the forests as their exclusive possession,—a certain extent to each man, that

* This rock, or rather hill, about 1000 feet high, is a striking feature in the beautiful scenery of Attapittia.

they might enjoy their favourite diversion of hunting. Such, it is believed, were the progenitors of the Weddahs, who, it is said, possessed originally more than human powers, but gradually degenerating, have become what they now are, — wild and savage.

There is, holding nearly the same rank as the Goewansè, and liable to the same services, though not strictly belonging to the caste, a certain description of Singalese Christians, who have been discovered lately at Wayacotté in Matelè, and at Galgomua in the Seven Korles; about two hundred in each village. In their dress, colour, general appearance, and manners, these people do not perceptibly differ from the rest of the Singalese. Their religion, there is reason to believe, is in a very rude and degenerate state. Their only minister is called Sachristian, — an ignorant man, who cannot read, and knows only a few prayers by heart. They worship the Virgin Mary, and pray before an image of Christ on the cross; they baptize their children, and marry and bury, according to the rites of the Roman Catholic church, conformably with whose doctrine they believe in a purgatory. To what extent their faith is contaminated by the superstitions of the surrounding people, it is not very easy to determine: I have heard it said, that they occasionally visit the temples of Boodhoo, and make offerings of flowers at his shrine; which it is easy to believe, knowing that their religion is not founded on judgment and reason, but on mere credulity, — the basis of all superstition. There can be no doubt that they are descendants of the numerous converts to Christianity made by the Portuguese, at the time they had so much influence in the Interior. It may be well supposed, that such a people, so situated, would, as soon as known, excite no small degree of interest. Their village in Matelè has already been visited by two clergymen of the church of England; one of whom, and their earliest visitor, the Rev. George Bisset, presented their little congregation with a copy of the New Testament in Singalese, the first they had ever seen.

2. The Nillemakareyea, or Pattea people, are generally considered by the natives rather as an inferior subdivision of the Goewansè, than a distinct caste. They are not very numerous; there are no families of rank amongst them; nor are they capable of holding any but low situations under government. Agreeably to their first occupation, that of shepherds, their business still is to attend to cattle; — besides which they are employed in cultivating the land. Their dues, in the king's time, they paid chiefly in rice, gee, tire *, and milk.

The different castes of the Kshoodra wansè appear as it were organized by the hand of government, for its own use, and that of the privileged Goewansè. According to the old system, each caste had certain dues to pay, certain services to perform, and was under the command of officers who were responsible for any neglect of duties.

1. The first of the low caste, according to the best authority I could consult, is the Carawè (men of salt water) or fishermen. Excluded from the sea in the Interior, the services they had to perform were the same as those required of the Marakkala or Moors, who, though of no caste, rank with this, which they greatly exceed in number and importance.

The Moormen are all Mahometans, and have always been allowed the free use of their religion. Neither their origin nor the

* Gee is clarified butter: — Tire is very similar to curd; it is milk coagulated by the addition of a small quantity of sour milk, or of a little tire of the day preceding.

period when they first came to Ceylon, is, that I am aware, well ascertained. They are a stout, active, shrewd, enterprising race; and, as the Goewansè monopolize the honours, so these people do the trade of the country. In dress, appearance, and manners, they differ but little from the Singalese. The whole department, including the Carawè, is called Madigè. It may be divided into two classes, — those who have lands, and are fixed; and those without lands, who are called Soolan baddé. * The chief wealth of both consists in cattle. For the protection which government afforded them, and for the lands they held, those of the first class were obliged to appear with their bullocks †, when required, to carry the king's rice and paddy to the royal store. Besides which service, they had a small tax to pay of salt, salt-fish, and some other articles. The Soolan Moors were employed as carriers, in times of emergency only; they were more frequently commissioned to trade for the king, with money furnished from the treasury.

2. The next caste, the Madinno, Chandos, or toddy-drawers, hardly deserve to be mentioned. Their occupation is to collect the sweet juice ‡ that flows from the decapitated flower-stalk of the cocoa-nut tree, and two other palms, for the purpose of fermentation. It being contrary to the religion of the Singalese to use fermented liquors, there are very few families of this caste

* Soolan, unsettled; literally, wind: — baddé, according to the best authorities, signifies a collection of men, from the Singalese verb, to tie or bind together.

† The bullocks of Ceylon are small and active, and well adapted to mountainous roads. They are the only beasts of burthen used in the country.

‡ This juice is called Toddy. It ferments with astonishing rapidity; in two or three hours it becomes intoxicating, and is much abused by the lowland Singalese. For raising bread there is no better yeast. Arrack is obtained from it by distillation.

in the Interior, excepting in one or two districts bordering on the maritime provinces.

3. The Achari, which I have placed the third, occupies, according to some, the first rank amongst the low castes. It is composed of silversmiths, blacksmiths, brass-founders, carpenters, turners, lapidaries, sculptors, &c.; — who are called by the general name *Achari*, as masters or teachers of the arts which they profess, such being the meaning of the word. For the lands which they hold they used to pay a land-tax in money, and annually furnish the king's stores with certain manufactured articles: — thus, the silversmiths had to furnish silver chunam boxes, and gilt and silver rings; and the blacksmiths had to provide betel knives, bill-hooks, and instruments for rasping cocoa-nuts. They were all obliged to work for the king, when required, without compensation of any kind, excepting the carpenters and sculptors; who, when employed, were allowed provisions, on the ground that their materials being wood and stone, articles of little or no value, they could not remunerate themselves like the rest, by pilfering a portion; — a system winked at, and even permitted in moderation, the Singalese being well aware that it cannot be entirely prevented.

4. The Hannawli, or taylors, are few in number. It was their duty formerly to make the splendid and barbarous dresses of the king and his court, for which they held lands.

5. The Baddahela badda, or potters, are pretty numerous. For their lands they had to pay a small tax in money, and to furnish the kitchen of the king and chiefs with earthenware. Owing to the influence and prejudice of caste, the consumption of this ware is extraordinarily great amongst the Singalese, who consider themselves disgraced and polluted if they drink out of

vessels that have touched the lips of their inferiors, — and, in consequence, after a feast at which people of different castes have been entertained, all the earthenware vessels used on the occasion are destroyed.

6. The Ambattea people, or barbers. — On account of the smallness of this caste, the term *badda* is not attached to it. They had a tax in money to pay for their land, and were liable to serve as baggage-porters, or, to use the Indian expression, as baggage-coolies. They are very little employed in a professional way, each Singalese being his own barber; one family, indeed, for land which it held, had a sacred duty to perform, which, ridiculous as it may appear, was the shaving of Boodhoo, at the great temple in Kandy, as a mark of respect. The duties of this office were executed by turns by the different members of the family. The manner of performing the operation was peculiar: — the barber stood in the anti-chamber, separated from the image by a curtain, whilst a priest within held a looking-glass to the face of the figure; the barber made appropriate motions with his razor, and thus, without seeing or coming in contact with the idol, went through the ceremony. I had this account from a priest, who related it in a mysterious whisper.

7. The Radabadda, or caste of washermen, is pretty numerous. They had to pay for their land one-twentieth of its produce in raw rice; for, were it scalded, it would be considered as dressed, and could not be used by the Goewansè, and much less by the royal family. Their particular duty was to furnish white cloths to spread on the ground, line rooms, and cover chairs, wherever the king or his chiefs were expected. Those families that washed for the court had lands free for

that service. Without payment, they were not required to wash for any of the superior castes; and, on no account would they degrade themselves by washing for any beneath them. The dress of all the preceding castes is the same as that of the Goewansè. In the dress of the females of this caste there is a little alteration: instead of using the single hala as a petticoat and scarf, they are obliged to substitute two short cloths, one to be wrapped round the loins, and the other to be thrown over the shoulder.

8. The Halee, or Chalias. — This caste is small in the Interior, and of no importance. By trade, the Chalias are weavers. For their lands they had to pay a pecuniary tax, and they were liable to be employed in the king's kitchen, in bringing fire-wood, cleaning chatties, and carrying provisions. The service imposed on the Chalias of the Seven Korles, about 500 families, was to furnish the king's stores annually with a certain quantity of salt-fish. The men of this caste were not allowed to wear caps, or cloths reaching much below the knees, and the dress of the women was similar to that of the potters. The men, but not the women, might marry into the caste immediately below them. The Chalias of the maritime provinces, having been employed as cinnamon-peelers, have received great encouragement from the government, in consequence of which their numbers have so increased, that they have acquired the name of Mahabaddé, and many of them have become wealthy and aspiring. Of the origin of the Chalias, different accounts have been given; according to the most respectable authorities, their ancestors were of the race of Paisecara weavers, who were brought to Ceylon from the continent of India, about 600 years ago.

9. The Hakooroo, or jaggery-makers, are pretty numerous. Their occupation is to prepare jaggery (a coarse kind of sugar) from the juice of different palms, but chiefly from that of the Ketoolga (Caryota urens), which contains the largest proportion of saccharine matter. For their lands they had to furnish a certain quantity of jaggery annually to the king's stores, and provide the chiefs with the same article, and with sweet toddy. Many families did service as coolies and palanqueen-bearers. It was from this caste that the Goewansè procured cooks, there being no impropriety in eating of dishes dressed by them.

10. The Hunubaddé, chunam or lime burners, are few in number. Their occupation is to burn lime and make charcoal. For the land they hold, they had to bring a certain quantity of each article to the king's store annually, besides paying a land-tax in money.

11. The Pannayo, or grass-cutters, are numerous. The services they had to perform for their lands, were to take care of the king's cattle, horses, and elephants; furnish the royal stores with vegetables once a fortnight, and provide mats, when required. They derive their name from Pan, a species of high grass which they cut.

12. The Velledurai constitute a small caste which is chiefly confined to the district of Neuracalava. They are, it is said, weavers; and, it is conjectured that they are descendants of Chalias.

13. The Dodda-weddahs, or hunters, are few in number, and inhabit some of the wildest parts of the mountainous regions. For the land which they held they were required to furnish the king with game.

14. The Paduas form a pretty numerous caste, who, for their

lands, besides paying a pecuniary tax, had to perform a variety of low services, as to build walls, and thatch the roofs of houses, carry loads, bring wood and ornaments for arches *, bear jingalls †, in processions, &c. — There is another description of Paduas, called Yamanoo, who are iron-smelters; and, for their lands had annually to furnish to the king's store, and to the chiefs of districts, a certain quantity of iron. There is, besides, a degraded portion of Paduas, named Gahalagambodayo, who are prohibited from eating and marrying with the rest, and had the lowest and vilest services to perform; thus they had to furnish executioners, and scavengers to keep the streets clean; and remove dead bodies. Even of this degraded race one set is considered lower than the other, and is held in contempt for eating beef. The Paduas, in general, are not permitted to wear a cloth that reaches below their knees; and their women are not entitled to wear one over their shoulders, or to conceal the upper part of their bodies.

15. The Barrawabaddè, Mahabaddè, or tom-tom beaters, are a pretty numerous caste. They are weavers by trade, and had to pay a tax in money for their lands, supply the royal stores monthly with vegetables, provide wooden gutters of the Ketoolga, and, in some districts, furnish a certain quantity of cloth of their own making. Particular families have lands for beating the tom-tom,

* The Singalese are extremely fond of ornamental arches, decorated with palm leaves and flowers; they erect them on all public occasions, in excellent taste, and with a very pretty effect.

† The jingall is a very small and long piece of ordnance, light enough to be carried with ease by a single man, and very well adapted for a desultory warfare amongst mountains. It is fired on the ground, resting on a long slender butt-end, and a pair of legs.

dancing and piping, &c. at the great festivals; and others have portions of church-lands, for performing at temples.

16. The Handee, few in number, were required to furnish the royal stores with baskets and winnows.

17. The Pallaroo are a very small caste, of which I have collected no particulars.

18. The Olee, very few in number, had no particular service to perform, but to carry in the procession, at one of the great annual festivals, the monstrous effigies of the demons called Assooriahs.

19. The Radayo is another very small caste, of which I can find no account amongst my notes.

20. The Palee, far from numerous, are the washermen of the low castes, inferior to the Rada badda.

21. The Kinnera badde is a very small caste, that had to provide the royal stores with ropes and mats. Their dress is similar to that of the other very low castes, with the exception that they are not allowed to confine their hair with a handkerchief.

Of the Out-castes of society who are shunned by the very lowest castes, and whose touch is pollution, there are two descriptions, — the Gattaroo, and the Rhodees.

The Gattaroo were such as were cast out of society by the king for infamous conduct, and at his pleasure might be restored. The terrible sentence was: — "Let the offender be exempted from paying taxes, and performing services; and be considered a Gattaroo."

The Rhodees or Gasmundo *, it is said, are the descendants of

* They are called *Gasmundo*, by those who forbear insulting them; the term meaning *tree*, and a kind of rope made by them, and which, when used for catching elephants, is fastened to a tree.

those who were punished by being made out-castes, for continuing to indulge in eating beef after its use was prohibited,—and of those who have since been degraded for high treason. Though considered the vilest of the vile, they are not entirely destitute of lands, nor were they quite exempt from taxation. For the little land they hold, they were required to furnish hides, and ropes made of hides, for taking elephants. To pay their tribute, they brought it to one side of the Mahawelle ganga, the king's jailor waiting on the opposite side, with his people, to see it deposited. Analogous too, to the castes, each village has a petty headman, called Hoolawalia, appointed by the same jailor, who was the only individual whose duty it was to communicate with them, and that at a respectful distance.

It may be well supposed, if their ancestors, with the certainty of utter disgrace staring them in the face, could not check their appetite,—that the present race, stimulated by want, and under no restraint in regard to diet, will not bridle theirs; indeed, they eat almost every thing that comes in their way, even the bodies of dead animals, if not putrid; and dead bullocks they consider their peculiar property. Besides those already mentioned, there are many other circumstances that mark the extreme disgrace and degraded state of these people. They are not allowed to live in houses of the common construction, but only in the merest sheds, completely open on one side, thus: 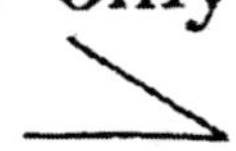 In carrying a pingo*, they are permitted to load it at one end only; and they are not only shunned by, but are required to avoid, others. When a Rhodia sees a Goewanse he must salute him with hands up-

* A pingo is an elastic stick about five feet long; loaded at both ends and poised on the shoulder, it is generally used in Ceylon for carrying burthens.

lifted and joined, and must move out of the way; or if the path be narrow, not affording room for both to pass at a distance, he must go back. But it is not true, as has been asserted, that on such an occasion he must prostrate himself for the Goewanse to walk over his body; indeed such a practice would be incompatible with the notion of impurity attached to their touch, and which is so firmly impressed on the minds of the Singalese, that they have been known to refuse to obey the orders of our government to make prisoners certain Rhodees suspected of a murder, saying, "they could not pollute themselves by seizing them, but they would willingly shoot them at a distance." The minds of the Rhodees, it is hardly necessary to remark, correspond with their wretched lot; and, excepting perhaps to one another, they seem to be destitute of all moral principle. Whether they possess any religious notions in common with the Singalese, it is not easy to ascertain. Prohibited from approaching temples, there is a solitary instance on record of a priest going and preaching to them, for which, having incurred his sovereign's displeasure, he replied, "Religion should be common to all." Wretched as is the condition of the Rhodees, they are said to be a robust race, and their women particularly handsome. On account of the beauty of the latter, and the art of fortune-telling which they profess, they are less shunned than the men. When rambling about the country practising their idle art, to attract attention they balance a brass plate on a finger, and holding it on high, twirl it round with surprising dexterity. The analogy between these people and the gypsies, in many points is obvious; but in all probability it is merely accidental.

It would be a work of supererogation to discuss here the origin of castes in general. Mr. Mills, in his elaborate work on British India, has satisfactorily pointed out one of its sources; referring it to the exertions of one man in an early stage of society, intent on its improvement, and conceiving classification and division of people and labour conducive to that end.*

Besides this source, — perhaps there is another, in the first instance the result of habit and mutual consent rather than of reason and authority: thus, in colonizaiton in early times, each individual of a settlement will have some profession or trade, which, without any enactment of government, will naturally become hereditary; and, the warmer the climate, the more indolent the disposition of the people, the greater the facility of supporting life, — so much the less disposition there will be to exertion and change. Custom may thus gradually fix what necessity or utility commenced; and, afterwards to perpetuate trades and endeavour to prevent their decline, as well as to derive all possible advantage from their division, government may come forward, aided by religion, to confirm and sanction the system.

The ideas of the Singalese respecting the origin of castes are very similar to those of the Hindoos, supposing them to be contemporary with the formation of society. Their account of the peculiarities of caste in Ceylon, and particularly of the absence of the brahminical caste, is less romantic, and is the most probable, perhaps, that can be given. They maintain that their island was colonized from the eastward about 2363 years ago; that the first settlers, with the exception of their leader of royal descent, were of the Goewansé; and that the great reinforcement of population that flowed into the island in

* History of British India, i. 108.

the reign of the fifteenth king, was also from the eastward, from a country where the Brahmens were not tolerated, and composed of eighteen different subordinate castes of the Kshoodrawansè.

As before observed, the Singalese experience less of the effects of castes than their neighbours the Hindoos; a very large proportion of the whole Singalese population being on an equality, and at liberty to pursue any liberal occupation. Respecting the effects of castes in general on society, it is extremely difficult to form a correct estimate, and to determine whether the evil or the advantages that result from them, in a hot climate, preponderate. As they check progressive improvement, and eternally degrade a large portion of the people, their operation is most injurious on society; but, as they preserve the arts, and tend to prevent farther deterioration, — as they repress the passions and ambitious desires, and promote order and tranquillity, their influence is beneficial, and almost moral. In a climate and country otherwise predisposed to advancement, their existence must be a curse; but in a climate and country of an opposite nature, more liable to decline, they may be considered almost a blessing. To which description Ceylon belongs, it is not easy to say; I am almost afraid to the latter rather than the former; and, consequently that the abolition of castes there, would not be desirable, unless powerful moral motives could be introduced as stimuli to counteract the deteriorating effect of physical circumstances. The system of castes is so wretched and humiliating in all its details, that only sheer necessity should induce one to support it: Englishmen have too much good feeling and generosity, and too correct notions of justice and liberty ever to err in improperly maintaining it; they are more likely to err in attempting prematurely its overthrow, before the people are ripe for the change, and prepared to benefit by its destruction.

CHAPTER V.

SUBDIVISIONS OF THE INTERIOR. — OLD FORM OF GOVERNMENT. — KANDYAN COURT — ITS CEREMONIES AND FESTIVALS.

Before engaging in a description of the old government of the Interior, it may not be unadvisable to notice the manner in which the country is divided.

The whole of the Interior is parcelled out into divisions of two different denominations, viz. Dissavonies and Ratties; the former signifying literally *side*, (perhaps, from their situation,) in an enlarged sense, may be translated province; whilst the latter strictly means country, or as we should say, county. These divisions, established by long custom, were occasionally, though very rarely, altered by the reigning monarch. The following is a list of each kind, according to their old arrangement:

Dissavonies.

Nuarakalawea.
Sat-Korlé, the Seven Korles.
Hattere-Korlé, the Four Korlès.
Korlé-tunay, the Three Korles.
Saperegamuay, Saffragam.
Ouva

Welassey.
Bintenney.
Tamankadada.
Matelè.
Walapany.
Udapalate.

Ratties.

Doombera.
Harasea-pattoowe
Toompanè.
Yatenuara.
Udoonuara
Kotmalè.
Hewahettè.

The relative situation and extent of the different districts is tolerably correctly laid down in the map which accompanies this work.

With the exception of two, viz. Walapany and Udapalate, all the Dissavonies, it will be perceived, according to the original signification of the word, are situated laterally in respect to the high country, and constitute, in every direction, the boundaries of the Kandyan kingdom; whilst all the Ratties are situated centrically, and in the mountainous region, and immediately surround the Kandyan capital.

Both Dissavonies and Ratties are farther divided into Pattoos, Korles, &c.; thus, Sat-Korlè, or the Seven Korles, is divided into the Eihala-dolos-Pattoo, the upper twelve Pattoos; and the Palaha-dolos-Pattoo, the lower twelve Pattoos; thus, Ouva is divided into the Kandapallè-Korle, Kandookara-Korle, Passera-Korle, Oodakinda, Medikinda and Yattikinda; and these minor divisions, in many instances, are themselves subdivided.

The old Kandyan government, at least two thousand years years old (if we may believe its historians) is now no more: it has probably perished for ever, and will be forgotten in a few years, in that very country in which it has existed so long. On these accounts it is the more necessary to describe it, and to give in detail respecting it as much information as possible. Without such details, the history of the Interior must always be obscure, and the character of the people, even much of their manners and customs, and modes of thinking, imperfectly understood. Independent of these local considerations, it is interesting, and deserving of being studied and recorded as a striking example of Indian monarchy unadulterated by foreign admixture.

In describing it, I shall endeavour to avoid abstract propositions, and make the account I have to offer, as descriptive as possible, and as little different, as is consistent with order and perspicuity, from the narratives of the chiefs from whom I collected my information.

The following scheme will give a pretty correct idea of the organization of the old government or regal establishment: —

	The King.	
	Ministers.	
Officers of the Palace.	Chiefs of Districts.	Officers of Baddies.
	Chiefs of Temples.	

Which, in detail, with the Singalese names and ordinary titles, is thus:

The King — Rajooroowo.

Ministers.

Pallegampahay	adikaram	mahatmeya.
Udegampahay	do.	do.
Siapattoowè	do.	do.

Chiefs of Districts.

Dissaves, Chiefs of Dissavonies.

Hattere-korlè maha-dissava mahatmeya.	
Satcorlay maha-dissava	do.
Ouva maha-dissava	do.
Matelè maha-dissava	do.
Saperegamuay dissava	do.
Korlè-tunay dissava	do.
Nuarakalawia dissava	do.
Tamankadada dissava	do.
Wellassè dissava	do.
Bintenney dissava	do.
Walapany dissava	do.
Udapalata dissava	do.

Rate-mahatmeyas, Chiefs of Ratties.

Udoonuara rate-mahatmeya.	
Yatinuara	do.
Toompanè	do.
Harasca-pattoowe	do.
Doombera	do.
Hewahettè	do.
Kotmalè	do.

Chiefs of Temples.

Mawligawé diwa-nilami.

Dewalay basnayeke-nilami.

Officers of the Palace.

Gajenayke nilami.		
Maha-lekam-mahatmeya.		
Attepattuay lekam	do.	
Wedikkara	do.	do.
Nanayakkare	do.	do.
Wadenatuakkoocava lekam mahatmeya.		
Padikara	do.	do.
Koodituakkoo	do.	do.
Bondikkulla	do.	do.
Doonoocara	do.	do.
Cooroowe	do.	do.
Madoowe	do.	do.
Coottaha	do.	do.
Aspantia mohandiram nilami.		
Hoodooharakpantiye mohandiram nilami.		
Patti widana nilami.		
Maha-aramoodalay-wannakoo nilami.		
Maha-gabada nilami.		
Uda-gabada nilami.		
Maha-haitepenega mohandiram nilami.		
Attepattoo-madoowe	do.	do.
Ranauda-madoowe lekam mahatmeya.		
Audagè-vannakoo nilami		
Diawadenè	do.	
Haloowadenè	do.	
Batwadenè	do.	
Paniveda-caruna	do.	
Baitgè mohandiram	do.	

Koonam-madoowe lekam mahatmeya.
Soodalia mohandiram nilami.
Mawroowaliye mohandiram nilami.
Naitoom-elangame do. do.
Kawiecara-madoowe do. do.
Wahala-elangame do. do.
Tamboroo-purampiettoo-cara mohandiram nilami.
Sinharak-cara do. do.

Subordinate Officers of the Palace under the preceding.

Maha-haitepenage cancawnam nilami.
Attepattoo-madoowe do. do.
Ranaude-madoowe do. do.
Maha-aramoodalè lekam mahatmeya.
Maha-aramoodalè cancawnam nilami.
Audagè do. do.
Sattambi.
Madappooli nilami.
Piha-rawla.
Gabadawe lekam mahatmeya.
Gabadawe cancawnam nilami.
Geba-rawle.
Coonam-madoowe sattambi.
Aspantia cancawnam.
Panikki atchilla.
Elangame mohandirama.
Cawicara-madoowe mohandirama.

Officers of Baddies.

Madigè-baddè nilami.
Kottal-baddè do.
Bada-hella-baddè do.
Rada-baddè do.
Maha-baddè do.
Hoonoo-baddè do.
Wie-baddè do.
Kinnere-baddè do.
Annilla-baddè do.
Soolan-baddè do.
Rahoo-baddè do.
Loonoo-baddè do.

The Singalese have no notion of any species of government, excepting the pure monarchical: they say, that a king is so essential, that without him there would be no order nor harmony, only confusion and dissension, that would soon prove fatal to society: and, supposing this species of government founded upon a kind of natural instinct, as well as on ancient custom, they remark, that even birds and beasts have their kings, — the anser * reigning over one, and the lion over the other.

No one, they conceived, was regularly qualified to sit on the throne, unless he were of the Rajah or Soorea wansè, either

* The anser is esteemed sacred by the Singalese: it is represented in their paintings like a goose. A Kandyan chief, who visited H. M. ship Minden, at Trincomalie, recognised the anser in a large stuffed albatross, hanging in one of the officers' cabins.

The late King of Kandy, from a drawing by a Native.

by the father's or mother's side: though there are instances of individuals of the Goewansè becoming kings; but these were not held in the light of precedents, — they were considered rather as brilliant exceptions, and as examples of extraordinary elevation and good fortune, the result and the reward of acts of piety and virtue in a former life.

Another qualification for the throne was being of the established religion, and a follower of Boodhoo.

The throne they considered hereditary, descending in succession from the father to the eldest son. The regular succession was not to be interrupted, excepting for very cogent reasons, and with the consent of the rightful heir; and, it was never doubtful, excepting when the king had no near relations: in such an instance, should not the king, before his death, have nominated his successor, the office of selection devolved on the ministers; it then became their duty to find out a proper person, propose him to the chiefs and people, and with their consent place him on the throne.

The rights and functions of the king were of the highest and most extensive nature: he was the acknowledged lord of the soil; he alone taxed the people, and determined the services they were to perform; all offices of government were at his disposal, and all honours, as well as power, emanated from him, and were enjoyed only during his pleasure. Notwithstanding this sway, he was not perfectly absolute and without check. On ascending the throne, he had to consider himself under certain restrictions: he was expected to follow the example of good princes; observe the customs of the country, and attend to the written rules handed down for the direction of kings. Of these rules the following are the principal: they are translated from the Pali, in which they are expressed in verse.

Sattara sangraha wastoo.

1. Be willingly charitable to the deserving.
2. Be mild of speech.
3. Let your conduct and actions be such as conduce to the good of your people.
4. Let the love of your people equal the love of yourself.

Sattara agati.

1. Favour no one to the injury of another.
2. Injure no one to benefit another.
3. Let not fear prevent your doing justice.
4. Avoid doing evil through ignorance, or the want of correct information.

Dasa rajah dharma.

1. Be munificent.
2. Strictly follow the rules of your religion.
3. Remunerate the deserving.
4. Let your conduct be upright.
5. Let your conduct be mild.
6. Be patient.
7. Be without malice.
8. Inflict not torture.
9. Be merciful.
10. Attend to good counsel.

Should a king act directly contrary to these rules, contrary to the example of good princes, and in opposition to the customs of the country, he would be reckoned a tyrant, and the people would consider themselves justified in opposing him, and in rising in mass and dethroning him; nor are there wanting instances, in extreme cases of oppression, of their acting on this principle, and successfully redressing their wrongs.

To have correct ideas of the old Kandayan monarchy, and of the regal establishment, it will be necessary to go into some details, and consider its subordinate component parts, a nominal list of which has already been given, that may well appal the reader by its length, amounting nearly to a hundred different offices, none of which were hereditary, all of them at the king's disposal, and the majority of them created, not for the purposes of government but for the use, convenience, luxury, and pomp of the monarch.

The officers of highest rank were the ministers, whom, in Ceylon, we familiarly call Adikars, whom the king called Adikaarams, and whom the Singalese honour with the title of Maha-nilami, or Maha-mahatmeya. In remote times there were four ministers: one to attend the king; one to take care of the city; one to administer justice; and one as minister of war. But for very many years prior to the reign of Raja Singha, there was only one minister: Rajah Singha added a second, and the last king added a third.

The first Adikar, Pallegampahay adikaram mahatmeya, derived his distinctive name from the five low villages * which belonged to his office,—low in point of situation, being lower down, in the course of the Mahawelle ganga, than Kandy.

* Pallegampahay is, literally, low, villages, five.

The second Adikar, Udegampahay adikaram mahatmeya, was so called from the five villages that were attached to his office, being situated higher up the river, and nearer Kandy. — Udè signifying both these circumstances.

The inhabitants of these villages were Katipooly-Lascoreens, who executed the orders of the ministers, and acted in the capacity of the gendarmerie of the country.

The third Adikar, Siapattoowe adikaram mahatmeya, was furnished with Lascoreens, from very many different villages; from which circumstance, probably, he derived his name, — Sia Pattoowe, signifying a hundred pattoos.

The only officers, that I have heard of, that were appointed by the ministers, were a Korleatchilla, and the Erigè-Cancawnam, and Dooreya, who had charge of the king's jail.

The office of the Adikars was very comprehensive; they had not only the duties of prime-minister to perform, but likewise of chief justices and commanders of the king's forces. The administration of justice was their principal occupation: according to a rule not very rigorously followed, the first Adikar should attend to cases from one half of the country, and the second Adikar to cases from the other half; whilst the third had a more general jurisdiction, it being his duty to receive all cases that might offer, and report on them to the king.

They were impowered to pass sentence in all cases but capital ones, of high treason and murder, in which the king alone could acquit or condemn. In every instance that satisfaction were not afforded, an appeal might be made from their decision to the king.

As the office of Adikar was not for life, — only at the king's pleasure, and as there was no emolument attached to it of any consequence, but the perquisites of the court, it may be easily imagined that the Adikars were not very pure judges; they are described, indeed, as completely corrupt, in the constant practice of taking bribes, and, excepting in the most flagrant cases, much more biassed in their opinions by gold than by argument, — insuring always to the richest man the better cause.

The pomp and state of the Adikars was next to that of the king; wherever they went, they were preceded by a person bearing their staff of office, — a crooked silver rod, and by a number of men carrying and cracking tremendous whips, emblematic of the punishment that awaited guilty offenders.

It may be worth remarking that, in some districts, where formerly there had been royal residences, and where there are still Kattipooli-Lascoreens, as in Ouva, Matelè, Bintenney, and Hewahettè, there were Adikarams, as they are even now called, appointed by the king to command the Lascoreens. They ranked in the districts next to the Dissaves, and acted under them in a judicial capacity. They were allowed to have whips carried before them; but, to denote their inferiority, they were not permitted to crack them.

The Dissaves, formerly called Dissave-pati, (chief of a side,) were the representatives of royalty, in the districts to which they were appointed chiefs; and were entitled, in their provinces, to all the honours of majesty itself, with the exception of prostration. Each chief was preceded by his peculiar flag, by a band of musicians, and by men bearing arms and jingalls, which were fired on his first entering his district, and each was attended by his guard, and a long train of followers.

The duties of these chiefs were, — to administer justice, collect the revenue, carry into effect the king's orders, and perform every other part of government. In their judicial capacity they were inferior to the Adikars only, to whom those dissatisfied with their decisions were at liberty to make an appeal.

Occasionally, on entering upon office, they made a present to the king; but I understand it is not correct, as it is commonly supposed, that they bought their appointments. The revenue of each district was fixed, and it was the duty of the chief to have it collected and paid annually to the treasury. He was responsible for any failure, and having the privilege of enjoying the surplus, he seldom failed to oppress the people.

Formerly the chiefs were not allowed to reside in their districts; they were kept in the capital, by a jealous monarchy, as pledges of the fidelity of the people under their command. The late King, to increase his revenue, indulged them with leave of absence from court, retaining their families as hostages.

The Disaves had the power of appointing the following officers to act under them; — three Mohottalas, viz. the Dissaway-Mohottala, the Attapatteé, and the Codituakka, and a certain number of Korawlas, Atu-corawlas, Mohandirams, Widahns, and Cancawnamas.

The Dissaway-Mohottala was the first officer under the Dissave, and, in his absence, exercised his authority. The Attapattee-mohottala commanded the Attapattoo-people, composed of the best Goewansé families, who constituted the body-guard of the Dissave, — thirty or forty of them being in constant attendance on him wherever he went.

The Codituakka-Mohottala had charge of the ordnance department of the district, and of the low-cast Paduas, whose duty it was to carry the jingalls. The Korawla was the head of a korle; the Atu-korawla was under him. Their duties were to collect the rents and dues of their little districts, and attend to its general concerns; acting, in their limited sphere, the same part as the Dissaway-Mohottala, to whom they were responsible.

The Mohandiram commanded the Dissavony Lascoreens, called Heywa-wassan, whose business it was to guard the king's timber-stores, cut timber, and plait the leaves of the cocoa-nut tree, called olas, to make roofs.

A Widahn was the head of a village; his duty was to attend to its police, execute the orders of the Dissave, and superintend the erection or preservation of buildings, intended for the reception of head-men, when travelling on service.

The Dooreyas were the petty chiefs of low castes, who were responsible for their conduct.

The Cancawnamas were petty officers, employed chiefly in aiding in the collecting of revenue.

In some Dissavonies, it may be remarked, there were officers who bore names different from any of the preceding; — thus in Newarakalawia, and in Tamankadada, there were Wanny-unnihays*, with the authority of Mohottalas; — thus, again, in Wellassey, Matelè, and Bintenney, there were Rate-rawles, whose rank and duties were very similar to those of Korawls.

The duties of Rate-mahatmeyas were similar to those of Dissaves, but their official rank was inferior, and less respect was required to be paid them by the people; strictly, they were not entitled to enter their districts in palanqueens, nor had they any right to flags, or to the beating of tom-toms, or the carrying of jingalls before them.

* Wanny, probably significant of a wild woody district; — unnihay, a term of respect, somewhat corresponding to our master.

The officers appointed by the Rate-mahatmeyas, to act under them were, a Liana-rawla, Undia-rawla, Korawls, Atu-korawls, and some inferior headmen, as Widahns, &c.

The Liana-rawla, (liana, to write; having to keep the accounts of the district) was in office similar to the Dissaway-Mohottala.

The Undia-rawla, next in rank, called in some districts Korlea, was employed in collecting the revenue.

The duties of the Korawls and of the inferior officers were the same in the Ratties as in the Dissavonies.

Under the old monarchy both the office of Dissave and Rate-mahatmeya, was confined to the first families in the country, partly from custom and partly because the people were averse to obey any excepting men of the most distinguished rank.

The chiefs of temples, the Mawligawe diwa-nilami, and the Dewalay basnayeke-nilamis, were laymen of high rank not appointed by the college of priests, but by the king himself, and held their office, (which was generally combined with some civil employment of consequence,) only during his majesty's pleasure.

The Mawligawè diwa-nilami had charge of the Dalada-mawligawe, (the chief temple of Boodhoo, at Kandy,) and of a large number of Pattea-people, whose services were confined to the temple and to the temple-lands. He had under him a Lekam-mahatmeya and several inferior officers; it was his duty to attend to the temporal affairs of the temple, assist at its religious rites, and take care that all the ceremonies of religion were duly performed. He himself, now and then, had to present offerings to Boodhoo; to prepare himself, he had to bathe, put on a clean topetty, and abstain from meat at least twenty-four hours, — not from the idea that these observances would be grateful to Boodhoo, but from the persuasion that the gods in whose keeping the temple is supposed to be, are particularly attentive to bodily purity, and resent highly its neglect. The morning offerings that were made by the chief, consisted of curry and rice, and flowers; and the evening, of flowers and of some light beverage and of betel leaves; — Boodhoo whilst alive having been in the habit of taking refreshment only twice a-day.

The Dewalay basnayeke-nilamis, in Kandy, were four in number, one for each of the Dewalays or temples of the gods, viz. of the Nata, Maha-Visnu, Katragam, and Patinĕ. In the charge of their respective temples, and of the people and lands attached to them, they were aided by petty and subordinate officers. Their duties differed very little from those of the Mawligawe dewa-nilami: but they themselves could not, as he did, present the offerings required of them, — greater mystery being observed in their temples, and none, but the officiating priests called Kappuralles, being qualified, or daring to appear before the idols; — but on this subject, more hereafter.

Besides these chiefs of the temples of the capital, there were others appointed to perform the like offices, and to watch over the temporal interests of religion in many of the districts.

The officers of the palace were as numerous and miscellaneous as the general wants of the monarch to whom they were subservient. A brief notice of each or of the principal, will be sufficient perhaps to satisfy the curiosity of the reader, and give an insight into the economy of the court of the old monarchy.

The Gajenayke nilami (elephant chief) was the first officer of the household department. His duty was to superintend the people who had charge of the royal elephants, of whom a register was kept by a subordinate officer, the Cooroone lekam.

The duties of all the different lekamships were (at least

originally) of a military nature. Each lekamship was commanded by a Lekam mahatmeya, whom the king called Mohottala, — and by a Lekamy mohandiram, and certain petty officers.

The six Lekams, that stand first in the list of these officers, had each the command of a certain number of men, whose duties latterly were nearly the same, and confined principally to carrying messages and conveying the king's orders.

The Coodituakkoo-lekam commanded the people who carried the king's jingalls, about one hundred in number.

The Bondikkulla-lekam was at the head of a department instituted by the last king, to take charge, as the word implies, of the iron cannon belonging to his majesty.

The Madoowe-lekam had the command of a class of men whose duty it was to keep watch round the capital. They mounted guard, armed with muskets, at fourteen different stations, about ten men to each post. Whilst they guarded the environs of the city, the king's foreign Malabar troops, about ninety in number, kept sentry round the palace, and protected his person.

The Aspantia mohandiram nilami was the master of the horse; and, with several subordinate officers, had charge of the royal stables.

The Hoodooharakpantia mohandiram nilami was intrusted with the care of the king's herd of white cattle, which were brought from the continent of India, and were much valued on account of their colour.

The Pattividane nilami had the superintendance of the king's cattle in general, in different parts of the country, under the care of the Pattea-people, and amounting, perhaps, to two thousand head.

The Maha-aramoodaly-wannakoo nilami, the king's grand treasurer, was an officer of the highest rank in the household establishment. There were five Lekams, and the same number of Cancawnams under him, appointed by the king, and all honoured with the title of Mahatmeya or Nilami. They were the king's receivers and paymasters-general, and had charge of all the royal treasures, of which they were required to keep the strictest account, and the greatest care. There were no people attached to them; when they wanted any, they had to make a requisition for men to the officer of the guard on duty.

The Mahagabada nilami was the chief of the king's store, and ranked next to the grand treasurer. His duty was to see that the king's dues in kind were correctly paid, and properly taken care of. He had under him four Lekams and four Cancawnams, appointed by the king at his recommendation, besides four Gayballanaralles and forty-eight workmen. The duty of the Lekams was to keep an account of the things stored and issued; that of the Cancawnams, to guard and open and shut the doors; that of the Gayballanaralles, to take care of the things within, in relation to their packing and unpacking and preservation; and, lastly, the forty-eight workmen, who were paid for their trouble, were employed in the ordinary business of the store, in carrying things forward and backward, cleaning, conveying messages, &c.

The Udagabada nilami had charge of the king's private store for the reception of the dues of the royal villages; and which was called Udagabadawe, having been first built on higher ground than that which the preceding officer superintended. From these two stores the king's household was supplied with every thing that it required, and that they could furnish.

The Maha-haitipenagé mohandiram nilami commanded the appohamies, or gentlemen in waiting on the king, and had under him a Lekam-mahatmeya, and a Cancawnam nilami. The duty of the former was to take care of the jewels that the king was in the daily habit of wearing; whilst that of the latter was to command the guard of appohamies about the king, under the direction of the Mohandiram. Formerly the number of these appohamies was not limited; by the late king, after the war of 1803, their number was reduced to forty-eight. The situation was considered honourable, and was in great request, and was always held by the sons of chiefs, and people of rank, whom the king promoted to higher situations as vacancies occurred. Their principal duty was to be in waiting to receive his majesty's orders, and communicate them to the chiefs; when called, they approached the king moving on their knees *, but having received their orders, they were allowed to rise and walk away. They had no immediate remuneration, excepting that their lands were exempted from paying duty to the Gabadawe.

The Attepattoo-madoowe mohandiram nilami, like the last officer, had the command of forty-eight appohamies, who were also the sons of chiefs. It was their duty to be in waiting in the Attepattoo-madoowe, a room near the king's, to convey his messages, and carry his "golden arms" in public. It must not be supposed that these arms were really of gold: the term was applied merely out of respect; and it is a common oriental court expression.

The Ranauda-madoowe lekam mahatmeya, with the aid of forty-eight young men of quality, kept a register of the royal

* The knees of some of the courtiers, from much practice, acquired a thick skin, not unlike that of the sole of the foot, and as callous.

arms, and took care that they were preserved in good order by the different kinds of smiths attached to the department.

The Audageywannakoo nilami, with two Lekam and two Cancawnam nilamis under him, had the superintendence of all the king's muskets and swords, and of all his iron and brass instruments.

The Diawadenè nilami was intrusted with the superintendence of the royal bath, and, when the king bathed, it was his duty to wash and comb and dress his majesty's hair. He appointed under him, with the king's permission, ten Satambis, and the same number of Pannivida-carayos. The former acted as the petty chiefs of the people (about 500 families) that were attached to the bath. Two Satambis were required to be in constant attendance in the palace; and, at the new year, when the king bathed as a ceremony, the presence of the whole ten was required. Their duty, besides taking care of the bath, was to pour water on the king; and those of the best families might touch him, and wash his feet. The Pannivida-carayos were employed in carrying messages to summon the services of the people of the bath.

The Haloowadene nilami had charge of the king's wardrobe, and was required to be present to aid in dressing his majesty. The ordinary dress of the late king was a shirt, a jacket over it with long sleeves, and a rich topetty in the Singalese fashion, or a loose trowsers in the Malabar: he wore a high four-cornered cap of a particular form, and ornamented with tassels.

The Batwadene nilami was the king's caterer. He had under him two Madapporales and many Piaharales. The business of the former was to dress the royal table, and arrange the dishes: the latter were master-cooks, who presided in the royal kitchen. The king's table was covered with a white cloth, and furnished with a service of gold plate. When all was prepared, the table was brought before his majesty, sitting with a white carpet under his feet, and a white canopy over his head. The Batwadenè nilami, using knives and forks and spoons, helped the king, who ate with his fingers off a fresh plantain-leaf that was laid on a gold plate. His principal dishes were different kinds of curries; his drink was water and cocoa-nut water. He always dined alone; occasionally he permitted, as a great favour, (and it was considered a strong mark of affection,) a favourite queen to perform the office of the Batwadenè nilami, who was excluded. and no one was allowed to be present.

The Paniveda-caruna nilami had the duty to perform of preparing "betel," and presenting it to the king. The ingredients of the royal betel, independent of the leaf which gave name to the whole, were the following:—the areka-nut, in four different states,—dried whole, dried in slices, fresh, and macerated in water; chunam, or lime; mandandoo, which is a mixture of the buds and roots of an aromatic plant; cardamums; camphor; kypoo, which is an astringent extract resembling catechu; catchoondam, a compound of different perfumes; and extract of liquorice. The king never used all these at once, but masticated them variously compounded, according to his fancy.

The Baitgay mohandiram nilami was at the head of the king's physicians, about fifty in number, and had the superintendence of the medical stores, to which forty assistants were attached, whose business it was to collect medicinal plants, and make medicinal preparations, under the direction of the physicians. Some of the physicians attended particularly to one disease, and some to another; thus, some to the diseases of the eye; some to the treatment of boils, and some to the removal of charms. There was no distinction amongst them of surgeon and physician. Some received their education in Kandy, and were taught the art by the Baitgay mohandiram; others were taught in the country, and, having acquired reputation for learning and skill, were summoned to the capital. It was only the Mohandiram nilami, and the most respectable of the physicians, who were allowed to come into the king's presence when it was necessary to prescribe for him; and it was only in cases of great emergency that any of them were permitted to see the queens; in general, they had to prescribe for the disease as it was described to them. Presents were made to them when they accomplished a cure; but if they failed, they had no remuneration.

The Koonam-madoowe lekam-mahatmeyas, two in number, were charged with the superintendence of the king's palanqueen, and were required to be constantly near his majesty. Ten Satambis were appointed under them, who did duty by turns, two at a time. The bearers of the royal palanqueen, consisting of three or four hundred families, were under their immediate orders.

The Soodalia mohandiram nilami, and Mawroowalia mohandiram nilami, each commanded a class of fencers; one called Soodalia, and the other Mawroowalia, — terms, the meaning of which I could not ascertain, and which were also applied to the people generally, the whole country having been formerly divided between the two parties. The champions on one side or party were always opposed to those of the other; their engagements were single combats, either with the fist, or with sword and shield, or with clubs. Formerly they exhibited before the court like gladiators, endeavouring to draw blood and inflict wounds. The bloody combat was discontinued, as it gave rise to serious quarrels and feuds amongst the people. Of each set of fencers there were ten maitres d'armes in different parts of the country to give lessons to all who wished to learn their art.

The Naitoom-elangamè mohandiram nilami had the superintendence of the king's company of dancers, who, according to the Malabar fashion, were women. It being contrary to the custom of the country (the Singalese disapproving of these exhibitions as indelicate), they were never much in vogue at court.

The Kawiecara-madoowe mohandiram nalami had the direction of the king's company of singers, about thirteen in number. The late king was fond of music, and his band frequently performed before him, playing on certain instruments at the same time that they sung.

The Wahala-elangamè mohandiram nilami had the command of about thirty men, performers of different kinds, some accomplished in slight-of-hand tricks, some in leaping, some in walking on stilts, and others in dancing, &c.

The Tamboroo-purampeetoo-cara mohandiram nilami commanded the king's drummers and trumpeters: it may be inferred from the title, that both the instruments from which it was derived, were borrowed from the Portuguese.

The Sinharack-cara mohandiram nilami had charge of a company of tom-tom beaters, formed by the late king for his own use: it was their duty to beat their noisy instruments at the palace eight different times daily.

Of the officers of Baddies little farther notice is required to be taken. It may be remarked generally, that in each Dissavony and Rattie, where there were many families of any Baddé, an officer was appointed to take the command of them, who, if commissioned by the king, had the title of Nilami, but if by the Dissave, only of Widane.

All the Baddies over whom there were chiefs have already been briefly described under the head of Castes, with the exception of two insignificant ones, viz. the Rahoo-baddé, and the Loonoo-baddé. The former consisted chiefly of about fifty families of tom-tom beaters, of whom the service required was to dance at the festivals of the gods, with bells about their ankles, from which circumstance they derived their name. The latter consisted of a few families of Paduas, whose duty it was to provide the royal kitchen with onions and with garlic.

All the preceding officers, who received their appointments from the king, were entitled to enter the hall of audience, and appear before the throne.

In no court, perhaps, was there ever a greater display made of barbarous pomp than in the Kandyan, or greater respect shown to a monarch, or more minute attention given to etiquette.

The royal throne was of plated gold, ornamented with precious stones. When the king appeared on state-occasions, he was either dressed in the most magnificent robes, loaded with a profusion of jewellery, or in complete armour of gold, ornamented with rubies, emeralds, and diamonds. To make the scene more impressive, and add to its solemnity, night was the favourite time for giving audience and transacting business.

The marks of respect required and shown to the Kandyan monarch were so unbounded, that one would suppose they were intended rather for a god than a man. The chiefs never approached the king without prostrating before him; and, in addressing him, Dewo (god) was an expression that they commonly used. His own proclamations were very characteristic; — "The most wealthy, — the protector of religion, whose fame is infinite and universally spread, and of surpassing excellence, exceeding the moon, the unexpanded jessamine-buds, the heavenly river, the white chanks, and the stars; — whose feet are as fragrant to the noses of other kings as flowers to bees; — our most noble patron and god by custom, — like Sakrea, who subdued the Assooriahs, sitting on the precious throne of the magnificent and prosperous city Sengada-galla, that possesses the beauty and wealth of all kingdoms, and is like the heavenly kingdom of Sakrea. — Ordered," &c. Thus commenced a *sanus* or deed of gift, of the last king, in which he assigned certain confiscated lands to one of his ministers, as a reward for his fidelity and good conduct.

Of the minute attention paid to etiquette and ceremonial at the Kandyan court, it is impossible to form an idea, excepting from details of the manner of proceeding on public occasions, — as on the election of the monarch, his marriage, and burial, as on the four great festivals annually solemnised in the capital, and lastly, on the occasion of giving audience to ambassadors. As these ceremonies illustrate both the point in question, extreme attention to etiquette, and, what is of more consequence, the character of the government and the manners of the people, I shall offer no apology for describing them.

On the death of a king, the ministers having issued a report that his majesty was ill, they assembled to deliberate respecting his successor, and to send orders for the principal people of the Ratties, who were entitled to be consulted on the election of a new monarch, to appear at Kandy.

Having come to a determination, the ministers directed a guard to be mounted before the house of the successor whom they had chosen; and this was the first public intimation of the important business in agitation. Their next step was to collect the chiefs, and inform them that the king was ill, and that it was right to be prepared for the worst that might happen. If there were an heir to the throne, about whose succession there could be no dispute, the chiefs remarked, "Such an one is heir apparent, we need not be consulted;" — if not, they observed, "We leave it to the Maha-nilamis to make choice of a proper person." Then the Adikars named the successor they had in view, and obtained the unanimous consent of the chiefs to his election.

Having done with the chiefs, they applied to the people of the different districts, sending for those of each district separately, and telling them the same story about the sickness of the king, and the necessity of being prepared for the event, should it prove unfortunate. The people, paying the greatest deference to the ministers, would remark: — "If there is a regular successor, we need not be consulted; and if not, the Maha-nilamis are the best judges of the prince who is most likely to make a good king." Then the prince selected was described, and one of the people of each district was sent to see him, that he might be known again, and they might be able to guard against future imposition.

The plot now opened fast; the chiefs were assembled in the

hall of audience, and the people were collected before the hall. The ministers came forward and informed the assembly that the king was very sick, and that it was their wish to know what arrangement the people chose to make. Then the people replied, "Such a one (naming the person chosen by the Adikars) promises to possess all the virtues of the sick king; or, is free from his faults." To which the ministers rejoined, "Well, remember it is your choice, do not blame us for it hereafter; we cannot refuse our assent."

Now it was pretty well understood that the king was dead. The Diawadene nilami, and the Haloowadene nilami, attended the prince, to assist him in bathing and in dressing himself in the robes and ornaments of royalty. He proceeded in the royal palanqueen to the palace, and getting out at the great arch-way, ascended the steps to the Dalada-malagowa, prostrated before the shrine, and made an offering of flowers to Boodhoo, to prove that he was of the established religion of the country. From the temple he went to the adjoining Pateripooa, the hexagonal pavilion at the head of the great square. A signal being given a curtain was drawn and the prince was disclosed seated, when jingalls were fired, and tom-toms, &c. played. The chiefs in the square below, arranged according to rank, prostrated themselves three times, and then went on their knees. The prince begging them not to mind the ceremonial, they prostrated again, and at his request went on one side. Then the people of the Ratties, drawn up in lines and formed into a square, presented themselves, and the first Adikar described the different districts to which they belonged. Now the chiefs repeated their prostrations, and were succeeded by tumblers, fencers, and dancers, who having first prostrated, performed before the prince. The chiefs having prostrated once more, the prince retired, and was conducted to the royal bed-chamber.

It was now publicly announced that the king was dead. A tent was pitched before the hall of audience, in which, on a piece of iron and a bason of mixed metal, a man stood by the side of a heap of paddy and beat the mourning tom-tom — the public signal of the event, warning the chiefs to dress themselves in black, and authorizing the people to give vent to their grief, and cry and lament aloud.

Till the body of the deceased monarch was consumed, it was contrary to custom for the prince to take any refreshment. The corpse, enclosed in a coffin, was carried in a palanqueen to the Awadana-madoowe, or royal burying-ground, attended by the chiefs, their wives and daughters. As the funeral procession moved on, two women standing on a platform, carried by four men, threw rice over the coffin. The priests of the different temples of Boodhoo were assembled at the burying-ground, and having offered up the proper prayer for the happiness of the deceased monarch in his metempsychosis, were presented with cloths, that were laid on the coffin, to be given them for discharging their pious office. The coffin was now placed in a kind of wooden cage, and was surrounded with wood; a person broke its lid with an axe, and a relation of the deceased set fire to the pile, which was fed with oil, and pitch, and sandal-wood, and various perfumes. When the whole was enveloped in flame, the chiefs retired, went to the great square, and informing the prince that the body was burnt, were ordered by him to go to their homes and purify themselves.

The mourning tom-tom was sounded, and the funeral fire was kept alive till the eleventh day, when the chiefs proceeded to the burying-ground with offerings of betel, areka-nut, and such articles of diet as might be presented to a king with propriety. The fire was now extinguished by pouring on it milk and cocoa-nut-water; some of the calcined bones were put into a pot or urn of earthenware, and covered and sealed, whilst the rest of the bones and ashes were collected and deposited in a grave with the presents brought for the deceased king.

The urn was placed on the head of a man masked and covered all over with black, who, holding a sword in his hand, and mounted on an elephant or horse, and attended by the chiefs, proceeded to the Mahawellé ganga. At the ferry called Katagastotte, two small canoes made of the kakoonga were prepared, lashed together, and covered with boughs in the form of a bower. The masked bearer, entering the canoe, was drawn towards the mid-channel of the river by two men swimming; who, when they approached the deepest part of the stream, pushed the canoe forward, and hastily retreated. Now the mask, having reached the proper station, with the sword in one hand and the urn in the other, divided the urn with the sword, and in the act plunged into the stream, and diving, came up as far as possible below, and landing on the opposite side, disappeared. The canoes were allowed to float down the river; the horse or elephant was carried across, and left to graze at large, never to be used any more; and the women who threw the rice over the coffin, with the men who carried them, were also transported to the other side of the river, under the strict prohibition of recrossing. The chiefs returned to the great square, informed the prince that the ceremony was ended, and were again ordered to purify themselves. If a near relation of the deceased monarch, the prince himself put on, and ordered the court to wear, deeper mourning than before; but if not, he threw off his mourning, with the exception of a black handkerchief, which he continued to wear about his head.

Another ceremony remained to be performed before the prince could be considered completely king; — it was that of choosing a name and putting on the regal sword. It was the duty of the royal astrologers to ascertain a fortunate period for the ceremony, and invent fortunate names; each individual being required to write a name on a plate of gold, set with precious stones, and deposit it in the Nata-dewalé. On the day fixed, which was sometimes a year or two after the election, the prince went in great state to the Maha-Visnu-dewalé, where he presented offerings and made prostrations to the god. Thence, he passed to the Nata-dewalé, and having gone through the same religious ceremony, he inspected the plates, chose the name that pleased him, and read it to the first Adikar, who proclaimed aloud, — "This is the name that the gods have chosen for the king to bear." Then the gold plate, the Nalalpate, on which the name was inscribed, was tied to the prince's forehead by a member of the Pilamè Talawè family, which being of royal descent, enjoyed this privilege and that of putting on the regal sword, which was attached to a belt that passed over the shoulder and came round the waist. The sword having been girded on the prince, the Kapuralle presented a pot of sandal-powder, in which the prince, who may now be called king, dipped his fingers and touched the sword; and this ceremony was performed in the Maha, as well as in the Nata-dewalé. From the temple, mounted on his elephant, the king went round the great square, and paraded through the illuminated streets of his capital, preceded by dancers, singers, and musicians of all kinds, and attended by his whole court, making the greatest possible display of pomp and splendour.

Coronation, it may be remarked, was not one of the ceremonies of the Kandyan monarchy, nor, I believe, of the eastern courts in general; nor is a crown named amongst the essential regalia, which are, the white umbrella, the chameraga or brush made of the tail of the Tibet cow, the gold sword, the gold forehead-plate, and the golden slippers. But though not essential, the use of the crown was not prohibited, and there was a handsome one of gold set with diamonds, rubies, and emeralds, that belonged to the kings of Kandy. It was seldom worn; and a cap, from superstitious motives, was generally substituted for it, — a king imagining that, in assuming a crown, he imitated the gods (who are supposed to wear crowns), and that unless he imitated them as well in his conduct, leading ever after the most correct and irreproachable and virtuous life, he should excite their highest displeasure, and draw down certain vengeance on his ambitious and unworthy head.

A Kandyan monarch, though restricted by religion to one wife, was permitted by indulgent custom to have any number he chose. It was necessary, however, that they should be of the Soorea or Rajah-wansé; in consequence, the kings of Kandy were obliged to procure queens from the continent of India; and Madura was the state that was usually applied to, to furnish princesses.

The marriage-ceremony, though long, complicated, and expensive, was a favourite ceremony, being attended with much festivity and enjoyment, and an unusual exchange of civilities, and an extraordinary relaxation of court-discipline.

The marriage having been determined on, and a princess procured, the Adikars directed the astrologers to calculate a fortunate day and hour for its celebration; ordered the people of the Dissavonies to get in readiness the presents it would be necessary to make on the occasion, and had the queen's apartment fitted up and decorated in the most splendid manner.

On the day fixed, the ladies of the court, the wives and daughters of the chiefs, and the chiefs themselves, assembled in the verandah of the queen's apartment, to receive the king; who, having entered and seated himself, the chiefs presented him with flowers, and the ladies rubbed sandal-powder and other perfumes on his arms; music, vocal and instrumental, not omitting tom-toms, playing all the while. On his majesty's departure, he was succeeded by the bride, who, taking a lower seat, experienced the same attentions as were before shown to the king. This ceremony was regularly repeated each day till the seventh, when the royal bridegroom and bride had to submit to have their nails cut, and all superfluous hair, including the beard of the former, removed — his barber operating on his majesty, and a female on the lady. This was done in conformity to a custom of ancient times, according to which neither the hair should be cut nor the nails pared before marriage. The barbers having completed the work, the royal couple bathed, and were clad in saffron robes, emblematic of purity and holiness. Having exchanged these for state-dresses, they proceeded to the verandah already mentioned, and seated themselves, the bride below the king, with a curtain between them. Now, two necklaces were carried round on a gold plate, each of the company in turn blessing them, saying, "May the pair enjoy long life and happiness." Then the father, or the nearest male relation of the bride's present, stepped forward, and pouring water on betel-leaves from a gold pot, declared, he relinquished his daughter to the king, who from that time might consider her his own. The mother was asked if she assented; and answering in the affirmative, the king took one of the necklaces from the gold plate, and standing up, he stretched his arms over the curtain, put the necklace round the neck of the bride, and clasped it, — an event that was announced to the public by the firing of jingalls. The curtain was now removed, and the royal bride and bridegroom saw each other for the first time; their little fingers were joined, and the ends of their clothes were tied together. This part of the ceremony was repeated four successive days: on the night of the fourth day, at the fortunate hour determined by the astrologers, the king put the second necklace on the bride and clasped it, and thus completed the whole of the marriage-rites.

On the day following, the king and queen amused themselves with throwing perfumed balls, and with squirting scented water at each other, — a diversion to which the wives of the chiefs were admitted, and of which they were allowed to partake, being quite at liberty to pelt and bespatter even royalty itself as much as they pleased. When the king was tired of the exercise, he retired to an apartment overlooking an adjoining room, in which vessels of scented water and small copper cups were prepared for use, and in which the chiefs were assembled, only waiting for the appearance of the king, to deluge each other with sweets.

The same night, the chiefs and their ladies were invited to sup at the palace; the former to be the guests of the king, and the latter of the queen. For each individual a mat was spread on the ground, covered with a white cloth to sit on; and for each was provided a fresh plantain-leaf, laid on a white cloth, as a table to eat from. They were regaled with separate dishes, the choice of two or three hundred different kinds of curries; and to drink, they had either milk or a sweet beverage, resembling lemonade. During the entertainment the king presided, seated in an elevated chair, and by his example encouraged mirth and facetious conversation. After the repast, dancers and dancing-girls, singers, and musicians, were introduced, and amused the company till the break of day with their performance.

The month following, it was the duty of the chiefs to make presents to the king and queen, every one according to his respective rank, situation and means. The presents should consist of trinkets, jewels, and embroidered cloths; and, it was requisite that each offering should be divided into two portions, one for the king and the other for the queen; and, that they should be presented at a certain time in the afternoon with all possible respect, and attended by musicians, dancers, and singers. At the end of the month, all the chiefs having made their presents, they and their wives were invited to another supper and entertainment at the palace, similar to the preceding; and at this, his majesty made them donations in return, and then closed the festivities on account of his marriage.

The four great national festivals kept annually in the capital were; 1st, the Awooroodu-mangallè, or feast of the new year; 2d, the Perraherra, a feast in honour of Visnu and the gods; 3d, the Karttie-mangallè, or feast of the fortunate hour, celebrated for the prosperity of the kingdom; and, 4th, the Aloot-saul-mangallé, or feast of new rice, kept in honour of the completion of harvest.

In describing these feasts, it is necessary to be in a certain degree minute, which can hardly fail being tedious, excepting, perhaps, to the curious few on the spot, who may be interested in these ceremonies, or to the philosophical few, who, even at a distance, may take an interest in such scenes, as illustrating the state of society, and the character of the people of the country and its government.

Before the approach of the new year, the king's physicians and astrologers had certain duties to perform. The former had to superintend the preparation of a thousand small pots of the juices of wild medicinal plants at the Nata-dewalè, from whence, carefully covered and sealed, they were to be sent to the palace, and distributed with much ceremony to the other temples. The duty of the astrologers was to form a Neykat-wattoroo, in which should be laid down, 1st, the day and precise minute of the commencement of the new year; 2d, the fortunate hour for washing with the medicinal juice; 3d, the fortunate hour for taking refreshment; 4th, the fortunate hour for commencing business; 5th, the fortunate hour of bathing; and, 6th, the fortunate hour of making presents to the king.

At the time appointed for the commencement of the new year, which amongst the Singalese is always in April, the king sat on his throne in state, surrounded by his chiefs; and the event was announced to the public by the discharge of jingalls.

At the hour appointed for the second ceremony, young women of certain families, with lighted tapers in their hands, and a silver dish containing undressed rice and turmeric water, stood at a little distance from the king; and when he directed his face to the south-east, with imbal-leaves under his feet and nuga-leaves in his hand, and applied the medicinal juice to his head and body, they thrice exclaimed, "Increase of age to our sovereign of five thousand years;—increase of age as long as the sun and moon last;—increase of age as long as heaven and earth exist." By the chiefs and people of consequence, this part of the ceremony was performed in a manner as nearly similar as possible.

At the hour appointed for the third ceremony, the king having first tasted of a dish on his table, called Dinaboejama, made for the occasion, and compounded of all kinds of legitimate food, he gave a portion of it to each of his chiefs, who were all assembled, and who, following the royal example, tasted it for the sake of the Nekata, or fortunate hour, (literally, star); and, the same night, they were invited to a feast at the palace, and were sumptuously entertained.

This hour happened sometimes on the first, and sometimes not till the second, third, or fourth day of the year. During the interval between the commencement of the year and the occurrence of this hour, no food could be used that had been dressed by fire.

This, too, was the fortunate hour for commencing trade or beginning business. The chiefs now sent rice, cocoa-nuts, fruit, &c. to the royal store, and received similar presents in return; and the people in general now made gifts to one another in a friendly manner, and were indulged in being allowed to carry on an exchange of little articles of property at the royal stores, which where thrown open for the purpose.

The fifth ceremony, that of bathing, was kept with the same formalities nearly as the second; and, as then, the juices of medicinal plants and perfumed oils were used, that had been prepared *secundum artem*, within the walls of the Nata-dewalé, and at an auspicious period.

In the course of a few days the last ceremony was performed. The king, seated on his throne, received his officers in succession according to their respective rank; each placed his present at the king's feet, and thrice prostrating, each time exclaimed — "May your majesty live as long as the sun and moon, and the heaven and earth exist." At the same time the king and the chiefs sent presents to the Maligowa, (the principal temple of Boodhoo.) The presents that the king received, were valued and deducted from the amount of what was due from each chief annually to the treasury.

The whole of the period of this festival was holiday time, and a season of rest and pleasure; during which both chiefs and people were exempted from public service.

The Perraherra, the next great national festival, and that which was observed with the greatest pomp and parade, was always kept in the month of July, whence it was properly called Eysalakeliyè, or the play of July. It was commenced on the day of the new moon in this month, in commemoration, according to some, of the birth of the god Visnu, which is supposed to have happened on that day, and was concluded on the day following the night that the moon was full.

In this instance, as in the preceding, there was a preparatory ceremony to be performed. A few days before the new moon mentioned, the people of the four principal Dewalés assembled and selected a young jack-tree that had borne no fruit, and the trunk of which was three spans in circumference. This they consecrated by fumigating it with the smoke of burning rosin, by smearing it with a preparation of sandal-wood, and by making an offering at its foot of a lighted lamp with nine wicks, of nine betel leaves, and of nine different kinds of flowers. This work of consecration was immediately followed by the operation of felling the tree, which was performed by the wood-cutter of the Maha Visnu-dewalé, dressed in a clean cloth, and purified by washing himself with lemon-juice. He divided the trunk transversely into four portions, each of which was carried to its respective dewalé, accompanied with the beating of tom-toms.

On the day of the new moon the piece of consecrated jack-wood at each dewalé was fixed in the ground, was protected by a roof, and covered and ornamented with palm-leaves, flowers, and fruits. During this and the three following days, the priests of each temple carried in pompous procession round the jack-wood the bows and arrows of the gods.

On the fifth day, all the chiefs assembled and thousands of people; the arms of the gods and the relic of Boodhoo, each placed in a ranhiligay *, were brought from their temples and carried in splendid procession, the composition and order of which was as follows: 1. The king's elephants, with the Gajinayke-nilami; 2. the jingalls, with the Kooditugakkoo-lekam; 3. the people of the Four Korles, carrying jingalls, muskets, and flags, with the Dissave and petty chiefs of that Dissavony; 4. the people of the Seven Korles; 5. those of Ouva; 6. of Matelè; 7. of Saffragam; 8. of Walapany; 9. of Udapalate; — all appointed and attended like the people of the Four Korles; 10. the Baumboos, or human images; 11. the elephant of the Maligowa, bearing the relic of Boodhoo, followed by other elephants, and by the people of the Maligowa, who went before the Diwa-nilami and the Nana-yakkara-lekam, with umbrellas, talipots, fans, flags, shields, tom-toms, drums, flutes, &c. accompanied by dancers;

* The ranhiligay is a small gilded dome or cupola, supported by pillars about four feet high, well proportioned, and handsomely made.

12. the elephant of the Nata-dewale, bearing the bow and arrows of the god, attended by the women of the temple, and followed by the Basnayeke-nilami, with the same pomp of attendance as the former; 13. the elephant, bow and arrows, and people and Basnayeke-nilami of the Maha-Visnu-dewalé, with a similar train; 14. of the Kattragam-dewalé; 16. of the Patine-dewale, both similarly attended; 16. the people of the Maha-lekam department, carrying muskets and flags, and preceding their chiefs; 17. the people of the Attepatuay department, similarly equipped, followed by the Attepatuay-lekam, and by the Rate-mahatmeyas of Udoonuara, Yatinuara, Tumpané, Harisea-pattoowe, Doombera, and Hewahatté; 18. the people of the Wedikkara department; 19. of the Wadena-tuakkoo department; and, 20. of the Padikara department, each followed by its respective lekam and petty officers.

This procession, for five days successively, paraded through the four principal streets of the capital and round the Nata-dewale, once in the afternoon and once at night: but the relic of Boodhoo did not join the nocturnal procession; indeed, till the reign of king Kirtissree, it did not appear at the Perraherra; he first ordered it to be brought out, at a time that some Siamese priests were on a visit to Kandy with the ostensible reason of doing honour to Boodhoo, as well as to the gods.

At the end of the five days, another and important part of the Perraherra commenced, called the Randoely-beyma. The procession just described was joined by the Randoelies or palanqueens, four in number, each dedicated to a particular goddess, and each furnished with a golden pitcher and sword, similarly dedicated. In the evening, the palanqueens followed the elephants bearing the arms of the gods; but by night they preceded them. They were attended not only by the women of the temple, but likewise by the ladies of the court and by the young wives and daughters of the chiefs, dressed in royal apparel, presented to them by the king. The king, who before was a spectator merely of the ceremony, now took an active part in it, and during the five days that the Randoely-beyma lasted, regularly joined the evening procession, in his golden chariot drawn by eight horses. According to the natives, this part of the Perraherra was extremely magnificent, the chiefs vying with each other in splendour of dress and in the multitudes of their attendants, and every party concerned, and the king in particular, using the utmost exertions to make the spectacle as brilliant and as imposing as possible. But to proceed: on the night of the full moon, the relic of Boodhoo for the first time joined the nocturnal procession; at the conclusion of which, it was not returned to the Maligowa, but deposited in the Asgirie-wiharé, a temple in the neighbourhood of Kandy.

The same night, offerings of boiled rice, curries, &c. were made in the Dewalés to the images of the gods; and the procession was immediately renewed, and proceeded towards the Mahawellé ganga, where, at the Gonaruwa ferry, a boat richly ornamented awaited its arrival, in which the Kappurawles of the four Dewalés, each with an attendant, rowed up the river, bearing the swords and golden pitchers of the goddesses. Here they waited the first blush of dawn; and, as soon as it appeared, the Kappurawles struck the water with the golden swords, and the attendants emptied the golden pitchers of the last year's water, and filled them with fresh, and with that very water to which the swords had been applied.

The procession now returned to the Asgirie-wiharé; and, being joined by the relic, and met by the king and his ministers, and all the chiefs who had not accompanied it to the river, it entered the city, and the Perraherra concluded.

The third annual festival,—the Karttie-Mangallè, "the feast of the fortunate hour," or "the feast of lamps,"—was celebrated in the month of November, on the day preceding the full moon. The fortunate hour for lighting lamps was previously determined and laid down by the royal astrologers in Nekat-wattoroos. In the morning of the day appointed, lamps and oil were brought from the royal store to the Nata-dewalé, where, the chiefs being assembled, and the Kappurawles of the four principal dewalés, the latter sung the Mangala-asta, a hymn of thanks and praise to the gods, and offered up prayers for the prosperity of the kingdom. They then distributed, with great ceremony, Neykat-wattoroos, with oil, to all the principal temples.

In the evening, at the fortunate hour pointed out, the great square decorated with arches, and the palace, the temple, the dewalés, and the four principal streets, were completely and brilliantly illuminated. During the night, the relic of Boodhoo and the images of the gods were carried in procession through the city on elephants, with nearly the same attendance, and the same honours, that were paid to them during the first part of the Perraherra.

The Aloot-saul-mangallè, the feast of new rice, the fourth and last of the great annual festivals, was observed in the month of January, when the moon was on the increase. A nekat-wattoroo was previously prepared by the astrologers, in which a fortunate hour, on two different days, was pointed out; one for bringing the new rice into the city, and the other for dressing and eating it. This document was sent to the king with the usual honours, and copies of it were carried by the chiefs to the royal farms in the neighbourhood. At these farms the ears of paddy and the new rice were packed up for the temples and palace, and king's stores, by the Gabada-nilamis and their officers. The ears of paddy, carefully put into new earthen pots, and the grain into clean white bags, were attached to pingos for the sake of more convenient carriage. Those intended for the maligowa were conveyed on an elephant; those for the dewalés were borne by men marching under canopies of white cloth; and those for the palace and royal stores were carried by the people of the king's villages, of respectable caste and well dressed, with a piece of white tape over their mouths, to guard against impurity. They started from the different farms under a salute of jingalls; were attended by tom-toms, flags, and other honours, and were met on the way by the adikars and chiefs, who attended them to the great square, to wait the Neykata hour, the arrival of which was announced by a discharge of jingalls; when the rice and ears of paddy were carried to the respective places for which they were destined. At the same fortunate hour, the chiefs and people brought new rice and paddy from their own fields and houses.

The Nekata for eating the new rice occurred two or three days after the preceding. The rice was dressed according to rule, and mixed with certain curries, and ate with the face in a particular direction; on all which points instructions were given in the Neykat-watoroo. The rice that was dressed and offered to the gods on this occasion, was either buried or consumed by the priests; not indiscriminately, but only by those who had led previously a life of purity.

In these annual festivals, which I have just described, as in most parts of Indian government, there is a curious blending of superstitious rites, pompous pageantry, and political institution. The first festival, in celebration of the new year, was evidently designed to prevent confusion of time. The second, the Perraherra, had a more secret object: — by obliging all the chiefs, and the principal people of all the Dissavonies and Ratties to appear before their sovereign in the capital at the same time, to take a part in a pompous religious ceremony, besides tending to excite national feeling and union, it had the effect of promoting loyalty, of keeping the ambitious in awe, and of checking rebellion; or, in case of the occurrence of symptoms of rebellion, it afforded an opportunity of apprehending the suspected, and of punishing the disaffected, — an opportunity that the late king, in a terrible manner, availed himself of. The third festival, no doubt, had the same political end as the second. The fourth requires no comment: it was clearly designed both to encourage the cultivation and the use of rice, — that staff of life in Ceylon and the East, on which, exclusively, the natives almost entirely subsist, and for the production of which the nature of the climate and country is peculiarly well adapted.

The manner in which the Singalese behaved themselves, during these festivals, is worthy of notice. — In 1817, I was present at the Perraherra, from its beginning to its end; and the conduct of the people throughout was decorous, and highly creditable to them: — during the whole time, though there were several thousand people assembled, I saw no scene of riot or disturbance, and no instance of drunkenness; the most modest might have looked on, without having occasion to blush; and the most refined might come away without having had their feelings shocked; which, I understand, is much more than can be said of the public exhibitions on the continent of India, that are generally indecent and licentious beyond description.

The last ceremony that I have to describe, at all characteristic of the old court, is that of receiving ambassadors. A few circumstances may be premised.—The king held his court in the hall of audience, and transacted all business with his officers seated on his throne. Behind the throne there was a secret door, by which his majesty passed unobserved; and before it seven curtains, which were not drawn up till the king was seated and composed, and in perfect readiness to appear. On ordinary occasions, all the curtains were raised at once; and after the chiefs had prostrated three times, they were desired to be at their ease, which was resting on their knees, and on which, when the business was over, they left the hall backward, his majesty remaining till all had departed. On the presentation of ambassadors, extraordinary pomp and ceremony were observed. A great concourse of people was assembled; the royal elephants were drawn out; all the guards were on duty, and the approaches to the palace were illuminated. On entering the hall the chiefs and ambassador had to prostrate before the curtains, which were now managed with peculiar finesse: they were all suddenly drawn up, and as suddenly let down, affording at first only a momentary glimpse of his majesty; after a pause, they were slowly drawn up, one after another, a certain number of prostrations being required for each, till the throne was disclosed, and the king exposed to view: then the ambassador, actually crawling, was led to the foot of the throne by the ministers, walking in the most submissive attitude; and, having delivered his letters, he had the troublesome task to perform of crawling backward.

It might be supposed that the amusements of such a court would have been characteristic and peculiar; but I am not aware that they were. Formerly, it is said, the kings of Ceylon delighted in games and sports; in seeing feats of horsemanship performed; in witnessing gladiatorial exhibitions, and the fights of animals, as of bulls, rams, and elephants: but latterly, particularly during the last reign, such diversions were discontinued. The late king devoted most of his time to business; and his leisure he spent listening to music, or in superintending his artists and workmen, a large number of whom he constantly employed in beautifying his grounds, and in enlarging and decorating his palace and city.

CHAPTER VI.

LAWS. — JUDICIAL PROCEEDINGS. — LAND-TENURES.

It has been already stated in fact, though not expressly, that the judicial and legislative power of government, as well as the executive, centered formerly in the king: a circumstance in which the Singalese strikingly differ from the Hindoos of the continent, and for a very obvious reason; — that the former are without Brahmens, who, wherever they have prevailed, have monopolized the powers in question.

The same cause, perhaps, may serve to explain another striking feature of the Singalese government; — viz. its having no written code of law, — being directed, in judicial matters, by ancient custom and precedent, and the common principles of equity acknowledged by all mankind.

A contrary opinion has been entertained by some writers, who have supposed that the Singalese, like the Burmas and the Hindoos, possess the laws of Menu.* They have, indeed, some of these laws, scattered here and there in their works on re-

* The Menu of the Burmas is, by the Singalese, called Manu. According to a learned native, the word has two significations; — it is used as a respectful generic term for man, *homo*, and as the name of a particular royal family, Manu-wansè; and in the latter sense it was usually employed in addressing the kings of Kandy.

ligion; but they are little known, rarely referred to, and never followed.

The common law of the Singalese, as far as I am superficially acquainted with it, and capable of judging of it, was far from being ill-adapted to the social state of the people; and, had it been administered with tolerable purity and impartiality, though there would have been ample room for improvement, there would have been little ground for complaint.

All officers, from the king to a Widane, exercised more or less judicial powers; and from all the subordinate ones appeal might be made to the superior, till it reached the king himself, whose sentences, in all instances, were decisive. Each officer of rank as an Adikar, Dissave, Ratté-mahatmeya, held an independent court, in which, with the exception of appeal, he acted without check or controul, and always in the double capacity of judge and jury. Only in two instances that have come to my knowledge, were courts formed of several individuals; one of these was nearly of the highest authority, and was composed of chiefs appointed by the king to investigate any particular cause; the other consisted of the principal men of a district, as the Lekam, Korawl, Widane; it was called Sakè-ballanda *, and had duties to perform in many respects similar to those of a coroner in England.

When a dead body was found, no one should touch it till it had been examined by the Sakè-ballanda, not even if the body were hanging, though by cutting it down suspended animation might possibly be restored. It was the business of these officers to endeavour to ascertain the cause of death, and all the circumstances connected with it. In a case of suicide occurring in a village, the suicide having been of sound mind, or subject to temporary fits

* Sakè, evidence; ballanda, to investigate.

only of insanity, the Sakè-ballanda inflicted a fine on the inhabitants of fifty riddies (about twenty-nine shillings), which were to be divided between these officers and the Dissave,— ten to the former, five to a Lekam if present, and the remainder to the Dissave; and the body could not be burnt or buried till the fine was paid,— a prohibition that insured its payment; for a heavier fine of one hundred or even two hundred riddies was imposed on those who allowed a corpse to decay unburied or unburnt. If the suicide were a confirmed idiot or lunatic, no fine was inflicted. In the first instance, the inhabitants were punished for want of attention to an individual who required it, and whose life might have been preserved had such attention been paid; whilst in the latter, they were excused, because they were not supposed to have time to spare to watch individuals who required incessant vigilance.

In a case of murder, the perpetrator of which was discovered, he should be sent to Kandy,— no one but the king himself having the power of passing sentence of death; but, generally, excepting in very atrocious and notorious instances, the Dissave, with an eye to his own profit, preferred inflicting on the criminal a heavy fine. When a murder was committed in a house or village and the murderer could not be detected, the inhabitants were fined as in the instance of a suicide, the amount varying a little according to circumstances. But if the jungle were the scene of a murder of this kind, no fine was levied, no one at a distance being considered in the least responsible for the prevention of acts of violence in a desert place. From all I could learn, neither suicide nor murder was common amongst the Singalese; an intelligent native, not a young man, who had lived constantly about court, informed me, that in the course of his life, the number of murders he recollected to have heard of did not exceed five, and that whole reigns had been known to pass without a single capital punishment.* The sentence of death, in cases of murder, was carried into effect by hanging; but for high treason, the only capital crime besides, the sword was used instead of the halter, and the criminal was decapitated.

Robbery, it is said, was not uncommon amongst the Singalese. The culprit, on detection, was obliged to restore the stolen property or its value; was fined in a certain sum, which was divided between the judge and the plaintiff; was sometimes imprisoned; and was often besides punished with a flogging, either with the hand, the rattan, or the Adikar's whip, having been previously led through the city or village, preceded by a tom-tom, with insignia indicating the nature of his offence, and the chastisement that awaited him.

The crime of adultery, by the Singalese, was punished in a very summary manner. The injured husband did not institute a suit at law to recover damages; if he caught the adulterer in his house, he might beat him soundly, or even cut off his hair and ears, or have him flogged in public, and his wife flogged in the royal store-house, the place of punishment of women; after which, by his own *ipse dixit*, he might divorce her, and in disgrace send her home to her own family.

Though acts of assault and violence are rarely heard of amongst the Singalese, they are a very litigious people; which perhaps arises rather from external circumstances than innate disposition. The circumstances that may be pointed out as naturally tending to promote litigation were, the former corrupt administration of the laws, the frequent changes of officers, the liberty of renewing

* This indeed is no decisive proof; as some Singalese monarchs, conscientiously acting up to the principles of their religion, refused to pass sentence of death.

trials almost indefinitely, and the privilege of appeal from one court to another.

In an ordinary dispute about land, which was the most common subject of litigation, the disputants usually commenced with referring it to be settled by the arbitration of their neighbours: if dissatisfied with the decision given, they might apply to the Korawl, and from the Korawl to the Mohottala, and from him to the Dissave: if still dissatisfied, they might apply to the Adikar, or even to the King: or, if unable for want of means to prosecute the suit, they might lie by and recruit, and wait the appointment of new officers, who would not hesitate, if well bribed, to reverse the sentence of their predecessors.

In difficult cases recourse was allowed to be had to trial by ordeal, which was practised in two different ways. In one, the parties took an oath in a Dewalé, declarative of innocency or of rights, and calling down vengeance on the head of the perjurer. In this instance, the party to whom any misfortune first happened, as the death of a wife, of a child, or of cattle, was supposed to be under the displeasure of the gods, was pronounced the perjurer, and sentence was given against him. The other mode of ordeal was by means of hot oil or hot cow-dung; the parties went to a Bogah (*ficus religiosa*), and each person, having tied an ola to his right arm, on which his claims were written, and a declaration made that no sorcery was employed to prevent the heat having effect on the skin, skimmed the hot oil or dung with his right hand and flung a little of it on a leaf, which, if it cracked, afforded proof that the temperature of the oil or dung was sufficiently high, and that the trial had been fairly made. The hands were washed for examination, and he was cast, on whose skin any burn could be detected; if both had their fingers burnt, the case was undecided, or the property litigated was divided. Trial by ordeal, amongst the Singalese, was not encouraged by those who had any pretensions to learning; they conceived, indeed, that truth might occasionally be discovered through the intervention of the gods; but in general that the result was accidental, and not to be depended upon.

Insolvency amongst the Singalese was very cruelly dealt with; slavery was its consequence. The creditor applied to the Dissave or Raté-mahatmeya, and having proved his claims just, and the debtor having acknowledged his incapacity to meet them, leave was granted to the former to make the debtor and his family his slaves, and to retain them and their offspring in slavery, till payment of the debt were made. The debtor could not be sold, but if he died, leaving his children in slavery, they and their children might be sold. No interest was allowed to accumulate for the original debt, the labour of the slaves being considered an equivalent. In respect to slavery, there was no privileged caste; it was a punishment to which all insolvent debtors were liable. It was not usual for the Goewansè to become the slaves of people of low caste; when in danger of this degradation, some chief generally paid the debt and made the debtors his slaves. The state of slavery is of course considered disreputable; by marrying a slave, a free woman would be utterly disgraced. The condition of slaves is, however, easy; they are kindly treated by their masters, well fed and clothed, and not required to do much work; and they are even distinguished occasionally, by being made the petty head-men of low castes. In consequence, they usually become attached to their masters, and soon cease to pine after liberty. What the total number of slaves may be in the Kandyan country, no register having ever been kept, it is impossible to estimate with any precision: an intelligent chief, from whom I collected the above particulars, guessed that they amount to about 3000. It would be worthy of our government to emancipate these people, though they may not ardently desire to be free; and altogether abolish slavery, by prohibiting the custom that gave rise to it.

Usury was not permitted under the old government. The relations of the late king practised it for some time, lending money at an interest of 40 per cent.; but it was no sooner complained of and made known to the king, than he prohibited it. The Moors, who are the principal money-lenders in the Interior, were allowed to receive an annual interest of 20 per cent. The Singalese themselves, when they lend money, do it on the single condition of its being returned augmented one-half, without attention to time, satisfied with the increase, if it be paid in twelve months or twelve years. Paddy and salt are occasionally lent on nearly the same terms; the agreement being to return three measures or three and one-fifth of the former, and four of the latter, for every two borrowed, and equally without relation to time.

The tenures of land amongst the Singalese were easy and favourable to agriculture. The king, it has been already remarked, was considered the sole proprietor of the soil; all the natives acknowledge this to have been the fact, and say he derived his title from the first king who conquered the island, and expelled the demons by whom he found it inhabited. All forests and chenas * were considered royal domains, and could not be cut down or cultivated without express permission. To cul-

* Ground overgrown with underwood, fit, when cleared, to bear crops not requiring irrigation, is commonly called Chenas, in Ceylon.

tivate a chenas, it was necessary to ask leave of the king, through one of his ministers. The cultivator was at liberty to improve it and convert it into paddy or rice ground. To secure this possession, he obtained a sanus * or deed of gift from the king. During the life of the first cultivator, no duty was paid for the reclaimed land. He was at liberty to sell it or give it away, without asking permission, except he wished to make a present of it to a Wiharé :—in this instance it was usual to petition the king in the following manner : "I am desirous of making this present to the Wiharé for my good, and I pray Your Majesty will permit me, as it is equally for your good."† The reason of this petition being necessary is obvious ; land granted to a temple being lost to the king, temple-lands paying no dues. If the original cultivator died intestate, or was guilty of rebellion, the land returned to the king. The king could dispose of this land in three different ways ; he might give it to a Wiharé, when it would be exempted from all dues and services ; or, he might bestow it on a favourite, or a deserving officer, as a reward, to be held at the royal pleasure, exempt from duties ; or, he might give the land to an indifferent person, without any exemption. In the latter instance, if the individual held it for thirty years, he would be entitled to retain it and dispose of it, as if he were the

* The modern sanus is generally of copper, and occasionally of silver gilt; some very old ones were of stone; there is one now extant, by which a large property is held, of this primitive material, on which the only inscription is Sree, the royal signature.

† The Boodhists suppose that by making an offering to a Wiharé, they will benefit themselves in a future life. They imagine also, that they can divide the benefit with another, or even give it away entirely: thus more than once a courteous priest, on meeting me, has said, "I have just made an offering of flowers to Boodhoo, and may you partake of, or reap the advantage it may confer."

original cultivator; in confirmation of which the Kandyans have a saying,—"That the devil himself may call a thing his own, that he has had possession of thirty years."

All tenures of land amongst the Singalese were similar to the preceding, and as far as I could ascertain, had nothing of a feudal nature: a great proprietor, indeed, might give land to individuals for certain services, to be held whilst those services were performed; but the individuals were not bound to the soil, owed no allegiance to the proprietor, and might quit his service when they pleased.

CHAPTER VII.

SINGALESE SYSTEM OF THE UNIVERSE.—BOODHOOS.—GOUTAMA BOODHOO.—PRIESTS OF BOODHOO.—WORSHIP OF GODS AND DEMONS.—DOUBTFUL POINTS OF THE RELIGION OF BOODHOO.

The religious system of the Singalese, which, without impropriety, may be called the Boodhaical system, is, in all its bearings, a highly interesting subject, and equally deserving of attention in relation to its influence on the character of the people, and in consideration of its acknowledged antiquity, the wide extent of country over which it is diffused, and its many and striking peculiarities.

The Boodhists, the followers of this system, do not believe in the existence of a Supreme Being, self-existent and eternal, the creator and preserver of the universe: indeed, it is doubtful if they believe in the existence and operation of any cause besides fate and necessity, to which, or to obscure negations, that are hardly to be distinguished from fate and necessity, they seem to refer all changes in the moral and physical world.

They appear to be materialists in the strictest sense of the term, and to have no notion of pure spirit or mind. Pranè and Hitta, life and intelligence, the most learned of them seem to consider as identical;—seated in the heart, radiating from thence to different parts of the body, like heat from a fire; — uncreated, without beginning, at least, that they know of; — capable of being modified by a variety of circumstances, like the breath in different musical instruments; — and, like a vapour, capable of passing from one body to another; and, like a flame, liable to be extinguished and totally annihilated. Gods, demons, men, reptiles, even the minutest and most imperfect animalcules, they consider as similar beings, formed of the four elements,—heat, air, water, and that which is tangible, and animated by pranè and hitta. They believe that a man may become a god or a demon; or, that a god may become a man or an animalcule; that ordinary death is merely a change of form, and that this change is almost infinite, and bounded only by annihilation, which they esteem the acmè of happiness. They suppose that plants are compounded of the same elements as animals; but do not admit that they possess pranè, and consequently, exclude them from the cycle of their metempsychosis.

This is not a rational system, nor do its followers attempt to support it by reason: if you ask a reason for any assertion, you may receive in answer a dogma in Sanscrit or Pali verse; if you are not satisfied, you may be amused with an allegory; and if you still persist and urge explanation, the Boodhist will take refuge in the mysteries of his religion, and in our very limited capacities to attain knowledge, and comprehend what is divine.

Farther, they are of opinion that the universe is eternal, at least, that they neither know it had a beginning, or will have an end; and that it is homogeneous, and composed of an infinite number of similar worlds, each of which is a likeness of the other, and each of which is in a constant state of alteration, — not stationary for a moment, — at the instant of greatest perfection beginning to decline, and at the moment of greatest chaotic ruin beginning to regenerate. They compare such changes to a wheel in motion, perpetually going round, of which they know no more than it is in motion, and have not the least idea when it began to move, or when it will stop; indeed, they say that they are directed not to make enquiries on a subject of which Boodhoo himself was ignorant.

Each world they consider as a complicated system of heavens and hells, of continents and seas, of rocks and rocky circles, inhabited by mortal gods, demons, and devils, and other strange varieties of fabulous beings.

A rock, Maha-meru-parwatè, they believe to be the centre of this sytem. Above this rock there are, they believe, twenty-six heavens; and under it, on which it rests, three rocks, — the Tri-koota, between which is the residence of the Asooras, the Asoora-bhawana. Under the Asoora-bhawana they have placed the residence of snakes, Naga-bhawana; and under it, a rock, Gal-pollowa, which rests, they believe, on water, which water rests on air. Round Maha-meru, they conceive, there are seven rocky circles; and round the whole world, a wall of rock, the Sakwalla-galla, all of which they believe to be separated from each other by seas. In the sea, between the seventh rocky circle and the wall of rock, they have placed four great continents, each surrounded by five hundred islands. Beneath this sea, one under another, they believe, that there are eight hells, — Aivichi-maha-narakè; and round them a hundred and twenty lesser hells, — Osoopat-narakè; and between every three Sakwallas, or worlds, a single hell, common to the three, called Locarnantarika-narakè.

With the details of this system a learned Singalese is perfectly conversant; as well and as minutely acquainted as with what relates to his village or family, and infinitely better than with the geography and history of his country and nation.

The heavens, in this system, are divided into Brachmea-lochès, twenty in number, and Dewia-lochès, six in number. The former are arranged in groupes of three-and-three, and four-and-four, rising one above the other. They are the abodes of the Brachmeas, beings of greater purity and higher rank than the gods who inhabit the six inferior heavens, which are situated one under the other, at the distance of 42,000 leagues, which is also the interval of space between the preceding groupes. The Brachmea-lochès, with few exceptions, and more particularly the Dewia-lochès, are paradises, provided in the oriental taste with palaces and gardens, and, in brief, with every thing delightful in nature and in art, and fitted to afford satisfaction to the beings that inhabit them.

The Brachmeas who reside in the lower Brachmea-lochès are all males, and are without female companions. In different heavens they vary in size, which is always most gigantic; they all resemble each other in being of great beauty, of a red colour, and of astonishing splendour, the light alone that radiates from one of their fingers being equal to that of 10,000 suns. Void of all passions and desires, they concern themselves about nothing, much less about our impure earth, and enjoy existence in perfect inaction and quietism.

In the highest heavens of the Brachmeas there are peculiarities in the character of the inhabitants that require to be pointed out. In the Brachmea-lochè, called Rootala, the Brachmeas resemble the others in form and appearance; but, being more perfect and in a happier state, they neither move nor think. In the next higher heaven, Arootala, they are without form, and resemble air; they speak and hear, but do not see. In the next superior heaven, Asanginnya, they are both without form, and neither see, hear, nor are conscious: and, in the next and highest heaven, Abhogata, which signifies *nothing*, life itself is in appearance annihilated,—but only in appearance and delusively, the Brachmeas in this heaven not having reached the summit of the wishes of true Boodhists, and being still liable to new births, and mutations of form.

The seven Dewia-lochès are called Wasawarti, Paranirmittia, Nirwanè-rattè, Toosita, Yama, Tawatinsè, and Chator-maharajikè. They are inhabited by gods and goddesses, who resemble men and women in form, but surpass them greatly in beauty. Their persons are tangible, but pure, like exquisite paintings, and without humours or fluids, without even blood, flesh and bone. The gods have hair on their heads, but no beards; — the goddesses are distinguished by their bosoms, and by their feminine form and dress. They eat and sleep in different degrees and manners: — some are satisfied with the fumes of meat, others prefer its flavour; none of them swallow food. There being no night in their heavens, they repose and sleep just when they feel inclined. They are not subject to pain, and are always easy and happy, leading a round of perpetual enjoyment, amused with dances and vocal and instrumental music, and every kind of sport and festivity that can afford delight. It may appear contradictory, but they are not without passions; they possess, in common, love, and anger, and selfishness, in which envy and covetousness are included. Their love is a pure bond of attachment between the gods and goddesses, the pleasures of which they enjoy in contemplation: their anger is excited by the vices of mankind; their selfishness and covetousness are gratified by devout worship, and rich offerings; and their envy is excited by the appearance of extraordinary merit and growing power in inferior beings. In respect to the perfections of their natures, and the enjoyment of existence, they vary in different heavens; the inhabitants of the higher being more powerful and beautiful, and longer-lived, and less annoyed by the violence of passion, than those of the lower. As before remarked, they are all mortal, and they must all die and appear on earth in human forms, before they can be qualified to ascend to higher states of existence.

The rock, Maha-meru, immediately under the lowest of the heavens, as already observed, and the centre of the world, is square, 160,000 leagues high, half in water and half in air. Its south side is blue, its north yellow, its west red, its east white, and its centre is of a golden colour. It is the property of the god Sacrea, who occasionally quits his heaven Nirwanè-rattè to enjoy himself on Maha-meru; where he has a palace, and a beautiful garden, an extraordinary tree and cow, a white elephant, and attendants of all kinds. Such are the rare qualities of the cow and tree, that the gods have only to visit them and express a wish, and it will be immediately gratified. The Singalese, it may be remarked, make frequent allusions to these two objects; if they wish to compliment a bountiful man, they compare him to the tree in the garden of Sacrea. The white elephant of Sacrea, well adapted to carry a god, has the power of passing from one heaven to another; and its flight is only limited above by the heaven of its master, and below only by the boundaries of the world. The attendants of Sacrea who live on Maha meru, are accomplished in the highest degree; some of them, as the Gandarwa, (his singers and musicians,) resemble men; others are peculiar in their appearance, as the Garuda, who constitute

Sacrea's guard, and have square faces, and noses and wings like hawks.

The Asoora-bhawené, below Maha-meru, and between the three spherical rocks the Trikootas, is 10,000 leagues in circumference. The Asooras, by whom it is inhabited, are degenerate Brachmeas, who have lost their beauty of form, though they still retain their powers, which are so great as to render them formidable to the gods, whom they occasionally attack and defeat. In war they multiply their species like the polypus, each limb or piece that may be lopped off becoming a complete Asoora. They retain much of their original splendour as well as power, and illuminate their abode with their own brightness. Their king, Asurendria, formerly devoured the sun and moon; now he no longer possesses that power, and causes eclipses by stretching out his hand and obstructing the light of these luminaries.

The Naga-bhawenè, that lies under Asoora-bhawené, is also 10,000 leagues in circumference. It is a hollow sphere, without mountains or hills, lakes or rivers, and entirely destitute of vegetation, with the exception of a single tree, called Parasattoo, that answers for all others, bearing not only an immense variety of flowers and fruits, but every thing else that is desirable. The Naga-bhawené is the abode of a numerous race of snakes, similar in kind to the hooded-snake, and of great size, beauty, and power; capable of passing from one part of the world to another, and shining like gods, so that though they have no light but that which emanates from their own bodies, they enjoy perpetual day infinitely brighter than ours. In their former lives on earth, they were persons of remarkable purity and goodness, almost deserving of becoming gods; but their high virtues were sullied by some vice, particularly that of malice, to which they owe their present forms. Though snakes, they are Boodhists, and are in possession of a relic, and worship in temples. They reside in well-furnished houses, and eat and drink, and enjoy society. By merely wishing, they immediately have any article of food they want; and whatever it may be, it always appears in the form of a frog. They are under a regal government, and are distributed into castes like the Singalese. Their king, Maha-killa-naga-rajaya, is in every respect superior to the rest; it was with his assistance that the gods and Asooras churned the milky sea; he wound himself round a rock, and they, pulling at his two extremities, set the mass in motion and accomplished their work. Were these snakes disposed, they could destroy the whole of the inhabitants of the earth by a single blast of their poisonous breath; but they are naturally mild and benevolent, and do harm only when provoked. In consequence, they are rather venerated than dreaded; and it is on this account that the common hooded-snake is so much respected.

The Gal-pollowa, on which the Naga-bhawené rests, and which is the rocky foundation of the world, is of a hemispherical form, and, including the rocks which it supports, it is 240,000 leagues thick. The subjacent water, on which it rests, is twice that depth, and the air that supports the water is twice the depth of the latter.

The seven concentric rocky circles that surround Maha-meru are, Ugandere̊, Eesadhere̊, Karaveeke̊, Soodassene̊, Nemindera, Winateke̊, and Assakanne̊. They are of different heights, their heights diminishing as their circumferences increase. The inferior gods and demons reside on them.

The seven seas, that separate the different circles, have each a name, and each is of a peculiar nature; thus, one resembles milk; another, the juice of the sugar-cane; and a third, arrack.

The Sakwalla-galla, the lateral boundary-wall of the Sakwalla, or world, rises above the surface of the ocean 82,000 leagues, and extends below it to the same depth; its circumference is 3,610,000 leagues, and the diameter of the world which it encloses is 1,200,450 leagues.

The four continents, that are situated in the ocean between the Sakwalla-galla and Assakannè, are, Poorwawidehay, to the eastward of Maha-meru; Aperakodawneya, to the westward; Citurukurudiwaina, to the northward; and Jamboodweapè or Dambadiwa, to the southward. Each of these continents, as has been already remarked, is surrounded by 500 islands, and each is separated from the other by unnavigable seas, preventing all ordinary communication.

Poorwawidehay is of a crescent form, 7000 leagues in circumference. It is inhabited by a race of men who do not differ from us, excepting in having faces resembling the form of their continent, and of a crescent shape.

Aperakodawneya is of an oblong form, and also 7000 leagues in circumference. Its inhabitants have oblong faces; like gods, they have only to express a wish and it is gratified; and in consequence, they are exempted from all toil and labour.

Citurukurudiwaina is square, and 8000 leagues in circumference. Its inhabitants have square faces, and in no other respect differ from ordinary men.

Jamboodweape or Dambadiwa, is of an oval figure, and 10,000 leagues in circumference. It derives its name from a jamboo-tree of gigantic dimensions which springs from it, the trunk of which is fifteen leagues round, its height one hundred leagues, and each of its branches fifty leagues long. This Dambadiwa is our earth, and corresponding to its form, our faces are oval; amongst the five hundred islands that surround it, there are fifty-six of considerable magnitude, in which large empires have been established. Ceylon itself is not one of them; it is only of the second magnitude.

To the eastward and northward of Ceylon is Hiemalè, which is 100 leagues high, and 3000 leagues* in circumference; as its name indicates, its mountains are covered with snow, which is supposed to be owing to its great height and its luxuriant vegetation. It is a land of wonders; its soil consists of gold and silver; its trees all bear delicious fruit; its horses and elephants are of a peculiar race, and have the power of flying through the air; in its centre is a lake covered with flowers, called Anota-hawilla, that pours forth four rivers, each of which winds seven times round its parent source; and lastly, to pass over its other marvels, its inhabitants are beings of supernatural powers, as Pasay-boodhoos, Moonies, Tapasayos, and Bhoomatoo-dewis. Pasay-boodhoos are men who, by extraordinary purity of manners, and complete abstraction from worldly pursuits, and profound religious meditation, have acquired the power of flying through the air, and of visiting any heaven; at the appearance of Boodhoo they will be privileged to make any request, with the certainty of its being fulfilled. The Moonies, by means of extreme purity and profound contemplation, have acquired extraordinary wisdom and knowledge; they are acquainted with the past and future to a great extent, and can look back on forty

* These and the preceding are Singalese leagues, one of which is equal to about four of ours.

kalpés, and look forward on the same number, which is beyond the power of the gods, and is exceeded by no one excepting by Boodhoo himself. The Tapasayos are devout men of different religions: there are three kinds of them; those who rank highest are neither dressed, nor move, nor eat — they are naked and fixed, absorbed in religious meditation, allowing ants to construct their hillocks over them, and the roots and branches of trees to entangle about them and cover them: those who rank next, remain stationary in religious contemplation, and eat nothing but the surrounding leaves on which they browse: those who rank lowest, walk about and live on fruits, bent solely on meditation. Those Tapasayos who are Boodhists, will be rewarded finally like the Pasay-Boodhoos; whilst those of other religions will imagine they shall enjoy the same reward, but instead will be translated to Abhogata.

The Bhoomatoo-dewis very much resemble the gods of the Dewia-lochès. They take a lively interest in what is passing on the earth, which they protect; and in the affairs of mankind, which they watch and superintend. Eiswara and Visnu, the two chiefs of these gods, have delegated their powers to others, and appointed Nata, Katragam, Samen, Pittia, and the goddess Patiné, as their ministers in governing the earth, and in watching in a particular manner over Ceylon. All these gods are worshipped by the Singalese, and with the exception of Eiswara, have temples erected to them. The worship they require is prostration, prayers, and offerings of flowers and money: no meat-offering must be made to them; and no one must appear before their shrines, unless he has lived on a vegetable diet many days previously, and is strictly pure. Prayers are addressed to them merely for temporal blessings; their power being

Nata.

Visnu.

Saman.

Patini.

From a Drawing by a Native Artist.

limited to the present, and not extending to a future life. The appearance and dresses of these gods are as they are represented in their figures; Visnu is blue, Nata and Samen are white, Pattinè is yellow, and Pittia and Kattragam are red. (Vide Plate VII.)

Dambadiwa, in general, is inhabited by men and demons. Of the latter there are five different kinds, viz. the Rawkshasa, Yakshyayo or Dewatawo, Bhootayo, Prayta, and Pisatcha. The Rawkshasa, in form resemble men, but they are hideous likenesses, and of gigantic size; though they have greatly dwindled, they are still as tall as palmyra-trees. Their dispositions are cruel and vicious. Furnished with teeth like lions, they feed on human flesh, and when they cannot procure meat, they eat dirt. They can descend to the bottom of the ocean, and walk under the sea, but they cannot ascend into or traverse the atmosphere. They dwell in a part of the eastern ocean that is unnavigable. They are never seen; and now they are not even heard, as they were formerly. The Yakshyayo or Dewatawo resemble the preceding, but are inferior to them in size and power. Unable to walk, they move along the surface like vapour, and are incapable of rising to any height. Their eyes are fixed and destitute of all motion. They inhabit every where, — houses, woods, and caves. With the design of creating terror, they make hideous noises, and sometimes appear, and occasionally even attack men. Of a malicious and revengeful nature, they suck the blood of men and other animals, and cause sickness and death. Though not worshipped, the timid, with the idea of warding off threatened danger, or any pressing misfortune, apply to some tom-tom beater, who officiates as their priest, and receives offerings on their account, which he of course appropriates and applies to his own use. * — The Bhootayo are so called from *bitaya*, fear; the Singalese fearing them very much. These beings have no form or figure, but resemble wind. They dwell in forests and in graves; and notwithstanding their airy nature, feed on dirt. They are capable of making noises and of frightening people, in doing which they are supposed to take delight.—The Prayta are ugly figures, composed of skin and bone; though unable to walk, they are capable of floating through the air. They have a desire for food and drink, but in attempting to satisfy their appetite, they are always tantalized, — their food and drink flying before them. Their power of doing mischief is limited to that of appearing and terrifying the timid.—The Pisatcha resemble air, and like air they abound every where. Like the preceding, they in vain attempt to satisfy a craving appetite, and like them too, they are only capable of exciting terror.

The infernal regions, the abodes of the guilty, are the only parts of the Saquela that remain to be described. Under the ocean, to the eastward of Dambadiwa, are situated the eight principal hells; viz. Sanjeewa, Kalasootra, Sanghata, Raurawaya, Maha-raurawaya, Pratapaya, Maha-pratapaya and Awichu. They are all metallic hollow squares, composed of different alloys of the common metals, and without any openings. In each there is an intense fire, which burns constantly without fuel. Though they do not differ in kind, they do in degree; the lowest being the largest and hottest, and the punishments inflicted in them proportionally more severe and of longer duration. Sinners are doomed to different hells according to the degree of their crimes;

* Vide Plate VIII. — It is a faithful copy of a portion of the wall of the Maha Visnu-Dewalé, in Kandy. The principal figures are representations of some of the demons alluded to in the text. It is a good example of the fantastic paintings with which their temples, in general, are bedaubed.

I. Clark sculpt.

Figures on the outer wall of the Maha Visnu Dewalé.

London, Published by Longman, Hurst, Rees, Orme & Browne, 1821.

thus, those who are merely guilty in thought and intention descend to the first hell; and as the crime deepens its dye, the sinner sinks lower. For each great sin, there is a particular kind of punishment:—for murder, the wretch is perpetually murdered, and the very act that he has been guilty of, in all its minute circumstances, is constantly repeated on him; for stealing, the sinner is punished by gems of great value in appearance, tempting him to seize them, and when seized, turning into fire; the drinker of spirituous liquors is drenched with melted lead; the liar is constantly tormented by the application of red-hot irons to his tongue; and the adulterer is punished perpetually by climbing up and down a thorny tree in pursuit of his paramour, whom, when he is below, he sees alluring him above, and whom, when he has forced his painful way through the thorns to the top, he sees practising the same arts below. Besides these particular punishments there are innumerable others. They all suffer dreadfully from intense heat, and from hunger and thirst, the pains of which are heightened by the expectation of gratification, which instead of enjoying they swallow fire. Besides, they are subject to be impaled on burning brands, and to be flogged whilst burning, and to be cut and chipped and fashioned like wood. Their tormentors are sinners like themselves, in the form of caffers, dogs, and crows, of the most monstrous appearance, and armed with teeth and claws of the most formidable kind. The most wicked are uncommonly fat and fleshy and attractive; whilst those who have sinned least, are extremely thin,—mere skin and bone—perfect natural skeletons, with little feeling and no charms for their hungry tormentors. The one hundred and thirty-six smaller infernal regions, that surround the eight principal, are similar to them, only differing in degree; and as they are smaller, so they are less terrible. The period of punishment, though not infinite, is of immense duration; even in the first hell, where life is shortest, it lasts several kalpès. Having expiated their sins, either in part or entirely, some will be born as demons, brutes, or men, and some even as gods. The Locarnantarika-narikay, the infernal region common to three worlds, is a general receptacle, and a place of extreme punishment. It is an immense hollow composed of walls of clay, without light or heat. Those who have committed the worst of all crimes are alone doomed to it; as the murderer of a parent, a priest, or a teacher; the scorner of Boodhoo or the gods; those who oppose their worship or injure their temples. The inhabitants of this hell are punished in utter darkness by the most intense cold and by the calls of a ravenous appetite, that urge them to bite and tear, and devour one another. As often as they die, they come to life again, changing their abode from one hell to another, without mitigation and without end.

Their physical system is conformable with the preceding. Rarely having recourse to natural causes, and never to any but of a monstrous kind, they suppose almost all the striking phenomena of nature either to be produced by means of particular gods, or to take place in consequence of the operation (if operation it can be called) of a fatal necessity.

Their theory of the tides is an instance of the first kind of explanation: over Sanjeewa, the uppermost of the infernal regions, they imagine an immense pit to receive the water of the ocean, and prevent its overflowing the land; the water in descending becomes heated, and before it has reached the bottom is inflamed and forced back in the state of steam and smoke, producing a violent commotion and regurgitation, — the cause of the phenomenon in question.

The phenomena of meteors and the heavenly bodies are explained on the more general and accommodating principle of divine agency. A god of wind, of clouds, of heat and rain, by mere willing, produce these meteors: when angry with one another, they set the elements to fight, and create storms. Their residence is in the lowest heaven, which, divided into twelve equal portions, revolves once every twenty-four hours, above and round Maha-meru. The sun, moon, planets, and stars, are supposed to be luminous gods, resident in the same heaven, in transparent mansions; all of which, excepting the abodes of the fixed stars, are constantly travelling at a certain regular rate, and in a precise direction, drawn by different kinds of animals, as horses, elephants, goats, deer, and bullocks; appearing when on our side of Maha-meru, and disappearing when on the opposite side. The milky way is supposed to be the light of a serpent, and a shooting star the death of a god.

What, in their fabulous system, are the greatest of all events,—the destruction and renovation of worlds,—are apparently referred to fate, and associated with the moral condition of mankind; the world degenerating and tending towards chaos as vice increases, and improving and becoming more perfect with the growth of virtue.

The time between one chaos and another, called a Maha-kalpè, is incomprehensibly long, and includes many revolutions or minor destructions, the periods between which, called anta-kalpês, though very subordinate to the greater, are still so immense, that man is unable to form any idea of their duration.

The chaos in which a Maha-kalpê terminates, is produced by the joint operation of the elements, ending in an almost universal conflagration, that spares no part of the world, with the exception of one of the Brachmea-lochès.

The fire having exhausted itself, the restorative process commences; the world is inundated with rain, which in due time subsides, leaving a surface of mud, clay, and rocks. The flower Naloon (a species of lotos) springs up, bearing suits of robes, for as many Boodhoos as are destined for the Maha-kalpè just commencing, and which vary in number from one to five. This flower grows to the height of the Brachmea-loche that during the general destruction remained uninjured. Eight Brachmeas descend by it to the earth, to become the progenitors of the next race of mankind. By feeding on a sweet mud with which the ground is covered, and a species of vegetation like a mushroom, they degenerate, become subject to change, acquire human passions and forms, become divided into sexes, and finally into castes, and, to be kept in order, require the controul of government.

The outline of one anta-kalpè will suffice for the whole. The human race by degrees degenerate farther, and become more vicious and shorter-lived, all animals and all nature degenerating with them. When at that pitch of depravity and degradation, that the majority of men are almost destitute of the moral sense, and the age of man is reduced to ten years, a warning voice will be heard all over the world, proclaiming, that in seven days there will be a great rain, and that all who are wetted by this rain will be converted into beasts and destroy each other. The few, who have any remains of virtue will listen to the warning voice, and by keeping themselves dry, escape destruction. They will begin to reflect on the effects of vice and to reform; as they get rid of their sins, their ages will be prolonged and the earth improved.

When in their greatest purity, their age will be of astonishing duration, and the beauty of their persons, the dimensions of their bodies, and their mental faculties, proportionably exalted. No state being permanent, when most perfect, they will begin to decline, and continue degenerating till the time arrive for the commencement of another anta-kalpè. Such is a very general outline of this system, with the exception of that part which relates expressly to the history of Boodhoo and his religion, and which is next to come under review.

The term Bouddou, or Boodhoo, is a generic term, signifying wisdom *, and applied to human beings of extraordinary faculties, attainments, and destiny; a certain number of whom is fated to appear in each Maha-kalpè, to reform mankind, and restore to its purity a religion, which is compared by its followers to a tree, not always in fruit, and sometimes even without leaves or indications of life.

The number of Boodhoos destined for the present Maha-kalpè is five. Of these all have appeared, with the exception of Nitrè Boodhoo, who remains to come, and will come in the next anta-kalpè, at a particular time predestined, after an immense period has elapsed. The fourth or last Boodhoo was Goutama, who is still, with strict Boodhists, the sole object of veneration, and even amongst the people is the chief object of worship.

The history of all these beings, — of those who have gone by, and of those who are to come, — is so similar, that one will convey a pretty correct idea of the whole; invention, in this instance, having wisely spared itself a great deal of trouble, —

* According to a learned native, Boodhoo is derived from the Pali word, bodie, wisdom.

altering a name, (Nitrè, for example, for Goutama,) without materially deranging the tissue of the story.

I shall endeavour, as briefly as is compatible with its oriental complexion and character, to give an outline of the life of the last Boodhoo, without some knowledge of which, no tolerably correct notion can be formed of the Boodhaical religion.

The individual who finally became Goutama Boodhoo, previously experienced every variety of state of existence, and was born an almost infinite number of times. In confirmation of the latter part of this statement, it is said, "were the bodies collected merely in each instance of abortion, which occurred to him in the common course of things, they would form a heap that would surpass in magnitude the earth itself."

In the life immediately before that in which he became Boodhoo, he was called Swata-katu, and was a god inhabiting Toosita-dewia-lochè. One thousand years before the event, the great sign announcing it appeared to the gods and Brachmeas in ten thousand worlds: the sign was, a man dressed in white, with a white crown on his head, flying through the air, proclaiming—"In a thousand years, Boodhoo will appear." This period in heaven seems as a moment only on earth. The gods no sooner heard the report, than they hastened to the dwelling of Swata-katu, told him that the destined time was at hand, and that his great actions rendered him worthy of the Boodhooship he was about to receive.

Swata-katu then reflected on five circumstances. He first satisfied himself that the time was really nearly arrived for him to appear, the age of man being 120 years: were it less — were it 100, mankind would have been too vicious to have been benefited by his instructions; and, were it much more — were it

100,000, too virtuous and happy to have required them. Farther, by reflection, having ascertained — that the world he was to be born in would be Dambadiwa, the country, Maddiadasè, the caste, the original royal caste of the Sakkea-wansè, and that his mother would be Mahayadavea, the queen of Sododen Rajahroo, residing at Kapilla-wastoo-poora, — he promised the gods assembled that he would become Boodhoo.

At the appointed time he disappeared in heaven, and was conceived in the womb of the queen of Sododen. The queen, towards the end of her pregnancy, in the flower-season, passing one of the royal gardens, was tempted in by the beauty of its appearance; she felt a wish to pluck a bunch of flowers from a tree in blossom, that struck her fancy; and the instant she experienced the wish, the branch bent down to be gathered. The moment she touched it, the pains of labour commenced, and were speedily over. The child, as soon as he was born, walked straight forward seven steps; and though the surrounding gods, who had assembled on the occasion, were in a circle, he appeared to each, at the same moment, to be advancing towards him.

When Sododen heard of the event, he sent for the Brahmens, his astrologers, that he might learn from them the exact time of his son's birth, and what was likely to be his lot in life. The astrologers replied, that the prince would be either a Chakkrawattè king *, or Boodhoo.

The sage, Kaladiwella, who dwelt in Hiemalè, having heard great rejoicings in all the heavens, that a prince was born, who

* A Chakkra-wattè king is king of the whole Sakwalla, and is able to visit every part of it in half-an-hour. Twenty-four, it is said, have already appeared in this kalpè, and the number is not limited.

was to become Boodhoo, paid a visit to Sododen, and begged to see the child. The king, in presenting him, tried to join the infant's hands to salute the sage, but in vain; — the young prince, to his father's horror and the sage's astonishment, put his feet on Kaladiwella's head, — a liberty that no being in the three worlds was entitled to take. The sage, discovering the two hundred and sixteen signs on the soles of the child's feet, and the thirty-two marks of beauty on his body, and the eighty inferior marks indicative of his destiny, and at the same time reflecting that he should not live to see it fulfilled, — that before that time he should be in Asanginneya, expressed the mixed feeling of pleasure and of grief that he experienced, by almost simultaneously laughing and weeping. Before he departed, he told the king that his son would be Boodhoo, and that he would see four things that would induce him to forsake his family, to prepare himself for his high calling; — viz. a sick man, an old man, a dead body, and a Tapissa.

The prince was called Siddhartè, and when sixteen, was married to Yassodevadavie, the daughter of a neighbouring monarch, and had a share in the government.

The brahminical religion at that time prevailed, and Sododen, ignorant of the nature and office of a Boodhoo, and fearful of losing his son, took every precaution to prevent it; he prohibited the approach of Tapissas; he removed all the old and sick from the city, and had the ramparts repaired, and a guard of a thousand men stationed at each of the four gates.

When in his 29th year, the Prince, preparing one day to step into his carriage with his minister, Channa, saw a very old and very infirm man tottering along, barely supporting himself with the aid of a stick. He begged an explanation of his minister, of this novel sight. Channa replied, "It is an old man, and we are all subject to old age." Siddhartè, instead of going to his pleasure-garden as he had intended, returned thoughtful and sad. Another day, on his way to the garden, he saw a man very sick, lying on the ground, unable to stand. The sight distressed him, and he suddenly returned home. Another day, going the same way, he saw a putrid dead body. Afflicted greatly, he proceeded to the garden, and there met a Tapissa. To his enquiries who he was, his minister replied; "He is a man who endeavours to get rid of the three evils we have witnessed, — old age, disease, and death." The prince remarked, — "It is good, Channa, for us to be like him;" and at that instant he resolved to depart and become a priest.

He returned to the palace full of grief and melancholy, which his father only aggravated by the dancing, singing, and feasting which he had introduced, with the hope of amusing his son. When about to depart, he heard that his princess, whom he loved exceedingly, was brought to bed; fearing it might shake his resolution, he resisted his longing to see her and his child, and set out privately by night, mounted on his horse Kandekka, with his faithful Channa behind him. The city gate voluntarily opened to let them pass. They did not stop till they reached the Anoma ganga, which the horse cleared at one bound.

On the bank of this river, the prince determined to throw off his royal robes, and put on those of a priest. With his sword he cut off his long hair, and threw it towards heaven. Sacrea, who was waiting, caught it in the air, and deposited it in a dagoba* in Toosita. The king of the Brachmeas, Maha-Brachmea, was in attendance, with a set of robes from the flower Naloon, that sprung up at the beginning of the world, and which he gave the prince, with every thing that a priest requires; viz. besides two robes, a cloth for the loins, a patrè or eating-dish, a straining-cloth to strain or filter water for drinking, a girdle to tie the robes, and a razor and needle.

Siddhartè, having thus become a priest and renounced power and pomp, intreated his minister to take back the horse, and return with his royal robes to his father, to acquaint him of all that had happened. Channa was with great difficulty persuaded to leave his master, and the horse was so grieved, that he died on the road, of sorrow.

Siddhartè proceeded alone to Rajahgha-neura, living on alms. The people who saw him, equally surprised at the beauty of his person and his noble presence, imagined he was a god come down to witness the miseries of mankind.

From Rajahgha-neura, he went to Ooroowella, where he stayed six years, performing the most difficult actions of the Tapessaays, — as, remaining stationary, and eating nothing but the leaves of the trees that dropped around him; — as, gazing on the sun, between four great fires, &c. This he did, not that he approved of such actions and considered them beneficial and laudable, but, on the contrary, to show the devotees present that he could accomplish them and despise them as vain and useless. By the severity of the trials he submitted himself to, his head had become bald, and his body excessively emaciated. He

* A dagoba is a kind of dome attached to the temples of Boodhoo, for holding relics. The word is said to be composed of *da*, relic, and *gaba* or *goba*, belly.

recovered his health, which appeared ruined, whilst performing another tapass, of a much less difficult kind, and better suited to his disposition. It was called Maddiama-prati-padarwa, and consisted in abstaining from evil, in practising what is good, in gaining a subsistence by such actions, in meditating on them and on good intentions, in the enjoyment of happiness resulting from the consciousness of having done good, in the absence of covetousness, anger, and rashness, and in an exemption from the passions. Whilst engaged in this tapass, he had five dreams, from which he plainly perceived that he was speedily about to become Boodhoo.

He next went to Senatini, and seated himself at the foot of a sacred Banyan-tree, called Ajapallé, at the time that a neighbouring princess, in compliance with a vow, was about to make an offering to it, expressive of her gratitude for being blessed with a child, after having been long barren. The offering was to be rice, dressed without water. The milk of 1000 cows, fed on liquorice leaves, was given to 500 cows; theirs to a smaller number; and so on, till the number thus fed was reduced to ten, and with their milk the rice was prepared. When the offering was ready, the princess sent a servant to learn if the tree were decorated according to her orders. The maid, seeing Siddhartè, supposed he was a god, and ran back and told her mistress that the god of the tree was out. The princess, believing this report, put the rice in a cup of the value of 100,000 pieces of gold, and presented it, not to the tree, but to the prince.

He next went to the river Niranjara, where, having made the rice he had received from the princess into forty-nine balls, he ate it, and threw the dish into the river, on the surface of which it floated *up* the stream.

The same evening he was presented by a Brahmen with eight bundles of kusa grass, which he carried to a Bo-tree to sit on. When about to be seated, a diamond throne, fourteen cubits high, rose from the earth to receive him. He was here visited by the gods, who remained with him till night, when they fled on the approach of Marea, prince of the infernal regions, who came to oppose him with ten bimberah of demons. Marea attacked Siddhartè in a variety of ways, with his elephant, with his Chakkra-yoodé (ring weapon), and with nine different kinds of showers, as of boiling mud, burning coals, sharp weapons, &c. but without the least effect. Finding violence useless, Marea claimed the throne as his own, saying, " Siddhartè, that seat is mine, not yours; I can produce evidence of it; and unless you can prove the contrary, you must acknowledge it mine." Then all the attendant demons yelled — " The throne is Marea's!" No one appeared for the prince; but suddenly, on his side there were thundering voices declaring for him, issuing from the earth, the mountains, and the heaven. Thus every way baffled, Marea and his infernal legions retreated, and the gods returned to pay their homage.

During the remainder of the night, Siddhartè acquired every species of wisdom, all of which are comprehended in the four principal, viz. the knowledge of his former births and eminent virtues, and those of others; the power of seeing the past and the future; acuteness of wisdom, enabling its possessor to penetrate and comprehend every thing; and the power of banishing all worldly passions, and the disposition to enjoy the happiness resulting from that state of exemption.

The following morning, Siddhartè became Boodhoo, and from the name of his family, he was distinguished by the title of Goutama Boodhoo. Besides this name, he had an immense number of other appellations, altogether amounting to 12,000; of which, those most frequently used by his disciples, are the following thirty-seven, in Sanscrit, written as they were pronounced by a learned native:

1. Boodha.
2. Dassabalha, - ten powers.
3. Sastroo, - guide.
4. Saster, - ruler.
5. Surwadnyia - all wisdom.
6. Dippadutama, - the majesty of two-footed beings.
7. Moneendra, - the chief of wise men.
8. Bagawanè, - the blessed.
9. Sregana, - great glory.
10. Natah, - the helper.
11. Sacksumah, - having eyes.
12. Angirassa, - sweet substance.
13. Loka-natah, - helper of the world.
14. Anadiwara, - sole ruler.
15. Mahhesèe, - the great noble.
16. Vinniaka, - one ruler.
17. Sammanta-chaksa, - surrounded by eyes, — seeing all things.
18. Soogata, - gone to a high place.
19. Bruree-panneah, - diamond of wisdom.
20. Mahrajè, - conqueror of Mahra.
21. Lokajè, - conqueror of the world.
22. Jinna, - the triumphant.
23. Tathagata, - he came the same (as other Boodhoos).

24. Sakkeasinha,	-	the lion of the Sakkea-wansè.
25. Narawera,	-	the skilful man.
26. Sammanta-badra,	-	surrounded by goodness.
27. Darma-rajah,	-	the king of doctrines.
28. Dewa-dewa,	-	god of gods.
29. Maha-dewa,	-	great god.
30. Dewatè-dewa,	-	great god of gods.
31. Rajatè-rajah,	-	great king of kings.
32. Brachmatè-brachma	-	great Brachma of the Brachmas.
33. Ouweahya-wadee.		
34. Sododennè,	-	son of Sododen.
35. Siddharta.		
36. Goutama.		
37. Arka-bandu,	-	another family name,— descendant of the sun.

During the first seven weeks, which he passed in meditation, Boodhoo ate nothing nor required any thing, the forty-nine balls he had previously taken, supporting him the whole time.

The remainder of his history, were it related the least in detail, would occupy volumes: I must confine myself to a very general abstract, which alone it is in my power to give.

The greater part of the remainder of his life Boodhoo spent in Kosol-ratta, residing in the city Sra-wasti-neura and in the temple Jetawanaramay, which was one of eighteen magnificent temples built for him in that city by a wealthy individual. He passed his time in meditation, in occasionally visiting other countries, and in preaching not only to men but the gods. Ceylon he is said to have visited three different times; and it is generally believed, that he left the mark of his foot imprinted on the rock on the top of Adam's Peak. His days he devoted to men, in preaching to them and converting them ; and his nights to the gods, who assembled to listen to him. He was so successful in convincing those whom he addressed of the truth of his doctrines, that he often daily converted many Asankeyas, (a number too immense to be comprehended.) The powers which he exercised in reforming mankind were more than human, and quite miraculous. He could assume any form he chose. He could multiply himself many hundred times ; or, produce the appearance of many hundred of Boodhoos, in every respect like himself, with rays of light issuing from every pore of their skin, differently occupied, — some standing, some sitting, and some preaching. He could go any distance in an instant, even as fast as thought, — through the air, under water, or under the earth. When he preached, his face appeared to all his audience, though surrounding him in a circle ; people of all languages understood him,—and all, however distant, heard him distinctly, excepting those who were too deep in vice to be reformed, and who were as the deaf, and, though close to him, heard nothing. A learned man, who followed him every where during six months to ascertain if he were the true Boodhoo, never saw the impression of his foot, not even a flower bent on which he trod, or a cushion pressed on which he sat. His good qualities equalled his extraordinary powers, and are said to have been boundless and to baffle description.

He expired in the eighty-fifth year of his age, after having been Boodhoo forty-five years, and accomplished the reformation of a great portion of the world and its conversion to his religion. On his death-bed, he called the god Sacrea to him, and bid him watch over and protect his religion, during the space of 5000 years, when his elements would re-assemble and arrange themselves in his image, under the very Bo-tree which shaded him when he became Boodhoo, and having performed many miracles, be dissipated for ever. Sacrea accepted the trust confided in him, and delegated it to Visnu and the other gods who guard the earth.

The funeral of Boodhoo was most magnificent. His body was deposited in a gold coffin, and covered with a pile of sandal wood 120 cubits high. The fire spared certain bones, which it is supposed are still preserved in different parts of the world, and converted the rest into pearls, and his flesh into grains of gold.

Boodhoo himself is said to be in Niwanè,—the final reward of all Boodhoos and of all perfectly just men, from whence there is no return. What this Niwanè is, is a religious mystery: priests are rather averse from answering enquiries on the subject; they say, it is forbidden to discuss its nature; and on the principle, that if men understood it, they would not like it, but prefer worldly things, as flies do bad smells. The word is said to be compounded of Ni, no, and Wané, thirst; it is occasionally illustrated by the putting out a fire,—the extinguishing of a flame; and the best informed and most learned Boodhists, who will express their opinions, seem to consider it identical with annihilation, and in reality, what Abhogata is merely in appearance.

This notion of annihilation as a final reward, at first view, not only appears extraordinary but monstrous. Monstrous, it certainly is, in relation to sound reason, but not in relation to the system to which it belongs, and with which it is very compatible; for, repulsive as it is, the mind revolts from it less than from a state of eternal existence, at the mercy of fate or chance, in perpetual change, without any security or permanency of enjoyment, and with the certainty only of a very large proportion of pain and misery.

The death of Boodhoo is one of the great eras from which the Singalese reckon. According to the best authorities I could consult, the present year, 1821, corresponds to 2364 A. B.

It is said that Boodhoo committed nothing to writing, and that no written records of his religion were made till many years after his death; according to some authorities, not till 218 years had expired, and according to others not till 400. In 400 A. B., in the reign of Wallagam Bahoo, king of Ceylon, those who maintain the latter opinion, say that the doctrines and traditions that had been carefully handed down by his disciples, were collected and written down by learned priests at Aloolena in Matele, altogether composing the five following works:—

1. Dik-sangia, - the long collection.
2. Medoon-sangia, - the middling collection.
3. Angottra-sangia, - the elementary collection.
4. Sanyoot-sangia, - the valuable collection.
5. Koodoogot-sangia, - the remaining collection.

These works, which contain a complete system of the religion of Boodhoo, are so extensive, that no individual has studied the whole of them; and so obscure, as to be frequently unintelligible; affording reason to the hostile Brahmens to remark, that "the Boodhists are like the dumb, who dream and cannot explain their dreams." Though they have become very scarce, they are still to be found in Ceylon, and all of them complete, with the exception of the Angottra-sangia, which was composed of twenty-five books, some of which have been lost. These sacred volumes are the guides and great authorities of Boodhists on all doubtful points of religion; and the Singalese maintain, that their own temple-establishment, their doctrines, and their forms of worship, are in perfect agreement with them.

In few parts of the world is the "establishment" of religion more regularly organized than in Ceylon. At Kandy there are two principal colleges,—the Malwattè-wiharè, and the Asgirie-wiharè *; to one or other of which all the priests in the island belong. Belonging to, and under the government of the former, it is conjectured, there may be about three thousand Upasampada priests; and belonging to the latter, about one thousand; three-fourths of the whole of which are supposed to be in the Interior. In the accuracy of these conjectures not much confidence can be put; for though all the priests that are ordained are registered, their deaths are not regularly returned.

The two colleges are independent, but not in the least in opposition. Over each are two chief priests, who were appointed by the king, called Maha-niakoo-unanci, and Anna-niakoo-unanci *, who are the only individuals in the priesthood who have official rank,—superiority being allowed to none besides, excepting on the ground of exemplary piety or learning. To these chief priests belong the superintendence and government of their respective colleges, in conducting which they have written and express rules and directions for their guidance.

Priests in general are of two kinds;—those of the superior

* A temple of Boodhoo is always called a Wiharè; whilst that of a god is distinguished by the name Dewalè.

† Unanci, lord, is a term of respect, applied to priests in general; niakoo is expressive of high rank.

order are called Upasampada, and are honoured with the title of Tirunnansè; those of the inferior are called Samenero, and have the title of Ganinnansè.* Only the Goewansè, as already remarked, can belong to the priesthood; not that religion excludes the rest, but pride, — people of the first caste not being able to condescend to pay the respect due to a priest to a low caste individual. There is, indeed, a description of pious men of low caste, who lead the life of priests, called Silvat, and perform some of their duties, but who are not ordained, or entitled to any distinctions.

The education and ordination of priests is regular and peculiar. A noviciateship is to be served before an individual can become a Samenero; and, before the latter can be made an Upasampada, he must qualify himself to pass certain examinations, and must be approved of by the king. The noviciateship is generally served in very early youth: — a boy, with the consent of his parents or nearest relations, puts himself under the care of a priest, whom he attends as a servant, or rather page, and by whom, in return, he is instructed. At the end of three years, if he has behaved correctly, he is made a Samenero. Having provided himself with yellow robes, and the same things that it is said Siddhartè was furnished with, when he turned priest previously to his becoming Boodhoo; and, having had his head and eye-brows shaved, and his body, before bathing, smeared with a variety of applications, he may address himself to his tutor, kneeling, and beg, in a Pali verse, to be admitted into the lowest order of priesthood. His request, after a trial of his attainments, being complied with, he is dressed in the appropriate

* Upasampada signifies almost full (of religion); Samenero, the son of a priest.

Samenero robes. His duties are comprehended in studying, in paying respect to his tutor, and in serving him; and, in attending the temple, and performing certain subordinate religious ceremonies. At the age of twenty, (reckoning from the commencement of his present existence; i. e. from his conception, and not birth,) if qualified and permitted, he may become Upasampada. Having prepared himself by throwing off his yellow robes, and putting on a white garment, (when he is called a Nagaya,) he proceeds to be examined. Having passed his examination before an assembly of at least twenty priests, and obtained the royal licence, he is paraded through the streets of the capital in great pomp, mounted on an elephant or horse, and attended by the chiefs. Lastly, on his return, having been examined afresh, he is invested in his Upasampada robes, which differ in some respects from those of the Samenero, and is considered one of the Upasampada order. *

Every priest possesses, or is attached to, a particular Wiharè; where, leading an indolent monastic life of celibacy, he performs his religious duties, and is supported either by the charity of the people, or the produce of the lands, the property of the temple. The number of priests belonging to any single temple varies from one to thirty, according to its size and opulence. A temple generally descends from the teacher to his pupil; it is not in the gift of any one but the actual possessor; and it is held for life.

What the number of Wiharès in the country is, it is not easy to determine: they are numerous, certainly; hardly the smallest district or village being without one. At each temple

* Fig. 8. Plate IX. represents a priest in his Upasampada robes.

the establishment is very similar: there is generally a neat pansol or dwelling-house for the priests; a poega, or a building in which the priests hold their meetings; a wiharè, containing one or more images of Boodhoo, and, occasionally, images of the protecting gods; a dagobah, near the wiharè, containing, as it is supposed, a relic of Boodhoo *, and a bo-tree contiguous. The

* A very ancient Dagobah, in ruins, and rather resembling a tumulus than what we may conceive its original form to have been, situated in the Raygam Korle, not very far from Colombo, was opened and explored last year, by C. E. Layard, Esq., to whose kindness I was indebted for seeing what was found in it, and for most of the following particulars: —

In the middle of the ruined Dagobah, a small square compartment was discovered, lined with brick, paved with coral, and containing, in the centre, a small cylindrical mass of grey granite, covered exactly with a rounded cap of the same stone; several small clay images of the hooded-snake; a common earthen lamp, similar to that used by the natives at present; a brass lamp; and a small obelisk, or four-sided truncated pyramid, solid, and composed of cement.

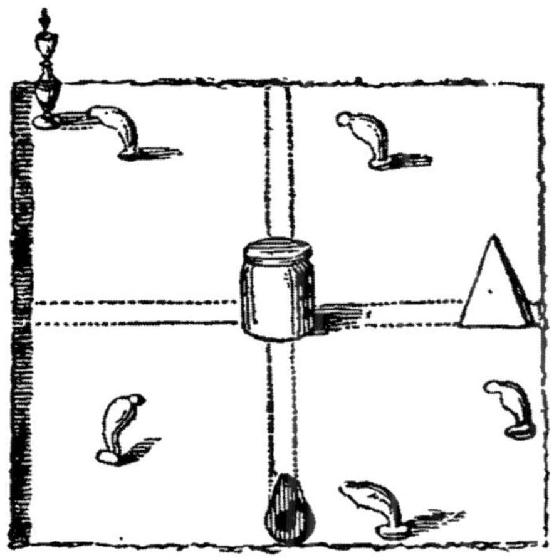

The top of the rude granitic vase, or carandua, was solid. The carandua itself was hollow, and was found to contain a small fragment of bone; bits of thin plate-gold, in which, probably, the bone was originally wrapped; some small gold rings; two or three very small pearls, retaining their lustre completely; beads of rock crystal and cornelian; small fragments of ruby, blue sapphire, and zircon; and pieces of situations are commonly judiciously chosen, in secluded places, amongst rocks, and near rivers; they are generally well planted, and shaded with a variety of elegant palms and luxuriant fruit-trees; they are always kept neat and clean; and their appearance is frequently beautiful, and often extremely romantic.

The duties of priests, both private and public, are peculiar. They are all required to observe the Triwededooscharitie and the Pratipatti. The first are prohibitory commandments, forbidding, 1. killing animals; 2. stealing; 3. committing adultery; 4. lying; 5. drunkenness; 6. eating at night; 7. resting on high beds; 8. amusements, as singing, dancing, &c.; 9. accepting gold or silver; and, 10. wearing flowers and using perfumes.—The Pratipatti order them to show, 1. the same attention to the relics and images of Boodhoo that were paid to Boodhoo himself whilst alive; 2. to respect religious books; and, 3. to respect elder priests like their own parents. Three times every day worship and respect should be paid by priests to Boodhoo, to religious books, and to senior priests. The worship of Boodhoo, of his relics and images, should be observed at about sunrise, and sunset, and at noon. It consists in presenting flowers before his shrine, in repeating certain prayers, in making a certain number of prostrations, and in observing a variety of forms, which it would be tedious to describe, and not

---

glass, in the shape of icicles, which had undergone, superficially, considerable change, having become crystalline, rather opaque, and infusible at a red heat,—in consequence, I suspect, of the loss of a portion of alkali.

The contents of this carandua are very similar to those of an urn found near Benares, and strongly confirm the conclusion of Mr. Duncan, that it belonged to a temple of Boodhoo; which, according to an inscription found in the same place, existed there seven or eight hundred years ago.—As. Res. tom. v. 131.

very easy to comprehend. I was once present in the Sanctum of the principal temple in Kandy, during the whole ceremony of the evening service; what I saw strongly reminded me of the ceremonial of high mass of the Roman catholic church; incense being burnt, perfumed water scattered about, &c. &c. The worship paid to religious books consists in offering flowers before them. So scrupulous are they in their respect to books, that they will not touch them till they have made their obeisance, as to a superior; nor sit down, unless the books present are placed, as a mark of distinction, on a shelf or table above them. The worship that priests pay to their seniors, consists in prostrations; on their knees, generally, with their hands uplifted, and the head bowed to the earth, they beg a blessing, which is bestowed by the elder priest stooping forward with his hands closed.

On each of the four holydays (pohoya) that occur in every lunar month, the priests should preach to the people assembled at the temple, inculcating lessons of morality and the duties of religion. The day should be kept like our sabbath, and devoted to religion and rest from labour; but it is not:— indeed, so little attention is paid by the people to a pohoya, that unless one were told of it, one would not suppose that they were acquainted even with the term.

Every fifteenth day, the priests of each temple should assemble in their poega, and hear the rules for the direction of their conduct read. Before the lecturer commences, the chief priest proclaims,—"If any one be present, whose sins will not permit him to sit whilst our doctrines are repeated, let him depart." Should an individual be guilty of a slight offence merely (and they reckon a million of this description), he may confess it immediately, and having been admonished, is at liberty to remain and sit down; but, if the offence be of the first magnitude,—if he be guilty of hypocrisy, or stealing, or fornication, or murder,—he must quit the assembly, and after trial be expelled the priesthood and punished. Once, annually, the priests in general of each college should be assembled by the chief priest, to be examined and exhorted.

During the period of three months, considered the rainy season, and called Waswassana *, priests are not allowed to be absent from their abodes more than six days, because of the weather,—travelling at that time being attended with many inconveniences and even with some difficulties, and it being considered indecorous for a priest to be walking about under a load of wet garments. Some individuals, to give a proof of their devotion, do not utter a word during the whole period. The people are expected to bring provisions to the temple for the support of the priests, while Waswassana lasts; and when it is ended, to present them with new garments. It is generally concluded by a great preaching. On such an occasion, the people are assembled from all the country round; night is the time generally chosen; two pulpits are prepared, which are either placed in a building constructed for the purpose, or in the porch of a Wiharè or Dewalè: two priests, in their full robes, attended by their companions, are carried to the pulpits, into which they are lifted; one priest reads texts from their religious books, and the other expounds them and preaches on them, exhorting the people to be pious and good, and correct and pure, in thought as well as action, and to subdue their pas-

* The term signifying rain (as the cause), and stopping (at home, as the effect).

sions, and be as like Boodhoo as possible, that they may obtain the same reward. *

The rank of a priest, next to that of Boodhoo, is considered the most exalted, — even superior to that of the gods: priests, in consequence, may sit in a dewalé; they never worship the gods; but when they preach, they invite the gods to be of their audience. No one should sit in their presence, not even a king; and, like Boodhoo himself, they are entitled to worship.

Their character in general is moral and inoffensive. The liberty they have of laying aside their yellow robes, and of quitting the priesthood at pleasure, has, no doubt, an excellent effect, and must tend greatly to exclude licentiousness and stop corruption, which (witness the old monasteries) are too apt to spring up and grow to a monstrous height, when no natural vent can be given to the violence of passion. Like the monks of Europe in the dark ages, they are the principal proprietors of the learning and literature of the country; and, like the same monks, their knowledge is chiefly of words and idle forms; their memories are more exercised than their judgments, and their reasoning powers seldom employed, except in defence of sophistry and error. As moral teachers, they appear in their best light; in this character I am not aware of any objection to them, and they form a striking exception to the priesthood of heathens in

* M. Joinville, in his account of the religion and manners of the Singalese, (As. Res. tom. viii.) has mistaken the nature of Waswassana: speaking of it, he says, "Priests must be three months during the year away from their ordinary habitation," that (he supposes) "they may spread their doctrines more generally." It is not easy to account for an error so complete.

general, who, ages ago, were justly accused of not teaching the people what even a poet exhorted them to learn :

> Disciteque ô miseri et causas cognoscite rerum ;
> Quid sumus et quidnam victuri gignimur.—

The people in general are not taught any of the mysteries of religion ; nor are they required to observe the Triwededooscharitie ; but they are expected to believe the Tisarana, and follow the Panchaseelè. The Tisarana are, — 1. Boodha-sarana, to worship Boodhoo, and acknowledge him to be all-wise ; 2. Dharmè-sarana, to have faith in his doctrines, as the means of salvation, or of avoiding misery and obtaining happiness, and finally niwanè ; and, 3. Sangha-sarana, to believe that priests are the disciples of Boodhoo, and qualified as guides to happiness. The Panchaseelè, which literally signify the five good qualities, are the same as the first five prohibitions of the Triwededooscharitie.

The people combine their worship with offerings, which they may make any day they choose, at morning or evening service. Their offerings consist of sweet-smelling flowers, which are delivered to the officiating priest, and by him arranged before the image ; whilst the people kneel, and either worship in silence, or, which is considered more devout, say or repeat after the priest, the Tisarana and the Panchaseelè, thus, — " I worship Boodhoo, and acknowledge him to be all-wise," &c. — " I do not deprive any animal of life." — " I do not steal," &c. Women as well as men may visit the temples for religious purposes ; and indeed, as in most countries where there is no restraint or prohibition, the Singalese women are to be seen at devotion more frequently than the men.

Besides the preceding rules, there are some others of a moral nature, that the people are expected to follow; such, for instance, as direct giving alms; meditating on the uncertainty of human affairs; living in a manner profitable to one's self and others; loving others as one's self, &c. &c.

It is certainly highly creditable to the Boodhaical religion, that its morality is so good and uncontaminated with vice and licentiousness. Considering its moral system only, it is to be regretted that it is not more strictly attended to and followed. Priests are frequently heard complaining on this head; but instead of exerting themselves to remedy it, they more easily satisfy themselves with accounting for it, and, on the sad principle of absolute fate and necessity, — the world, according to them, being now in its decline, yearly becoming more degenerate, vice and misery gaining strength, and virtue and happiness dwindling away. Another source of regret is, that such a system of morality should be associated with such a monstrous system of religion, — a compound of the coldest materialism, and the grossest superstition, offering nothing consolatory, or intellectual, or dignifying, or rational.

Boodhoo, as already remarked, is not alone worshipped by the Singalese: the gods, the guardians of the island and of the national religion, are worshipped also; as Nata, Visnu, Kattragam, Samen, Pittia, and the goddess Patinè. Whilst the people address themselves to Boodhoo for favour in another state of existence, for advancement in the next life, or for final happiness, they beseech these gods to confer on them immediate blessings or to remove or ward off present misfortunes or dangers. Knowing the influence and impression of the pressing calls of the moment, and the little thought that most men take of the distant and uncertain future, one cannot be astonished that these gods of the day, though less respected than Boodhoo, or even his priests, should be more feared and more zealously worshipped. The Kappurales *, the priests of dewalés, are not particularly respected as such: they are not educated for their office, or regularly ordained; no qualification worth noticing being necessary on their part, with the exception of caste and the observance of a certain mode of life considered essential to purity. The priests of Kattragam should be Brahmens, and of the other gods either Goewansé or Pattea-people. Of all the gods, the Kattragam god is most feared: his temple in the eastern part of the island is resorted to by pilgrims, not only from all parts of Ceylon, but from many parts of the continent of India; and, such is the dread entertained of this being, that I was never able to induce a native artist to draw a figure of him. Besides his common name, derived from the village where his principal temple is, this god has a thousand others; and it is a privilege of all of them to have a variety of names, the numbers being generally proportionable to the rank or the estimation in which the individual is held.

The combination of the worship of Boodhoo and of the gods, is a curious feature in the history of the religion of Ceylon, and, particularly, as it may be considered not merely tolerated, but quite orthodox; accordingly, it is not uncommon to see a Dewalé and a Wiharé contiguous, or even under the same roof.

Besides the preceding, there is a third order of beings, viz. Demons or Devils, who are worshipped by the Singalese. The

* According to the conjecture of a learned native, this word is a compound of kappu, proper, and ralle, chief.

principle of this species of devotion is completely fear; and, it is chiefly had recourse to in cases of extraordinary sickness or misfortune, in producing which the demons are supposed to be concerned: — thus, in a case of epilepsy or insanity, the individual, it is believed, is actually possessed by a devil; thus, again, in the instance of any great mortality among cattle, demons are considered the agents of the mischief. On such occasions, the ignorant and deluded people apply to designing knaves who pretend to the means of expelling or appeasing the devils. For the purpose, they institute a farce called a devil-dance, which generally lasts a whole night, and consists of a variety of mummery, the most essential parts of which, besides dancing and praying, are the cutting of lemons and the making an offering of a cock. This species of superstition is not approved of by the more enlightened; it is forbid in the religion of Boodhoo, and it is highly reprobated by the priests; yet it is much followed, and in some parts of the country there are even small temples, called Covillas, erected to these imaginary malignant beings.

The antiquity of the Boodhaical religion, the quarter in which it originated, and the direction in which it spread, are interesting subjects of enquiry, and still unexhausted, notwithstanding the learned labour and ingenuity that have been employed already in investigating them.

The pretensions of the Boodhists themselves, on the subject of the antiquity of their religion, are of two kinds, — one probable, and the other absurd in the extreme. In the latter, they associate it with their monstrous system of the universe, and consider it, in its various revolutions, as old and as durable as the universe itself: whilst, in the other, they only reckon from the time it was established, or, as they say, restored, by the Boodhoo whom they now worship, and who lived only about 600 years before the commencement of the Christian era. These latter pretensions may be admitted without difficulty: and, if admitted, it follows that the Brahminical religion is the more ancient of the two, which the Boodhists themselves do not deny, as they allow that their own religion was extinct when Boodhoo appeared to revive it, and that the Brahminical was the prevailing religion.

Is Boodhoo an incarnation of Visnu? Is the religion of Boodhoo grafted on, and a heresy of the Brahminical? Several oriental scholars of eminence maintain the affirmative. The Boodhists themselves are positive in holding the negative. Where all is probably fiction, one assertion may be opposed to another. The Boodhists contend, that the last Boodhoo was never Visnu; but that their present Visnu is fated to become a Boodhoo. In respect to the second question, — the mythological portion of the Boodhaical system in Ceylon does appear to be a graft of the Brahminical; but that which is purely Boodhaical seems to have had an independent origin: it is different in principle; it is as directly opposite as the doctrines of the Sadducees to the Pharisees, and surely cannot with propriety be consid l a heresy.

The question in what part of the world this religion first appeared is still involved in considerable obscurity. The majority of oriental scholars are in favour of its western origin, and maintain that it is derived from some part of Africa, — probably Ethiopia. A very few hold the contrary opinion, that the north of Asia was its birth-place and cradle.

The principal argument of those who maintain the first opinion, is derived from the appearance of some of the images

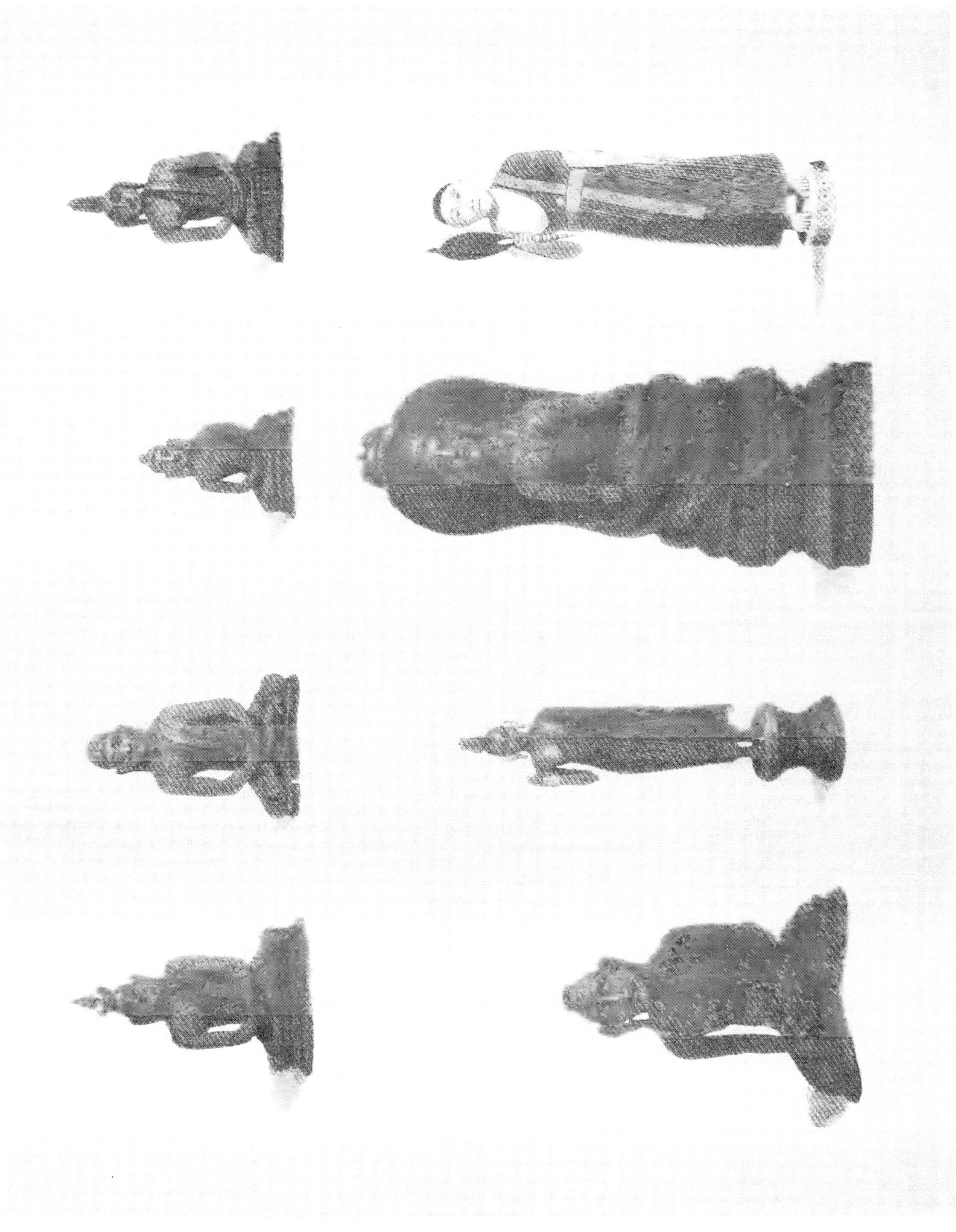

of Boodhoo. It is said, they show that Boodhoo was an African, having marked on them the short woolly hair, the flat dilated nostrils, the thick fleshy lip, and indeed every feature of the African countenance. If this be generally so, it certainly is strong evidence. I have paid particular attention to innumerable figures of Boodhoo, made in Ceylon; I have seen several from Ava and Siam; two or three of Foh, from China; one of Mahamoonie, and of a Lama, and a Dalai Lama, from Tibet *; and the result of my observations is the persuasion, that the asserted resemblance is either accidental or fanciful. The features of the Tibetian, Burman, and Chinese images, are more or less Tartar; and those of the Ceylon figures, Singalese: — and, it is worthy of remark, that the more carefully and ably the figures are made, the more complete is the copying of the national features. † The argument, therefore, from the African countenance, appears to me untenable; and I know no other of force in favour of African origin, which the Boodhists themselves will not patiently listen to, considering even the supposition a species of insult,—their ideas of the African (of the Kaffer) being very low, and full of contempt, as is evident, from their giving him the office of tormentor in the infernal regions, in common with dogs and crows. If questioned respecting the hair of Boodhoo, they say it was like their own, and that the object of artists is not to represent curly, woolly hair, but hair cut short, as

* These interesting figures from Tibet are in the possession of Charles Hatchett, Esq. and were brought to Europe by Pallas.

† Vide Plate IX., in which are several figures of Boodhoo, carefully copied from the original, with the view of illustrating the statement in the text. The six first are from small images in brass, which I procured in Kandy. The seventh is from an image in stone, which I found in the Wiharé, at Kattragam, where it was called by the attendants a female Boodhoo!

Boodhoo's was when he became priest; and, to prove this, they observe, that one long hair or lock was left uncut on his forehead, which is represented as a circle or curl, in all images that are correctly executed.

The opinion, that the religion of Boodhoo had its origin in the north-east part of Asia, has been advanced by Dr. Hamilton, in his valuable paper on the religion and literature of the Burmas.* It is the opinion of the Boodhists themselves. To my enquiries respecting Kosol-ratte where Boodhoo is said to have resided, and from whence he is supposed to have propagated his religion, a learned native replied,—"It is to the eastward of Ceylon, and further northward." He arrived at this conclusion, from circumstances mentioned in religious books. From these books it appears, that there was frequent intercourse between Kosol and Ava, and Bengal. Whence it may be inferred, that the former country could not be very remote from the two latter. In the same books certain directions of Boodhoo are preserved respecting woollen robes, and the times of bathing: in Kosol, he allowed his disciples to bathe only once in fifteen days; but in hot countries, once daily,— a most convincing proof that the climate of Kosol must have been at least cool, and not tropical. Were stronger evidence required, the same source affords it:—according to a passage in these works, in Kosol, in the month of September, at noon precisely, when the sun is at its greatest altitude, the shadow of man was six times the length of his foot. Hence, it is evident that Kosol was pretty far north; in confirmation of which, allusions are made in these works to snow and ice.

The extent of country over which the Boodhaical system has

* As. Res. vi. 261.

spread is immense: even now, variously modified, it is perhaps more widely extended than any other religion. It appears to be the religion of the whole of Tartary, of China, of Japan, and their dependencies, and of all the countries between China and the Burrampooter.

What its exact modifications are in all these countries, in a great measure, still remains to be ascertained. There is some reason to believe, that in Ava and Siam the system is least contaminated and of the greatest purity, and that in China, it has undergone the greatest adulteration. In the former countries, there are no temples erected to the gods, and no worship permitted excepting of Boodhoo; and, it may be added there are no distinctions of caste.* It has been supposed, that the system in general is equally pure, that the worship of Boodhoo and th gods could not come in contact, and that caste is unknown to Boodhists. That this supposition is not quite correct, is evident from the state of religion in Ceylon, where the worship of Boodhoo is connected with that of the gods, and associated with caste; and, I suspect that Ceylon is not, or at least was not a solitary example of the kind. It is highly probable that a similar combination of worship formerly existed on the continent of India, wherever the Boodhaical system prevailed. On such an idea may be explained, in a satisfactory manner, "the singular fact," as Mr. Erskine expresses it, and to which he has called the

* According to a native of Ceylon, who received his education as a priest in Siam, both in Siam and Ava the same notions are entertained respecting the gods as in Ceylon; he even stated that in Siam, Visnu is worshipped as in Ceylon, and that the dewalé-worship is followed; this was in conversation: in a written account of the peculiarities of religion in the two countries, the statement he made was that adopted in the text.

attention of enquirers, "of the existence of temples of opposite characters and of different and hostile religions, only a few miles from each other, and in some instances, as at Ellora, even united in the same range."* By the analogy of Ceylon, the fact is explained, with the rejection of the inference of the hostility of the two establishments, on which its apparent singularity depends.†

The extension of the religion of Boodhoo to the most eastern parts of Asia is more than probable: how far it has ever extended in an opposite direction is not perhaps an easy question to determine. I am not aware that it has been traced, in a satisfactory manner much to the westward of the Indian Caucasus.

What are we to think of the opinions of those eminent men, who have imagined its extension over all Europe as well as Asia, and have identified Boodhoo with Fro, Thor, and Odin, the gods of the Scandinavians? What analogies are there between the Boodhaical and the Scandinavian systems? The points of resemblance, if any, are certainly very few, whilst those of dissimilitude are innumerable. What two beings can be more different in character than Boodhoo and Odin: the one subduing his passions, and resigning a princely vest for a priest's robe; the other a conqueror and founder of a kingdom: the one teaching the annihilation of existence, as the final reward of virtue; the other inculcating the immortality of the soul: the one living a life of the greatest abstinence, exhorting his followers to imitate his example, and forbidding them the use of fermented liquors; the other, in Valhalla, leading a life the most jovial, drinking wine himself and regaling his companions, the Einheriar, (the ghosts of the brave slain in

* Trans. Lit. Soc. Bombay, i, 249.

† There is some reason to believe that the worship of the gods is combined with that of Boodhoo, or of Maha-moonie and Foh, both in Tibet and China.

battle,) with mede and beer, which they drank out of human skulls after feasting on pork: the one prohibiting the killing of any animal, even the minutest, and on this principle straining the water he drank, to save the lives of the animalcules, he might otherwise swallow,—inculcating humanity and mercy, and accepting no offerings but flowers; the other, the god of war, delighting in bloodshed, esteeming valour the first virtue, and gratified with no offering so much as that of human sacrifices:—the contrast might be carried farther, were it necessary;—even the periods of their existence do not agree; Boodhoo having flourished little more than a century after the founding of Rome; whilst Odin, according to his historian, did not emigrate from the East with his family and people, till the time of Pompey.* Were there any similarity of system, both might have had a similar origin; but where no similarity appears, but total difference, is it reasonable to suppose that the two sprang from the same root? Dr. Hamilton, from such considerations, has already opposed the notion, that our ancestors were Boodhists; and, I cannot help thinking, that every one who will give the subject a careful consideration, unbiassed by hypothesis, will adopt his conclusion. The argument from the name of a day, on which the analogy between Boodhoo and Odin or Woden is chiefly founded, is hardly worth noticing: I may remark cursorily, that Wednesday, (Woden's day,) in Ceylon, is generally called Sawummia-dinna, wind-day, on the idea that wind was created on that day; if it is ever called Boodhoo's day, I believe it to be not in reference to the being worshipped, but to Boodahoo, the mild god or planet, who is supposed to preside over Wednesday.

* T. Bartholini, Antiquit. Dan. &c. 4to. Hafn. 1689.

CHAPTER VIII.

SINGALESE LANGUAGE. — LITERATURE. — MUSIC. — ARITHMETIC. — WEIGHTS. — MEASURES. — CURRENCY. — ASTROLOGY. — MEDICINE. — PAINTING. — STATUARY. — ARCHITECTURE. — JEWELLERY. — IRON-SMELTING. — BLACKSMITHS. — SALTPETRE. — GUNPOWDER. — POTTERY. — WEAVING. — AGRICULTURE.

THE subjects that have just passed in review, — government and religion, are, in respect to those which follow, and which I purpose now briefly to consider, viz. literature, sciences, and the arts, so much in the relation of cause and effect, that a correspondence may always be traced between them. In no part of the world is this correspondence more distinct than in the East; and in no part of the East is it more obvious than in Ceylon.

The language of Ceylon, the Singalese, is not as Mr. Bartolacci supposes, the same as the Siamese *; it is distinct and peculiar. Like most of the Indian languages, its root, in the opinion of the best judges, is the Sanscrit. By those who understand it, it is much admired; its words are harmonious, its compound words very significant, its variety and power of expression great;

* Bartolacci on Ceylon, p. 40.

and as a whole, though complicated, it is not deficient in regularity. The variety of words and expressions in it is so very remarkable, that it may almost be said to contain three distinct vocabularies; — one for use in addressing majesty, another in addressing the ministers of religion, and a third for general use in the common intercourse of society. The distinctions of the language do not terminate here; as the Singalese have high castes and low castes, so they have a high dialect and a low dialect. The former is chiefly employed in serious writing; the latter in familiar conversation: with the former, the inhabitants of the maritime provinces are almost entirely unacquainted; and, in consequence, when one is holding a conversation with a Kandyan priest or chief, on religious or political matters, it is not unusual to hear a common interpreter apologise for inability to do his office, saying, "the language is too high for me." Farther, religion has a distinct language of its own, — a learned and dead language, — the Pali, derived from and said to be very similar to Sanscrit, and common to the priests of Ava and Siam, as well as of Ceylon.

Language is considered of such consequence in the Interior of Ceylon, that it is almost the only subject which is carefully and pretty generally studied there. Very many of the natives are said to be grammatically acquainted with Singalese; every Upasampada priest should be, and is more or less acquainted with Pali, and a few of them are conversant with Sanscrit. Reading and writing are far from uncommon acquirements, and are almost as general as in England amongst the male part of the population, to whom they are chiefly confined: they do not form a part of female education, and in consequence, the very few women who can read and write have taught themselves after marriage.

The Singalese write very neatly and expeditiously, with a sharp-pointed iron style; and, they colour the characters they have scratched by rubbing them with an ink made of lamp-black and a solution of gum. Their books are all manuscript, and actually formed of leaves of trees, and confined by boards. The leaf most used, as best adapted to the purpose, is the immense leaf of the talipot-palm, occasionally nearly thirty feet in circumference. It is well and slowly dried in the shade, rubbed with an oil, and cut into pieces of suitable dimensions, the length of which always greatly exceeds the width; near the two extremities each piece is perforated, that they may be connected by means of a cord, to which the boards also are attached, to form a book. The boards are generally neatly painted and decorated. Occasionally, but rarely, their books are made of thin copperplates.

Figure of a Singalese Book and Style.

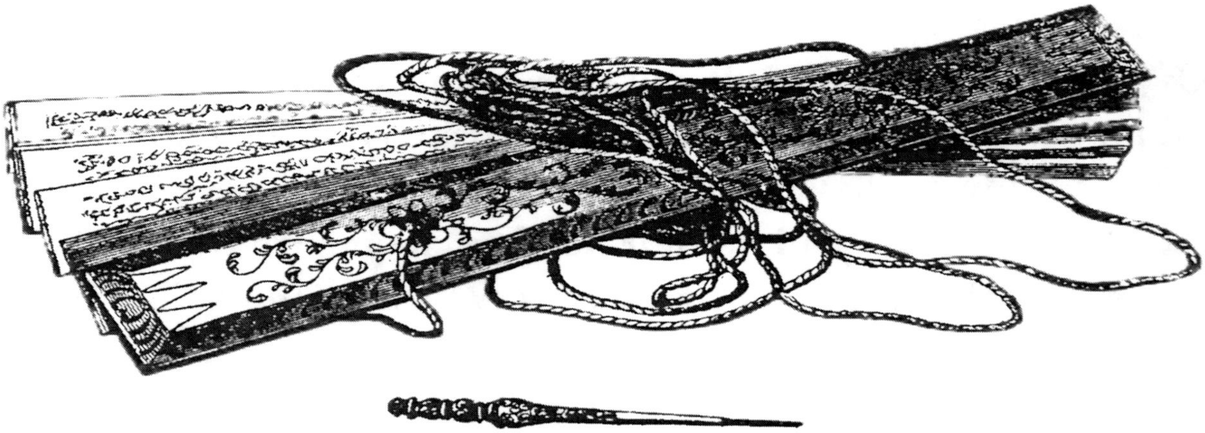

The materials of their writings are durable, and they last much longer than ours, particularly in Ceylon, where our paper is so apt to be destroyed by insects, and our ink to fade. Their books are pretty numerous, and though much more expensive than our printed works, are very much cheaper than MSS. were in Europe before printing was invented.

The subjects of their writings are various; chiefly theology, poetry, history, medicine, and astrology. They compose both in prose and verse. Their compositions on religion are principally in the former; on other subjects, mostly in verse. Whether in verse or prose, their style is completely oriental; and, if I may presume to judge from translations, equally gaudy and obscure. They are extremely fond of intricacies of style, and the more artificial the more it is admired: I have heard a poem spoken of with delight as an extraordinary effort of genius, the peculiar merit of which was, that it admitted a great variety of readings, from the left to the right, up and down, and in many other ways, each way making sense. Those too, who are learned, are very fond of variety of languages as well as of perplexity of style, and will interlard their composition with abundance of Pali and Sanscrit.

Almost every Singalese is, more or less, a poet; or, at least, can compose what they call poetry. Love is not their great inspiring theme, but interest;—a young Kandyan does not indite a ditty to his mistress's eye-brows; the bearded chief is the favourite of his muse, to whom he sings his petition in verse, whether it be to ask a favour, or beg an indulgence. All their poetry is sung or recited: they have seven tunes by which they are modulated. Their most admired tune is called "The

Horse-trot;" from the resemblance which it bears to the sound of the trotting of a horse.

Of their music, which is extremely simple, they are very fond, and prefer it greatly to ours, which, they say, they do not understand. The whole amount of their tunes does not, I believe, exceed the number already mentioned.

Their most common instruments are those of which figures are given:—

1

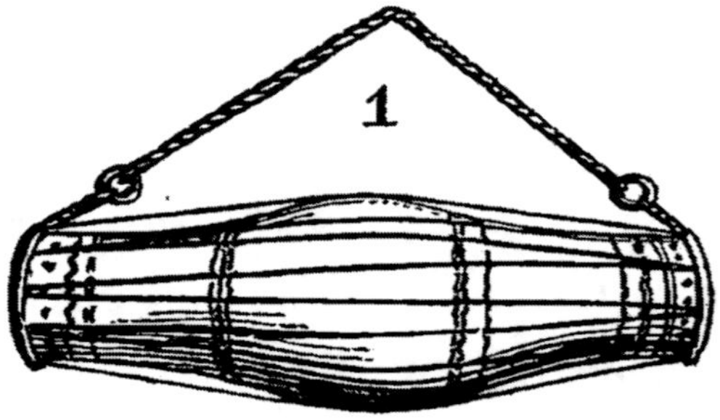

2

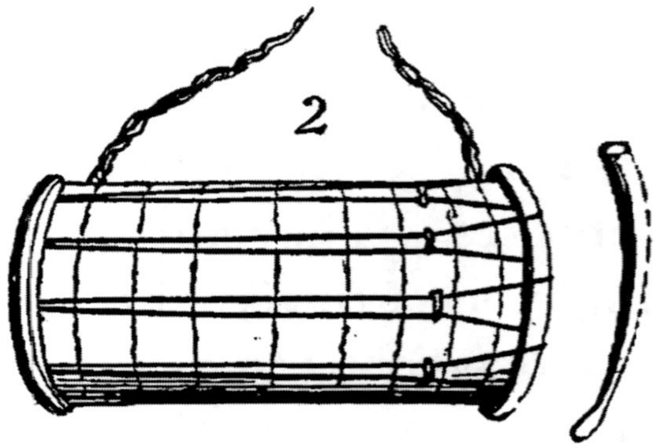

3

4

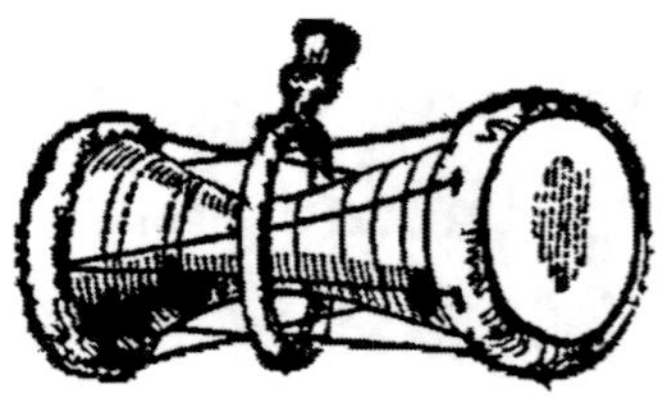

No. 1. The Berrigodea, a kind of long drum, is made of jack-wood, covered with deer's skin, and beat with the hands.

No. 2. The Doula, made like the former, is beat at one end with a stick, and at the other with the hand.

No. 3. The Tam-a-tom, is beat with two sticks, the extremities of which are bent to form circles, and kept in a state of tension.

No. 4. The Udakea, is beat with the fingers.

5

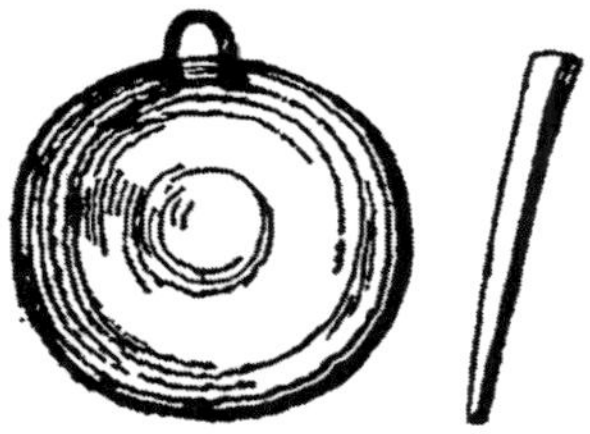

6

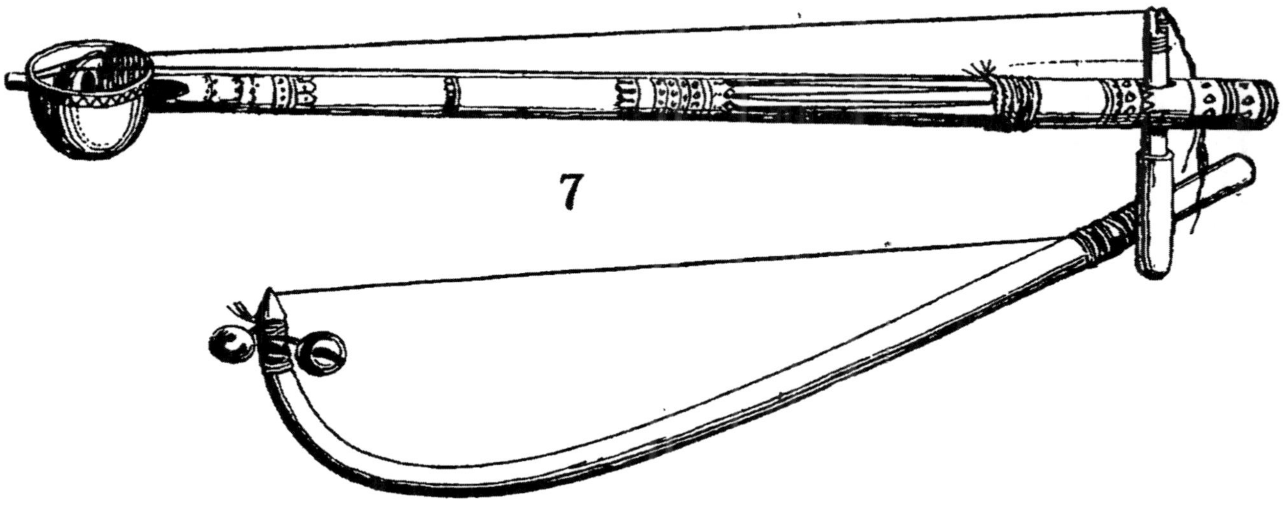

7

No. 5. The Tallea, made of brass, is beat with a stick.

No. 6. The Horanawa; its mouth-piece, is of talipot-leaf, its middle-piece of wood, and the other parts are of brass. The fusiform piece of wood attached, is to separate the bits of leaf forming the mouth-piece, and enlarge the orifice.

No. 7. The Venah, or Venavah, has two strings of different kinds, one made of a species of flax, and the other of horse-hair, which is the material also of the string of the bow, which with bells attached to it, is used as a fiddle-stick. The hollow part of the instrument is half a cocoa-nut shell, polished, covered with the dried skin of a lizard, and perforated below.

All these instruments, with the exception of the Venavah and Udakea, are very noisy, and are seldom used, excepting in temples and in processions. Each kind of drum has a different sound. The Horanawa, the Kandyan pipe, is extremely shrill, and its notes are not unlike the Highland bagpipe. The Venavah is rarely seen, excepting in the hand of some strolling lame or blind son of Apollo, who wanders about the country from house to house, amusing the villagers, and supporting himself by his simple instrument. The Udakea is the favourite domestic instrument. It is usually beat during the recital of a poem, and is the general accompaniment of the song. At night, it is often to be heard in the houses of the Singalese, particularly of the better sort; many of whom spend hours together listening to it, and are in the habit of being lulled to sleep by it; for "nothing (they say) is so tranquillising as sweet poetry, and the gentle Udakea."

The sciences can hardly be said to exist among the Singalese. Of the mathematics and geometry, they appear to be entirely ignorant; even of arithmetic, the extent of their knowledge is extremely limited. They have no figures of their own to represent numbers; and, according to their own method, they are obliged to use letters. These, proving very inconvenient, have fallen into disuse; and, instead of them, they have adopted the Malabar, or Tamul figures, which are on the decimal principle, and simple to express the cardinal numbers, and simple also to express 10, 20, 30, &c. up to 100; and farther, to express 100 and 1000: the intermediate numbers are expressed by combinations of the simple characters; and all sums beyond 1000 are written at length. From the Malabars, too, they have borrowed tables of multiplication and subtraction; but, in the little arithmetical operations they have occasion to make, they use these tables much less than their fingers, which, for purposes of calculation, they manage with great dexterity.

It may be taken for granted, that where arithmetic is in so low a state, weights and measures and currency have had little attention paid to them. Weights are very little employed, except by their gold and silversmiths, and their medical men. By the former, the weights used are, a seed and a brass weight, (the Kalandè,) equal to twenty-four seeds. The seed is red, hard, and heart-shaped, the produce of a large tree, called by the natives Madatea-gah. Different specimens of it, that I have tried, have varied in weight, from 3 to 3.9 grains; their average is about 3.6. The weights used by their medical men are different from the preceding; but of what nature, I did not learn.

Their smallest measure of quantity, whether dry or liquid, is the hundua, equal to a handful; two hunduas are equal to one nellea; four nelleas to one punchy-laha; and one and a half punchy-laha to one lochoo-laha. Farther, ten lochoo-lahas are equal to one pala, and four palas to one ammomam. These latter are merely nominal, to express large quantities. The lochoo-laha is the largest dry-measure in actual use; and, the nellea, equal to eight hunduas, the largest liquid measure. Both kinds are employed only in measuring grain and oil. For grain, the measure is made of rattan; for oil, of bamboo. Their measures vary, like their standard, the human hand, so that no two are to be found exactly alike.

They have in use different measures of distance and space, none of which are very precise. In estimating the distance between place and place, their smallest measure in common use is the whoo, a loud hollo; two of which are considered equal to an attakmè; four of the latter to a gow, and five gows make a day's journey, i. e. about five-and-twenty or thirty miles. The bamba and the bandera-bamba, which are occasionally used, are rather more precise measures of distance. The former is considered equal to the space between the arms extended, measuring from the tips of the fingers, and is about six feet; and, the latter, about nine feet, is equal to the height to which a man can reach above his head with his hand. The bandera-bamba, 500 of which make an attakmè, was employed on one or two occasions by the late king in measuring roads. Besides the preceding, they have other measures both smaller and larger. Their smallest measure is the seventh part of a veetè (a grain of paddy); seven veetès are equal to one angula; seven angulas to one veata; nine veatas to one doona *; 500 doonas to one attakmè; four attakmès to one gow, and four gows to one youdoona. Carpenters and some other artists have measures of their own. The carpenter's angula is equal to the space between the second and third joint of the fore-finger; and his wadduranea is composed of twenty-four angulas, and is divided into four

* The Singalese bow (doona) is usually about nine feet long.

parts. Strictly, they have no land-measure; they apply that of grain to land, and taking the nature of the soil into account, form their estimate by the quantity of seed required; an ammomam of land being that which requires an ammomam of seed.

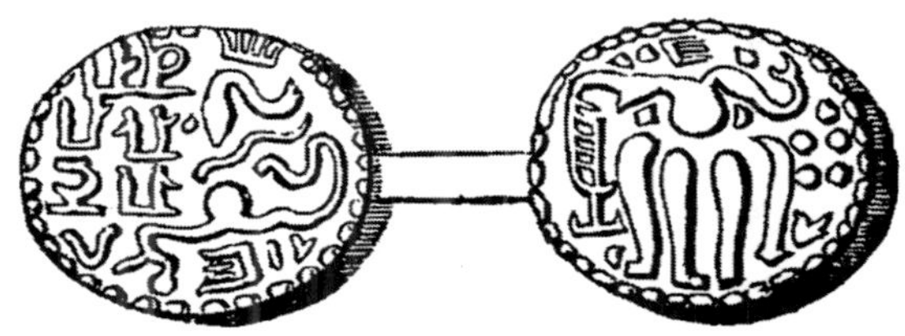

The Singalese currency consists of gold, silver, and copper coin. The Indian pagodah is the only gold coin now to be met with. Lately, an antique gold coin, called a Dambadinia rhatra, was found in the neighbourhood of Dambadinia in the Seven Korles, which was probably struck there, when it was a place of royal residence. This coin exactly resembles in size and appearance the Dambadinia chally, which will be mentioned presently. The silver coin in circulation, called a riddy or rheedy, is worth about seven pence English, and is equivalent to sixty-four Kandyan challies. Its form is singular; it resembles a fish-hook, and is merely a piece of thick silver wire bent. The chally * is a copper coin, of which two kinds are to be met with, — Dutch challies, which are common, and the Dambadinia challies, which are scarce. The characters on this ancient coin, of which a fac-

* Rhatra signifies gold; Riddy, silver; Chally, copper.

simile is given, resemble more hieroglyphics than letters; the natives are ignorant of their meaning, which has not yet been ascertained. In the habit of bartering what they have superfluous for what they want, money is but little used by the Singalese; and the quantity of it in their possession of every kind must be extremely small, particularly of gold and silver. One may form an idea of this by the circumstance, that the total revenue in specie of the late king, who exacted as much as possible, did not exceed in value 1,500l. sterling.

Slight notice has already been taken of the ideas which the Singalese entertain of the heavenly bodies. Ignorant of astronomy, they are very much addicted to astrology. Each of their seven days they have put under the superintendence of a planet; and each of the sixty hours, into which they divide the day, under that of a star. They have an astrological as well as a lunar month, divided into twenty-seven days, corresponding to the number of their astrological stars or constellations, and like them called nekat; and each of these days, or each nekata, is divided and subdivided in a very complicated manner. No people ever were, or can be more devoted to this delusive art than the Singalese: their faith is implicit in it, and the stronger, since they can assign no reason for it; it is fixed, they say, that the stars should influence the affairs of mankind, and their agency is the necessary consequence of certain relative positions. Their practice is conformable to their faith, and a strong proof of their complete conviction. Their actions, in consequence, are in a great measure regulated by the movements of the stars. It is as common, almost, for a native to enquire the nekata of the time, as to ask the hour of the day. The first object of parents on the birth of a child, is to have his nativity cast and his horoscope made out, which is of more importance to the Kandyan through life than any certified extract from a parish register is to an European. Not the hour of celebrating a marriage can be fixed, nor indeed a match be made in high life, without the aid of the astrologer, who, in more than one instance, has prevented the union of those whose circumstances were most suitable, but were unfortunately born under hostile stars. We have already seen the important part which the astrologer acts in the great national festivals: in private life the calls on him to determine fortunate hours are innumerable; and a man would be considered very imprudent, were he to begin sowing a field, or were he to set out on a journey, in ignorance of the nekata of the time: indeed, in all the affairs of life, astrology is consulted, from the most important down to the most trivial, and in public matters as well as in private. It is worth remarking, that their astrologers, by means of tables of the places of the sun and moon, introduced from the continent of India, can calculate eclipses with considerable precision.

Their knowledge of medicine, and of its collateral branches, is of a piece with their astrological knowledge; and, as on the one subject, so on the other, they have built up a system of their own, founded merely on fancy, and equally complicated and erroneous.

As they have an abhorrence of dead bodies, by the mere touching of which they consider themselves polluted, they are completely ignorant of anatomy; and are no better acquainted with the true structure of the human body, than they are with that of the universe.

Nor can they be said to have any knowledge of chemistry; besides making infusions, decoctions, and extracts, the only chemical operation they are acquainted with, is distillation, which is occasionally practised to procure distilled waters for medical purposes, but more frequently to obtain an intoxicating liquor, which too many of the natives drink, though prohibited by their religion. The still they use is of earthen-ware, and of the simplest construction; the only one I ever saw was of this kind:

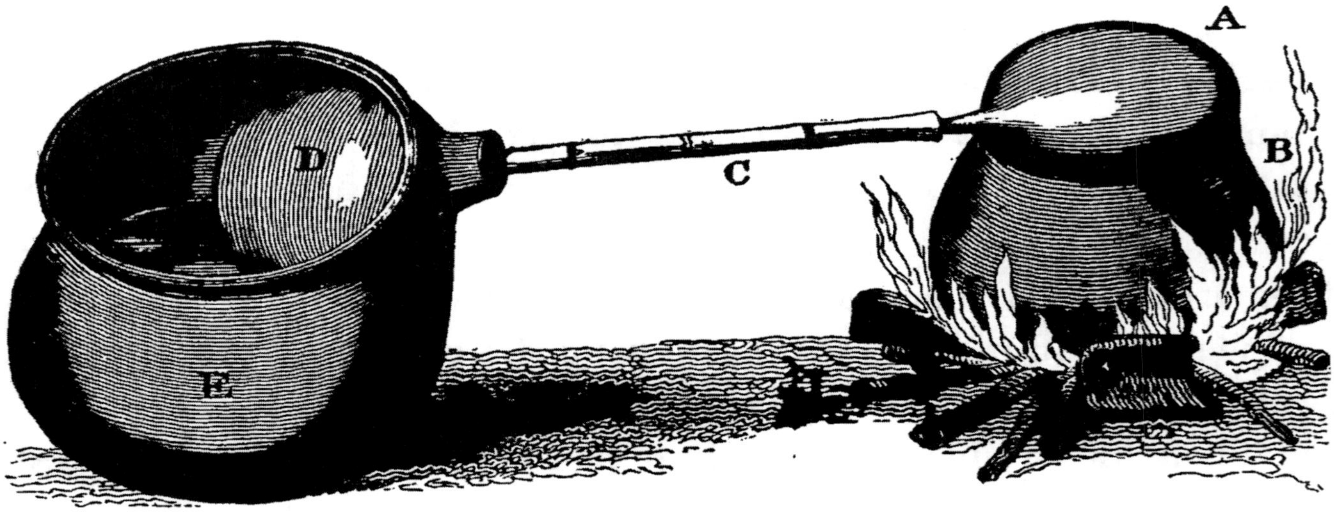

An alembic and capital luted together; a refrigeratory and receiver, of one piece, and the latter connected with the capital by a bamboo. With this rude apparatus, an ardent spirit (arrack) is procured with the greatest facility from toddy, the fermented juice of the cocoa-nut tree.

Their knowledge of pharmacy is equally limited. The articles of their materia medica consist chiefly of simples, in the form of powders, infusions, and extracts; of a few fixed oils, obtained by expression or boiling; and of a very few metallic preparations, as mercury, incorporated with some fat or viscid substance;

arsenic, in the state of white oxide; and copper, gold, and silver, in the form of powders.

Surgery amongst them is in an extremely rude state. The surgical operations they perform are chiefly those of cauterizing and cupping, and opening boils; even bloodletting is seldom practised by them; and, during the last forty years, the only great operation performed in Kandy was the amputation of a leg, which was accomplished in the ancient manner, by means of a knife heated to dull redness.

Their physiology, as might be conjectured, is of the most fanciful kind. By means of their four common elements,—earth, water, air, and fire, to which some add a fifth,—ether; by means of their seven elements, or proximate principles of the animal body, viz. skin, blood, flesh, fat, bone, marrow, and the spermatic fluid; and, lastly, by means of their three humours, phlegm, bile, and wind, they conceive that they can account for every function of the animal economy, and for all the actions of the system, whether regular or deranged, whether in health or sickness.

Their pathology is of the same notional kind, and is entirely founded on the wild hypothesis of the preceding principles. They have imagined 572 different combinations of circumstances, or causes of disease, and the same number of diseases corresponding to them; of these, 140 they suppose arise from errors of the three humours, and the rest from faults of the humours and elements, and excrementitious parts conjointly.

Their nosology, embracing these 572 diseases, is founded on their pathology. In it, diseases are not considered as combinations of symptoms; on the contrary, almost each symptom and each modification of a symptom, is considered a distinct disease;

and, thus, with the help of imaginary causes, their catalogue of disorders is so prolonged.

Their practice is rather theoretical than empyrical, and is directed to obviate causes, rather than palliate symptoms, or to attempt a cure on the ground of experience alone. The general indications, in their practice, are, first, to ripen or maturate the disease; and, secondly, to remove it. As they leave a great deal to nature, their ignorance and false principles are not very mischievous; and they probably do, on the whole, though little good, more good than harm. The education and qualifications of a physician are most strongly characteristic of the state of the art. Besides an acquaintance with all that has been alluded to, a Singalese, to be an accomplished and scientific physician, should be an astrologer, that he may know what concern the stars have had in producing a disease, what are the best times for exhibiting medicines, and what are the most appropriate periods for culling simples. He should be a physiognomist, that he may form a judgment of any case he may be called to, as well from the countenance of the messenger, as of the patient himself. He should be an adept in interpreting deams, that he may anticipate the future relative to the fate of his patient, form a correct prognosis, and avail himself of any hints the gods may be pleased to send through this obscure channel. And, he should be endowed with the faculty of inferring, from the first appearance of the disease, whether it be the result of a temporary cause deranging the humours, or the consequence of some crime committed in a former state of existence. All this is too absurd to dwell on; and every part of their system of medicine is full of such absurdities; so that one can derive certainly no satisfaction, nor gain any useful knowledge, from considering it;

excepting, perhaps, so far as it shows the extraordinary errors and delusions the human mind is liable to, when it follows fancy as a guide, instead of reason, and exercises implicit belief without judgment.

In the arts, the Singalese have made more progress than in the sciences; particularly in some of the ornamental or fine arts. Of these, painting is the least advanced. Ignorant of perspective, they rarely attempt landscape-drawing; and, even at representing single figures they are far from successful, their drawing being always faulty from the erroneous rules by which they are guided. Not acquainted with the effect of light and shade in colouring, their only aim is gaudiness of effect. The pigments which they employ, are few in number, and of a pretty permanent nature: their yellow paints I have ascertained to be orpiment and gamboge; their blue, a preparation of indigo, containing a good deal of earthy matter; their red, cinnabar and red ochre; their white, a native mineral already described, (a mixture of carbonat of lime and carbonat of magnesia, nearly in the state of chalk); and their black, lamp-black. All these paints they use mixed with gum. Of oil-painting they are entirely ignorant. Some notion may be formed of the state of the art amongst the Singalese from the specimens of their paintings contained in this work; for the best of which, — that representing the late King of Kandy about to take the air, surrounded by his courtiers, — I am indebted to my friend Mr. Finlayson, who got it executed by an artist of high reputation amongst his countrymen for skill and talent. (Plate V.)

Lacker-painting is an art much used by the Singalese, and of which they are very fond. The lacker they employ is a substance which has never yet been examined, I believe, and which possesses some peculiar properties. It is called by the natives kapitia; and is procured from a shrub of the same name, (*Croton lacciferum*,) of very common occurrence in most parts of Ceylon. It exists in the sap of the plant, as I have ascertained by experiment. Occasionally exuding, it collects on the branches in drops like common gum. It is either of a light yellow colour and translucent, or of a dirty brown and opaque. The drops are generally hollow, strongly adhering, and neither easily broken nor detached. They have no taste; but a slight, peculiar, and agreeable aromatic smell. After fusion, to get rid of entangled air, I have found the specific gravity of this substance to be 1024. When heated, it begins to soften at 150° Fahrenheit; at 220° it is almost liquid, and may be drawn out into the finest threads. In this state it is extremely adhesive. On cooling, when its temperature is reduced below 150°, it becomes solid and hard. Strongly heated, it takes fire and burns with a bright flame. From the experiments I have made on it, it proves to be a resin, that is pretty soluble in ether and alcohol, and almost insoluble in oil of turpentine. In the translucent drops, in which it is almost pure, I could detect only slight traces of gallic acid, and of extractive. In the dirty-brown opaque drops it contains more of these substances, and a good deal of woody fibre, probably derived from the bark. To purify it for use, the natives macerate it, about twenty-four hours, in an infusion of the alburnum of the *mimosa cæsia*, which is slightly acrid, and dry it, after having well rubbed it in a coarse cloth and washed it frequently with the infusion, to separate as much as possible of the adhering impurities. To purify it still further, they put the dried kapitia into a long cylindrical linen bag, open at one end, and at the other fixed to a stick. This they hold over a charcoal fire; and, when the kapitia is sufficiently softened by the heat, they twist the ends of the bag different ways, applying pressure by torsion, till the whole of the resin has exuded, which is scraped off with a blunt knife as it is expressed. They have succeeded in imparting to kapitia four different colours, green, red, yellow, and black: an attempt, they say, was once made to invent a fifth colour, but it failed. The colouring matter is incorporated by beating with a hammer, the heat produced by the percussion being sufficient to keep the kapitia soft. It is coloured red with cinnabar; black, with lamp-black; yellow, with orpiment; and green, by beating together a portion of yellow resin and of resin coloured of a dirty bluish-green with indigo. The lackerer, when about to exercise his art, seats himself on the ground by a charcoal fire, and arranges his materials around him, — as pieces of kapitia differently coloured, a small stick to fasten the resin to that he may expose it to the fire, and a bit of the leaf of the Palmyra-palm as a polisher; and besides these, with the exception of a very long nail on the thumb of his left hand, which he uses as a cutting instrument, he requires nothing else for his most delicate work. Whether it be wood or ivory that he undertakes to lacker, it must be perfectly clean. The resin is drawn out into round threads and flat filaments of various dimensions, as required, and applied cold to the heated surface, to which it immediately adheres. Many of the Singalese perform this kind of work with a good deal of skill and taste, and often produce a very pretty and brilliant effect. It is chiefly used to ornament bows and arrows, spears, sticks, ivory boxes, priests' screens or fans, and wooden pillars. The excellence of this species of lackering is its great strength and durability; it lasts as long as the surface to which it is applied, and retains its brilliancy of colouring to the last. Could it be collected in sufficient quantity, (I am afraid it cannot,) it might be worthy of trial in this country.

From the greater facility of attaining a certain excellence in the art, and from the greater encouragement given to it, the efforts of the Singalese in statuary have been more successful than in painting. As in ancient Greece, their religion offers a never-failing subject, and every temple affords employment. Boodhoo is the most common subject of their statuary: figures of him of all sizes are to be seen in their temples; gigantic ones of masonry, twenty and thirty feet long; others no larger than life, of clay, wood, or marble; and very many of a diminutive size of more precious materials. Artists are restricted in their designs to three postures, the standing, sitting and recumbent, and to the priestly costume; and they would be guilty of impiety, were they to introduce in the representation of the object of their worship any the least innovation. They are in the constant habit of colouring their statues, which adds much to their lively appearance; and they give a pupil to the eye, which animates the figure still more. The finishing the eye is considered an important and mysterious operation, and it is performed with a good deal of ceremony. Before it is accomplished, the image is merely an image — a stock or a stone; but when it is completed, it is esteemed by all but the priests, as something more, as something divine; and, not till then the artist falls down and worships the work of his own hands as a god.

The art of casting amongst the Singalese is certainly not behind that of sculpture. It is chiefly exercised in making small figures, many of which, of brass and copper, are very neatly executed. There is now in Kandy a figure of Boodhoo in copper, in a sitting posture, as large as life, so well done that it would be admired even in Europe.

In architecture, I am not aware that the Singalese can be said to have any national or any very peculiar style. In no country is much greater variety to be seen, or much stronger marks afforded to trace the progress of the art. Rock-temples, which are very numerous in the Interior, may, with the exception of their embellishments, be considered rather the work of nature than of art. Buildings in the Hindoo style, next to the rock-temple the least artificial, are here and there to be met with in ruins. In viewing the dewalés, or the temples of the gods, one is occasionally reminded of Grecian architecture ; and in viewing their wiharés, one is often strongly reminded of the Chinese style of building ; indeed, the temples of Boodhoo in general have a very Tartar aspect. In some old ruins, the arch is to be seen without the principle of the arch, formed of stones laid horizontally, and projecting one beyond the other on each side till they meet above ; and in some comparatively modern buildings, the arch regularly constructed with a key-stone may be found. Judging from the remains of antiquity that are to be met with here and there in Ceylon, it may be inferred, that architecture, for at least one or two centuries past, has been on the decline. All the public buildings that are now in a state of preservation in the Interior, are comparatively small ; and few, if any of them excite a lively interest in the spectator. Many of their rock-temples are much more curious and impressive, particularly one which will be described hereafter, and which may be considered one of the wonders of Ceylon. Their domestic architecture is of the most unassuming character, in which appearance is sacrificed to convenience and economy. Their best houses, those of the chiefs, are of mud with tiled roofs, raised on a low terrace, and always of a single story, built in the form of hollow squares; presenting externally a dead wall, and internally bordering the open area a verandah, with which the side-rooms communicate by narrow doors. A large establishment consists of many such squares communicating by passages inside, and having only one or two entrances from without. Most of their rooms are dark, or only furnished with windows hardly large enough to admit the human head. The floors are of clay plastered with cow-dung*, and the walls are either covered with the same composition or with a wash of white clay, the use of lime for the purpose being prohibited, and appropriated solely to royal palaces and temples. The dwellings of the people in general are much on the same plan, and differ little, excepting in size, and in the circumstance that they are invariably thatched; only those of the highest rank being permitted to have tiled roofs. The royal palaces too were constructed nearly on the same model, and differed very little more from the residences of the chiefs, than these did from the dwellings of the people.

The accompanying wood-cuts will give some idea of the different kinds of building alluded to. — No. 1. is a sketch of a small portion of an ancient Hindoo pagoda that still remains at Trincomalie, situated on the extreme and lofty point of the promontory on which Fort Frederic stands. No. 2. represents a small dewalé in the neighbourhood of Trincomalie, dedicated to Ganesa, and to which most of the dewalès in the Interior bear

* To an European this may suggest the idea of filth, but erroneously; it is used for the sake of cleanliness and to keep off insects, and answers the purpose extremely well.

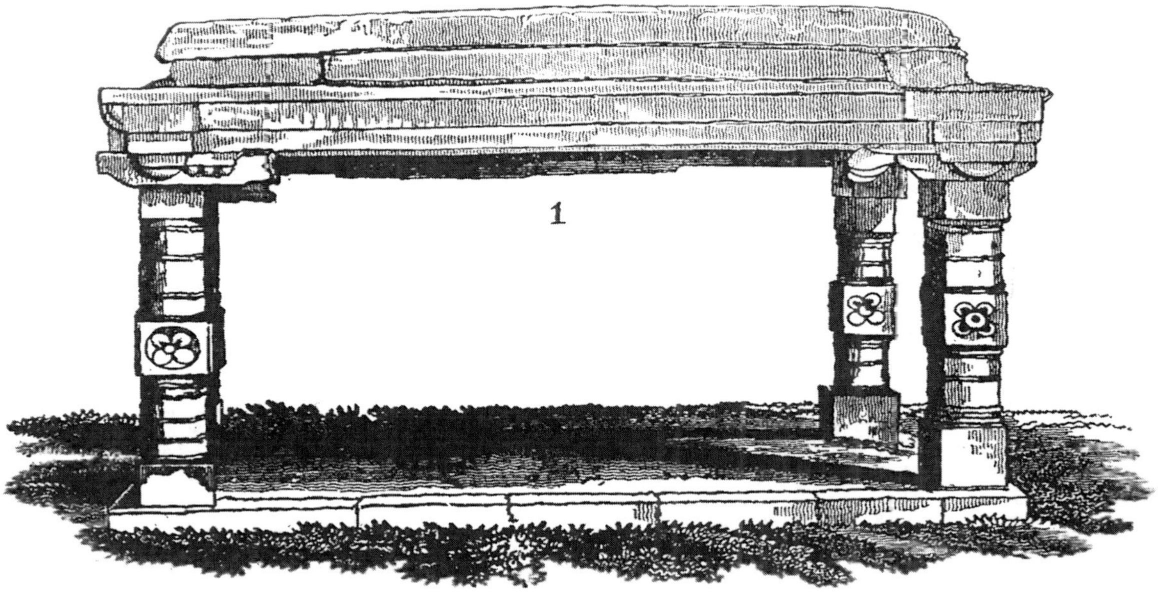

1

2

a close resemblance. Nos. 3, and 4. are sketches of two wiharés or temples of Boodhoo in the neighbourhood of Kandy: the

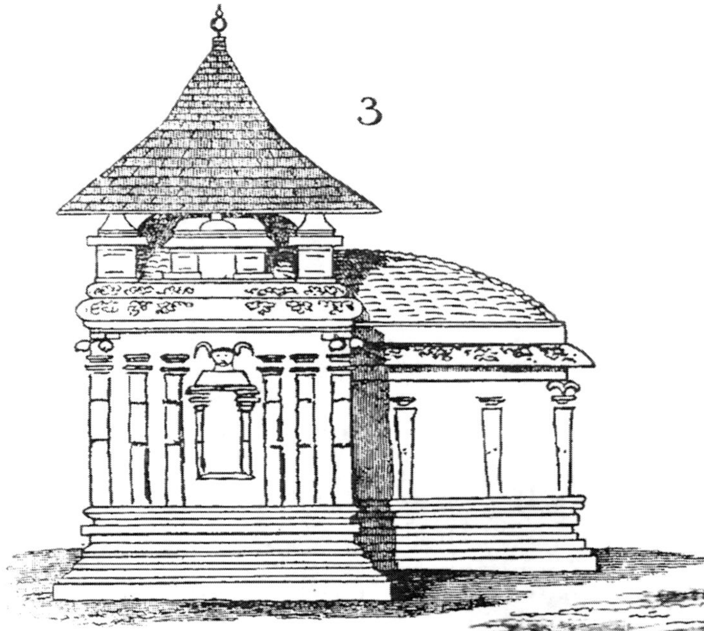

3

4

5

latter is the more common form of the wiharé; the former is built rather in the style of a dewalé. No. 5. represents the

Dagobah, which is generally attached to a wiharé, and is the receptacle of a relic. No. 6. is a Singalese farm-house.

6

The Singalese work in gold and silver with considerable dexterity and taste; and, with means that appear very inadequate, execute articles of jewellery that would be admired certainly in this country, and not very easily imitated. The best artist requires only the following apparatus and tools: — a low earthen pot full of chaff or saw-dust, on which he makes a little charcoal fire; a small bamboo blow-pipe, about six inches long, with which he excites the fire; a short earthen tube or nozle, the extremity of which is placed at the bottom of the fire, and through which the artist directs the blast of the blow-pipe; two or three small crucibles made of the fine clay of ant-hills; a pair of tongs; an anvil; two or three small hammers; a file; and, to conclude the list, a few small bars of iron and brass, about

two inches long, differently pointed for different kinds of work. It is astonishing what an intense little fire, more than sufficiently strong to melt silver and gold, can be kindled in a few minutes in the way just described. Such a simple portable forge deserves to be better known: it is perhaps even deserving the attention of the scientific experimenter, and may be useful to him when he wishes to excite a small fire, larger than can be produced by the common blow-pipe, and he has not a forge at command. The success of the little Singalese forge, I hardly need remark, depends a good deal on the bed of the fire being composed of a combustible material and a very bad conductor of heat.

The Singalese excel rather in the setting than in the cutting of the precious stones; and, particularly the Singalese of the Interior, who have had little practice in the art, it having been the fashion at the court of Kandy to wear jewels uncut, or at least only rounded and polished.

In the account I have given of the gems of the island, I did not mention the manner in which they are sought for. The mode is so simple, that it hardly deserves the name of an art. It is only in alluvial ground, it has been remarked, that these scarce and beautiful minerals have yet been discovered in Ceylon.

Where there is a probability of finding them, pits are sunk from three to twenty feet deep; the coarse sand and gravel through which they are generally disseminated, is collected and carried in baskets to an adjoining stream, where it is well washed; the lighter particles are got rid of by a rotary motion given to the basket in the operation; and the residue, still wet, is transferred to shallow baskets for careful examination. Not only gems, the great object of the search, are collected, but every stone that has the least chance of finding a purchaser in the market. Like mining in general, the occupation of searching for gems is a very precarious one: in Ceylon it cannot be considered a profitable pursuit; and there is good reason to believe that the individuals engaged in it, who are not very numerous, and chiefly moormen, would be better employed in cultivating the ground that they ransack.

Ores of iron and of manganese, it has been observed, are the only ones that have yet been discovered in Ceylon. With the mode of reducing the former, and of working the iron which they extract, the natives are well acquainted. Their process of smelting iron, like most of their other processes, is chiefly remarkable for its simplicity. The most complete Singalese smelting-house

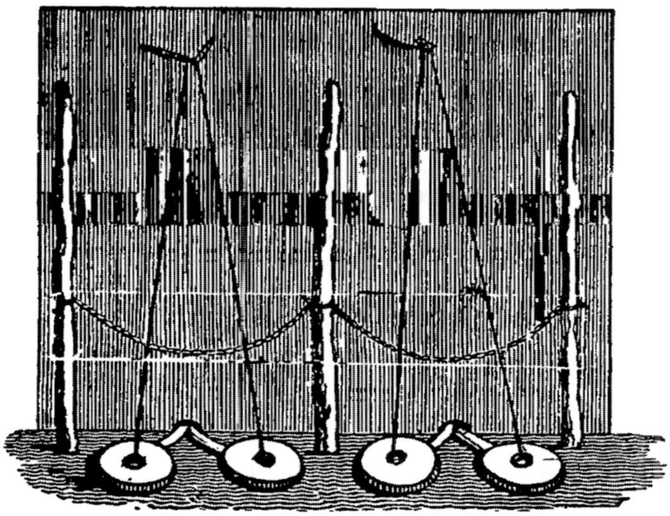

that I ever visited, consisted of two small furnaces under a thatched shed.

Each furnace, at its mouth, was about one foot four inches, by eight inches in diameter; about three feet deep, and terminated in the form of a funnel, over a shallow pit inclining outwards. They were made in a bed of clay, about three feet high and three feet wide, against which a light wall, about ten feet high, was raised, to protect the bellows and operators, who were situated immediately behind. Each bellows consisted of a circular rim of wood, about six inches in diameter, and scarcely two high, fixed on a clay floor, and covered with moist cow-hide; in the centre of which was a hole to admit air, and to receive a cross stick, to which a cord was attached, that was fastened above to an elastic stick. Each pair of bellows was worked by a boy, who rested his back against a rope, for the purpose of support, and stepped alternately from the orifice of one bellows to that of the other, at each step forcing a blast of air into the furnace, through a tube of bamboo. The furnaces were charged with a mixture of iron ore, broken into small pieces, and charcoal. The fires were kept up as strong as possible, till the ore was reduced, and the fused metal collected in a cake in the ash-pit. Here the labour of the smelter terminated: he sold the crude metal, without subjecting it to any farther operation; leaving it to the blacksmith to purify and bring to a malleable state, fit for working. It is generally remarked, that the ruder the method employed in any country for the reduction of iron, the better the quality of the metal is: the observation holds good in Ceylon; and there is a pretty obvious reason why it should be correct. Where the art is little advanced, the most tractable ores must be selected, and charcoal is the fuel always used, — circumstances alone which are sufficient to account for the iron obtained being excellent. The mode of purifying the metal, employed by the blacksmith, consists merely in the repeated operation of heating it in a charcoal fire, and of hammering it till it is sufficiently malleable. Whether the Singalese know how to make steel, I have not ascertained in a satisfactory manner: I rather think they do; they are in the constant practice of case-hardening, which they accomplish by cementing the soft iron, covered with a paste, composed of a variety of vegetables, in a charcoal fire. It is of little consequence, probably, what vegetables are used for the purpose, though the artist, who considers the process a mystery, and keeps the particulars of it secret, is of a different opinion.

The Singalese blacksmith, in the exercise of his art, is far from unskilful: he is on a par, perhaps, with the common country blacksmith in any part of Europe; and his smithery is almost as well provided with tools. I do not believe that he ever employs, or is even acquainted with, the vice. He uses an instrument for drilling holes in iron and brass, called Tarapane, that answers the purpose extremely well, and is really ingenious.

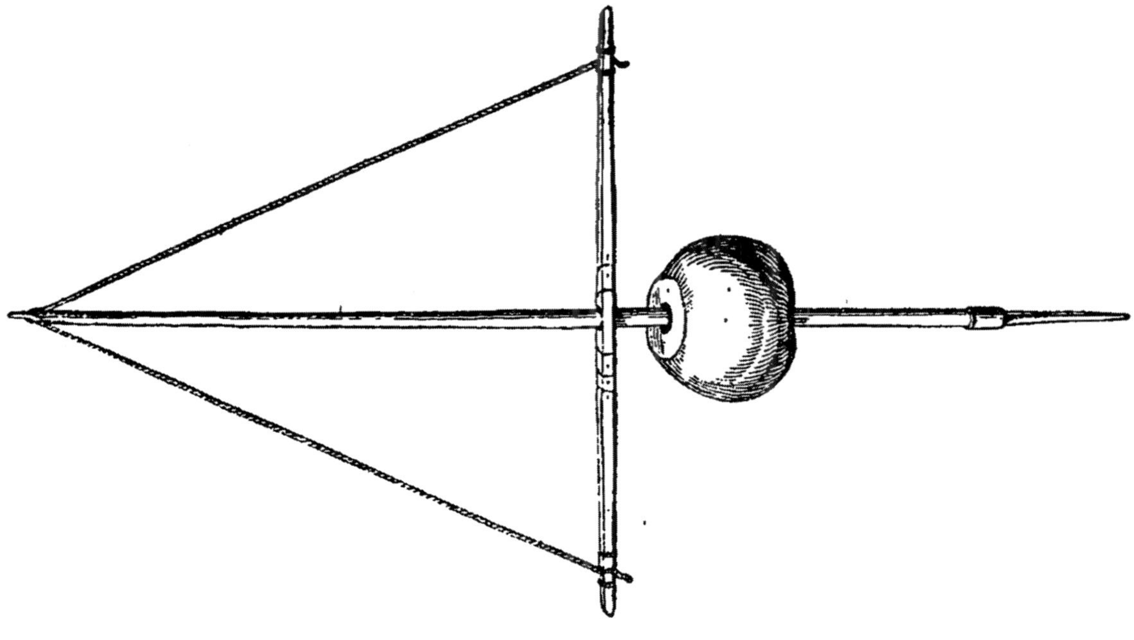

It is about two feet and a half high: the cord attached to the cross-stick is made of slips of hide twisted. The round weight, to give momentum, in the instrument I examined, was of compact gneiss, neatly cut. Any kind of borer can be fixed to the extremity of the wooden rod. The instrument is worked on the principle of torsion. No blacksmiths, perhaps, have a greater variety of bellows than the Singalese. Occasionally, they use the one already described; occasionally, one resembling a common English bellows; and sometimes, as a substitute, a couple of bags made of bullocks' hides, each furnished with a bamboo nozle and a long slit as a mouth, with wooden lips, that are opened and drawn up, and shut and pressed down alternately, by the hands of a person sitting between the pair, who keeps up a constant blast by the alternate action of the two.

It would be tedious to enumerate the variety of work a native blacksmith is equal to; — locks, and even gun-locks and gun-barrels, do not exceed his abilities. The workmanship of them is indeed coarse, and not to be praised; but still, they answer pretty well the purpose for which they were intended, and give satisfaction to those unacquainted with better. The smiths use a composition, as a hone for sharpening knives and cutting-instruments, that is worth noticing. It is made of the kapitia resin, and of corundum. The corundum, in a state of impalpable powder, is mixed with the resin, rendered liquid by heat, and well incorporated. The mixture is poured into a wooden mould, and its surface levelled and smoothed whilst it is still hot; for when cold it is extremely hard. It is much valued by the natives, and preferred by them to the best of our hones. The method which the Singalese smiths, and, indeed, people in general, employ to prevent iron tools from rusting, is also not undeserving of notice. They cover them with a thin coating of melted bees-wax, and either bury them, or leave them in the open air, quite secure of their being out of danger of spoiling.

The preparing of saltpetre, and the manufacture of gunpowder, are arts which the Singalese for many years have constantly practised. A list of the principal caves has been given, in which saltpetre has been made. The process of preparing the salt, in different parts of the country, was very similar. When the salt occurred impregnating the surface of the rock, as in the cave near Memoora, the surface was chipped off with small strong axes, and the chippings, by pounding, were reduced to the state of a powder. This powder, or the loose fine earth which, in most of the caves, contained the saline impregnation, was well mixed with an equal quantity of wood-ash. * The mixture was thrown

* Such a quantity must appear very large; but I do not believe it is more than is required to decompose the whole of the nitrat of lime, that accompanies the salt-

on a filter formed of matting, and washed with cold water. The washings of the earth were collected in an earthen vessel, and evaporated at a boiling temperature till concentrated to that degree, that a drop let fall on a leaf became a soft solid. The concentrated solution was set aside; and when it had crystallized, the whole was put on a filter of mat. The mother-lye that passed through, still rich in saltpetre, was added to a fresh weak solution, to be evaporated again; and the crystals, after having been examined, and freed from any other crystals of a different form, were either immediately dried, or, if not sufficiently pure, re-dissolved and crystallised afresh. The operations just described were generally carried on at the nitre-caves. In the province of the Seven Korles, besides extracting the salt at the caves, the workmen brought a quantity of the earth to their houses, where, keeping it under a shed protected from the wind and rain, without any addition excepting a little wood-ash, they obtained from it, every third year, a fresh quantity of salt. After twenty-one years, or seven repetitions of the operation, the earth was considered unfit for farther use, and was thrown away. Whether the Singalese found out themselves, or learnt from the Portuguese, the advantage attending the addition of wood-ash, in the manufacture of saltpetre, and the possibility of extracting from the same earth, after rest, fresh quantities of salt, it is not easy to determine; certainly, in their process they exhibit more address than could be expected from them, and much more than

---

petre. The proportion of alkali in the ash of large trees in Ceylon, which are usually burnt for the purpose in question, is very small: in one specimen that I examined, I found only three and a half per cent. of carbonat of potash; carbonat of lime was the principal ingredient.

is exhibited by the natives of the continent of India, whose invention, perhaps, has been less stimulated, — the source from which they extract their nitre (the general soil of the country) being richer, and, on account of its extent, inexhaustible. What quantity of saltpetre the Singalese obtained from their different caves, it is impossible to calculate with any precison; no doubt it was considerable, and equal, if not more than equal, to the consumption of the article, for none was imported. Since we have had possession of the country, the manufacture has, in a great measure, been stopped; and lately, on account of political motives, it has been prohibited. Now the Interior is again tranquillized, I believe the workings might be renewed with advantage, and with profit to the government. It is hardly necessary to give the particular reasons that could be assigned for such an opinion, as the subject is not of general interest, nor, comparatively, of much importance.

In their mode of manufacturing gunpowder, which is very generally understood, there is not the least refinement. To proportion the constituent parts, scales are used, but not weights. The proportions commonly employed are, five parts of saltpetre, and one of each of the other ingredients, — sulphur and charcoal. The charcoal preferred is made of the wood of the parwatta-tree (*pavetta indica*). The ingredients, moistened with very weak lime-water and a little of the acrid juice of the wild yam (*arum maerorhizon*), are ground together between two flat stones, or pounded in a rice-mortar. After the grinding or pounding is completed, the moist mass is exposed to the sunshine to dry. Nothing farther is done to it; no attempt is ever made to granulate it; and, it is used in the state of a very coarse powder, or impalpable dust. Considering the rudeness of the method, the gunpowder is better than could be expected : some specimens of it that I have examined have inflamed readily, exploded pretty strongly, and have left little residue. Why they use lime-water, or the acrid juice of the wild yam, they themselves cannot assign a reason. Perhaps the latter is employed with the idea of rendering the powder more active; and, what corroborates the notion, is, that in some parts of the country arrack is used instead. According to their own account, they first learnt from the Portuguese the use of fire-arms, and the art of making them, and of manufacturing gunpowder; of both which they were completely ignorant before they had any intercourse with Europeans.

The pottery of the Singalese is coarse and unglazed, and rather useful than ornamental; though the forms of some of their vessels are elegant, and of a very antique appearance.

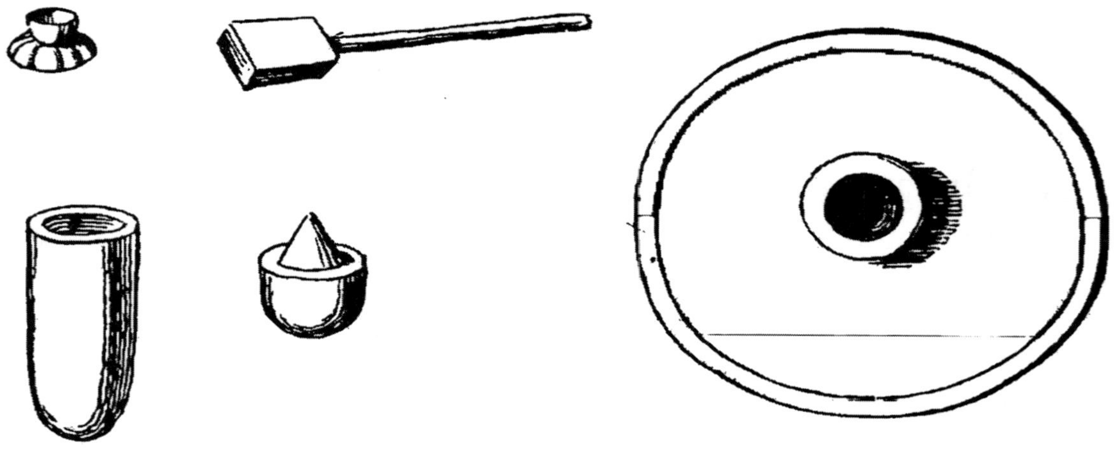

In the manufacture, besides a wooden mallet, and a smooth stone to oppose to it, they use only a wooden wheel, which is turned by the hands of an assistant, and revolves on a neatly formed pivot of stone, that moves in a cavity of a cylindrical stone, fixed in the ground, and sunk to the depth of two-thirds of its whole length. The cavity is well smeared with oil. The head of the pivot is firmly attached by the glutinous matter of the jack-fruit, to a cavity in the middle of the under-surface of the wheel These two stones, called by the Singalese koodogalle, are the most valuable parts of the apparatus; they last in continued use about forty years, and constitute the present which is usually given by a potter to his son on his marriage.

The art of weaving has made very little progress amongst the Singalese. Their loom is of the rudest construction, resembling the primitive loom, that may be seen still in some parts of Ireland; it is worked by the artist sitting on the ground, with his legs in a pit, dug for the purpose of receiving them.

No muslins are made in the country, and no kind of cloth excepting the coarse, strong, and serviceable cotton-cloth, which is worn by the common people.

Agriculture, the most important and the last of the Singalese arts that require particular mention, is in no part of the world more respected or more followed than in the Interior of Ceylon. In common with all the other arts, it is marked by its great simplicity. The cultivation, in which the natives engage, is almost exclusively of two kinds, — dry and wet. The former kind is chiefly carried on on the sides of hills, or on plains where there is no command of water. When the ground is covered with underwood, as it usually is, it is called a Chenas. The operation of cultivating such ground commences, in the dry season, with cutting down the underwood, strongly fencing, and burning in heaps the dried wood not used in making the fence. No sooner is the surface thus cleared, than the ground is dug up and sown. During the whole time the crop is in the ground, it is nightly watched, to defend it from wild animals, as deer, hogs, elephants, &c. which abound in most parts of the country, and are the farmer's greatest enemies. Some of the dry crops are weeded; and, this excepted, nothing is done to them from the time of sowing to that of reaping, or, when the straw is not saved, of gathering the heads of corn. The grains most cultivated in dry grounds are corrican or natchiné, a variety of rice and Indian corn. The same ground will not bear two years successively, partly for want of manure, which the natives never use; but chiefly on account of the underwood, which not having been eradicated in the first instance, presently springs up, and before twelve months have expired, is a luxuriant crop of itself. The cultivation of dry crops is chiefly engaged in by the poorer people, and is of very little importance in comparison with the wet kind, which is solely devoted to rice, or paddy, as this grain is called in the husk.

Most of the operations in the cultivation of paddy, which is carried on wherever water for irrigation can be procured, are connected with or have some relation to the element on which its success depends. The farmer commences with repairing the banks of the paddy-field. He then admits water in sufficient quantity to be an inch or two deep over the whole surface. After the ground has been well macerated and softened, he ploughs it, still under water. After farther maceration, it is ploughed again, or merely trampled over by buffaloes, till reduced to the state of mud. Its surface is now levelled and smoothed. The water is drawn off, and the paddy, having been previously steeped in water till it has begun to germinate is sown with the hand, and is scattered as equally as possible over the moist surface of mud. When the seed has taken root, and before the mud has had time to dry, the openings through which the water was drawn off are closed, and the field is again inundated. When the paddy is two or three inches high, it is weeded; and, where the seed has failed, the vacant spots are planted from those parts which are too thick and require thinning. The irrigation is continued till the paddy is nearly full-grown and about to ripen, when openings are made in the banks and the field is drained. As soon as ripe, the paddy is cut with reaping-hooks, and immediately carried to the threshing-floor, where the grain is trampled out by buffaloes. From the moment the seed is sown till the period of harvest, the paddy-field, like the chenas, requires constant nightly watching to protect it from the depredations of its wild enemies. In the low country, where the cultivation of paddy is in a great measure dependent on the rainy season and on artificial reservoirs for a farther supply of water, only one crop is procured annually: but amongst the mountains, in situations where perpetual irrigation is at command, the seasons are less concerned; the farmer can sow when he please, and from good ground annually obtain two, and I have heard, even three crops.* The hilly and mountainous districts, in consequence of being well supplied with water, are thus particularly favourable for the cultivation of this important grain: and it is a most fortunate circumstance that they are so; otherwise the coolest, most salubrious and most beautiful parts of the Interior would, instead of being cultivated to a certain extent, be quite neglected and deserted. In the low country the paddy-fields are generally of a large size, and apparently quite flat; and, every crop being in the same stage of vegetation, or nearly so, the whole exhibits very little variety of surface. Amongst the mountains it is quite different; — paddy-fields there are a succession of terraces or flights of steps; and in each field the crop may be in different stages of growth; — in some just vegetating, in others full-grown, ripening, or ripe; there, at the same time you may see the labourers at all their different operations, — banking, ploughing, sowing, weeding, reaping, and treading out the grain. I do not know any scene more interesting than a highland valley thus cultivated, or more beautiful, when (as it generally is) it is surrounded by the bold, wild, and frequently savage scenery of untamed nature. In the low lands the labour and skill required to cultivate paddy, are less than are necessary in the high lands. In cutting terraces in the sides of hills, the perseverance and industry of the mountaineer are often in a striking manner displayed.

* One crop a-year of the best paddy, which requires seven months, is most common; when two crops are procured, they are of an inferior grain, that comes to maturity in three or four months.

Many of his beds are actually walled up, and many of them are not four feet wide, and though generally long, occasionally they are so short, from the nature of the ground, as well as narrow, that one would not suppose they were worth the labour of keeping in repair and much less of making. In bringing water to his fields and insuring them a constant supply, the judgment and skill of the cultivator are most exercised. Sometimes it is conducted two or three miles along the side of a hill, and occasionally it is even carried from one side of a mountain to another by means of wooden pipes.

The implements of husbandry employed by the Singalese are few in number, and of a very simple construction.

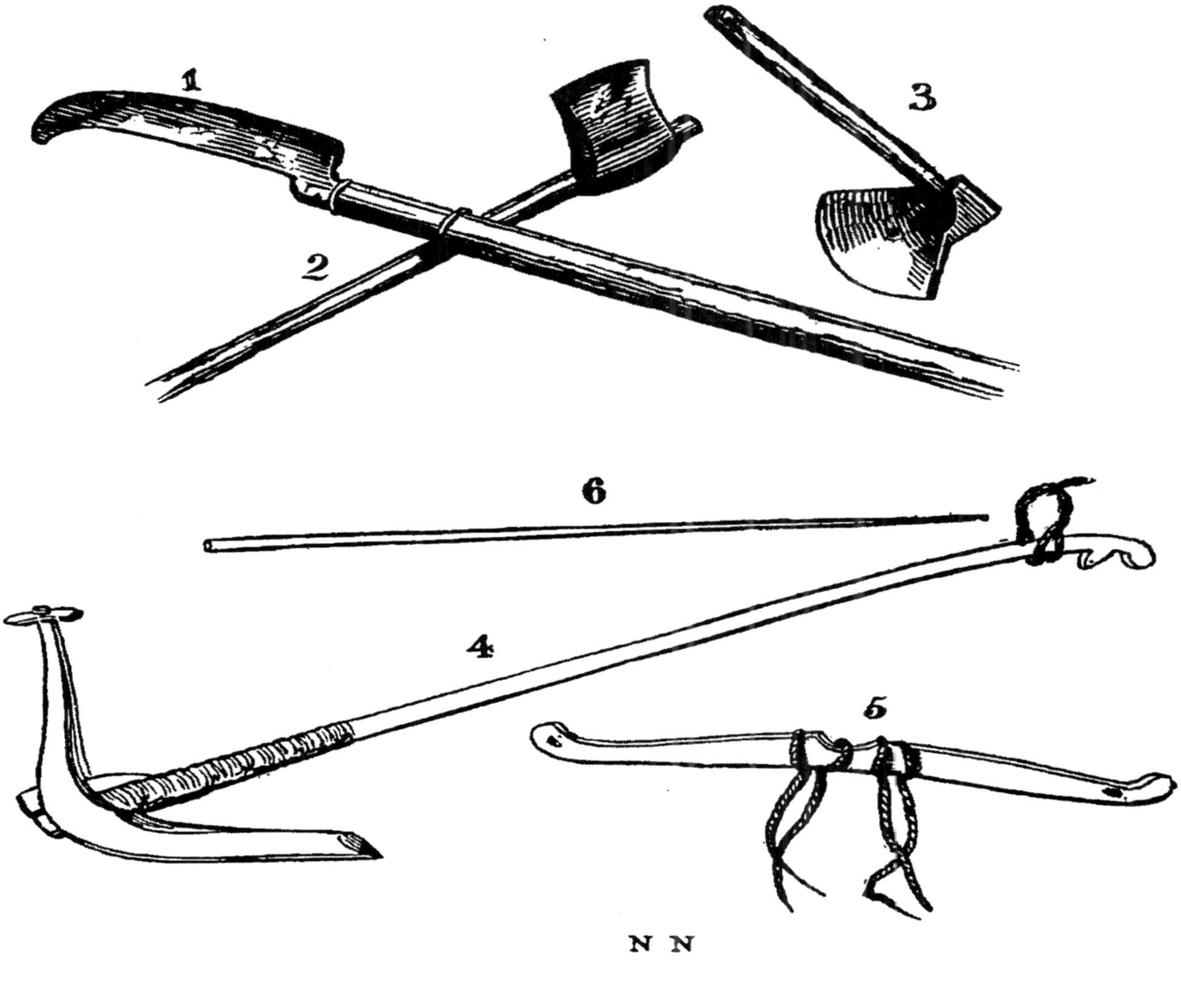

For cutting down trees and clearing underwood, they have two very serviceable instruments, a jungle-hook, wal-dakat, (fig. 1.) and an axe, proa, (fig. 2.) For digging where the plough cannot be used, and for banking, they employ their udala, (fig. 3.) Their plough, naguela, (fig. 4.) is of the simplest and lightest kind: with one hand the ploughman holds the plough, which is attached to a pair of buffaloes by a yoke, veaga, (fig. 5.) and in the other hand he holds a goad, kaweta, (fig. 6.) with which and his voice he directs and stimulates the animals.

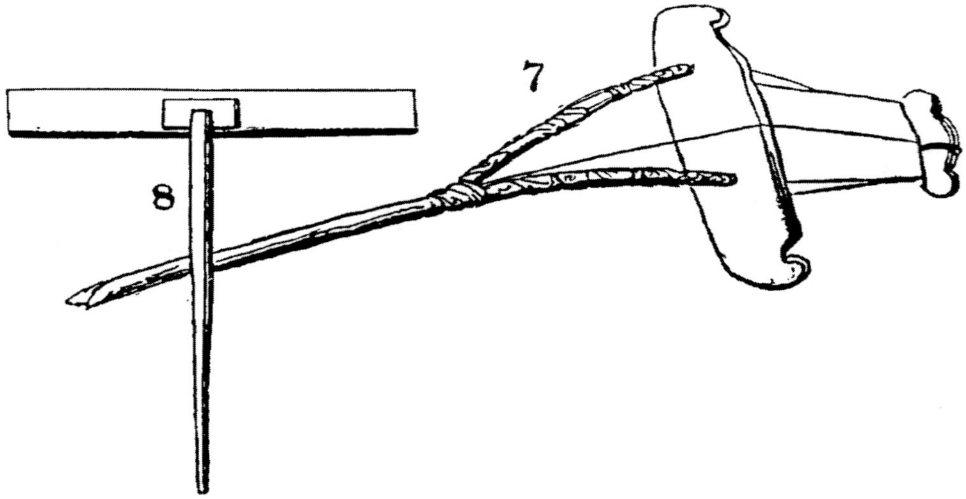

10

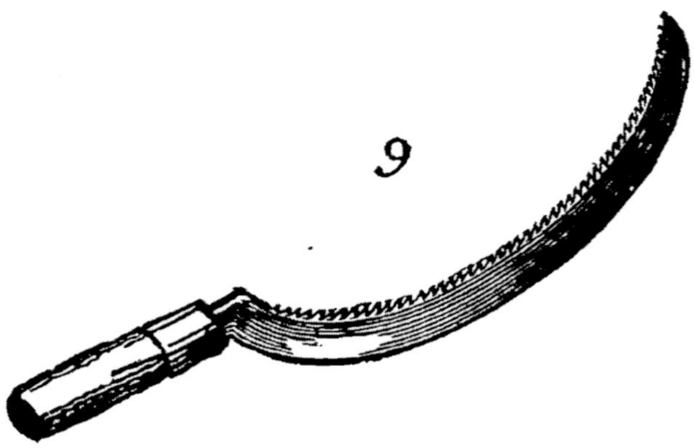

For levelling ground after ploughing, the anadatpooroooa, (fig. 7.) is used; which, like the plough, is drawn by a pair of buffaloes.

the driver sitting on it to give it momentum. For smoothing the surface of the mud preparatory to sowing, the light hand-instrument the atpoorooa, or goelalè (fig. 8.) is employed. The reaping-hook used, called guygon-kopana-dakat, (fig. 9.) has a fine serrated edge, and is very similar to ours. Their winnow, coola, (fig. 10.) is composed of strong matting and a frame of tough twigs.

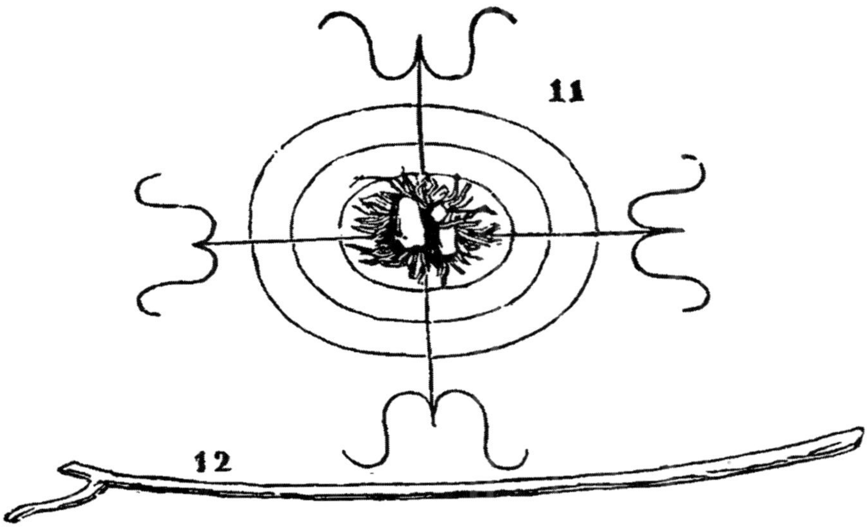
11
12

The floor is made of beat clay, on which the paddy is trampled out. Preparatory to the commencement of this operation, a superstitious ceremony is performed;—the commata or charm (fig. 11.) is described on the middle of the floor, with the notion of defending the grain from evil demons. The figure is made with wood ashes, which is poured on the ground from a leaf; a bit of wood of the kohomba tree, and two or three small pieces of quartz are placed on a little paddy-straw in the inner circle, and covered with the same; the owner walks once round the circle,—stops,—with uplifted hands, makes repeated salems to the offering in the centre,—prostrates before it,—mutters a prayer, and entreats the demon neither to steal the grain nor injure it. After this mummery the corn is heaped on the circle, the buffaloes are driven in, and the work begins in earnest. The primitive fork called datalla, (fig. 12.) and which is merely a branch of a tree, is used to gather the straw under the buffaloes' feet.

Gardening amongst the Singalese is hardly known as an art: they plant, indeed, different kinds of palm-trees and fruit-trees round their houses, and flowering shrubs about their temples; and they occasionally cultivate a few vegetables, as yams, sweet potatoes, and onions, in their fields; but in no part of the country is a garden according to our ideas to be seen.

CHAPTER IX.

DOMESTIC HABITS AND MANNERS. — MARRIAGE RITES. — POLYGAMY. — TREATMENT OF CHILDREN. — CEREMONY OF GIVING NAMES. — UNJUST ACCUSATIONS. — FUNERAL RITES. — CHARACTER OF THE SINGALESE.

In this chapter, I purpose to give a very brief sketch of the manners, habits, and character of the Singalese. Well aware of the difficulty of the subject, and of my inability to do it justice, I shall at least endeavour not to be unjust to the people, in measuring their moral height by our own, or any arbitrary standard; or, from the vices of a few individuals, hastily generalising, and passing sentence of condemnation on a whole nation. To avoid these rocks, on which we are all, more or less, apt to run, in the mist of prejudice, I shall confine myself as much as possible to facts, and to such simple inferences as are almost obvious truths. When character is at stake, whether it be of an individual or a people; in whatever circumstances, however exalted or humble, near or remote; one surely cannot be too cautious in making assertions, or too anxious to avoid error.

The Singalese of the Interior are rarely found collected in large villages. Kandy, the capital of the country, may be considered a large village; but, besides it, I know of no other.

From time immemorial, the natives have been able to indulge a preference, natural and common to all agricultural people, of living either in very small villages, consisting of a few houses, or in detached habitations, separated from each other only by the extent of land of each individual.

Their dwellings are generally in low, sheltered situations, bordering on their paddy-fields, to be as near their work as possible, and the crop they most value, and to be defended from wind, of which they have a great dislike, conceiving exposure to it highly prejudicial to health.

Each dwelling is a little establishment of itself; and, each little district or village, as far as its wants are concerned, may be considered independent. A family have, about them and in their neighbourhood, almost every thing they require;—rice, their staff of life, they have in abundance from their own fields; milk, from their cows and buffaloes; and fruit and oil from the trees that immediately surround and shade their houses. The blacksmith of the village or district, the weaver, potter, &c., furnish them, in barter, those articles with which they cannot supply themselves; and, by the same mode of barter they procure, from the travelling moormen, the few comforts or luxuries they indulge in, and which the country does not afford;—as salt, and, perhaps, a little salt-fish and tobacco, and a smart handkerchief or cloth for holiday occasions.

The economy of a Singalese family is very simple, and the occupations of the different members of it well defined. The more laborious operations of agriculture fall to the lot of the men,—as ploughing, banking, &c.; and the lighter to the women,—as weeding, and assisting in reaping. The care of the house, and the management of the household affairs, belong almost exclusively to the latter, and constitute their peculiar duties. It is their business to keep their dwelling neat, to prepare the meals of their family, to milk, and spin.* These remarks relate chiefly to the middling classes. In families of rank, the ladies lead nearly a life of idleness; and, in poor families, the life of the females is one of extreme drudgery.

The furniture of their houses, which is equally plain and economical, consists chiefly of a couch or two, for lying on; of two or three stools; of a few mats; of two or three porcelain dishes; and, amongst the higher ranks, of some plate, and other articles of luxury. Their kitchen apparatus, besides baskets and coarse earthenware vessels, are principally the following:—

A wang-gadea, or rice-mortar and pestle, for pounding paddy, and depriving it of its husk. The mortar is occasionally made of stone, but more generally of wood.

* They prepare the cotton-thread, of which the family linen is made by the village weavers. The spindle they use is of the most primitive kind.

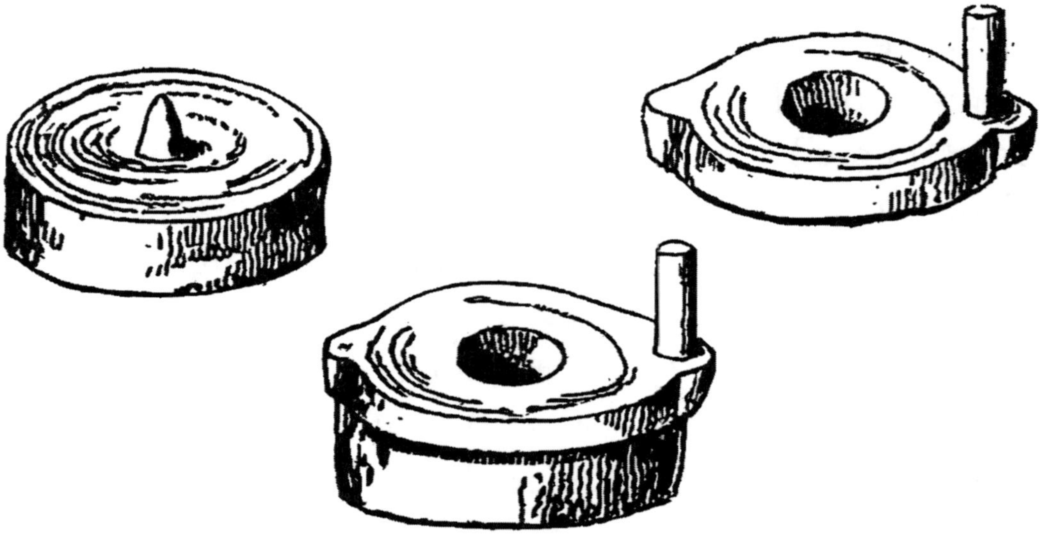

A corrican-galle, or stone handmill, composed of two parts, which is used for grinding corrican and other small grain, and which is very similar to the old Celtic querne, that is still employed in some parts of Ireland and the Highlands of Scotland.

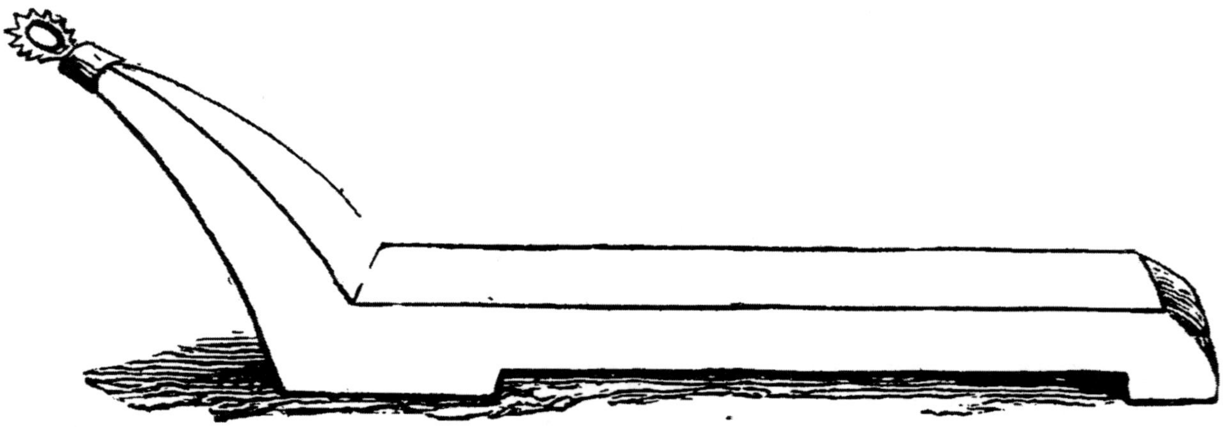

A heromané, or cocoa-nut scraper, consisting of a circular iron rasp, fixed into a wooden stand. It is used for the purpose of reducing the ripe cocoa-nut to a minced state, as an ingredient of curry, into the composition of which it always enters. Besides this, a couple of smooth stones are used, one small and the other large, for mixing together intimately, and grinding finely, all the different ingredients of their curries.

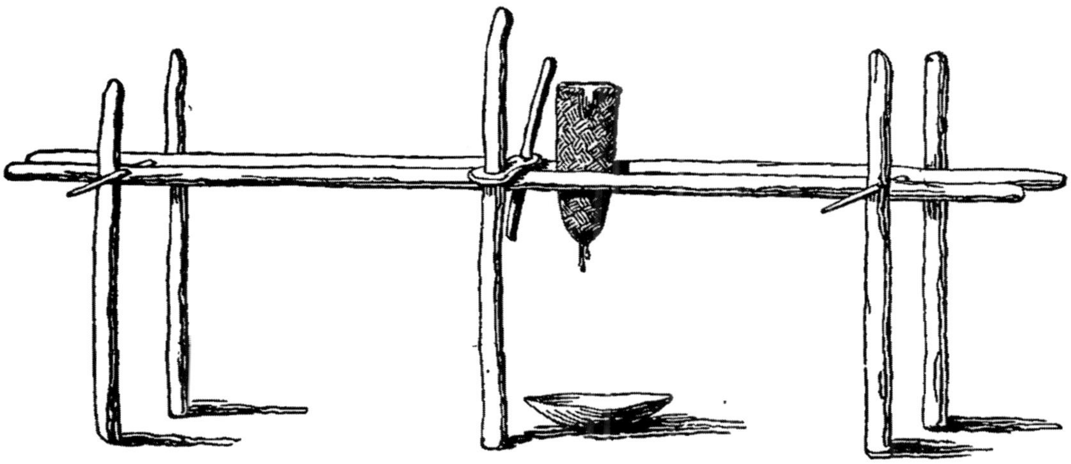

And, lastly, may be mentioned, an apparatus for procuring oil, by the compression of two or three different kinds of seed in a rattan bag, which answers the double purpose of a receptacle of the material, and a filter for the oil. The pressure is made on the bag by the action of a perpendicular lever.

The Singalese rise at dawn of day, and retire to rest about nine or ten o'clock at night. They sleep on mats, either on the floor or on couches, with a fire generally in the room. Their principal meal is at noon: it consists chiefly of rice and curry, which is commonly composed of red pepper, salt, lime-juice, and the dried skin of the gorka.* The higher ranks make use of a variety of curries, and eat animal food, as eggs,

* The following are the ingredients of a Singalese curry-stuff of a more elaborate composition, and which is much approved of by many of my countrymen:— a piece of green ginger, two cloves of garlic, a few coriander and cummin-seeds, six small onions, one dry chilly or capsicum, six or eight corns of pepper, a small piece of turmeric, half a dessert-spoon of butter, half a cocoa-nut, half a lime.

fowls, and different kinds of game. Beef they strictly abstain from; not that it is contrary to their religion to use it, but because it was forbid by one of their kings, who, they say, was nursed by a cow, and to express his gratitude made the prohibition in question. Besides at noon, some eat early in the morning, and almost all have a meal between seven and eight o'clock at night. Many other articles of food are used besides those that have been mentioned, particularly milk, of which, in its coagulated state, the Singalese are fond; cheese they do not appear to be acquainted with, nor with butter, excepting clarified, when it is called gee, and is a frequent addition to their curries. Their meals are short and unsocial: the master of the house, the father of the family, is first served; at his solitary repast he is waited on by his wife, who helps him and supplies him with what he wants. The turn of the mistress of the house is next, and of the younger children, who cannot help themselves and require a mother's care; the rest of the family eat last, and their portion is what remains. Amongst poor people of low caste these distinctions are little attended to, and father, mother, and children eat together; occasionally, even in families of the highest rank, the master and mistress of the house associate at meals, but it is not approved of; it is considered uxorious and indecorous.

Though not a convivial, the Singalese are a social people, great gossips, and when not occupied seriously, visiting and conversation are their principal amusements. On such occasions the men and women form their respective circles; they are never seen mixed in society. People of rank who have a great deal of leisure, pass their idle time either in playing cards, which they probably learnt from the Portuguese, or in hearing stories, or in listening to poetry and music. Idle ladies amuse themselves with talking, or at a game somewhat resembling backgammon. Chewing betel on such occasions is never omitted by either sex; it is a practice indulged in almost constantly by all classes of people, and it is considered quite indispensable. What is called *betel*, is a variously compounded masticatory; it most commonly consists of betel-leaf, areka-nut, quenched lime, tobacco, and catechu. Each chief has a servant, whose duty it is to supply his master with this article. In the preparation of the masticatory, two instruments are used:

1

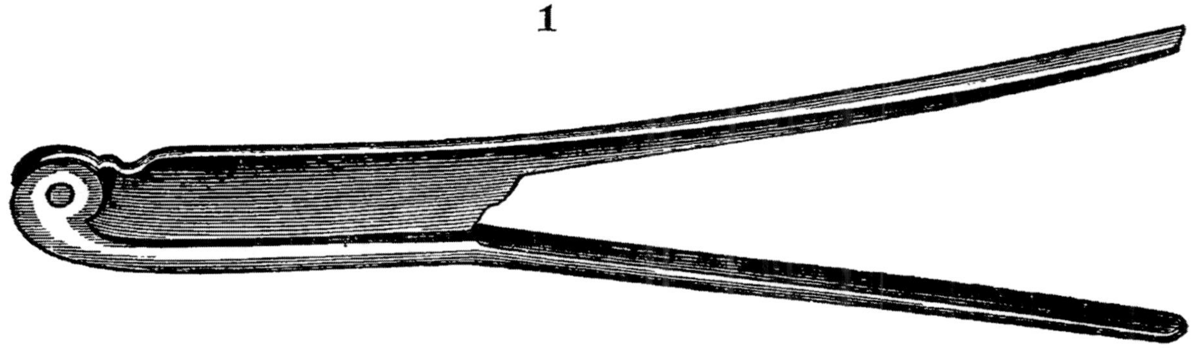

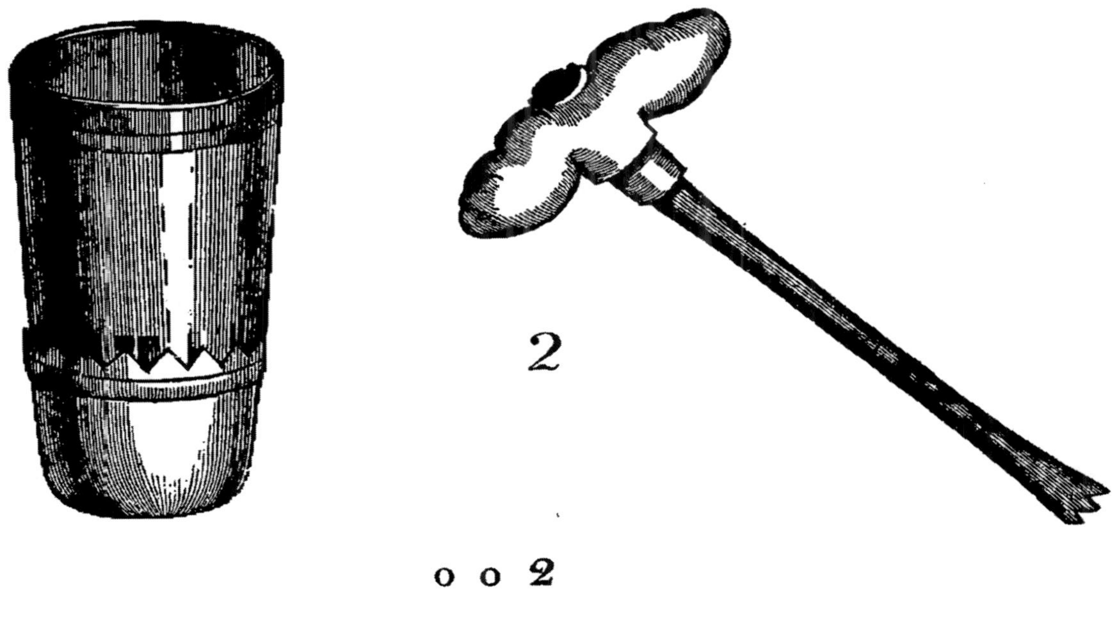

2

The girri, (fig. 1.) for cutting the areka-nut, and the wanggedi and moolgah, a kind of mortar and pestle, (fig. 2.) for mincing and intimately mixing the ingredients together. The boxes of the higher ranks, in which the materials are kept, are generally of silver, and very handsomely wrought.

The Singalese are a courteous and ceremonious people, and whilst they attend most particularly to all their minute distinctions of caste and rank, they are mutually respectful: the man of rank is not arrogant, nor the poor man servile; the one is kind and condescending, and the other modest and unpresuming. The friendly intercourse of different ranks is encouraged by religion, and strengthened by the circumstance, that, on one side there is nothing the great are so ambitious of as popularity; and on the other side, nothing the people are so desirous of as favour.

But though a courteous, they are not a gallant people; gallantry, and the refined sentiment of love, do not belong to a tropical climate, and are almost peculiarly characteristic of European manners. Old bachelors and old maids are rarely to be seen amongst the Singalese; almost every man marries, and marries young, and the wife not of his own but of his father's choice. The preliminaries of the union are entirely settled by the parents. When a young man has reached the age of eighteen or twenty, he is considered marriageable, and it is the duty of his father to provide him with a proper wife. The father having selected a family of his own caste and rank, pays the master of it a visit, and if the information he receive respecting the lady's dower be satisfaetory, he formally proposes his son. Soon after, the father of the lady returns the visit to learn the circumstances of the young man, the establishment he is to have, and his prospects in life. If both parties are so far satisfied, the father of the young man makes another visit to his friend, to see the lady, and enquire respecting her qualifications, age, and disposition. He is contented if she is younger than his son, in good health, free from ulcers and corporal blemishes, possessed of a pretty good disposition, and acquainted with the ordinary duties of a housewife. On his return home, he desires his son to go clandestinely and see her: if the young man enter the house, it is under a feigned name; and if he see his intended, he must not address her. The day of the marriage being fixed, and the hour determined by an astrologer, the bridegroom and his family, their relations and friends, proceed to the house of the bride, accompanied by people carrying provisions, and by four men in particular bearing a large pingo laden not only with all sorts of provisions, but likewise with a piece of white cloth, and with jewels and ornaments, varying in number and richness according to the means of the individual. The party set out in time to arrive towards evening: they find a mandoo (a temporary building) prepared for their reception, a feast in readiness, and the friends of the lady assembled to meet them. In the middle of the mandoo, which is covered with mats, the men of both parties seat themselves round a large pile of rice, placed on fresh plantain leaves, and garnished with curries of different kinds; the ladies do the same, collected within the house. Both parties help themselves with their hands, and eat from the common pile. This mode of eating, peculiar to the marriage-feast, is esteemed proof of good fellowship; and, should any one hesitate to partake, he would be considered an enemy, and be driven away. After the repast, the bridegroom enters the house, meets the bride attended by her friends; they exchange balls made of rice and cocoa-nut milk; and he presents her with the piece of white cloth and with the jewels and ornaments he has brought.

All this having been transacted in silence, she retires, and he returns to the mandoo. The night is passed by the company in telling stories and in conversation; the next morning the bride, led by the bridegroom and accompanied by all their friends, is conducted to his father's house, where the ceremony is concluded with another feast similar to the preceding. The woman's dower generally consists of household goods and cattle, but rarely of land. The ceremonies observed on the marriage of chiefs (at least at Kandy) are in some respects different from those just described. The first preliminary consists in comparing the horoscopes of the parties, it being essential to the union that the two agree. After having made certain presents to the bride, the bridegroom conducts her home and entertains her friends: the first fortnight that they live together is a period of trial, at the end of which the marriage is either annulled or confirmed. If the latter, the pair stand on a plank of jack-wood, the husband pours water on his wife's head, and having exchanged rings and tied their little fingers together, they are firmly united for life. Amongst people of the lowest rank, little attention is paid to the marriage ceremony, and no formality is observed excepting that of asking leave of the parents to part with their daughter.

Though concubinage and polygamy are contrary to their religion, both are indulged in by the Singalese, particularly the latter: and, it is remarkable, that in the Kandyan country, as in Tibet, a plurality of husbands is much more common than of wives. One woman has frequently two husbands; and I have heard of one having as many as seven. This singular species of polygamy is not confined to any caste or rank; it is more or less general amongst the high and low, the rich and poor. The joint husbands are always brothers. The apology of the poor is, that they cannot afford each to have a particular wife; and of the wealthy and men of rank, that such a union is politic, as it unites families, concentrates property and influence, and conduces to the interest of the children, who, having two fathers, will be better taken care of, and will still have a father though they may lose one.* After the preceding remarks, it is hardly necessary to observe that chastity is not a virtue in very high estimation amongst the Singalese women, nor jealousy a very troublesome passion amongst the men. Infidelity, certainly, is not uncommon, and it is easily forgiven, unless the lady disgrace herself by forming a low-caste attachment, which is considered unpardonable, and always ends in divorce. It might be expected that extreme licentiousness would mark the manners of the Singalese. Were their society constituted like ours, such undoubtedly would be the result; but constituted as it is, the conclusion is hardly admissible, excepting, perhaps, in the capital; which, like most other capitals, is rather distinguished for the polish than the correctness of its manners.

As fathers and mothers, as sons and daughters, the Singalese appear in a more amiable light. Their families are generally small, one woman rarely bearing more than four or five children: a fact that does not at all agree with the assertion that has been made, that the women of Ceylon are remarkably prolific. The care of the children is almost equally divided between the parents; and an infant is more frequently seen with its father than mother. Mothers almost universally suckle their own children, and for the long period of four or five years, either in

* These reasons were once assigned to me by a very acute old Kandyan chief, who, with his brother, had one wife only in common. The children called the elder brother "great papa," and the younger "little papa." There appeared to be perfect harmony in the family.

part or entirely. The only exception to this custom, when health permits, is in the instance of some fine ladies, who, even in the Interior of Ceylon, are occasionally more obedient to the voice of vanity than of nature; and, to preserve a little while a fine form of bosom, relinquish the first duty and most endearing office of a mother. Children, though well attended to, are at first very backward in learning to speak and walk: it is considered a forward infant who, at two years, can stand alone, and articulate *ama*, *apa*; but, having once fairly commenced, their progress is rapid.

Children are generally named when they commence eating rice, and sometimes when only a half-year old. This early name is called *batnamen*, the rice-name; and the conferring of it is attended with some ceremony. At a fortunate day, that has been calculated, the relations and friends of the family assemble; and, at a fortunate hour, the grandfather, or, should both grandfathers be dead, the father, takes a little rice in his fingers, puts it into the child's mouth, and at the same time gives it its name. An entertainment is made on the occasion, at which the men sit down together, and before the women; and each is served with the best the house affords, on a piece of fresh plantain-leaf. The name given varies according to the rank of the family; and, excepting in low castes, is composed of a general name applicable to all of that rank, and of a trivial name to distinguish the individual. Thus all boys of respectable caste and family are either called *rale* or *appo*, and are distinguished each by some trivial addition, as *lochoo*, great; *punchy*, little; *kalu*, black; — and in the case of girls the same rule is followed; they are all called *etanna*, lady; and besides have some distinguishing term, expressive of beauty or value. The "rice name" is used only in infancy. The Singalese being without family names, grown-up people are called either by the names of the places of their abode, or of the offices which they fill.

Amongst few people, I believe, are family attachments more strong and sincere: there is little to divert or weaken them; and they are strengthened equally by their mode of life and their religion. A family is the focus in which all the tender affections of a native are concentrated. Parents are generally treated with the greatest respect and regard; and children with extraordinary affection. During the late rebellion, very many instances occurred of fathers voluntarily delivering themselves up, after their families had been taken. I have heard an assertion made, not at all compatible with the preceding statement, that the Singalese sometimes expose their children. The result of my enquiries is, that they hold the crime in abhorrence; and, that it is never committed, excepting in some of the wildest parts of the country; and never from choice, but necessity, — when the parents themselves are on the brink of starving, and must either sacrifice a part of the family or die altogether. I have heard another assertion made, of a character with the preceding, and no better founded, viz. that the natives neglect their sick relations, — indeed not merely neglect them, but cruelly turn them out of their houses, or throw them into the jungle to perish. This erroneous notion arose perhaps from the circumstance, that a person dangerously ill is frequently placed in an adjoining temporary building, that, should he die, the house may escape pollution. Generally they are attentive to their sick, especially their parents and children, and are not wanting in any kind offices towards them. They have been charged, too, with a shameful neglect of their dead. To help to refute this accusation, which I believe to be true in the instance only of the lowest and most degraded of the people, I shall notice briefly their funeral rites.

Their attentions to the dead commence as soon as the fatal event has taken place. As Boodhoo came from the east, they lie, during life, with their heads in that direction; and, as they think it is not right that the living and the dead should lie the same way, their first duty is to turn the head of the corpse to the westward. Then they decently compose the limbs, tie the great toes together, place the expanded hands on the chest, wash the body, dress it in its best clothes, and deck it with the ornaments worn during life. Every respectable family burns its dead. The funeral pile consists of a layer of cocoa-nut shells, a layer of the husks of the cocoa-nut, and an upper layer of wood, altogether about three feet high, confined by strong stakes. The body, dressed and decked as described, is laid on the pile and covered with wood, to the height of about three feet more. If the dead were a person of high rank, as a Maha-nilami, or Dissave, the corpse is carried in a palanqueen, preceded by the mourning tom-tom: in all instances, it is followed by the male relations, and it is generally attended by a priest. The funeral fire is kindled by the nearest relation of the deceased; and the priest recites prayers for the happiness of the deceased in a future state of existence. When the body is consumed, the friends return to their homes, after having surrounded the ashes with slips of the young leaf of the cocoa-nut tree, supported on sticks, to point out that the spot is sacred. At the expiration of seven days, they come back with priests, and having collected the ashes into a little heap, cover them with a pile of stones, a few feet high. Sometimes they remove them in an earthen pot, and deposit them near some Wiharè, or in the family burying-ground. The priests conclude the ceremony with a moral discourse, inculcating resignation, the doing of good, the shunning of evil, and attention to the duties of religion. Generally, men alone attend funerals. If there be an exception, it is in the province of Doombera, where I was informed by a native, that the corpse is carried by females; and, indeed, that all the last and sad offices of humanity are performed by the tender sex. Low-caste people are not allowed to burn their dead; they bury the corpse, with little ceremony, in a grave three or four feet deep, with its head to the west.

Respecting the degree of civilization of the Singalese, and their moral character, I know from experience that a variety of opinions is entertained, by individuals who have been a good deal amongst them, though not in circumstances, perhaps, generally favourable for forming correct conclusions on such difficult subjects. In candour, I must premise, that my opinion is more favourable than that which is more commonly adopted; and, such as it is, it has been formed, I trust, in a dispassionate manner, — not in a moment of heat during a period of rebellion, but from all I have seen, and from the best information I could collect. In civilization, the Singalese appear to be nearly, if not quite, on a par with the Hindoos. They hardly admit of just comparison with any European nation. In courtesy and polish of manners, they are little inferior to the most refined people of the present day. In intellectual acquirements, and proficiency in arts and sciences, they are not advanced beyond the darkest period of the middle ages. Their character, I believe, on the whole, is low, tame, and undecided: with few strong lights or shades in it, with few prominent virtues or vices, it may be considered as a compound of weak moral feelings, of strong natural affections, and of moderate passions. This is a very general statement. It is intentionally so; I do not feel qualified to make one more particular and precise. If it be difficult to know one's self, — to know completely a bosom friend; how much more so is it to know a people, and pronounce on their character, and especially of such a people as the Singalese, with whom our acquaintance has been short, our intercourse slight, and our opportunities of judging extremely imperfect.

CHAPTER X.

SKETCH OF THE HISTORY OF CEYLON, FROM THE EARLIEST PERIOD ON RECORD TO THE PRESENT TIMES.

The Singalese, like the nations of Europe in the middle ages, and like the people in general of almost the whole of Asia and Africa at this instant, possess no accurate records of events, are ignorant of genuine history, and are not sufficiently advanced to relish it. Instead of the one, they have legendary tales; and, instead of the other, historical romances, which are the more complete the more remote the period is to which they belong. Agreeably to this remark, the details of the earliest periods are not only the most monstrous, but also the most clear and precise, without mystery and without obscurity; whilst those of later periods, approaching the present times, on the verge of authentic history, are less monstrous and wonderful, and proportionably scanty and obscure.

Their historical romance, in which the Singalese have implicit faith, commences with the first king of Ceylon, Wijeya Coomarayo, whose father and mother were brother and sister, and the children of a princess of the Soorea-wansé, by a lion. Wijeya, banished by the king, his father, on account of his profligate and cruel conduct, left his country, Wagooratta, with seven hundred companions; embarked to seek his fortune at random, and sailing westward, reached Ceylon, where he landed at a spot which they called Poottalama.* This happened in the first year of Boodhoo, and seven days after his death. Wijeya found the island uncultivated, and inhabited only by innumerable demons. A beautiful female demon, Koowanè, fell in love with him, and became his mistress. By her advice, and with her assistance, mounted on her transformed into a mare, he attacked the devils, routed them, and put them to death. The weapon which he used on this occasion, the natives believe to be the state-sword, which, if not brought to England, is still in Ceylon. He built Tammananeura, in Neurakalaweya; and, at the solicitation of his companions, procured from Madura a princess, and seven hundred young women. The vain lamentations of the fair demon, which this connection gave rise to, are recorded *verbatim*:—"It was foretold, that when I should see the man destined to be my husband, one of my three breasts would disappear; one breast did disappear, when I saw you; and did not you become my husband? Have I not been a faithful wife, and loved you dearly, and respected you? Why, then, talk of our parting? Can you be so cruel to one who brought you from a banyan-tree to a palace—who complied with all your wishes, supplied all your wants, sacrificed every thing to your welfare?—Oh gods! where shall I go—where shall I find an asylum and support for myself and my children?† Oh, cruel Wijeya! where can my heart find comfort!" The discarded Koowanè, intent on revenge, watched her opportunity; and one night, when the

* Now Putlam. The name signifies a society of young men, such as the king's was.

† These children, the history relates, were counterfeits, made by her to please the king and retain his affections.

king and queen were sleeping together, in the form of a tiger with a diamond tongue, she darted through seven doors, and was in the act of piercing the hearts of the royal pair, when Tissa *, one of the king's companions, who was on guard, with a blow of his sword cut off the organ of the intended mischief, and deposited it under a lamp. The tiger vanished; but re-appeared the next morning, when Wijeya uncovered the tongue. A battle ensued, in which the king was victorious, and his mistress fell. Wijeya died without issue, 38 A. B., and was succeeded by a nephew.

It would be tedious and unprofitable to follow this historical romance through all its details: it will be sufficient to pause at those parts which have something peculiar to recommend them to notice.

During the two following centuries, the country was improved and peopled, and several cities were built, as Anooradapoora, by Prince Anoorada; and Coornegalle, Doondera, and Gampola, by his brothers.

In 236 A. B., Dewinepatissé, the fifteenth king, commenced his reign, which was remarkable for the introduction of the religion of Boodhoo. The event is minutely related, and with the usual admixture of the marvellous. A Rahatoon (a priest of Boodhoo, of extraordinary sanctity and powers), called Mihidoomaha, with the title of Maha-Tironansy, having been commissioned by Darmasóka, king of Maddadisay, a country to the eastward of Ceylon, to visit the island and convert its inhabitants to the true faith, passed through the air, and alighted on a rock in the neighbourhood of Anooradapoora, just when the

* The family of this Tissa is still living, it is said, in a village of that name in the Seven Korles.

king was passing, returning from hunting. His appearance in yellow robes, his head and eyebrows shorn, puzzled the party not a little, and made them doubt whether he was a man or a demon. He told the king his commission, and to sound the depth of his majesty's understanding, to ascertain if he were qualified to comprehend the discourse he meditated, he asked him a few questions: — Rahatoon: "Have you relations? The King: "Many." — R. "Have you people, who are not your relations?" K. "Yes." — R. "And besides your relations and those who are not related to you, are there any else in your kingdom?" K. "Only myself." Satisfied by the manner in which these and other questions were answered, that his majesty possessed a quick understanding, the Rahatoon addressed him on the subject of religion, and preached on the beauty and propriety of the actions of Boodhoo, till he converted him and all his people. Temples and dagobahs were quickly built, and Ceylon soon became a sacred island. The Rahatoon brought from Sacrea's heaven the jaw-bone of Boodhoo, and deposited it in a dagobah 120 cubits high; and Darmasoka sent a branch of the identical bo-tree, under which Siddhartè became Boodhoo, in charge of eight princes and five hundred Rahatoons, and accompanied by eighteen different castes of people, ninety thousand blacksmiths, and a proportional number of other kinds of artists. This branch was planted at Anooradapoora, in a bed eighty-six cubits high; where it took root contrary to the nature of the tree, which can be propagated only by seed, and it has lived ever since, — even to this moment, it is said, always green, neither growing nor decaying. Letters were introduced at the same time.

In the reign of the twenty-third king, the country was invaded by the Malabars of Soleratte, on the coast of Coromandel; who pushed their conquests to the Mahawellé ganga, and subdued the whole island, with the exception of the parts to the southward of this river and of the Kalany ganga.

Soon after this invasion, in the reign of Kalany-tissa, who built Kalany, a great catastrophe took place. In consequence of a chief priest having been unjustly put to death by this king, the sea, it is said, invaded the land, destroyed four hundred fishing-villages, and seventy villages of pearl-fishermen, and overwhelmed twenty-four miles of country; reducing the distance between Kalany and the sea from twenty-eight miles, that it was previously, to four, which it is at present. The king himself was drawn down to the infernal regions by a flame of fire; and his beautiful daughter, of whom he had made an offering to the ocean, floated to Roona, in the Magampattoo, and was married to the prince who succeeded her father.

Whilst the Malabars held the northern parts of the island, the natives concentrated in the southern extremity of it, and in those very districts which are now almost deserted. Under the command of Dootoogaimoonoo, one of the sons of the princess just mentioned, they defeated the Malabars, drove them out of the island, and re-occupied Anooradapoora.

During three successive reigns, the country was tranquil, and flourished; and numerous tanks were formed, and temples raised, both in the northern and southern districts.

About 430 A.B., the Malabars renewed their inroads; recovered their former conquests, and retained them thirty-two years, when they were expelled by Wallagam-bahoo, with a force which he had collected in the Udoo-rattè, or Highlands.

The reign of Sakka is the next most memorable one. His predecessor was an apostate to his religion, and in every respect an infamous character. For his cruelties, and particularly for having put to death a Brahmen, with whose wife he was enamoured, the whole country was visited with a drought of twelve years' duration. During this period, a priest, on his journey, stopt at the house of Sakka, then a private individual residing in the Haraseapattoo. There remained of his store only one scanty meal of rice, which, without hesitation, he ordered to be dressed for his guest. His charity was rewarded: his little modicum became inexhaustible, and supported his family and all the country round, as long as the drought and famine lasted. His good fortune did not stop here. Though a Goewansè only, the people, out of gratitude, raised him to the throne; and, as a perpetual memento, they made the commencement of his reign an era, which is still in common use. The first year of Sakka corresponds with 621 of Boodhoo, and with 78 of our era.*

In the first century of Sakka, the Malabars made a fresh incursion into the island, and carried off twelve thousand prisoners of both sexes; but not with impunity. King Gaja-bahoo, armed with an iron rod weighing five hundred pounds, and accompanied by a giant, visited the enemy's capital, and seized double the number of the inhabitants, with whom, and the gold dish that was presented to Siddhartè the day before he became Boodhoo, and the bangles of the goddess Patinè, he returned triumphant. The captives were distributed amongst the different provinces; and, the names which several of them now bear were given, it is said, at that time, from the number of families placed in them;

* By some, a different explanation, evidently borrowed from the Hindoos, is given of the origin of this era. The story is a fiction equally indelicate and monstrous.

thus, Hewahettè is expressive of sixty; Toompanè, of one hundred and fifty, or three fifties; Haraseapattoo, of four hundred; Pancea-pattoo, of five hundred; and Matelè, of many — a multitude.

The monotony of several succeeding reigns is interrupted only by an extraordinary legend, which for wildness of fiction may compete with any monkish production, fabricated in the most credulous period. Three young princes are told by a blind sage, who draws his conclusions from the sound of their feet, that they are destined to be successively kings. The eldest succeeds his father and speedily dies. The second, Sirisangabo, the hero of the story, and a perfect model of virtue and piety, ascends the throne. After having performed many extraordinary actions, finding that his younger brother, in his impatience to fulfil the prophecy of the blind sage, is plotting his destruction, he abdicates in his favour, and retires to a hermitage. Not satisfied of the permanency of his power as long as Sirisangabo is alive, the young prince offers a reward of 5000 pagodas to the person who would bring him his brother's head. Many heads were presented, but not one was acknowledged as genuine. A very poor man, who knew the place of the king's concealment, went at the instigation of his wife, tempted by the promised reward, with the design of murdering him. In the Hinna-korle he met with the king, and ignorant of his person entered into conversation with him; and, when questioned, freely confessed the nature of the business on which he was abroad. They presently came to Attanagallé, where the king said they would stop and eat together some rice, which he perceived the poor man had provided himself with. The king took a handful of it and throwing it down, said; — "If I am destined to become Boodhoo, this rice will immediately spring up;" and it instantly vegetated. After their repast the king said,—"I am the man you seek,—I am Sirisangabo; do what you intended: carry my head to my brother; and should he be incredulous, as he probably will be, many attempts having been made to deceive him, put my head on a white cloth, on a chair, and it will answer for itself." The poor man now repented, and refused, for all the riches in the world, to be guilty of the deed he meditated. Then, the king laid hold of his own hair and said,—"If I am to become Boodhoo, let my head separate from my body." It came off; but the body did not lose its life and powers till the hands had given the head to the man. He carried it to Anooradapoora and presented it to the prince, who declared that, like all the rest, it was an imposture. The poor man following the directions he had received, requested it might be put on a white cloth on a chair; which having been done, the lips opened, and the head three times cried aloud,—"I am the King Sirisangabo!" The miracle of course was conclusive. The prince repented, went to Attanagallé, burnt the body of his brother, and built a dagobah, which remains to this day; and rice, it is said, still grows there spontaneously.

The next remarkable reign was that of Mahasin, who by means of charms, it is said, controlled demons and compelled them to labour for the public good. With their assistance, he constructed 150,000 tanks, many of which were of large dimensions. The tank of Mineré is mentioned as an instance of them, which is of that vast size, that it more resembles a great lake than an artificial piece of water; and, by a superstitious people, might naturally be referred to agency more than human. This king was the last of the family of Wijeya that reigned in Ceylon.

The race became extinct on his death, which happened in 846 A. B.

In the reign of the next king, who was a descendant of one of the princes who accompanied the branch of the Bo-tree, a memorable event occurred: Ceylon became possessed of the famous relic, the tooth of Boodhoo, which in the estimation of Boodhists is the most precious thing in the world, and the palladium of the country, the whole of which is dedicated to it. It was brought by the daughter and nephew of the king of Kalingoonratté, when in danger of falling into the hands of a neighbouring monarch, who made war for the express purpose of seizing it.

During the next sixty reigns, — excepting a partial invasion of the Malabars, the elevation of a person of low caste to the throne who made an excellent king, and the attachment of a royal poet to a poetical friend, so strong as to impel the one, and that the monarch, to throw himself into the funeral fire of the other, — little deserving of notice is recorded.

The next remarkable event is the conquest of the whole island by the Malabars, with the exception of Magam and Roona in the Magampattoo. After eighty years' submission, the natives rose in arms, and under Maha-wijeya-bahoo expelled their enemies. Owing to the religious persecutions of the invaders, who were of the Brahminical persuasion, hardly a priest was to be met with, and not one well acquainted with the doctrines of Boodhoo. In this emergency twenty Upasampada priests were procured from the Carnatic, who instructed a youth from each village, and in a few years completely remedied the evil and made several thousand priests.

For several successive reigns Ceylon flourished, till it was again visited by its old enemies, the Malabars, who took the king prisoner, plundered and ruined the country, and conquered the whole of it, excepting the southern districts. After nineteen years, Wijeya-bahoo appeared, "like a flame bursting out of darkness," defeated the Malabars, and drove them into the northern extremity of the island. The period of this event is not mentioned. Anooradapoora was never again a royal residence; and, from this time, its decay and ruin, and that of the adjoining country, have been progressive. *

Between this event and the landing of the Portuguese, little occurs worth repeating. The country, for a considerable time, was disturbed by the war carried on with the Malabars, with various success, till it was concluded in a very chivalrous manner by Prince Areachakrawartè; who, mounted on a black horse, alone, sword in hand, invaded Jaffnapatam, put thousands to death, and subdued the district. The court was established at Cotta. One king ruled over the whole island, and several princes had subordinate commands in different parts of the country, particularly at Gompalla, in the high country, in the Seven Korles, and in Jaffnapatam.

As my object is not to attempt to give a complete history of Ceylon, but merely a rapid historical sketch, with a view to illustrate the state and character of the inhabitants, and some of the peculiarities of the country, I shall proceed as I have begun; and, in the period extending from the first appearance of the Portuguese on the shore of the island to the expulsion of the Dutch, I shall notice only the most memorable events.

* Anooradapoora, so long the capital of Ceylon, is now a small mean village, in the midst of a desert. A large tank, numerous stone pillars, two or three immense tumuli, (probably old dagobahs,) are its principal remains. It is still considered a sacred spot; and is a place of pilgrimage. This information was collected partly from the natives, and partly from an officer who visited it during the rebellion.

In the beginning of the 16th century, in the reign of Derma-prakkrama-bahoo, the Portuguese arrived off Colombo.* The description given of them is not a little amusing. The natives who first saw them went to Cotta, and informed the king "that a new people was arrived, white and beautifully made, who wore iron coats and iron caps, and drank blood and ate stones; who gave a gold-coin for a fish, or even a lime; and who had a kind of instrument that could produce thunder and lightning, and balls which, put into these instruments, would fly many miles, and break ramparts, and destroy forts."

By the advice of the king's brother, who examined them in disguise, the Portugese were well received, and permitted to trade and establish a settlement at Colombo.

During the remainder of this reign, and the whole of the next, which was a short one, the Portuguese had very little influence in the country, and they remained in their original capacity of traders. In the next reign, that of Boowanyka-bahoo, in consequence of dissensions in the royal family, they began to gain ground and acquire political power. Engaged in a war with his brother Mihidoony, who refused to acknowledge the king's grandson as his successor, he sent an embassy to Portugal, with a figure of the infant prince in wax, begged protection for the child and his kingdom, and requested aid, which was most readily granted. The young prince was christened Don Juan Derma-pali. Troops were sent to Ceylon, with abundance of ammunition, to make good the promise that had been given.

* Ceylon was first discovered by the Portuguese in 1505. They do not appear to have attempted a settlement till after 1518; nor to have been firmly established till about 1536. Vide the History of Ceylon, by Philalethes, A.M., for the details of these events, extracted from Valentyn.

For some time, wherever the Portuguese appeared they were victorious. The king himself was almost one of the first to fall, by the new engines of war introduced; he was shot through the head when going to oppose his brother. He is said, by the native historian, to have ruined his country and religion, by his unnatural policy of having recourse to the Portuguese.

During the life of his successor Derma-pali, the island was in the most disturbed state. Mihidony proclaimed himself king, and established himself at Avisahavellé; he had to contend not only with the Portuguese on one side, but with native princes on the other, who strove to become independent: and he kept his ground manfully. His successor, Rajah Singha, of Sittawakka, carried on the war with great vigour: he overcame all the native princes who opposed him; took Cotta, and destroyed it; besieged Colombo, and reduced the Portuguese to great straits. After his death, the Portuguese were again successful; they took Avisahavellé, possessed themselves of the whole of the maritime provinces, and of a great part of the Seven Korles, and seemed to have a fair prospect of becoming masters of the whole island. The only obstacle in the way of their ambition, was Maha-Wimmala-derma, a native prince of spirit and abilities, who, in the civil wars of the Interior, when very young, had taken refuge at Colombo, from whence he was sent to Goa, and from thence, when the Portuguese were in danger of being driven out of the country by Rajah Singha of Sittawakka, he was sent back to Ceylon, to make a diversion in the high country in favour of his friends. He accomplished this, and more than was desired; he established himself at Singada-galla or Kandy, as an independent monarch, and governed the greater part of the country now included in the Kandyan provinces. As the most likely means of accomplishing their ends, the Portuguese brought Donna Catharina from Jaffna, where she had taken refuge with her father, Verasoora, the former Prince of Kandy, and sent her with a large force to oppose Wimmala-derma. The Portuguese owed much of their success to an enterprising native called Janiere, and by the Singalese Jayè Vera Banda, with the title of Maha-Modiansi, who went over to Derma-pali, in consequence of ill treatment. Wimmala-derma, to get rid of him (of whom he had the greatest apprehension) had recourse to a stratagem, which proved successful. From a forged letter that he had thrown in their way, the Portuguese hastily inferred the Maha-Modiansi to be a traitor, and put him to death.* The king attacked them in Yattineura, defeated them completely, and took the princess, whom he afterwards married: thus, the expedition formed to crush him, had the effect of strengthening his throne; indeed, were its consequences traced still farther, it might be considered as one of the remote causes of the final expulsion of the Portuguese; for the king whom the natives call "the Great Rajah Singha, who expelled the Portuguese," was the son of this princess.

On the death of Derma-pali, the Portuguese who actually governed his dominions took possession of them formally, as a dependence of Portugal.

Wimmala-derma died after a reign of twelve years. Though he left sons, he was succeeded by his brother Sennerat, who married his widow, Donna Catharina, by whom he had the Rajah Singha already alluded to. The dominions of Sen-

* According to Valentyn, he had formed a plot, in conjunction with the King of Kandy, to ruin the Portuguese, on the discovery of which he was assassinated by the orders and in the presence of the Portuguese commander. Philalethes, p. 68.

nerat at the time he ascended the throne, consisted of Ouva, Wellassey, Bintenney, Mately, Wallapané, Oudapalate, Oudooneura, Yattineura, Toompany, Harasea-pattoo, Doombera, and Hewahettè. The remainder of the island, and by far the greater part of it, belonged to the Portuguese. The king fixed his residence at Diatilika, or, as it is more generally called, Hangranketty. During the whole of his reign of twenty-five years, hostilities were carried on with the Portuguese. The latter under Simon Coerea *, entered Kandy seven different times, and burnt the town; and they built two forts in the neighbourhood, on the Mahawellè ganga, one at Pairawdenia, (of which the ruins are still to be seen,) and another at Gannoroowè. Thus far they were generally successful; but a reverse of fortune was near at hand: a large Portuguese force, led by Don Constantino, was completely defeated, with the loss of its general, at Wellawaya, in Ouva, by the Kandyans, under the command of Rajah Singha, (then only seventeen years old,) and of his two brothers-in-law, sons of Wimmala-derma. The young princes followed up their advantage; they besieged and took the forts on the Mahawellè ganga, invaded the Four Korles, and in fact did not remit their exertions till they had recovered the whole of the island, with the exception of the strongly fortified places, — Galle, Colombo, Jaffna, and Trincomalie. On the day that the fort at Gannoroowé was taken, Rajah Singha, who exposed himself very much, had a narrow escape of his life: a Kaffer aimed at him, and sent a bullet through his cap; the prince returned the fire with effect. For very many years the cap was kept as a court-curiosity,

* He was the brother of a leading Mohottala, in the Seven Korles; was taken prisoner by the Portuguese, sent to Goa, baptized, and married to an orphan of the Orphan-house.

and the gun which the prince used may be in existence even now · for it was in the late king's armoury. It was left-handed, as the prince was; there was this inscription on it: "This is the gun with which Rajah Singha killed the Kaffer who fired at him at Gattambè."*

Whilst carrying on the war in the Four Korles, Sennerat died, and was succeeded by the princely triumvirate, each of whom had his separate command.

To expel the Portuguese entirely, the princes formed an alliance with the Dutch. The conditions of the treaty which was made by Rajah Singha on board the Dutch fleet off Batticaloa, were; that the Dutch aided by the Kandyans, having driven the Portuguese out of their remaining possessions, should have all the maritime provinces, with the exception of Batticaloa and Putlam, which were to be retained by the princes, with the whole Interior of the island; and farther, that they should live peaceably as allies, and annually send ambassadors to each other. Galle first surrendered to the Dutch fleet; and in about sixteen years the Portuguese power was totally annihilated in Ceylon. This happened A. D. 1658.

Shortly, in consequence of the death of one prince, and the abdication of the other, who preferred forsaking his native country to engaging in a civil war with his ambitious brother-in-law, Rajah Singha became sole king of the Interior. He attained the great age of ninety. His government was so severe, that it gave rise to more than one rebellion. Though he had frequent quarrels with the Dutch, they were generally amicably adjusted. He was remarkable for a fine person, great strength, an enormous

* Another name of the place, particularly applicable to the right bank.

nose, violent passions, and a jealous temper. Till seven days before he expired, he kept it a secret that he had a son. Then, he produced the prince to the court at Hangranketty, where he latterly resided; and, to convince the chiefs, who had their doubts, that no imposition was committed, he was the first to prostrate and acknowledge his successor.

His son and successor Wimeladarmè, who usually resided at Kandy, reigned twenty-two years. He bore a high character; and is said to have governed piously, wisely, and justly. During the whole time he was on the throne, not an individual was put to death, and the country was neither disturbed by war nor rebellion. Owing to the long wars carried on with the Portuguese, the religion of Boodhoo was at an extremely low ebb*; its doctrines were forgotten, its ceremonies were in disuse, and its temples were without ministers. With the assistance of the Dutch, the king sent an embassy to Siam, and procured twelve Oupasampada priests, who came to Kandy, and instructed and ordained forty natives of the Oupasampada order, and very many of the Sameneroo.

It is stated as a remarkable event in this reign, that a large ship with a rich cargo, without a crew, without a single man on board, was driven on shore at Batticaloa. She was not plundered, but taken possession of in the king's name. The iron cannon, that are still to be seen at Bintenny, Haipola-cadavetté and Meddamahaneura, belonged to her.

Wimeladarmè was succeeded by his eldest son, Narendaré Singha, commonly called Condisali, — Condisali having been his

* This may be inferred from another quarter, — from the account which Knox gives of the state of religion in Ceylon, in the reign of Rajah Singha, when our countryman was so long detained a prisoner in the Interior.

favourite residence. He reigned about thirty-five years. He was addicted to cruelty and drunkenness, and was remarkable for his vices only. In one instance, many of his principal chiefs rebelled, and placed his brother on the throne; but they failed in their enterprise, and were all put to death. He had no offspring, and he was the last of the Singalese race of monarchs.

The next king was Sree-wijeya Rajah Singha, the younger brother of one of the queens of the late king, who was called to the throne by the general consent of the chiefs and people assembled in Kandy. He was generally named Hangranketty, having lived a good deal at that place as a private individual. During a short and peaceable reign of seven years, he gained the affections of his people by his just and virtuous government. He had three queens from Madura, but died childless.

Kirtisserè Rajah Singha, the younger brother of one of his queens was chosen to succeed him. He reigned forty years. The early part of his reign was licentious and cruel, and gave rise to insurrections which he had the good fortune to put down. After reading some religious books he reformed completely, and became as remarkable for virtue and piety as he had been before for vice and the neglect of religion. He sent an embassy to Siam for priests to restore the religion of Boodhoo, which, in Ceylon, was still in a very degenerate state. Three different missions arrived, by whose exertions the evil was in a great measure remedied. He vainly flattered himself, that he had it in his power to expel the Dutch from the island; and went to war with them, deaf to the remonstrances which they made, on his breach of faith. On neither side were hostilities carried on with any vigour: the king failed in his attack on the maritime provinces, and the Dutch were obliged to evacuate Kandy which they had taken.

On the whole, the Kandyans were the greatest sufferers by the war, particularly as they lost Batticaloa and Putlam, which the Dutch afterwards kept in their possession. The king was remarkable for a fine person and for great strength and activity. He particularly excelled in managing a horse or an elephant. Riding in the streets of Kandy a spirited vicious horse, that had been sent him by the Dutch, he was thrown, and after lingering some months, died of the injury he had received. This happened A.D. 1778. Though he had several queens, he had no children.

His brother was chosen to succeed him. He ascended the throne with the title of Rajadi Rajah Singha. He bore the character of an indolent, voluptuous man, addicted to love and poetry, and devoted to nothing else. His reign of twenty years was tranquil, and undisturbed, either by insurrections or hostilities, excepting on one occasion, that the Dutch made an unsuccessful inroad into Saffragam; and, on another, that his forces invaded the low country, to co-operate with us when we took possession of the maritime provinces in 1796. It is in relation to this event, and no other, that the period of his reign will ever be memorable in the history of Ceylon. It is hardly necessary to mention the embassies to the court of Kandy, that preceded our landing, or the expectations of advantages that the unsagacious monarch founded on the transfer of power from the Dutch to the English. It is sufficient to remark, that he gained from us no sea-port, as he had anticipated, and no accession of territory; that all political relations between him and us continued the same as they had been between him and the Dutch; and that the only alteration of consequence was the exchange which he made of a weak for a powerful neighbour. He died at Kandy in 1798; and without a child by either of his five queens.

During the last twenty-two years, Ceylon, like Europe, has had its portion of change: — a king has been dethroned; we have taken possession of the whole island; a rebellion has broken out, and has been subdued; the old constitution of the country has been in a great measure set aside, and a new one has been given to it. These important events, with the principal circumstances that either led to them or were connected with them, I shall endeavour to describe succinctly, accurately, and candidly.

On the death of the former king, it was for some time doubtful who would be chosen to succeed him. The nomination, according to the etiquette of the court, rested entirely with the first Adikar, who, in the present instance, was Pilimé Talawè, an ambitious and intriguing courtier. He seemed to have decided very early the choice he should make, if we may judge from a conversation which he had with the chief priest, an able and upright man, in the presence of a Dissave, during the former king's illness. — Chief Priest. "The king's case is desperate; he can live only a few days. What are your plans respecting his successor?" First Adikar. "I have a good plan in view: we will have a king who will listen to us, and not ruin the country." — Chief Priest. "Yes: such a one as you contemplate will attend to advice and be tractable at first; but if his education be not good, your plan will fail: he will finally follow his own bent, and the country will suffer." First Adikar. "There is a remedy for the evil you anticipate: if the king turn out ill, we can apply to the English; they will check him." — Chief Priest. "What you propose might answer in the time of the Dutch, but now it is out of the question. Rest assured, if the keeper do not take care of his elephant, not only the lives of others, but his own will be endangered. In choosing a king, do not proceed a step without deliberation: you must choose one who will take care of religion, the country, and yourself." — The individual selected by the minister, according to his own principles, was a young man, only eighteen, called Kannesamy, a sister's son of one of the queens-dowager; uneducated, and having nothing to recommend him but a good figure. He was, as usual, regularly proposed to the chiefs and people; and, as usual, accepted, and publicly acknowledged. He was raised to the throne by the name of Srèe Wikrimè Rajah Singha.

The minister immediately made the young king the tool of his nefarious designs. Murder, that for many years had not appeared on the political stage of Kandy, again shewed its face. Arawavali Adikar, and Damagomoowa Dissave, were way-laid and assassinated; and Carpa, a faithful servant of the former, was hanged. Instigated by his minister, the King even gave an order for the imprisonment and execution of his uncle, Gampola Naika, whose only offence was that of giving good advice. The persons to whom this order was secretly communicated, had the virtue and courage to obey the first part of it only. Of a piece with this monstrous conduct, the King selected the two daughters of this very uncle for his queens; who, in Matelè, on their way from Madura, when they heard of their father's confinement and refused to proceed, were brought by compulsion to Kandy.

It is unnecessary to dwell on the disastrous war between us and the Kandyans in 1803, or on the unsuccessful embassy of General M'Dowal, which preceded it, and there is reason to suppose, partly conduced to it. Both have been pretty minutely described.* I shall notice only such circumstances of the terrible catastrophe, that followed the capitulation at Kandy, as are either not generally known, or tend to develope the character of the Kandyan monarch.

On the 24th of June, 1803, Kandy, then occupied by the English force under Major Davie, was attacked by the Kandyans in great numbers, in presence of the king and his court, stationed on an adjoining hill. After about seven hours' fighting, a flag of truce was displayed on our side. A conference ensued. Major Davie was required to quit the town immediately, even without his sick, who, it was promised, should be sent after him. Major Davie, after some objections, yielded at length to the terms imposed on him, and left Kandy with all the troops able to march. The king instantly ordered the chiefs to assemble. He knew that the river, the Mahawellé ganga, was flooded, and that the English could not pass without assistance. Taking advantage of this circumstance, he ordered certain chiefs to go to Major Davie, and demand the surrender of Mootosamè, (the brother-in-law of the former king, and whom we had proclaimed king,) and five other relations who had accompanied him, and a Kandyan deserter. They were given up, it is said, unconditionally. Pilimè Talawé and Malawa were directed to bring them before the king at Oodawellé, in the neighbourhood of Kandy. When they appeared, the king desired Eheylapola, to ask Mootosamè, "If it were proper for him, who was of the royal family, to join the English." The unfortunate Mootosamè made no defence, replying, "He was at the king's mercy." He was next

* Vide Percival, p. 375., and Cordiner, vol. ii. chap. vi.

asked if any Kandyan chiefs were connected with him. He answered,—"A few letters had been received from Pilimé Talawè." To which the king remarked, he could not believe it; and ordered his Malay Mohandiram to take the prisoners away to execution. The deserter was impaled, and the rest were put to death by the krises of the Malays. This is the first act of the tragedy. Speedily, the king again summoned the first Adikar and Malawa before him, and bid them follow the English, and put them to death. The minister objected to the order, remarking, "It is highly improper for those who have submitted, to be put to death."—"What! (said the enraged king) are you siding with the English again?" The minister then left the royal presence, observing, "Since he urges the measure, what can we do?"—He made another attempt to dissuade the king, by means of a favourite, who went in and represented the impropriety of such proceedings. On this second application the king became furious, and starting from his seat, cried aloud, "Why am I not obeyed?" The order now was too soon obeyed. Having hastily collected a force, the two chiefs proceeded to Watapaloga, where the English were stopped by the height of the river, and were without the means of crossing it. The chiefs desired Major Davie and the principal officers to come to them. Strange to say, Major Davie complied; and, with two captains, and a native captain of Malays, was sent to Kandy. The Malay Mohandiram, in the Kandyan service, and Maniseram, a spy, persuaded our Malays and Sepoys to desert. Having thus deprived our men of their officers, and weakened them by the seduction of the native troops, they hastened to the bloody catastrophe. They told the soldiers that their officers were gone to the Katisgastottè to cross at that ferry; that they must lay down their arms; and that they should be conducted the same way. Too weak to resist, they did as they were desired, went over unarmed to the Kandyans, and were immediately massacred. About the same time, the hospital in Kandy, containing 120 men of the 19th regiment, was entered by the enemy, who, in compliance with orders, threw the dead, dying, and sick, all into a deep pit, prepared to receive them. Major Davie and his companions, whose lives were spared, were detained, and died of sickness, one after another, in their cruel captivity.

Elated by his success at Kandy, and encouraged by the native officers who had deserted, and were anxious, with their men, to return to their old masters, the king resolved to invade our territory and attack Colombo. His army approached within eighteen miles of the seat of our government, when its progress was stopped by the little post of Hanwellè, defended by a few invalids. After vain exertions to take the place, the king, convinced of the impracticability of the enterprise he had engaged in, retreated to the mountains, but not without having previously sacrificed to his disappointment and anger Lookè Dissave, and his companion, Palipanerale, who were put to death by his order, for sitting under a tree instead of leading their men, during one of the attacks on Hanwellè.

In the desultory warfare that followed, and which was continued during several months, on a principle rather of retaliation and revenge than with any political object in view, nothing presents itself deserving of being adverted to, with the exception of the gallant conduct of a detachment under the command of Captain (now Lieutenant-Colonel) Johnston, that in the latter end of 1804, penetrated into the Interior, and without any of the support and co-operation which it had a right to expect, marched through the heart of the country from Batticaloa to Kandy, which it entered, and from Kandy to Trincomalie, overcoming every obstacle that it had to encounter, and proudly displaying what valour is capable of accomplishing when directed by talent*.

Between 1805 and 1815, the armistice, or mutual suspension of hostilities, in which the unfortunate war of 1803 terminated, experienced no serious interruption. During this period of mutual and gloomy forbearance on each side, little that is interesting occurred relative to Kandyan affairs, except in the court of Kandy itself, where the worst passions of human nature were in horrible operation, — agitating the breast of a tyrant on one hand, and of conspirators on the other; and producing deeds quite diabolical, and, did not truth require the relation, too terrible to be described.

About 1806, Magasthenè, second Adikar and Dissave of the Seven Korles, died. In his office he was succeeded by Eheylapola. The vacant dissavony was divided between this chief and Molligoddè Dissave, to the great offence and discontent of the people. Such a division, they said, "was contrary to custom; — it was a grievance, as two Dissaves would require double the services and duties of one, and that they would resist it:" a rebellion in the Seven Korles was the consequence. On this occasion, Pilimè Talawè assured the king, that were the district transferred to him and his nephew, Ratwattè Dissave, they would soon make the people submit to his orders. The experiment was made, — the minister was as good as his word; for he immediately brought the people back to their duty. His success excited the king's

* Vide Colonel Johnston's "Narrative," &c. for a very interesting account of this perilous expedition.

suspicion and jealousy, and heightened the aversion he had some time begun to feel towards his old benefactor. The chief, nettled by the altered manner of the king, reminded him, who had placed him on the throne; and told him, he did not behave as he ought, nor listen to him and pay him that attention that he was wont to do. The monarch did not receive his reprimand patiently; he retorted — "He was not to be led by his chiefs, but they were to be directed by him." Farther, the minister expressed his disapprobation of the public works which the king was then engaged in, on the ground that they were vexatious to the people and oppressive. The works in question were several new roads; the lake of Kandy, which was made at this time; many new buildings, particularly the present Pattiripooa, &c. These bickerings between the monarch and his minister, created mutual hatred, which was soon coupled with mutual dread; the one imagining his life insecure from the machinations of the other. The king, who had little controul over his passions, soon gave them vent. When the minister expressed a wish to unite his son to the natural grand-daughter of King Kirtisserè, his majesty, taking it for granted that this was merely a step to the throne, assembled the chiefs, enumerated various grounds of complaint against the minister, charged him of mal-administration, and accused him of being the author of every thing cruel and unpopular, that had been done during his reign; then suddenly relenting, he told the Adikar, that he forgave him all his offences, and as a proof he conferred new honours upon him. But this relenting and these new honours were merely delusive. Presently, having neglected some little trivial duty, the minister was summoned to appear before the king and chiefs assembled in the great square. His offences were recapitulated; he was deprived of all his offices, and sent to prison, from whence he was liberated in eight days, and permitted to go to his country residence, and lead a private life. The disgraced and irritated chief did not remain quiet at home. He soon hatched a plot to murder his ungrateful sovereign. He bribed the Malay Mohandiram and sixty of his Malays to attack the king on a certain day and assassinate him; and he prevailed on the headmen of Oudeneura and Yattineura to raise the people of these districts in arms, about the same time. On the day and hour appointed, Ballinwattella-rallefinding the king awake, when it was expected he would have been asleep, begged the conspirators, whose spy he was, to wait a little. The two provinces just mentioned prematurely broke out in rebellion and marred the plot. The king instantly sent for Pilimé Talawé, his nephew, and son; and had them secretly conveyed by night to different prisons, in the most difficult parts of the country. The Malay Mohandiram and his men fled to Colombo. The incipient rebellion was suppressed, and the ringleaders apprehended. Pilimé Talawé and his nephew and son were sent for to undergo trial. The two former arrived together; and, in the presence of the king and chiefs, were confronted with the ringleaders, and were sentenced to death on their confession. They were immediately beheaded, and six petty chiefs were hanged and impaled around their bodies. The son, who was imprisoned farther off, was capitally condemned, at the same time; but not arriving till after the execution of his relations, and on a holiday, he was reprieved; and at the intercession of the chiefs his life was spared, but his lands confiscated. The execution of Pilimé Talawé and the ruin of his family, the first act of retributive justice, took place in 1812.

Eheylapola succeeded Pilimé Talawé as first Adikar. The king now became more suspicious and tyrannical than ever. Terrified by the past, apprehensive of future danger, and intent on his own security alone, without any regard to consequences, he ordered, that there should be no communication between the provinces which he considered tainted with the leaven of revolt, and the loyal ones of Hewahetté, Doombera, Ouva, Kotmalé, and Walapané. Farther, he ordered, that no moormen, and that no priests, should remain in the latter provinces; and that all women, not born in these provinces, should also quit them, and return to their native districts. These orders were enforced in the same spirit in which they were issued. Wives were separated from their husbands, mothers from their children; the young bride and the aged parent,—all, indiscriminately, were torn from the bosom of their families, and driven from their homes; producing scenes of distress, and feelings of anger and discontent, which might well shake the firmest loyalty. Intent on the same object, his personal security, the king made a great change in his household; he removed to distant situations all officers who belonged to the lately rebellious or suspected provinces, and would allow no one to be near his person, who was not a native of those he considered his loyal, as well as mountain districts and natural fortresses.

He had formed certain secret suspicions of the first Adikar, which the confessions of the conspirators in Pilimè Talawè's plot had given rise to, and which, suppressed at the time, fermented inwardly, and produced cordial hatred of the minister. Having lost two sons and two daughters by his first queens, he married two more at the same time, and sisters. On the occasion of the chiefs making their presents after the celebration of the nuptials, the king's ill-will towards the minister first showed itself; his present, though rich, was called mean, and unworthy of acceptance.

A crisis was now fast approaching. The people in general were disaffected; most of the chiefs were anxious for a change of government, either from hatred of the king, or as an easy way of getting rid of debts to his relations, of whom many chiefs had received large loans; the second Adikar's debt alone (Molligoddé's) amounting to six thousand pagodas.

In this state of affairs, just after his marriage, the king sent the chiefs into their respective districts, to superintend the cultivation of the country, and the improvement of the revenue. Eheylapola, in a discontented mood, hastened into his Dissavony (Saffragam), and presently began to act his part. Many circumstances, about the same time, gave rise to an open rupture between the king and his minister: — a village of Saffragam, belonging to one of the queens, refused to pay its dues, and ill-treated her agent; the revenue derived from areka-nuts was not duly paid into the treasury; a charge was brought against the Adikar, by a Malabar merchant, of his having unjustly deprived him of a large sum of money, which the minister was required to disprove, or refund the amount; farther, he was ordered to return to Kandy, and bring with him the people of his district, who had neglected the payment of various dues to the king, particularly on the occasion of his marriage. The Adikar's answers were not those of a submissive subject, and widened the breach. A favourite in his district, which is almost entirely cut off from the other Kandyan provinces by mountains inaccessible, excepting by two or three difficult passes, he began to think of opposition: he opened a correspondence with Colombo, and made preparations for defence, with the concurrence of the people, who promised to risk their lives in his support. Intelligence of his measures soon reached the king, who instantly deprived him of all his offices, imprisoned his wife and children, appointed Molligoddé first Adikar and Dissave of Saffragam, and ordered the invasion of the province by the new minister. Molligoddé obeyed with alacrity: he entered Saffragam over the loftiest point of the island, and the most difficult pass — the summit of Adam's Peak. The hearts of the natives failed them on his approach; and he met with but little opposition. Eheylapola, with some of his adherents, fled to Colombo, and Molligoddé returned to Kandy with a crowd of prisoners, forty-seven of whom were impaled. This happened in 1814. Now, one scene of horror and bloodshed rapidly follows another, till the tragedy is wound up, and retributive justice again appears on the stage. Pusilla, Dissave of Neurakalawea, had excited the king's displeasure, by a present that, through the ignorance of his brother, was offered in a disrespectful manner. The brother was imprisoned: the Dissave was soon suspected of correspondence with Eheylapola, and a letter from this chief, abusive of the king, having been found in the possession of one of his attendants, Pusilla was considered guilty, his eyes were plucked out, his joints cut, and after this torture he was beheaded. The old offence of the Seven Korles was again ript open; all the headmen supposed to have been concerned in the rebellion which Pilimé Talawé suppressed, were summoned to appear at Kandy. They were tried by a commission of three chiefs, of whom Molligoddé, whose authority they had opposed, was one, and were condemned to death: after a severe flogging, about seventy were executed, all of them men of some consequence in their district. These transactions are horrible; but what remains to be related is worse. Hurried along by the flood of revenge, the tyrant, lost to every tender feeling, resolved to punish Eheylapola who had escaped, through his family, which remained in his power: he sentenced the chief's wife and children, and his brother and his wife, to death,— the brother and children to be beheaded, and the females to be drowned. In front of the queen's palace, and between the Nata and Maha Visnu Dewalé, as if to shock and insult the gods as well as the sex, the wife of Eheylapola and his children were brought from prison, where they had been in charge of female jailors, and delivered over to the executioners. The lady with great resolution maintained her's and her children's innocence, and her lord's; at the same time submitting to the king's pleasure, and offering up her own and her offspring's lives, with the fervent hope that her husband would be benefited by the sacrifice. Having uttered these sentiments aloud, she desired her eldest boy to submit to his fate; the poor boy, who was eleven years old, clung to his mother, terrified and crying; her second son, nine years old, heroically stepped forward; he bid his brother not to be afraid,—he would show him the way to die! By one blow of a sword, the head of this noble child was severed from his body; streaming with blood and hardly inanimate, it was thrown into a rice mortar; the pestle was put into the mother's hands, and she was ordered to pound it, or be disgracefully tortured. To avoid the disgrace, the wretched woman did lift up the pestle and let it fall. One by one, the heads of all her children were cut off; and one by one, the poor mother —— but the circumstance is too dreadful to be dwelt on. One of the children was a girl; and to wound a female is considered by the Singalese a most monstrous crime: another was an infant at the breast, and it was plucked from its mother's breast to be beheaded; when the head was severed from the body, the milk it had just drawn in ran out mingled with its blood. During this tragical scene, the crowd who had assembled to witness it wept and sobbed aloud, unable to suppress their feelings of grief and horror. Palihaparïè Dissave was so affected that he fainted, and was expelled his office for showing such tender sensibility. During two days the whole of Kandy, with the exception of the tyrant's court, was as one house of mourning and lamentation; and so deep was the grief, that not a fire (it is said) was kindled, no food was dressed, and a general fast was held. After the execution of her children, the sufferings of the mother were speedily relieved. She, and her sister-in-law, and the wife and sister of Pusilla Dissave, were led to the little tank in the immediate neighbourhood of Kandy, called Bogambarawave, and drowned. Such are the prominent features of this period of terror, which, even now, no Kandyan thinks of without dread, and few describe without weeping. Executions at this time were almost unceasing; the numbers put to death cannot be calculated; no one was perfectly secure, — not even a priest, — not even a chief priest; for Paranataley Anoonaika-Ounnansi, a man, in the estimation of the natives, of great learning and goodness, fell a victim to the tyrant's rage. To corporal punishments, imprisonments, &c. — those minor causes of distress, — it is unnecessary to allude; in the gloomy picture they are as lights to shades.

Disgusted and terrified by the conduct of the King, the chiefs and people were ripe to revolt; and only waited the approach of a British force to throw off their allegiance.

Acquainted with what was going on in the Interior, it was impossible for our government to be unconcerned. His Excellency Lieutenant General (now General Sir Robert) Brownrigg prepared for hostilities, which seemed to be unavoidable. He had stationed a force near the frontier, in readiness to act at a moment's notice; and he had made arrangements for invading the Kandyan provinces should war break out.

Cause for declaring war soon offered. Several of our native merchants, who in the way of trade had gone into the Interior, were treated as spies, and sent back shockingly mutilated *; and very soon after, a party of Kandyans passed the boundary and set fire to a village within our territory. The declaration of war against the Kandyan monarch immediately followed this act; it was made on the 10th of January, 1815. On the day following, our troops entered the Kandyan territory; they found the Three and Four Korles in a state of revolt, and they were soon joined by Molligoddé, the first Adikar, and many of the principal chiefs. Almost without the least opposition, our divisions reached the capital; on the 14th of February our head-quarters were established there; and on the 18th, the king was taken prisoner. Forsaken by his chiefs, he fled on our approach into the mountainous district of Doombera, accompanied only by a very few attendants. Driven by heavy rain from a mountain where he concealed himself during the day, he descended and took shelter in a solitary house in the neighbourhood of Meddah-mahaneura, not aware that there was a force at hand lying in wait for him. The party was a zealous one, composed of natives of Saffragam, headed by a stanch adherent of Eheylapola: as soon as intimation was given of the king's hiding-place, the

* Ten were thus treated: — the noses of all of them were cut off; besides which, some were deprived of an arm and others of their ears. Two only of these unfortunate men reached Colombo, presenting a most miserable spectacle, — the amputated parts hanging suspended from their necks; the other eight died on the road.

house was surrounded and the monarch seized. He was sent to Colombo, and from thence to Vellore, where he is still in confinement. He may be justly considered an example of the perfect tyrant: wrapped up in selfishness, — possessed of ungovernable passions, — destitute of religious feelings, — destitute of moral principles, — and without check, either human or divine.

A fortnight after his capture, on the second of March, in a convention held at Kandy, by his Excellency the Governor on one side, and the Kandyan chiefs on the other, the tyrant Sree Wikrimè Rajah Singha was formally dethroned; the king of Great Britain was acknowledged sovereign of the whole island of Ceylon; the preservation of the old form of government of the Interior was guaranteed on our part, as well as the protection of the customs, laws, and religion of the people.*

A board, composed of three civil servants, was soon established at Kandy, consisting of a resident, and of a commissioner of justice and of revenue; — the first, the representative of the governor; the other two, the presidents of their respective departments. The board, with the Adikars and the principal chiefs, formed the great court of justice, from whose sentence there was no appeal, except to the Governor. Besides the board, and a subordinate agent of government in Ouva, Saffragam, and the Three Korles, the civil authority of the country was exercised as before, by the native Dissaves and Raté-mahatmeyas.

The military force which was kept in the Interior, was inconsiderable, seldom exceeding 1000 men, who were confined to a few stations where we had established military posts, — altogether

* Vide Appendix, No. I. for the Articles of the Convention.

not exceeding eleven in number. The offices of first and second Adikar were filled by Molligoddé, the former prime-minister, and by a chief of the name of Kappawattè. Eheylapola, to whom the first appointment was offered, begged to decline it. There is reason to believe that he looked higher, and that he expected to have been made king. Be this as it may, he married again, and resided in Kandy; where he lived in considerable state, and was regarded by the natives as the great chief of the country.

Between March 1815 and October 1817, the Kandyan provinces remained quite tranquil. The terms of the convention were strictly adhered to by us; and the chiefs and people seemed contented under our mild and indulgent government. But these appearances were delusive. Having by our means got rid of a tyrant, — having enjoyed a little rest, — they seemed to have considered themselves sufficiently refreshed to try their strength, and attempt the expulsion of their benefactors.

Circumstances considered, such a desire, however ungrateful, was not unnatural on their parts. There was no sympathy between us and them; no one circumstance to draw or bring us together, and innumerable ones of a repulsive nature. The chiefs, though less controuled than under the king, and exercising more power in their districts than they ever before ventured to exert, were far from satisfied. Before, no one but the king was above them; now, they were inferior to every civilian in our service, — to every officer in our army. Though officially treated with respect, it was only officially; a common soldier passed a proud Kandyan chief with as little attention as he would a fellow of the lowest caste. Thus they considered themselves degraded, and shorn of their splendour. The people in general had similar feelings on this score; at least, the respectable and most considerable portion of the population, viz. the Goewansè part. Ignorant of their distinctions, high caste and low caste were treated alike by most Englishmen who came in contact with them: and, undesignedly and unknowingly, we often offended and provoked them when we least intended it; and particularly in our mode of entering their temples, and in our manner of treating their priests, who require respect amounting almost to adoration. Accustomed to the presence of a king in their capital, to the splendour of his court, and to the complicated arrangements connected with it, they could ill relish the sudden and total abolition of the whole system. The King of Great Britain was to them merely a name: they had no notion of a king ruling over them at the distance of thousands of miles: they had no notion of delegated authority: they wanted a king whom they could see, and before whom they could prostrate and obtain summary justice. These are a few only of the leading circumstances which tended to render the natives averse from us and our government, and anxious to attempt to throw it off.

In October, 1817, such an attack was commenced, and there is reason to believe, prematurely, owing to accidental circumstances, without previous combination or system. In the beginning of this month, a moorman employed under our government, who had gained the ill-will of the natives of the remote district of Welassey, was seized by the people of the country, carried before a man who had assumed the title of king*, and condemned to death and executed. The Agent of Government of Ouva, who was the first to learn of this transaction, instantly

* In the course of the rebellion it was ascertained, in a [illegible]isfactory manner, that this pretender to the throne was a native of the Sev[illegible]orles, and had been a priest of Boodhoo.

went into the district with a small party of military, to investigate the matter. He found the inhabitants armed with bows and arrows, and averse from conference. He was the next victim who fell, and the officer and his men, with considerable difficulty, made good their retreat to Badulla.

Such were the unfortunate circumstances under which the rebellion of 1817 began. Justice, to say nothing of policy, absolutely required that active measures should be taken to punish the guilty and apprehend the impostor,—the pretender to the throne. Active measures were accordingly taken by the Governor to this effect, but not with the desired success. The rebels were speedily joined by Kapittipola, Dissave of Ouva, an active, enterprising, intriguing, ambitious, and unprincipled man, the brother-in-law of Eheylapola, and his intimate friend, and connected with many of the best families in the country. Every day, notwithstanding all our exertions, the spirit of insurrection expanded itself, actually increasing in magnitude, in proportion to the opposition it encountered. Before six months had expired, the rebellion was truly alarming, both from the rapidity and extent of its progress, and the number of chiefs who had joined it. In March, 1818, all the country was in arms against us, with the exception of the lower part of Saffragam, the Three and Four Korles, and Oudeneura, and Yattineura; and, with the exception of the first Adikar, every chief of consequence had either joined the rebel standard, or was under arrest and confined by us, for favouring, or being suspected of favouring, the rebel cause: Eheylapola himself, and the second Adikar, Kappawattè, were of the latter number. During the three following months, our affairs assumed a still more melancholy aspect. Our little army was much exhausted and reduced by fatigue, privation, and disease; the rebellion was still unchecked; all our efforts had been apparently fruitless; not a leader of any consequence had been taken, and not a district subdued or tranquillised. This was a melancholy time to those who were on the scene of action; and many began to despond and augur from bad to worse, and to prophesy (what indeed was far from improbable) that the few districts not yet against us, would join the enemy; that the communication between Colombo and our head-quarters at Kandy would be cut off; and that we should be very soon obliged to evacuate the country, and fight our way out of it.

This gloomy prospect was of short continuance: the aspect of our affairs brightened with the same rapidity that they had become overcast. Kappitipola was defeated in several attempts which he made about this time with all the force of the country he could command, often amounting to several thousand men. Dissensions sprung up amongst the leaders of the rebellion. Kappitipola and the pretender were seized and imprisoned by another rebel chief, and another pretender to the throne was set up in opposition to the first. Now all our efforts were as eminently successful as they had been the contrary before: hardly a day passed but some rebel chief was taken; district after district submitted, till, in October, Kappitipola was seized, and the relic which had been clandestinely removed from Kandy, recovered, and the whole country completely tranquillised.

It would be difficult to give the English reader an accurate idea of the manner in which, during the rebellion, hostilities were carried on on either side. It was a partisan warfare, which, from its very nature and circumstances, was severe and irregular; particularly when at its height, and after lenient measures had been tried in vain. When a district rose in rebellion, one or more military posts were established in it; martial law was proclaimed; the dwellings of the resisting inhabitants were burnt; their fruit-trees were often cut down, and the country was scoured in every direction by small detachments, who were authorised to put to death all who made opposition, or were found with arms in their hands. The natives, on their part, never met us boldly and fairly in the field; they had recourse to stratagems of every kind, and took every possible advantage of the difficult nature of their country, and of their minute knowledge of the ground. They would way-lay our parties, and fire on them from inaccessible heights, or from the ambush of an impenetrable jungle; they would line the paths through which we had to march with snares of different kinds,—such as spring-guns and spring-bows, deep pits, lightly covered over, and armed with thorns, spikes, &c.; and, in every instance that an opportunity offered, they showed no mercy, and gave no quarter. Such a system of warfare as this, of which I have partially sketched the outline, had better not be given in detail. There were certain redeeming circumstances occasionally exhibited, on which one might dwell with pleasure; traits of heroism amongst our men, and of undaunted courage, that have never been exceeded; and traits of parental attachment amongst the natives, and of cool resignation to their fate, that have seldom been surpassed.

For the same reason that I have not entered into details of the warfare, I shall notice only in the most summary manner, the sufferings and miseries inflicted and endured on both sides, whilst the conflict lasted. We suffered most from the harassing nature of the service; from fatigue and privation; and from the effects of these, and of night-marches, and of an unwholesome climate, producing disease. The sufferings of the natives were of a more severe kind and complicated nature. In addition to the horrors of war in its most appalling shape, they had to encounter those of disease, want, and famine, without chance of relief. Our loss, from disease alone, amounted nearly to one-fifth of our whole force employed.* The loss of the natives, killed in the field or executed, or that died of disease and famine, can hardly be calculated; it was, probably, ten times greater than ours, and may have amounted, perhaps, to ten thousand.

When one considers this rebellion and its consequences, one almost regrets, that we ever entered the Kandyan country. The evils immediately resulting from it, certainly greatly exceed the original benefit we conferred on the natives, in removing a tyrant from the throne. One source of consolation to the local government is, that the rebellion was not the effect of oppression or misrule, but of the innate propensities of the people, concealed till they burst out and showed themselves in acts of violence, that required to be repelled by force. In candour, too, it must be remarked, that our government was hardly answerable for the irregularities committed on our side whilst hostilities lasted: they were contrary to express orders, and never had the countenance of any officer high in command; and, I sincerely

* Till towards the conclusion of the rebellion, when reinforcements were received from the continent, our whole force in Ceylon hardly amounted to five thousand men; and I believe it is not too high to estimate our total loss at about one thousand.

believe, seldom reached the ear of the Commander of the Forces, who, through the whole of the distressing affair, was not less remarkable for mildness and forbearance, than for constancy and determination, and unremitting exertion. The future, it is to be hoped, will rationally afford another and the best source of consolation for the past: but to lay open this prospect, it is necessary to revert to the conclusion of the rebellion, and to notice the political changes which immediately followed that event.

After the capture of Kappitipola and all the principal leaders of the rebellion, with the exception of the upstart pretender; and after the recovery of the sacred relic, the possessor of which is considered by the natives the master of the country that is dedicated to it, the whole of the Interior, as has been already remarked, was speedily tranquillised. Kappitipola, with two other rebel chiefs of note, (Madugallé and Pilimè Talawé,) were tried by a court-martial, and were condemned to death. The two former were beheaded: Pilimè Talawé (the same who had escaped execution under the late king) had his life again spared, and was banished, with some other rebel leaders, to the Isle of France. On the 21st of November, 1818, a new constitution, or, rather, a modification of the former convention, was given by His Excellency the Governor to the people of the Interior; the principal articles of which were the following:— 1st, relating to the revenue; that all personal services, excepting those required for making and repairing roads and bridges, were to be abolished, and that all taxes were to merge in one,— a tax of one-tenth of the produce of the paddy-lands: 2d, relating to the administration of justice, which, throughout the country, was to be conducted by the Board of Commissioners in

Kandy, and by the agents of government in the provinces, aided by the Dissaves, subordinate to our civil servants, and remunerated, not as before, by contributions of the people, but by fixed salaries. * These were great and important alterations; and our government still reserved to itself the power of making such farther changes, from time to time, as circumstances might seem to require.

It is in this change of system, that a prospect opens of amends in future, for the immediate evils and misfortunes, the result of the rebellion. Whilst the old system lasted, whilst our hands were tied by the articles of the convention, and the chiefs were the rulers of the country, we had little power to do good. The chain of custom, fixed for centuries, preventing all progress, and keeping the people stationary, is now happily broken; the Interior is now in the same political state as the maritime provinces; and we shall have much to answer for, both politically and morally, if we do not exert ourselves, and, availing ourselves of the capacity, ameliorate the condition of the people, and improve the state of the country. By attending to the education of the rising generation, much may be done for the diffusion of useful knowledge, and of Christian principles, amongst the people; and, by encouraging agriculture and horticulture, the Interior may be made the granary and garden of the island, productive of grain equal to the wants of the whole population of Ceylon, and of cinnamon and coffee to almost any extent; and thus, from being a source of expense and loss, it may be changed into one of profit and wealth to the island in general, and to the

* Vide Appendix, No. II. for a copy of the proclamation of Government, enacting the changes stated in the text, and many minor ones.

British government. If these sanguine anticipations be nowise realised, the natives may well rue the day we crossed their mountains, and deplore the time when their old system of government was overturned. I will hope better things, and that, as we nobly commenced with dethroning a tyrant, so we shall continue to be the benefactors of the country.

PART II.

TRAVELS IN THE INTERIOR OF CEYLON.

CHAPTER I.

SET OUT FROM COLOMBO, FOR ADAM'S PEAK. — BORDER-COUNTRY. — RATNAPOORA. — APPROACH TO ADAM'S PEAK. — PALABATULA. — ASCENT OF THE MOUNTAIN. — PROSPECT FROM THE SUMMIT. — DESCRIPTION OF THE PEAK. — PILGRIMS, AND THEIR MODE OF WORSHIP. — DESCENT. — MISCELLANEOUS REMARKS ON THE MOUNTAIN.

It is not my intention to give an account of all the ground that I went over during my residence in Ceylon, but only of such excursions as are likely to be most interesting to the reader, and are best adapted to afford illustrations of the condition and manners of the people, and of the state of the country, and its most remarkable scenery.

The first excursion which I made into the Interior after my arrival in Ceylon, was to Adam's Peak, the highest mountain in the island, and one that cannot fail to excite the interest of the traveller; its name being known, and its fame spread all over the world, and being an object of veneration almost equally to the Boodhist and the Hindoo,—to the Mahometan and the nominal Christian of India; each of whom considers it a sacred mountain, and has attached to it some superstitious tale.

On the 15th of April, 1817, at dawn, I set out from Colombo in company with my friends, the Rev. George Bisset, William Granville, Esq., and Mr. Moon: on the 17th we reached Ratnapoora, and, on the evening of the 19th the summit of the Peak, distant from Colombo only 66 miles.

Our mode of travelling varied with the nature of the road and country. The first sixteen miles we went expeditiously in gigs, over an excellent road, through a populous country, delightfully shaded the greater part of the way by the rich and beautiful foliage of extensive groves of cocoa-nut trees, which form a deep belt round the south-west part of the island.

On leaving the great maritime road at Pantura to strike into the Interior, we exchanged our gigs for the indolent Indian vehicles, palanqeens, in which we were carried as far as Ratnapoora, in Saffragam, about 43 miles from Colombo, over a pretty good new road, through a country low and yet hilly, in general overgrown with wood, very thinly inhabited, (having been a border-region,) and little cultivated; and, excepting here and there, exhibiting few objects, and little scenery of an interesting nature. At Horina, where we slept the first night in our palanqueens, we noticed the remains of a Hindoo building of the simplest kind of architecture, the style of which has been already alluded to. The next morning, at dawn, just before sunrise, from a hill over which we were passing we had a splendid view of a tropical wilderness, — hills, dales, and plains, all luxuriantly wooded, bounded by blue mountains, fleecy clouds resting on the low grounds, and a brilliant sky over-head. The charms of the prospect were heightened by the coolness and freshness of the air, and by the animation of the scene, produced by the notes of a variety of birds, some of them reminding one of the blackbird, others of the song of the thrush, and others of that of the redbreast; with which were mixed the harsh cries of the wild peacock, jungle-fowl, and parrot, — the soft cooing of doves, and the shrill sounds of innumerable insects.

Ratnapoora is a military post, and we were indebted to the officers of the little garrison for a most hospitable reception. The post is situated on a low hill, on the right bank of the Kalu ganga; it is surrounded by fertile little plains, beautifully wooded hills, and magnificent mountains; and consequently, it is in the midst of very exquisite scenery. It has many advantages of situation; the adjoining country is fertile and productive, the climate, though hot, is remarkably wholesome, and the river is thus far navigable for large boats. Though not eight miles in a straight line from the summit of Adam's Peak, the river here is hardly fifty feet above the level of the sea.* Lower down the

* In March, 1819, when I visited Ratnapoora a second time, a long mountain barometer, which I then had with me, at three P. M., just above the river, stood at 30.10 inches, (thermom. 82°,) which, it may be conjectured, was about .10 or .05 lower than at the level of the sea.

river, about half a mile, is a village composed of twenty or thirty mean huts, and a dewalé of some size, built on the ruins of an old Portuguese fort, and dedicated to Samen, who seems to be the provincial god of Saffragam.

At Ratnapoora we left our palanqueens, and proceeded towards the mountains, each in a chair lashed to two bamboos and carried on men's shoulders. In this manner we travelled about nine miles as far as Palabatula. The first half of the way the country is most romantic. We were constantly ascending and descending hills and deep valleys; — now, traversing the thick jungle, through which the sun's rays could not penetrate; — now, toiling up and down narrow, rocky passes; — sometimes along the edges of precipices with the river foaming beneath, and sometimes under overhanging rocks. About a mile on our way, we passed the Balangoddé Wiharè, finely situated above the river, on a little height, amongst enormous masses of rock and shady wood. There was an air of gloom and melancholy about the place well adapted to inspire or heighten devotional feeling. Four miles from Ratnapoora, we stopped to breakfast at Gillemallè, a beautiful spot: it is a little green plain, about a mile in circumference, skirted by a border of different kinds of palms and fruit-trees, amongst which are the dwellings of the natives, and surrounded by wooded mountains. The latter half of the way is almost one continued ascent by a narrow rocky path, shaded either by an impenetrable jungle, or by trees so covered with parasitical plants that each resembles a bower. This kind of luxuriant vegetation is probably connected with the dampness of the climate, and the frequent and heavy showers which fall in this part of the country. Owing to the same cause, the country is infested with leeches, from which the naked legs of our bearers suffered not a little, and from which we did not escape completely. Palabatula is the last inhabited station on the way to the Peak. We gladly sought shelter there from a heavy thunder-storm, which had deluged us with rain for more than two hours. There is a little Wiharè at this place, and two open amblams or rest-houses: one small, where we took up our quarters; and the other pretty large, where we found assembled at least two hundred pilgrims of both sexes and of all ages, either going to, or returning from, the Peak.

At dawn, the next morning, we started for the summit on foot, — the mountain-path we had to ascend admitting of no other mode of travelling. About a quarter of a mile beyond Palabatula, immediately after crossing a considerable torrent by a single plank, the steep ascent commences by a narrow foot-path, rugged and rocky, through a forest with which the mountain is clothed from its base to its top, and which in general shades the road so densely as to exclude the direct rays of the sun and intercept the view of the adjoining country.

After toiling up this steep gloomy path about two miles, we came to a halting-place on a little platform above a precipice, from which we had a prospect of the country below, that was at once grand and beautiful.

About half way up the mountain, we crossed a small torrent, that flows over an immense tabular mass of rock; and, about a mile farther, having ascended a considerable height and descended over very irregular ground, we came to the bed of a much larger torrent, the Setagongola, which may be considered the parent-stream of the Kalu ganga. This river-scene was a very impressive one and extremely picturesque: — the torrent, with fine effect, rushed from a wooded height down a channel obstructed by great masses of rock, on which were assembled numerous groupes of pilgrims, variously employed,—some bathing, some making a frugal repast on cold rice, and others resting themselves, laying at length, or sitting cross-legged in the Indian fashion, chewing betel. Both the air and the water here were most agreeably cool and refreshing; at one P. M. the former was 74°, and the latter 57° 75′; and it had all the other good qualities of the water of a mountain torrent. A short mountain-barometer was here stationary at 25.6 inches.

About half a mile from the river we crossed a little glen. The descent, which is very steep, was facilitated, in the most difficult parts, by rude wooden ladders. The opposite ascent was in appearance of a much more formidable nature; it was over an enormous rock, the smooth face of which, from the hardness of its surface and the steepness of its declivity, was quite naked and without any traces of vegetation. The danger of scaling this rocky height (which in its natural state would not have been inconsiderable) is entirely removed by steps having been cut in it. By four different flights of steps we ascended with ease. The three first were short, composed collectively of thirty-seven small steps. The fourth, to which the preceding led, had something grand in its appearance, from its regularity, height, and extent;—it consists of ninety steps. About half way up the rock, on the left-hand side, is the figure of a man rudely cut, and an inscription in Singalese, both commemorating the king by whom the steps had been made. From the top of this bare rock we were once more gratified with an extensive view. A thunder-storm was gathering; the scene was magnificent and awful, and of a nature to baffle description. I shall mention merely some of its features,—as deep precipices, overhanging woods, mountains rising above mountains, all covered with wood; extensive valleys, in which a dense white mist exhibited the appearance of lakes and rivers frozen and covered with snow; the whole overshadowed by a dark threatening sky, which with distant thunder foreboded the approaching storm.

Very soon after leaving the rock, the storm commenced, attended with very heavy rain, and with thunder and lightning extremely loud and vivid. There being no shelter, it was useless to halt: we continued ascending without intermission; the difficulty of the path increasing with the height.

The storm lasted till about half-past two, when we had reached a little flat, covered with stunted wood. Whilst we stopped here to rest ourselves a few minutes, under a rude shed made for the use of the pilgrims, the weather rapidly improved; the rain nearly ceased, the thunder was to be heard only rolling at a distance, the mists and clouds were dispersing, and we presently had the pleasure of seeing the object of our toil immediately above us — the Peak, of a conical form, rising rapidly and majestically to a point.

Wet and cold, the thermometer at 58°, the wind piercing, we speedily renewed our exertions. This last stage of the way is the most difficult of all, and the only part attended with any danger. Near the summit, the ascent is so precipitous, that were it not for iron chains fixed to the rocks, small indeed would be the number of those who would complete their pilgrimage: even with the help of these chains, accidents occasionally occur, and lives are lost; only a fortnight before, (we were told,) two natives perished here; looking down, they became giddy and frightened, fell, and were dashed to pieces.

We arrived on the top of the mountain a little after three

o'clock. The rain was over, the air clear, and the sun shining. The magnificent views of the surrounding scenery amply repaid us for a laborious march, and all the little difficulties we had to contend with. No description, and I doubt if any pencil, could do justice to the scenery, the prospect of which was perfectly uninterrupted in every direction. Looking immediately down the side of the mountain, two or three thousand feet deep, the eye wandered with delight over an irregular surface of foliage, variously and beautifully coloured, of different tints of green, brown, and red, to features more distant and more impressive, — the mountain-ridges and valleys, of very various forms, and of as many different hues and appearances, according to their distance, and their situation in respect to the descending sun. The nearest mountains — those only two or three miles off, we could observe minutely, and distinguish, through the clear atmosphere, their smaller features, — as the trees with which they were covered; their projecting rocks; deep ravines; and the rills and torrents, which, after the heavy rain, glittered in every hollow. From these there was a transition, sometimes abrupt, sometimes gradual, to the most distant mountains of the Interior, which terminated the view in that direction, and had the blue aerial tint of the sky, differing only in being of greater intensity. As the mountains faded with the distance, and almost vanished in air, so did the valleys and lowlands, in mist and vapour. The mountain valleys within a few miles were still occupied with dense strata of white mist, and had the appearance before remarked, of frozen rivers and lakes: indeed, so strong was the resemblance, that they vividly brought to my recollection the winter-scenes of my native country.

From the surrounding scenery our curiosity soon led us to examine the summit of the mountain, and the object which induces thousands annually to undertake this weary pilgrimage. The summit is very small; according to the measurement made by Lieut. Malcolm, (the first European who ascended the Peak,) its area is seventy-four feet by twenty-four. It is surrounded by a stone wall five feet high, built in some places on the brink of the precipice. The apex of the mountain is a rock, which stands in the middle of the inclosure, about six or eight feet above the level ground. On its top is the object of worship of the natives, the Sree-pada, — the sacred impression, as they imagine, of the foot of Boodhoo, which he stamped on his first visit to the island. It is a superficial hollow, five feet three inches and three-quarters long, and between two feet seven inches and two feet five inches wide. It is ornamented with a margin of brass, studded with a few gems, of little value: it is covered with a roof, which is fastened to the rock by four iron chains, and supported by four pillars; and it is surrounded by a low wall. The roof was lined with coloured cloths, and its margin being decked with flowers, and streamers, it made a very gay appearance. The cavity certainly bears a coarse resemblance to the figure of the human foot: were it really an impression, it is not a very flattering one, or the encomiums which are lavished on the beauty of the feet of Boodhoo are very improperly bestowed. It is hardly worth enquiring how it was formed; and whether it is entirely or only partly artificial. From its appearance and other circumstances, I believe it to be partly natural and partly artificial. There are little raised partitions to represent the interstices between the toes; these are certainly artificial; for a minute portion, which I secretly detached, was a mixture of sand and lime, similar to common cement, and altogether different from the rock itself. Lower down, on the same rock, there is a little niche of masonry, dedicated to Samen, who is also worshipped on the Peak, being considered the guardian god of the mountain. Within the enclosure is a small house of one room, the residence of the officiating priest; and this, and two small huts outside the parapet, is all the shelter that the mountain affords. There is nothing else on the summit deserving of notice, that I am aware of, excepting a grove of rhododendrons, (*rhododendron arboreum,*) which, studded with large red flowers, made a very handsome appearance. It is situated on the east and north-east side of the mountain, immediately outside the parapet, and is considered sacred. This shrub, or rather tree, the natives say was planted by Samen, immediately after the departure of Boodhoo; and, that it is peculiar to the Peak, and found in no other part of the island. The latter assertion I have since ascertained to be quite erroneous; the tree is common on all the higher mountains of the Interior, and it occasionally makes its appearance at elevations little exceeding 2000 feet above the level of the sea.

We passed the night on the mountains; and, it was the first night, since I had entered the tropics, that I had occasion to complain of cold. There was no moon, the sky was cloudy; stars of the first and second magnitude only making their appearance: once or twice, that we looked out, we saw what might be called "darkness visible," and the giant forms of the mountains, sublime in obscurity. The next morning, just before sun-rise, we were awoke by the shouts of a party of pilgrims, just arrived. Having no toilet to make, we were in the open air in an instant. It was indeed a glorious morning; and we had reason to thank the pilgrims for waking us. The rising sun painted the sky with gold and purple, and threw over the whole scene such a rich purple light, that I never before saw equalled.

The party of pilgrims that had just arrived consisted of several men and women, all native Singalese of the Interior, neatly dressed in clean clothes. They immediately proceeded to their devotions. A priest, in his yellow robes, stood on the rock close to the impression of the foot, with his face to the people, who had ranged themselves in a row below; some on their knees, with their hands uplifted, and joined palm to palm, and others bending forward, with their hands in the same attitude of devotion. The priest, in a loud clear voice, sentence by sentence, recited the articles of their religious faith, and duties; and, in response, they repeated the same after him. When he had finished, they raised a loud shout; and, he retiring, they went through the same ceremony by themselves, with one of their party for their leader.

An interesting scene followed this: wives affectionately and respectfully saluted their husbands, and children their parents, and friends one another. An old grey-headed woman first made her salems to a really venerable old man; she was moved to tears, and almost kissed his feet: he affectionately raised her up. Several middle-aged men then salemed the patriarchal pair; these men were salemed in return by still younger men, who had first paid their respects to the old people; and lastly, those nearly of the same standing slightly salemed each other, and exchanged betel-leaves. The intention of these salutations, I was informed, was of a moral kind,— to confirm the ties of kindred,— to strengthen family love and friendship, and remove animosities.

Each pilgrim makes some offering to the impression of the foot, and to Samen. I observed several of them: one presented a few small pieces of copper coin, another some betel leaves, another some areka-nuts, another some rice, and another a piece of cloth. The offerings were placed on the impression, and almost immediately removed by a servant who stood by for the purpose; they are the perquisites of the chief priest of the Malwattè Wiharè.

Before the pilgrims descend they are blessed by the priest, and exhorted to return to their homes, and lead in future virtuous lives.

It was our intention over night to spend the day on the mountain, and descend the following morning; but we were overruled by our followers, who found the air too cold for them, and considered the spot too sacred. The excessive cold was the burthen of their complaint, concealing their superstitious dread, which I have no doubt influenced them most; it being a current opinion amongst the natives that none but a priest can pass a night on the Peak with impunity; sickness, they imagine, being the general consequence, and often death.

Obliged to yield to their entreaties, we began to descend at eight o'clock in the morning, and we reached Palabatula about four in the afternoon, weary and wet, having been overtaken by another thunder-storm. We returned to Colombo the same way we came.

Whilst on the mountain, I did not neglect to observe a barometer and thermometer with which I was provided. I suspended the former instrument in a little temple on the top of the rock: at six in the evening, after sufficient exposure to acquire the temperature of the air, which under the roof was 52°, it stood at 23.70 inches; and at seven the next morning, when the air was 58°, at 23.75. Unfortunately, I had no long barometer to compare the short instrument with, and no one at Colombo was possessed of a barometer to make an observation at the same time; consequently, the estimate of the height of the mountain made from the preceding observations, and which I have given in a former part of this work, can be considered only as an approximation to the truth. The extraordinary heights assigned by some old authors to Adam's Peak of twelve and fifteen thousand feet, are certainly erroneous. According to a rough trigonometrical measurement, made by a very able observer, (the late Lieut. Col. Willerman,) the perpendicular height of the Peak does not exceed 7000 feet; and thus confirming the barometrical estimate. *

The observations which I made on the temperature of the air, are the following:

TIME.	TEMPERATURE.	WIND.	
3 h. P. M.	54°	N. E.	Moderate.
4 - - -	52	N. N. E.	Do.
6 - - -	51	Do.	Gentle.
9 - - -	51	Do.	Do.
5 30 m. A.M.	53.5	Do.	Fresh.
7 - - -	59	Do.	Gentle.

The Mahometans, there is good reason to believe, first assigned the name to this mountain, by which it is generally known amongst Europeans. The moormen of Ceylon still call it Adam

* The height assigned, p. 4., is merely the approximate height of the mountain: supposing the barometer, at the level of the sea, at 6h. P. M., to be 30.1, and the thermometer 80, the estimated height would be about 6680 feet.

Malay: they say, that Adam, when turned out of Paradise, lamented his offence on the summit of the Peak, standing on one foot (of which the impression remains) till he was pardoned by God. The superstitious belief of the natives has already been alluded to: conformably with this belief, they call it either Siripada, or in Pali, Sree-pada, in relation to the object of their worship, the imaginary impression; or Samennella or Hamennella, (the sound of S and H being indiscriminately used,) in relation to Samen, the guardian god of the mountain.

The learned Bryant, in his Analysis of Ancient Mythology, lays great weight on the latter name; he says, "The Pike of Adam is properly the summit sacred to Ad Ham, the king or deity Ham, the Amon of Egypt. This is plain, to a demonstration, from another name given to it by the native Singalese, who live near the mountain, and call it Ham-al-el: this, without any change, is Ham-eel-El, (Ham, the Sun,) and relates to the ancient religion of the island. In short, every thing in these countries savours of Chaldaic and Egyptian institution." *

Were this hypothesis (partly founded on a name) correct, traces of the ancient worship, one would suppose, might still be discovered. The result of particular enquiry on the subject is, that there is nothing peculiar in the mode of worship followed on the Peak, Samen being worshipped like the other gods, and the Sree-pada as Boodhoo. The name which afforded Bryant demonstration, when correctly written, seems to be rather a refutation of his hypothesis; Samennella (the rock of Samen) being supported by the similar Pali name, Somané-koota, and by the Sanscrit, Samanta-koota-parwatti.

I shall conclude with transcribing the exordium of a curious

* Analysis of Ancient Mythology, vol. iv. p. 266.

Sanus, written in the time of King Kirtisseré, relative to and descriptive of the Peak:— "Our Boodhoo, who acquired Niwané; who came into the world like other Boodhoos; from whom is derived the food of life (religion); who is celebrated for his thirty-two great manly beauties, and for the eighty-two signs connected with them, and for the light which shines a fathom round his body, and for the beams of light that dart from the top of his head; who is the preceptor of three worlds; who is acquainted with the past, present, and future; who, during four asankeas of kalpés, so conducted himself as to be an example of the thirty great qualities; who subdued Mareya and his attendants, and became Boodhoo:— in the eighth year from that event he rose into the air, spread beams of light, of six different colours, round his person, and stamped the impression of his foot, bearing the noble marks Chakkra-laksana, and the one hundred and eight auspicious tokens, on the rock Samanta-koota-parwate;— which is celebrated for the cold and lovely waters of its rivers, for its mountain torrents, and for its flowery groves, spreading in the air their sweet-scented pollen;— which is the crown of the Virgin Island, rich in mines of all kinds of precious stones, like a maid decked with jewels."

CHAPTER II.

DEPARTURE FROM COLOMBO FOR KANDY.—AVISAHAVELLE'. —SITTAWAKKA. — RUWENWELLE'. — MODE OF TRAVELLING OF THE GOVERNOR. — FORT KING. — ELEPHANT-SNARE. — AMANAPOÒRA. — APPROACH TO KANDY. — DESCRIPTION OF KANDY. — EXCURSION INTO DOOMBERA. — NITRE-CAVE OF MEMOORA. — LEAVE KANDY FOR TRINCOMALIE. — AT-GALLE' PASS. — FORT M'DOWALL. — DESCRIPTION OF COUNTRY BETWEEN NALANDE' AND MINERE'. — LAKE OF MINERE'. — DESCRIPTION OF COUNTRY BETWEEN MINERE' AND KANDELLE'. —LAKE OF KANDELLE'. — RETURN FROM TRINCOMALIE TO KANDY. — BREAKING OUT OF REBEL-LION. — TRANQUILLITY RESTORED. — RETURN TO COLOMBO.

My next visit to the Interior was in attendance, in a medical capacity, on His Excellency the Governor, who left Colombo in company with Lady Brownrigg, for Kandy, on the fifth of

August, 1817. Little aware of the rebellion, which was on the eve of commencing, we set out as on a party of pleasure, expecting that the whole journey would be such; and instead of being détained, as we were fifteen months, that we should return in a few weeks.

The distance of Kandy from Colombo, by the common road which we went, through the Three and Four Korles, is eighty-five miles. The first stage is to Hanwellè, a little fort on the Kalany ganga, eighteen miles off. The country, thus far, is either flat or gently undulating, and is liable to be inundated by the flooding of the river. It is generally well inhabited. The greater part of the way the road is most agreeably shaded by the fine foliage of fruit-trees, and especially of cocoa-nut trees, which, with the exception of being here and there interrupted by paddy-fields, form a continuous line of grove for many miles along the river.

Between Hanwellé and Avisahavellé, the next stage, distant about eleven and a half miles, the country has a wilder aspect. It was a border-country, between the Kandyan and our old possessions; and, in consequence, almost a desert. Its wild scenery is very beautiful, similar to the corresponding part of Saffragam, and most remarkable for the richness and variety of forest and jungle with which its hilly surface is almost universally covered.

Avisahavellè is an inconsiderable village, romantickly situated almost at the base of bluff hills of black naked rock, which rise precipitously from a surface of rich foliage to a height perhaps of 1000 feet. On a low but steep conical hill, just by the Rest-house, there are the remains of a small military post, which has been unoccupied and neglected since we have had possession of the Interior.

About half a mile beyond Avisahavellé, is Sittawakka, where

there is a ferry over a pretty considerable river of the same name. The ferry is provided with a large boat, which is plied backward and forward, not by oars or poles, but by means of a strong flexible cane, stretched across and fastened to the opposite banks, by pulling on which the boatmen effect a passage with great facility. *

Sittawakka, once a royal residence, and a place of considerable consequence, is now merely a name. No traces of what it once was are now to be seen by the traveller passing along the road; and, for a considerable time none were supposed to exist. Lately, some remains of buildings have been discovered. In June, 1819, when travelling this way the third time, I was conducted by the natives to an old fort, concealed by wood, situated on a tongue of elevated ground, formed by the confluence of a small deep stream with the river. I went in a boat, and ascended from the river by a short flight of hewn-stone steps, and after walking about a hundred yards, came to the building, which I found to be nearly square, formed of three walls, one within the other, thus:

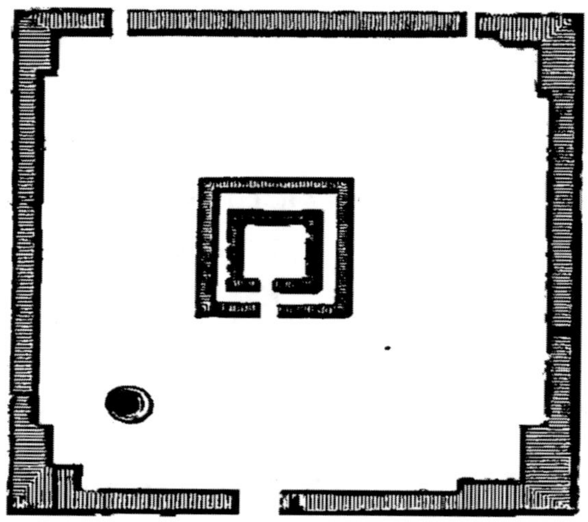

* This cane, which has been seen 300 yards long, is jointed, and of equal dimensions throughout; it grows wild in the woods in damp places. The one used at the ferry was about half an inch thick. As it is very tough and strong, it is a good substitute for rope, and is much employed as such by the natives.

The walls were of kabook, as the stone is called by the natives; and in this instance, as in most others, appeared to be clay, strongly impregnated with red oxide of iron, to which, probably, it owes its property of hardening by exposure to the atmosphere. The outer wall was between eight and ten feet high, and six and eight wide. It was widest at its angles, where it communicated with the enclosure by steps. Between this wall and the next, the distance might be twenty-four or thirty feet; the space was overgrown with bushes. Here I observed a deep well, carefully made, and its sides lined with masonry. The second wall, only a very few feet from the inner, seemed intended for its defence. The inner enclosure was probably roofed, and was the donjon-keep of the fortress. There were no marks of its having been divided into different compartments, and, indeed, it was hardly large enough to admit of it. The natives, who call this ruin Kotua (a fort), have a tradition, which is probably correct, that it was built and occupied by the Portuguese when the neighbourhood was the arena of bloody contention between these bold invaders and the princes of Sittawakka. The nature of the building, the circumstance of there being a good well within its walls, its situation on the Columbo side of the river and nearly opposite to the spot on which there is reason to believe the palace and town of Sittawakka formerly stood, seem to be proofs of the correctness of the tradition. Be this as it may, the ruin was not uninteresting, and might have been worth preserving; I say, might,—knowing that the work of destruction has commenced, and that the walls which two centuries, at least, had spared, have been pulled down either in part or entirely, and their stones removed to build a new rest-house. The curious traveller will complain of this measure; whilst the indolent one will bless his stars for being saved the trouble of forcing his way through thickets to see an old ruin, the materials of which, newly arranged, afford him a comfortable shelter. In August, of the same year, in my last excursion into the Interior, I visited some ruins on the right bank of the river, distant from it about a hundred and fifty yards, and nearly opposite to the fort. These remains were, I undertand, first noticed by Mr. Maitland. The jungle, with which they were completely overgrown, has been partially cleared by Major Bayley, the commandant of the district, by whom they were pointed out to me. The approach to them is by a bridge, composed of large flat stones, each about fifteen feet long, three or four wide, and about two feet thick. At the distance of about twenty yards, on a rising ground, there is an enclosure (a parallelogram, a hundred and twenty feet by ninety) surrounded by a wall formed of large blocks of hewn stones. In the centre of this area are the foundations, and parts of the walls of a small and handsome temple, probably a dewalè, which was substantially and neatly built of cut and carved stones. Judging from the appearance of its remains, it was evidently pulled down, and not ruined by the slow operation of time, of which there are few marks. Popular tradition refers its destruction to the Portuguese, who, we very well know, showed their religious zeal, whenever occasion offered, by overthrowing the works of Indian superstition. Other ruins are said to exist in the adjoining jungle; they are probably the remains of temples, or of the royal palace of Sittawakka, and not of the town itself, the clay-walls of the houses of the natives being even more perishable than their inhabitants.

Ruwenwellè, the next stage, is eight miles and a half from Avisahavellè. The intermediate country is little cultivated, and thinly inhabited, and generally overgrown with wood. The road, a great part of the way, is through a valley, which here and there on the right is bounded by a lofty rocky ridge. About a mile and a half from Ruwenwellè there is an extensive plantation of cocoa-nut trees, the property of government. The trees are very inferior in size to those on the sea-shore, justifying the popular notion that the sea-air favours their growth. Farther, it may be remarked, that they appear to be less flourishing than those about the dwellings of the natives, who have a saying, that cocoa-nut trees do not thrive unless "you walk amongst them, and talk amongst them." *

Ruwenwellè, which three years ago was almost a desert spot, is now a flourishing station. It is advantageously situated on a point of land at the confluence of the clear Kalany ganga and the turbid Gooragooya oya. A fort is nearly completed, in which there are excellent quarters for officers and men; and, a bazar has been established, in which two or three hundred families have settled, attracted by the prospect of gain. We were agreeably surprised, on our arrival, at the rapid growth of this little town, and at its gay and festive appearance. In honour of the Governor, the day was a holiday; the natives were clothed in their best; the street which leads from the river to the fort, was ornamented in the Singalese simple and beautiful style, with

* The cocoa-nut tree on the sea-shore is certainly larger and more productive than in the Interior of Ceylon. In the former situation it frequently grows to the height of a hundred feet. Its flourishing most in this situation, and close to the dwellings of the natives, is probably connected with the circumstance, that its leaves, in a healthy state, contain a very large portion of saline matter. The Singalese are well aware of this; the washermen burn its leaves for the sake of its alkaline ashes, and it is a common practice, in planting a cocoa-nut, to put a little salt into the pit.

arches of young cocoa-nut leaf, scented with the sweet and elegant white blossom of the areka-palm, and supported by plantain trees, which, transplanted entire, full of leaves and fruit, looked as fresh as if growing in their native soil. In the evening, when the Governor and Lady Brownrigg visited the bazar, it was quite splendid, and like a fairy scene, ornamented as described, and brilliantly illuminated with lamps made of cocoa-nut shells, and fed with cocoa-nut oil, and placed amongst the vegetable arches and before the humble shops of the natives. On his return to the fort, the Governor received the Dissave of the Three Korles, who had come from Kandy on the occasion. He was a young man of a prepossessing appearance, notwithstanding the disguise of his rich but far from graceful dress. He seated himself in a chair when desired; behaved with much decorum; and did not refuse tea, though in all probability he had never before tasted it. According to the Indian custom, he remained till he was told he might depart; and, according to the same custom, before he took leave he made a present, which consisted of fruits, eggs, and confectionary, brought on plates of leaves, and arranged on the ground for inspection.

Idamalpanè, the next stage, is eleven miles. The country between Ruwenwellè and Idamalpanè is better cultivated and more populous than any we had yet passed through, with the exception of the immediate neighbourhood of Colombo. The road the greater part of the way is level, and through meadows or paddy-fields, which at the time had a most refreshing appearance, being covered with young paddy, the verdure of which surpasses in beauty that of any other plant with which I am acquainted, and had a very pleasing effect, contrasted with the dark-green of the woods on the adjoining hills. Idamalpanè is a small military post, ill situated amongst jungly hills by which it is commanded. About two miles from it, we passed Arranderrè, where the Dutch had established a fort, of which slight traces still remain, and where the Governor has since built a cantonment, preferring the situation to that of Idamalpanè, which has been evacuated.

Hettymulle, another small military post, is only five miles from Idamalpanè. All the intervening country is extremely hilly, almost mountainous; and in consequence the road is rugged, difficult, and fatiguing. The lover of nature will find remuneration for his fatigue in the beauties of the wild scenery, which are lavishly scattered over this bold and romantic part of the country.

Fort King, the next stage, is seven miles distant. The character of the country between, is hilly, picturesque, and difficult, though in a less degree than the preceding, and better cultivated. One or two of the valleys we passed, were very deep, and so narrow that persons on one hill might almost converse with those on the other. I was induced by curiosity to stop on the brow of one of the nearer hills to look at the cavalcade passing on the opposite; — it made an imposing appearance; and I shall briefly describe it, to give an idea of the manner in which a Governor travels in Ceylon, — and in this instance, an individual particularly averse from all show and display. First, slowly ascending the hill, appeared three tusked elephants gaily caparisoned, each with a bell hanging from his side which made a clear and mournful sound. Next followed a party of the Ceylon light dragoons, who, though well mounted, had a very diminutive appearance compared with the elephants; their brisk gait, too, was as great a contrast as their size with the grave and measured motion of the huge animals going before them. The Governor, next came in view, carried in a tomjohn *; then followed Lady Brownrigg in a similar vehicle; the officers attending the Governor rode after, and the rear was brought up by another party of dragoons. But the procession was not yet finished; — another party immediately appeared, consisting of the Dissave of the district, mounted on a horse with bells to its neck and with very gay furniture, led by two grooms, and surrounded and followed by a large number of his people dressed in their peculiar costume, and bearing the insignia of his office, as flags, talipot leaves, &c. Lastly, the irregulars followed, successively ascending without order, and for so long a time that my impatience mastered my curiosity; — some in palanqueens, some on horseback, but the majority on foot, being chiefly servants or baggage-coolies. Persons of refined taste may justly find fault with this oriental mode of travelling, and exclaim, — what barbarous pomp! The exclamation is just; but it is the pomp which the natives are accustomed to respect and associate with power, and in consequence it would not be very politic to neglect the observance of it. The numerous attendants necessary in travelling in Ceylon, is an evil inseparable from the state of the country, — without inns, and where you are under the necessity of carrying with you every thing you want, as in a campaign, or in journeying on the desert.

Fort King, deriving its name from Captain King, R. S. C., who planned and superintended the works, is quite a recent creation and still unfinished. The fort is building in the most substantial manner, on a low hill that commands the ferry of the Maha-ohio,

* A tomjohn is very like a sedan-chair: it is open in front and on each side, and is carried by a single pole on men's shoulders.

a considerable stream, on whose banks many a bloody battle was fought between the Singalese and Portuguese. In a picturesque point the situation of the fort is unrivalled, being surrounded by a fore-ground of gentle hills, and bounded on every side by bold mountains, combining in one view the beautiful and the grand. The country round is productive; and the bazar, which like the fort has sprung up where jungle only was to be seen three years ago, is already large and well supplied. This part of the country is elevated about 631 feet above the level of the sea *; owing to which circumstance and the proximity of mountains, it enjoys a climate far more agreeable than that of the sea-coast,—the nights being generally cool, and the days seldom oppressively hot.

Amanapoora, eight miles from Fort King, is the next stage, the Bellany mountain intervening. At Gannithenè close to the foot of the mountain, we went off the road about half a mile over paddy-fields, to visit an elephant-snare, situated in a narrow part of the valley. The snare is merely a square space of small dimensions surrounded by strong palisades, having a tree in the middle and one narrow entrance. The manner in which elephants are here taken is very simple. The wild animials are first driven to Kandy, and then, if approved of, to this place. When an elephant enters the enclosure, he is fastened to the tree by means of a noose, and his feet are properly secured by strong ropes. From the enclosure he is led to an adjoining spot; a shed is built over him; his feet are tied firmly to trees, and he

* At Fort King, on the 26th November, 1819, at 9 A. M., a mountain-barometer was 29.35 inches; it had acquired the temperature of the air which was 77.5: the following week, the same instrument at Colombo, observed at the same time of day, was about 30.07, and the air about 78°.

is not allowed to lie down. We found six elephants in progress of taming — their limbs more or less shackled, according to the subjugation effected. They were all extremely lean, and miserable objects to look at. More than half of those caught, die during their confinement: they seem to pine for the lost blessing of liberty; they refuse to eat, and generally die of starvation. If they can be prevailed on to take food, the difficulty of the task is got over, and they are soon tamed. Great as the mortality is in this instance, it is small in proportion to that which takes place in a large snare, such as is used in the low country. *

The Bellany mountain may be about three thousand feet above the level of the sea. Its ascent is laborious, but less so than I expected; and infinitely less than it was before the new road was made. The Governor and Lady Brownrigg were carried in their tom-johns all the way, without being obliged to get out once; and it is possible, though not humane or considerate, to ascend it on horseback. The toil of the ascent is amply rewarded: the traveller breathes a fresh, cool air; is shaded by noble forest-trees, with which the whole mountain is covered; and, when he stops to rest himself, he enjoys, every now and then, magnificent prospects. Till you reach the top, there are only two small descents; one, into a narrow, deep glen, through which a torrent rushes, and the other, into a hollow, where a few soldiers are stationed for the purpose of felling trees and making shingles for the buildings at Fort King. The torrent in the first glen divides the Four Korles from Yattineura. It is difficult to imagine a wilder and grander tropical scene than this pre-

* Vide Cordiner, vol. i. chap. vii. for a description of the manner of hunting and taking elephants in the maritime districts.

sents: in the rocky bed of the torrent, you have merely a glimpse of the sky; you look up, and see on each side a mountain towering above, and on each side an overhanging gloomy forest. In the hollow, where the soldiers are stationed, you are surprised to find human beings, and still more, Europeans. The men had made themselves comfortable huts; they had connected themselves with native women, who came out with their children, and looked in good circumstances, and contented. The sun-burnt countenances of the soldiers were very striking; they were so dark, as to equal almost the fairest of the natives, and would almost persuade one, that the different shades of colour of the human race may be owing merely to climate and mode of living. When we had reached the top of the mountain, we had a very extensive view of that part of the country we had travelled over. It looked like a map, laid out on a magnificent scale, with a glow of colouring, warmth of light, and charm of landscape, that we rarely see combined, excepting in the paintings of the first masters. The native chief of the district had chosen this elevated spot to pay his respects to His Excellency; and, as if inspired with an unusual degree of boldness by the grand scenery surrounding him, he stood, I observed, in his sandals, which is contrary to the custom of the natives in addressing a superior. It was a singular pleasure to ascend this mountain with the General who had first passed it, and returned in triumph, after having overthrown, without bloodshed, a most cruel and tyrannical government; it was highly interesting to hear his officers compare the past state of the road with the present, and to hear them relate little anecdotes of events connected with different spots. After ascending the mountain, the road for two or three hundred yards is nearly level. The descent is short, and pretty gradual.

You have an extensive view of the country before you, extremely hilly, and bounded by distant and apparently lofty mountains, but, altogether, not so grand as the scenery on the other side. You see Amanapoora quite close to you, on a steep hill, merely divided from that on which you stand by a deep glen: the British flag was flying on the fort; and we could observe distinctly a number of officers assembled, watching the Governor's approach. We soon descended one hill, and ascended the other. On the Governor's entering the fort, a salute was fired, consisting of several discharges from a brass cannon, the effect of the reverberation of which amongst the hills was very remarkable. The troops, consisting of two companies, — one European and the other native, were drawn up to receive His Excellency. It was a pleasure to observe the fresh and healthy looks of our countrymen, with whom this mountain-air seemed to agree extremely well.

Amanapoora is a considerable military station. The fort, situated on the top of a precipitous hill, about two thousand feet above the level of the sea, has a very commanding aspect, and is naturally strong. The works designed to protect it are not yet completed. At the foot of this hill is a cantonment, consisting of officers' quarters and soldiers' barracks; and close by there is a considerable village and bazar. The country, to some extent round Amanapoora, excepting towards the Bellany, consists of small green hills, of rather irregular forms, pretty free from jungle, and apparently affording good pasture: in the lower grounds there are paddy-fields, and at a distance, lofty grey mountains. Towards the Bellany, the scenery is of a different character; every feature is grand, particularly the huge Bellany, covered with forest, which you view across the deep intervening

Plan of the Town and Lake of Kandy.

I. Clark sculp.t

London, Published by [illegible] Orme & Browne, 1821

glen, and the lofty Narran-gallé-kandy, a little more distant to the right, shooting its angular rocky top into the very clouds. This is a mountain noticed by Knox, and which, in his Map of Ceylon, makes a very conspicuous figure.

Kandy is twelve miles from Amanapoora. The country between the two places is hilly and difficult. The hills, in general, are covered with wood; the valleys, which are narrow and deep, are cultivated with paddy. Five miles from Amanapoora, we passed Dodanwellè, through a delightfully cool avenue of iron-trees, many of which have attained a great size. These constitute a sacred grove, and belong to two or three small wiharés that are built under their shade. Not quite three miles from Kandy, we crossed the Mahawellé ganga, at the Gannoroowé ferry. The river here is about two-thirds the size of the Thames at Richmond; its course is pretty rapid, and its banks finely wooded. On the Kandy side of the river, a large concourse of chiefs was assembled, with numerous followers, in great state, waiting to receive His Excellency. I was too late to see the meeting; but I overtook and passed most of the chiefs on their return to Kandy, and had an opportunity of noticing their manner of travelling. They were all robed in their court-dresses, glittering with gold and jewels. Some rode on horse-back; others were carried in palanqueens; and one or two of them, if I recollect rightly, were on elephants. The furniture of the horses was as gay as necklaces of small bells, and the gayest colours, could make it. The rider did not use a saddle, but a pad without stirrups, and made little use of the reins — the horse being led by two horse-keepers. The palanqueens were equally tawdry and overcharged with ornament; most of them were open on each side, and exposed to view the great man, sitting or lying at his ease within. I passed one chief just as he was getting into his vehicle, and just at the moment that an attendant was washing his feet, which had been dirtied by standing in the mud, by pouring a small stream of water upon them from a vessel for the purpose, that very much resembled a tea-kettle. All the way from the river to the town, the road was crowded with people,—chiefs with their retinue moving forward, natives come to satisfy their curiosity, and many British officers, who had rode out to meet the General, and see their friends. The nearer we approached Kandy, the more animated the scene became. The crowd was enormous, and not very well behaved: in passing the arches, many of which were erected across the roads, made of cocoa-nut leaves, plantain and areka-nut trees, and ornamented with different kinds of fruit, the mob became quite unruly; and, in their eagerness and contention to take the fruit, almost stopped the way, and sometimes nearly upset our palanqueens. The long street by which we entered was full of natives of both sexes; the men in general conspicuous by their large beards, and the women, in many instances, by their light colour and feminine beauty.

Kandy, the Maha-neura, (the great city,) the capital of the Interior, is in the district of Yattineura, at the head and widest part of a pretty extensive valley, and about 1400* feet above the level of the sea. Standing on the border of an artificial lake, made by the late king, and surrounded by wooded hills, and mountains varying in height from 200 to 2000 feet, its situation

* At the hospital at Kandy, on the 24th April, 1819, at ten A.M. the barometer was 28.50, when it had acquired the temperature of the air which was 77°. Many other observations which I made differed little from this. The average height of the same instrument at Colombo, at that hour, was 30.10 inches, the thermometer 78°.

is beautiful and romantic ; but, in a military point of view, very ill chosen and insecure, and hardly admitting of defence. The accompanying plan will give a better idea, than words can afford, of the size of the town, the arrangement of its streets, and the localities of its principal buildings. The houses which constitute the streets are all of clay, of one story, standing on a low terrace of clay, and are all thatched, with the exception of the dwellings of the chiefs, which are tiled ; in brief, they are all constructed on the plan described when treating of the buildings in general of the natives. The only street that requires particular mention is Astawanka-weediye, or, as we call it, Malabar-street, — having been exclusively inhabited by Malabars, relations and dependants of the king, in whom, their interests being intimately connected with his, he could put more confidence than in his Singalese subjects.

The principal objects in Kandy worthy of any notice, are the palace, and the different temples of Boodhoo and the gods. The palace did occupy a considerable space of ground. Its front, about 200 yards long, made rather an imposing appearance : it looked towards the principal temples, and rose above a handsome moat, the walls of which were pierced with triangular cavities for purposes of illumination. At one extremity, it was terminated by an hexagonal building, of two stories, called Pateripooa, in which the king, on great occasions, appeared to the people, assembled in the square below. At the other extremity, it was bounded by the women's apartments, on the front of which the sun, moon, and stars, (not out of gallantry, but as insignia of royalty,) were carved in stone, and in which, at the public festivals, the king and his ladies stationed themselves to witness the processions. The intermediate space was occupied chiefly by the great entrance to the palace, and by the temple (the Dalada Malegawa) a little in the rear. The entrance was by a drawbridge over the moat, through a massive arch-way, on one hand, up a flight of huge steps, and through another arch-way to the hall of audience; and, on the other hand, up another flight of steps to the temple and the hexagonal building. The buildings in the back-ground, with the exception of the hall of audience, exhibited nothing peculiar; they were chiefly sleeping-rooms, offices, and baths, and were most of them dark, small, and mean, and have almost all been destroyed. The hall of audience, where the king usually transacted business and kept his court, is a long room, in which nothing ornamental is now to be seen, excepting the carved wooden pillars by which the roof is supported.

Kandy abounds in temples. Under the old government, the alliance of church and state was as strong as possible: in corroboration of which remark, it may be observed, that the Singalese seem to consider the temples of the gods as necessary appendages of a royal palace. Accordingly every royal residence had its orthodox number of temples, which, in two or three instances, have survived the palaces to which they were attached. The principal temples in Kandy and its immediate neighbourhood, are the Dalada Malegawa, the Malwatté, and the Asgirie Wihares,—and the Nata, Maha-Visnu, Katragam, and Patiné Dewalés. The Dalada Malegawa, was the domestic temple of the king, and is the most venerated of any in the country, as it contains the relic, the tooth of Boodhoo, to which the whole island was dedicated, and which is considered by good Boodhists as the most precious thing in the world. The temple is small, of two stories, built in the Chinese style of architecture. The sanctum is an inner room,

View of part of the Palace, including the Patirippoo ... of the Nata Dewale from the great Square.

Drawn by Lieut. Lyttleton, H.M. 73 R.

Front of the Palace in Kandy.

London, Published by Longman, Hurst, Rees, Orme & Browne, 1821.

about twelve feet square, on the upper story, without windows, and to which a ray of natural light never penetrates. You enter it by folding doors, with polished brass pannels, before and behind which is a curtain. The splendour of the place is very striking; the roof and walls are lined with gold brocade; and nothing scarcely is to be seen but gold, gems, and sweet-smelling flowers. On a platform or stage, about three feet and a half high, and which occupies about half the room, there is a profusion of flowers tastefully arranged before the objects of worship to which they are offered, viz. two or three small figures of Boodhoo, — one of crystal, and the other of silver-gilt, and four or five domes or caskets, called karanduas, containing relics, and similar in form to the common Dagobah, of which a figure has been given already. All but one of the karanduas are small, not exceeding a foot in height, and wrapped in many folds of muslin. One is of much greater size, and uncovered, and, with its decorations, makes a most brilliant appearance. It is five feet four and a half inches high, and nine feet ten inches in circumference at its base. It is of silver, from three-tenths to four-tenths of an inch thick, and gilt externally. It consists of three different pieces, capable of being separated from each other. Its workmanship is neat, but plain, and it is studded with very few gems, the finest of which is a valuable cat's-eye on its top, which is rarely seen. The ornaments attached to it are extremely rich, and consist of gold chains, and a great variety of gems, suspended from it. The most remarkable of these is a bird hanging by a gold chain, and formed entirely of diamonds, rubies, blue sapphires, emeralds, and cat's-eyes, set in gold, which is hid by the profusion of stones. Viewed at a little distance, by candle-light, the gems about the karandua seem to be of immense value; but when closely inspected, they prove in general to be of bad quality, and some of the largest merely crystal, coloured by a foil. This great karandua is the receptacle of the dalada, 'the tooth,' as it is considered, of Boodhoo. Through the kindness of the Governor, I had an opportunity (enjoyed by few Europeans) of seeing this celebrated relic, when it was recovered, towards the conclusion of the rebellion, and brought back to be replaced in the Dalada Malegawa, from which it had been clandestinely taken. The accompanying figure will give some idea of

its size and form. It was of a dirty yellow colour, excepting towards its truncated base, where it was brownish. Judging from its appearance at the distance of two or three feet, (for none but the chief priests were privileged to touch it,) it was artificial, and of ivory, discoloured by age. Never a relic was more preciously enshrined; wrapped in pure sheet-gold, it was placed in a case just large enough to receive it, of gold, covered externally with emeralds, diamonds, and rubies, tastefully arranged. This beautiful and very valuable bijou was put into a very small gold karandua, richly ornamented with rubies, diamonds, and emeralds: this was enclosed in a larger one also of gold, and very prettily decorated with rubies: this second, surrounded with tinsel, was placed in a third, which was wrapped in muslin; and this in a fourth, which was similarly wrapped; both these were of gold, beautifully wrought, and richly studded with jewels:

lastly, the fourth karandua, about a foot and a half high, was deposited in the great karandua. Here, it may be remarked, that when the relic was taken, the effect of its capture was astonishing and almost beyond the comprehension of the enlightened: — "Now (the people said) the English are indeed masters of the country; for they who possess the relic have a right to govern four kingdoms: this, for 2000 years, is the first time the relic was ever taken from us." * And the first Adikar observed, "That whatever the English might think of the consequence of having taken Kappitipola, Pilimé Talawé, and Madugallè, in his opinion, and in the opinion of the people in general, the taking of the relic was of infinitely more moment."

The Malwattè and Asgirie wiharés, it has already been mentioned, are the two heads of the Boodhaical establishment in Ceylon. Both are situated at a little distance from the town; the former on the border of the lake, and the latter in a little dell, two or three hundred feet above the lake, near the western redoubt. The Malwattè is a monastery or college in which about forty priests usually reside, in strict subordination to their chiefs and the rules of their order, principally occupied in religious duties, and in studying and teaching. Their dwellings are of the best kind of Kandyan houses, and are kept very neat. There are two small temples belonging to the Malwattè on the same side of the lake, and a very large poegah †, or hall of meeting, within its en-

* They deny the accuracy of the story told by the Portuguese, and say that when Cotta was taken the relic was secretly removed to Saffragam. It may be said, since the relic was in our possession before, how was this the first time it was taken? To which they would reply, that they had never surrendered it, and that they considered it in their possession till we took it from them by force.

† A sketch of this building is given in the vignette of this chapter.

closure, the roof of which is supported by sixteen stone pillars, each a single stone about twenty or twenty-five feet high. The Asgirie is in all respects like the Malwattè, but on a smaller scale. Close by the residence of the priests, is the temple — a handsome square building, the overhanging roof of which is supported by sixteen square pillars of masonry, four on each side. In the temple there is a recumbent figure of Boodhoo, about thirty feet long, and several smaller figures of the same, in the standing attitude: they are all painted bright yellow, with the exception of one, whose robes are red. The walls and ceiling of the temple are painted with the brightest colours, and in a very elaborate manner. Contiguous to this temple there is a very small wiharé, containing an image of Boodhoo in the sitting attitude, cross-legged, about as large as life, extremely well executed, particularly the face, which is handsome and quite Singalese, with a very mild expression of countenance; on each side and above him, many of the gods are represented in high relief in attendance.

With the exception of the temple of Kattragam, which is surrounded by houses, the dewalès that have been mentioned are situated intermediately between the palace and the town, to both which they are ornamental; not indeed so much by their buildings as by the groves of cocoa-nut trees, and the immense solitary and venerable bo-trees, which are carefully preserved in their grounds, particularly in those of the Nata and Patinè dewalès. As these temples are closed to the profane vulgar, (no one but the priests daring to appear before the shrines of the idols,) I can give no account of their interior. The approach to the Nata dewalè by two massive arch-ways, through courts shaded by noble trees, has rather a fine effect: but generally, externally they have little to recommend them to notice; and without drawings it would be impossible by description to give any tolerable idea of their appearance.

No census has yet been made of the population of Kandy. Since we have had possession of the Interior, the number of the inhabitants of the town has almost constantly been in a state of fluctuation, ebbing and flowing with the contingent circumstances of the day; alarm driving very many families to their dwellings in the country, and the assurance of safety having a contrary effect. Perhaps when fullest, just before the rebellion broke out, the total population did not exceed three thousand souls.

Though from the time of our entrance into Kandy our object has been to improve the town, what we have done has generally had a contrary effect. We have pulled down much and built up little; and, taking no interest in the temples, we have entirely neglected their repair: the consequence is, that Kandy has declined very much in appearance during the short time it has been in our possession, and to the natives must seem merely the wreck of what it once was. In a few years, in all probability, not a vestige of the old town will remain, and an English town will rise on the ground it at present occupies. Hitherto only three permanent edifices have been built by us:—two houses, one for the Governor and the other for the Commandant, both good of their kind, particularly the latter, and a jail, which, to the surprise of the natives, is the finest-looking building in the country. It was in contemplation to construct barracks for the troops and a place of worship, both which are much required, and by this time probably have been commenced.

Of the beautiful scenery and of the few objects of slight interest in the neighbourhood of Kandy, I shall not now stop to take notice, but hasten to pursue my travels.

Whilst the Governor remained transacting business in Kandy, I had the pleasure of undertaking a little excursion into the hitherto unexplored district of Doombera, in company with the Reverend George Bisset, chiefly for the purpose of examining a nitre-cave, which, we were told, was at the distance of two days' journey.

On the 1st of September we set out, and crossed the Mahawellé ganga at the Lewellé ferry, about a mile from the town, just after a native had been drowned by the upsetting of the crazy ferry-boat, into which too many had crowded. Beyond the river we mounted our horses, and rode about eleven miles, to Teldenia, a royal farm, prettily situated at the foot of a mountain in the fertile valley of the Hulu ganga. The country through which we passed was not of uniform character: the first half of the way it was beautiful; its surface consisted of green hills gently rounded, without jungle, spotted here and there with clumps of trees, and well cultivated. The latter part of the way, the ground was more rugged and rocky, and pretty generally overgrown with forest, in going through which we saw many traces of elephants. We took up our quarters at Teldenia, in the Atua, or granary, close to the river, in a grove of cocoa-nut trees, and almost surrounded by paddy-fields, which were nearly ripe, and very like corn-fields in harvest-time in England. The Atua was pretty extensive, and afforded our party good shelter. The buildings formed a hollow square, in the middle of which was the principal granary: it was a room with a strong wooden floor, standing on short stone pillars; its entrance resembled a window, being near the roof, and only just large enough to admit the grain, which being introduced, the shutter is closed, tied, and sealed with a piece of soft clay, on which, I believe, is impressed the royal signature, Sree. To take out the grain, it is necessary to make a breach in the wall. In the evening, just before sunset, we walked about half a mile, to the Bamberra-galle wiharé, romantically situated on the side of a steep hill, amongst great masses of rock, interspersed with fruit-trees. An immense overhanging rock formed the roof and walls of the temple, with the exception of the front wall, which was of masonry. The cavity of the rock, very prettily and gaily painted, was divided into two compartments; in the largest of which was a recumbent figure of Boodhoo, about twenty-five feet long.

On the morrow, about sunrise, we prosecuted our journey. Having crossed the Hulu ganga, which is a considerable stream, and, when flooded, not to be forded, we commenced the ascent of a mountain by a path so steep and rocky, that before we had proceeded a quarter of a mile, we thought it right to send back our horses. About half a mile from the river, we passed through Rabookwellè, where there was a neat little wiharé in the charge of four priests, a small amblam, or rest-house, several scattered dwellings surrounded by fruit-trees, and a considerable extent of ground in cultivation, and then covered with green paddy. The ascent beyond this village was steep, and the mountain was entirely covered with forest. In two hours we reached its summit, from which we had a grand view of wild and wooded mountain-scenery. On the other side, a steep and difficult path led us to the village of Meddahmahaneura, at the bottom of the hill, consisting of a single street of about twenty houses, and containing about sixty inhabitants. The houses were neat and comfortable, and in front of each there was a little inclosed spot, in which were a few cocoa-nut trees. Passing through this village, which is about five miles from Teldenia, and wading across a mountain-torrent close by, we were led to a building in a ruinous state, in the wildest situation, on its bank, which the late king had constructed as a hiding-place, and in which our guide intended that we should stop; but, though fatigued and hungry, we preferred ascending and descending another hill, and taking up our quarters in the first hut we came to in the cultivated valley of Beaumuri. Here, after visiting a solitary house, in which the late king was made prisoner by his own subjects, I lost the pleasure of Mr. Bisset's company; he being obliged to return to Kandy, not having leisure to go farther in pursuit of the nitre-cave, which we were now told was three days' journey off, in the midst of an immense jungle of difficult and dangerous approach, on account of leeches, elephants, precipices, cold, and hurricanes, which, with other evidently exaggerated circumstances, were successively enumerated by one of the natives, the only individual who pretended to know the exact locality of the cave.

On the following morning I left Beaumuri, and before evening reached Hanwellè, distant about ten miles. The country through which I passed was mountainous, and very difficult of access. The ascent was first through a steep valley, which had a very remarkable appearance, from the admixture of the wildest scenery with the most artificial cultivation. No contrast could be stronger than the numerous paddy-fields, ascending by steps and terraces the steep sides of the mountain, and the natural features of the country, — the cloud-capped mountain, the overhanging wood, and the rapid torrent. Another peculiarity in the valley was, that one might here see, at the same time, paddy in its different stages of growth. Water being in abundance all the year round for purposes of irrigation, the farmer was independent of seasons, and each sowed when it was most convenient: in consequence, in some fields the corn was ripe, and in others green; in some they were reaping, and in others sowing. Ascending still higher, we left the cultivated region, and entered a gloomy forest, through which we travelled three or four miles over most irregular ground. The air was cool, varying between 68° and 70°: it had a chilling effect when at any time we stopped for a few minutes to rest ourselves; and the water of the many streams which we crossed was almost cold, varying in temperature between 66° and 68°. In the middle of the forest we passed through a strong cadavettè, or gateway, which, in the king's time, was fortified by a thorn-gate, and constantly guarded. It was flanked on each side by a thick stone wall, and there was a large overhanging rock in its rear, under the shelter of which the guard was stationed. Suddenly emerging from the forest, we had the unexpected pleasure of seeing an open country before us, as bold as any I had yet witnessed, and not less remarkable for want of wood, than that which we left behind was for excess. The eye with delight ran over this novel kind of scenery, from the foreground, covered with long, sweet-smelling lemon-grass, to a deep and large valley, pretty generally cultivated, and spotted with farm-houses and clumps of cocoa-nut trees, to the boundary green hills and more distant blue mountains. Descending very little, our path led us along the side of the mountain, and in about an hour brought us to the scattered village of Hallèhalè. Here we found a large concourse of people (about 500) assembled from the surrounding country, celebrating a fête with tom-toms, pipers, and dancers.

My sudden approach and appearance in a place, where I was told a white man had never been before, excited no little surprise and disturbance. On the part of the women, who were collected within a circle of stones, under the shade of a large bogah, there was a general rush backward to conceal themselves; and forward on the part of the men to see me. They were very civil and conducted me to a little amblam lined with coloured cloths. Close by was a small rustic temple, constructed of the branches of trees and lined with cloths, in which a priest of Boodhoo was officiating before an image of that being on an altar decked with flowers. In front, outside, were two very large earthen vessels full of hot rice, which I was informed, had been blessed by the priest, and was to be distributed amongst the poor, to whom it was a donation from the wealthier proprietors, in gratitude for favourable crops, to express which was the occasion of the holiday they were now keeping. Almost immediately on my arrival, the man who appeared to have most influence amongst the people, and who had brought me his little girl smartly dressed, as a mark perhaps of his confidence, desired that my gun might be fired in honour of the day. When both barrels were discharged, the people seemed greatly pleased, lifting up their hands joined, and bowing their heads as when they worship. I wished to be a spectator of their sports and told them so; but finding they did nothing but look at me, I retired to a neighbouring house to take some refreshment, preparatory to continuing my journey and whilst my people were cooking their rice, — an important operation in travelling, for which not less than two hours can be allowed.

From Hallèhalè I proceeded to Hanwellè about four miles distant, by a path that led over a mountain, one side of which was bare and the other covered with forest, and through a valley pretty generally cultivated. I had for my guide a Widhan, a handsome, active, and intelligent young man, from whom I procured all the information I could wish respecting the country, and particularly respecting the nitre-cave, the working of which he superintended.

At Hanwellè I found shelter for the night in a government atua; contiguous to which, in a state of decay, were a tiled house that did belong to the king, a small dewalé, and an amblam; and in the neighbourhood there were many paddy-fields and several farm-houses. In the evening I received a visit from the Widhan of the village and the Korawl of the district, attended by several country-people, to whom I was an object of considerable curiosity. The Widhan, I may remark, brought with him a boar which he wished to present me, that had been taken in the woods when very young, and so completely tamed, that it followed its master like a dog. I had now the satisfaction to learn, that the nitre-cave was not more than six or eight miles distant, and that on the morrow I might reach it with ease.

On the morrow we set out for the cave. A continued ascent through a stunted jungle brought us to a little plain, covered with fine grass and beautifully spotted with clumps of trees, from which we had an extensive and interesting prospect. Behind, towards Kandy, and on each side, were lofty mountains, and in front the low country of the Mahaweddah-rattè, presenting as far as the eye could reach an uninterrupted surface of wood, with the exception of one spot of water about 10 miles off, which I was told is the lake or rather tank of Bintennè, said to be six or eight miles in circumference. The sky in the opposite directions was in appearance remarkably contrasted, and a true index of the difference of climate amongst the hills and in the plains: over the latter, which at this season are parched, the sun was shining brightly through a clear unclouded atmosphere; whilst the tops of the mountains in our rear were all hid in dense mist, from which a cool moist wind descended with considerable force, occasionally blowing so strong that it required some exertion to stand against it. The natives of our party, whilst we stopped to look at the country below, had an inexhaustible theme of conversation in its wonders; — such as the large alligators of the tank, the herds of elephants that abound in the plains, the barbarous Weddahs who inhabit the woods, and the demons that haunt particular rocks, and delight in every kind of mischief. Ascending from the little plain by a steep and dangerous path, we came to the narrow ridge of the mountain, hardly three feet wide, bounded on one side by a naked precipice perhaps five hundred feet deep, almost perpendicular, and on the other by a very steep declivity covered with entangled wood. Crossing this giddy ridge about thirty yards long, we descended on the other side, through a thick forest, where the view was limited to a few yards, where no sound was to be heard but what we ourselves made in passing, or the occasional note of a solitary bird, or the loud bassoon-like voice of a monkey; and where no traces of man were to be distinguished, excepting in the path, which more resembled a track made by wild animals, and in half-consumed trees still burning, set fire to for the sake of their ashes: I never saw before so perfect a specimen of wild forest-scenery! The trees were of different kinds, sizes, and ages; some saplings, some dead and decaying, and some of very great bulk and height towering above the rest in their prime. When we had descended about half a mile, the path divided; we quitted that most trodden, which led to the secluded village of Memoora, and entered another, just perceptible, leading off to the right, before which a few withered boughs were strewed to show that the way was prohibited. After an hour's hard walking over most difficult ground, we arrived at the object of our search. The first view of the place was exceedingly striking. A large cave appeared in a perpendicular face of rock about three hundred feet high crowned with forest, at the base of which was a stage or platform of rubbish, that seemed in danger of sliding into a deep wooded valley, closed in by mountains of considerable elevation and remarkable boldness. The cave was two hundred feet deep, and at its mouth, which was nearly semicircular, about eighty feet high and one hundred wide. Its floor was rocky and steep, rapidly ascending inward, and its extremity was narrow and dark. To facilitate the ascent, ladders were planted in the most difficult places. I have already described the nature of the rock of which the walls of the cave are formed, and the process followed by the natives to extract saltpetre from its surface.* The workmen, whom I found at their labours, sixteen in number, were the rudest set of artificers I ever witnessed; their bodies, almost naked, were soiled with dirt, and their bushy beards and hair were matted and powdered with brown dust. When I arrived, they were occupied, not in the cave, but on the platform before it, attending to the operations that were then going on in the open air, — of filtration, evaporation, and crystallization. The apparatus employed was curious for its simplicity and rudeness. A small stream of water was led from

* Vide pp. 32 and 265.

a distance to the place by a pipe of bamboos; the filters were of matting, in the shape of square boxes supported by sticks; and the evaporating vessels, and, indeed, all the vessels used, were the common chatties of the country, of which a great many were assembled of various sizes. The cave may be considered partly natural and partly artificial. I was informed, that during the last fifty years, for six months in the dry season, it has been annually worked, and that each man employed was required to furnish a load of nitre, which is about sixty pounds, to the royal stores.

Having gratified my curiosity as far as my limited time would permit, I hastened to rejoin my people, who waited for me at a little village high up the mountain, called Costanè, about three miles from Hanwellè, where I passed the night; and on the day following set out on my return to Kandy.

On the 26th of September the Governor, having brought to a conclusion some urgent business which detained him in Kandy, His Excellency continued his journey, with Lady Brownrigg and suite; and, on the 3d of October, arrived at Trincomalie, distant 128 miles.

The first stage was thirteen miles to Kohimbeaweletenè, a small village in Matelè, where a handsome Bungalow had been prepared by the natives for the Governor's reception. Crossing the Mahawellè ganga at the Watapaloga ferry, we proceeded through a beautiful part of Doombera to the Atgallè Pass, which, by a continued descent of about three miles between the lofty Hoonisgirikandy * on the right, and mountains of

* This mountain, which is better known by the name of Doombera Peak, has been considered the highest in the island. In January, 1818, in company with Lieut. Atkinson, I succeeded in reaching its summit. A short mountain-barometer, which

minor magnitude on the left, leads directly from the high or mountainous country into the low, or rather hilly region, between which there is a difference of perpendicular elevation, of about 1000 feet. It was by this pass that Captain (now Lieutenant-Colonel) Johnson effected his hazardous retreat, with the little force he had marched from Batticaloa to Kandy, in 1804. The conversation, as we travelled along, naturally turned upon the exploit, and on the exertions made and the difficulties overcome in this very pass, where they were greatest, and of a most appalling kind. We had no little pleasure in reflecting on the change that had taken place since that time: the same Kandyans who had attempted his destruction were now running to pay their respects to an English Governor; — the same road which he had passed with an armed force, with so much danger and loss, was now travelled by a lady in her tomjohn; and was now open to all the world, which was then closed even to the natives, and prohibited on pain of death. Between the bottom of the pass and the halting-place, the road led through a valley partially cultivated, between hills of no great elevation, overgrown with jungle, the favourite cover of elephants, that are here numerous, and very troublesome both to the traveller and farmer.

The next stage was to the little military post of Nalandé, distant from the preceding about fifteen miles. The intermediate country is a continuation of the valley that we had entered

---

I carried with me, indicated that, instead of being the highest mountain in the island, it was at least two thousand feet lower than Adam's Peak. The mountain was too low for the barometer to act freely, the top of the column of mercury disappearing as soon as its vibration had ceased.

below the Atgallè Pass, and its features are very similar, excepting that it exhibits less cultivation, and its scenery is more wild and wooded. About two miles on the road, in the neighbourhood of the only extensive paddy-fields that we saw, the ground was pointed out to us where a military post had been established in 1803, called Fort M'Dowall. Little did those who constructed that fort imagine, that in so short a time hardly a trace of it would remain; and, little did we think, that in a still shorter period its buildings would re-appear, and a busy scene start up in the midst of the jungle: — this is actually the case. Fort M'Dowall is now a permanent station, where an agent of government for the province constantly resides, with a detachment of troops. About a mile farther, close by the road, we visited an old wiharé, romantically situated amongst immense masses of rock, the overhanging side of one of which constituted the roof of the temple. The wiharé was extensive, and divided into a number of compartments, the principal of which were crowded with images of Boodhoo, and very gaily and prettily painted. This temple appeared to be of great antiquity, and formerly of much more consequence than at present. It was the best specimen of the rock-temple I had then ever seen in the Interior, but it is not to be compared with one in the same province, which I shall describe hereafter.

The post of Nalandé is on the confines of the hilly region of the Interior. In point of climate, it resembles more the plains than the mountains; having its unwholesome periods, and being liable to long droughts. In corroboration of the latter circumstance it may be mentioned, that leeches, which are common at Fort M'Dowall, and occur sparingly within three miles of Nalandé, are never seen in the immediate neighbourhood of the post, nor in the country beyond it; a long drought being incompatible with their existence.

From Nalandé to Mineré, a distance of forty-three miles, and a fatiguing journey of two days, there is surprisingly little variety of country or scenery. Forest extends the whole way, only diversified here and there by little grassy plains (the oases of this desert) or by dry sandy channels, the beds of rivers in the rainy season, or by a hill here and there of grotesque form, rising above the outline of wood. The forest, in general, is very little obstructed by underwood, and abounds in noble trees, particularly the ebony-tree, which grows something like the elm, has a dark rough bark, and a small leaf like the plum. Man has almost entirely deserted these woods, and given them up undisputed to wild animals, as the elephant, buffaloe, hog, deer, &c. The only inhabited spots we passed were three, divided from each other by an interval of several miles; these are Naycombera, Gonava, and Pecolam. Each of these has a little paddy-ground that affords one crop annually, and is the chief support of the few families whom the tie of nativity still binds to these little enviable spots. Close to Mineré, the scenery alters very much in its character, and greatly improves in its appearance. The last three miles, the path leads across long narrow plains alternating with wood. After having been confined two days in a close forest, such as has been described, we had no small pleasure in entering a comparatively open country. The mind, as it were, expands as the sphere of vision increases, and feels more free as the eye has more liberty. The prospect of a considerable expanse of water was still more agreeable than that of the plains: no sight is so refreshing in a tropical climate, especially in Ceylon, where it is so rare. Yet, independent of association.

this piece of water, where we first approached it, is not remarkable for beauty. Its form is irregular, without islands or rocks, or any bold features, surrounded by a flat green plain, which is generally bounded by gently-rising ground covered with wood.

Mineré is situated on low marshy ground, in paddy-fields, about half a mile from the lake, and on the banks of a stream that flows out of it. The village, consisting of a few scattered huts, is very like the preceding, but it has the distinction of possessing a small kovilla or temple, dedicated to Mahasin-maha-rajah, and said to contain the image and "golden arms," of this king; who, according to tradition, (as has been already noticed,) made 150,000 tanks, of which the lake of Mineré is one. Of the few inhabitants whom we saw, not one had escaped fever, which is the prevailing disease of the country. They all, I perceived, wore something wrapped up and tied to the arm. On enquiry what it meant, they said, "it was a charm to defend them against sickness and wild beasts." This place was occupied by a detachment of our troops in 1803; and since, during the late rebellion. In both instances, it proved excessively unhealthy; and, indeed, in the former, fatal to the majority of those stationed here.

The lake or tank of Mineré is a very interesting object. Its great size, fifteen or twenty miles in circumference, entitles it to be called a lake; but, as it is artificial, its waters, being kept in by an embankment, it is strictly a tank. The embankment is about a quarter of a mile long, and about sixty feet wide at its top. In general it is overgrown with forest-trees and thick jungle. Judging from those parts of it which are not thus concealed, it is made of stones of moderate size. On our way back from Trincomalie to Kandy, I visited it, and examined, as well as circumstances would permit, the outlet through which the water of the tank has vent. Guided by a native of the place, with some difficulty I made my way through the close jungle to the principal outlet, of which I could procure a good view only by wading in the stream that bursts out of it. The adjoining sketch will give some idea of its construction, composed of large masses of rock,

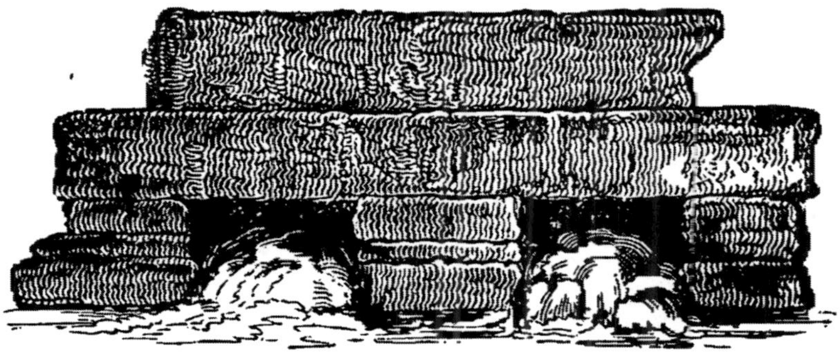

coarsely cut. As it is at the base of the embankment, and probably lower than even the bottom of the tank, it ensures a constant flow of water. I wished to examine the work on the opposite side of the embankment, towards the lake, but was prevented by the thick jungle intervening. The stream, which is always running from the tank, is of considerable size; at least twelve feet wide at its source, and two or three feet deep. It flows into the Mahawellé ganga, through the district of Tambankadduwe. Formerly, when its waters were directed by man, and applied to cultivation, it was a source of fertility, probably, to the whole tract through which it passed; but now, running waste, forming swamps, and only supporting rank vegetation, it may be considered one of the causes of the unwholesomeness of this part of the country.

The manner of my guide, who led me to the embankment, was very characteristic, and not a little amusing. He kept always a little in advance, walking cautiously, as if on an enemy's ground; his eye constantly wandering about and penetrating the thickets, as if to avoid being surprised by an elephant, bear, or leopard. The only wild animals I saw during our walk, with the exception of a few monkeys, were four or five large alligators. Turning round a little headland of the lake, we suddenly came within a few feet of them, as they lay on the sandy shore, basking in the sun. The instant they saw us, and heard the report of my rifle, they plunged into the lake, and disappeared under water: a circumstance that may convince even the timid, that on land, at least, they are not dangerous, particularly when I mention that we were only two in company; that they were in the act of flying even before the rifle was fired; and that the sand where they were contained their eggs. This we discovered accidentally: walking over the sand, we heard distinctly feeble cries from beneath; some egg-shells lying on the shore immediately suggested the cause, and, on digging in the sand from whence the noise issued, two or three young alligators made their appearance, and we found several eggs. It was curious to observe the propensity of these animals to use the weapons with which nature has furnished them; they all bit at the stick with which I touched them; savage from birth, and shewing more instinctive hardihood than their runaway parents. The egg was about the size of a goose-egg, but larger, and at its extremities more rounded. Its earthy shell was brittle, and easily separated. Like the shell of the eggs of all the other lizards that I have examined, as well as that of the turtle, and of birds, it consists chiefly of carbonat of lime, and a little albumen, with very slight traces of phosphat of lime. The membrane beneath the outer shell too, like that of other lizards and of the turtle, was thick and remarkably tough and strong. The alligator of Ceylon is never seen in rivers amongst the mountains or hills; it is confined to the low country, and abounds most in the lakes and tanks in the northern and southern parts of the island. It appears to be the *Crocodilus biporcatus* of M. Cuvier. * It occasionally attains a great size: I have heard of one taken that was seventeen feet long. Even in its own element, it rarely attacks man; but there are instances of its carrying off individuals; and the large one, just alluded to, had seized and swallowed a native.

Kandellé, distant from Mineré twenty-nine miles, is a journey of two days. The country between Mineré and Pulian-Kadavettè, the intermediate halting place, is a very agreeable succession of wood and plain. It is low, and in the rainy season a great part of it is under water. The extremity of Mineré lake, in this direction, is far more picturesque than in the other. When we passed early in the morning, the prospect of the calm lake, with its numerous projecting promontories, girded round by green wood, and bounded by the lofty blue mountains of the Interior, had a most charming effect. About six or seven miles on the road, we crossed a pretty extensive plain. On the left, it had very much the appearance of a morass, and was covered with long grass four or five feet high. Here, at a distance, we saw several wild buffaloes feeding; they were so large, that we at first mistook them for elephants. On the right, this plain is bounded by jungle, in which, on our return, I accidentally discovered a great embankment, exceeding in magnitude that of Mineré. The mouth of the outlet of the old tank is a massive work, and still nearly in perfect preservation. It is a square

* Regné Animal, tom. ii. p. 20.

well, with walls formed of large stones, some of which are twelve feet by four, neatly cut, and most nicely adapted to each other, — to use the technical phrase, " rabbited together." I regret I could not cross the embankment and examine the vent of the outlet on the opposite side. At a very little distance, and nearer Mineré, I observed in the jungle an immense hollow, like the bed of a great river, intersected by pretty steep ridges of quartz-rock. Its bed was composed of fine sand, and was full of deep pools of clear water. How far it extended I cannot say; the rocks, water, and jungle, preventing rapid examination, and I had not time to prosecute any other. On the spot it occurred to me, that it might be the quarry from whence the stones were procured for the construction of the great embankment adjoining. On this idea, even the appearance of the insulated ridges of quartz-rock may be accounted for, on the supposition that the more valuable gneiss only was quarried.

Pulian-Kadavettè is the counterpart of one of the wretched little villages on the former part of the road. Here we felt, in a very sensible manner, the sudden transition we had made from the cool air of the highlands to the hot atmosphere of the plains. In the afternoon, the wind was westerly and hard; its temperature was 88°, and being very dry, it had a parching effect, and excited thirst greatly, in a place where there was only a little muddy water to allay it.

Between Pulian-Kadavettè and Kàndellè is the little village of Permamadua. The intermediate country is more generally covered with wood than the preceding stage. Three or four miles from Kandellé the scenery again improves. The path leads across an open grass plain, in which there is a small tank that was crowded with water-fowl. The tank was a most agreeable object to our thirsty followers, particularly the palanqueen-bearers, who no sooner saw it, than they raised a shout of joy, and impatiently ran to it to take a draught of its water.

Kandellé is a scattered village, similar to the preceding. It contains about sixteen families, who subsist on the produce of one large paddy-field. The lake or tank of Kandellé, which is close by, is a great work, and the best example of the kind of work, that I have ever seen. The lake is about three or four miles in circumference, and, like that of Mineré, skirted with green plains. The embankment by which the water is confined is a mile and one-third long. It extends nearly in a straight line, from a rocky hillock at one extremity, to a high ledge of rock at the other. Its perpendicular height may be about twenty feet; at its base, it may be a hundred and fifty or two hundred feet wide. Its face towards the lake is naked, sloped at an angle of about 45°, and composed of stones that rise one above the other like steps. The stones are of the same size nearly; from two to three feet long, about two high, and from one to two wide. They are of the same kind as the adjoining rock. It is, perhaps, worth remarking, that they have no sharp angles or asperities of surface; they have the appearance of quarried stones, rendered thus smooth by the action of the elements in long process of time. On the land-side the slope is very gentle, and the embankment is of gravel and earth. The stone face of the embankment is shaded by trees of great size; the other side is covered with large forest-trees and thick underwood, in most places impenetrable. Besides the great embankment, there is a small one detached from it about a quarter of a mile, and nearly at right-angles to it, similarly constructed.

The lake has two outlets; the principal one about a hundred yards from the rocky ledge, through which a river is constantly flowing; and another near the opposite extremity of the embankment, which is commonly dry, and carries off water only when the lake is unusually high.

The great outlet or sluice is constructed with much art and of vast strength; the channel is beneath a platform of masonry that projects into the lake about six feet beyond the line of the embankment, and is about twenty-four feet long. It is built of oblong stones from five to seven feet long, well wrought and nicely adapted to each other without cement. The top of the platform is flat; it contains a small cylindrical well, communicating directly with the channel below, and in which the water, in passing, rises of course to the level of the lake. The water passing through the embankment, appears on the other side gushing out in a noble stream through two apertures formed by a transverse mass of rock supported by three perpendicular masses. The transverse mass, which is now cracked in two, is about twelve or fourteen feet long, and four or five thick; and the other masses are of proportional size. The water rushing out in a considerable volume with great force, dashing amongst rocks beneath, in a deep gloomy shade produced by overhanging trees, makes altogether a very striking scene. The work itself has a simple grandeur about it which is seldom associated with art; it looks more like a natural phenomenon than the design of man.

The other outlet being dry, afforded an opportunity of seeing the entrance of the channel. At the foot of the embankment there was a circular pit, almost filled with leaves and branches;

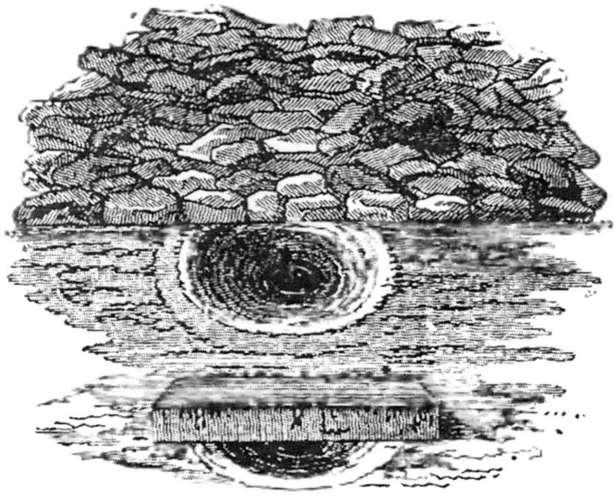

and a little anterior to it another small pit, the mouth of which was almost entirely covered and defended by a large long mass of hewn stone. The Kandellé river flows into the bay of Tamblegam. At Tamblegam a good deal of rich paddy-ground is still irrigated by this stream ; but with this exception, and the solitary field at Kandellé, instead of conveying fertility through its whole course, it runs entirely waste.

The occurrence of these great tanks, in a country now almost entirely desert, makes a forcible impression on the mind of the traveller, and excites greatly his curiosity to know the causes of that change which has evidently taken place. The works themselves indicate that, at some former period, this part of the island must have been inhabited by a numerous people under a regular and probably an absolute form of government, and who had made considerable progress in the arts ; and this is confirmed by the history of the country. What the causes were that produced the change, are not all of them very obvious ; one cause pointed out by history seems certain ; and that may have been the cardinal one on which all the others hinged : I allude to the wars which the history of Ceylon, vague as it is, decidedly shows were carried on for a long series of years in the northern parts of the island. During this disturbed period, reasoning from too certain analogy, it may be taken for granted that industry was checked, that disease and famine were the consequences, that the tanks were neglected, that morasses formed and the jungle encroached on the cultivated land, that the climate became permanently deteriorated, and the population diminished; and thus, probably, by a progressive increase of destructive causes, the change in question was produced.

The next stage beyond Kandellé, at the distance of thirteen miles, is Tamblegam, a small village near the shore of the bay of the same name. The country between Kandellé and Tamblegam is very uninteresting; being low, wooded, and uncultivated.

From Tamblegam the Governor and his party proceeded to Trincomalie, distant fourteen miles, by water, across the bay, in the Admiral's barge.

On the 20th of October His Excellency quitted Trincomalie to return to Kandy. The wet season was about to set in; some rain had already fallen, which had produced a very decided effect: the grass, which in many places on our way down had a completely withered appearance, was now generally green; the air was comparatively cool; the ground, before baked up and indurated, was now moist, and in low places not easily passable; and water was beginning to run in the channels which were before without a drop. The nearer we approached the mountains, the stronger the symptoms of the alteration of season appeared: at Nalandé the rain met us and poured down in torrents; and we found the Mahawellè ganga so swollen that we had some difficulty in crossing it.

It was at this time that the rebellion broke out: the Governor had the first intimation of it at Kandellé; at Mineré the accounts brought were of an alarming nature; at Naycombera we appeared to be in great danger. The chief, Eheylapola, who was also returning to Kandy, was in the neighbourhood, with a large body of followers; and, he had just been guilty of an act of rebellion; he had disgraced the Dissave of the district, deprived him of the insignia of his office, and in fact suspended him. We fully expected that this measure was merely preparatory to his heading the rebellion, and taking the Governor and Lady Brownrigg, and all the party prisoners; which, he was aware, he could have done with perfect ease, as His Excellency travelled without an escort, attended only by four or five orderly dragoons. Fortunately, the result did not confirm our apprehensions; we proceeded without molestation to Nalandé, where Eheylapola appeared in great state, with several elephants and two or three thousand people. He waited on the Governor most submissively, and apologized for his extraordinary conduct in the best manner he could.

I shall pass over in silence the anxious period that elapsed between the 26th of October, when the Governor re-entered Kandy, and the 25th of November the following year, when he left it for Colombo. The journey down was delightful: the whole country was tranquillized; we passed through districts which had not experienced any of the horrors of war, which appeared improved since we had seen them in going up, and which poured their inhabitants forth on the road, as it were, to congratulate His Excellency on his success. The entry into Colombo was quite triumphal; — under beautiful arch-ways, — through the streets of the Pettah, lined with troops, and crowded with the inhabitants in their holiday-dresses, — the cannons of the ramparts firing, and the bands of two or three regiments playing. The scene had as much life, animation, and gaiety as an ancient triumph could possess: and, if it wanted the ancient splendour, it was not disgraced by its barbarities.

CHAPTER III.

DEPARTURE FROM COLOMBO FOR OUVA. — DESCRIPTION OF COUNTRY BETWEEN AVISAHAVELLE′ AND RATNAPOORA; BETWEEN RATNAPOORA AND BALANGODDE′; AND BALANGODDE′ AND KALAPAHANE′. — THE IDALGASHENA - PASS. — VELANGAHENA. — HIMBLEATAWELLE′. — BADULLA. — NAMINA-COOLI-KANDY. — AN INSTANCE OF HEROISM. — PASSERA. — ALIPOOTA. — EXCURSION INTO THE MAHAWEDDAHRATTE′ OF OUVA AND INTO WELASSEY. — DESCRIPTION OF COUNTRY BETWEEN ALIPOOTA AND KATRAGAM. — KATRAGAM. — DESCRIPTION OF COUNTRY BETWEEN KATRAGAM AND GAMPAHA. — NITRE-CAVE NEAR WELEWAY. — KIRRIWANNAGAMME′. — RETURN TO UPPER OUVA. — DAMBAWINNE′. — FORT M'DONALD. — DESCRIPTION OF COUNTRY BETWEEN FORT M'DONALD AND

MATURATTA.—HINTS ON THE IMPROVEMENT OF THE INTERIOR.—NITRE-CAVE IN THE VALLEY OF MATURATTA. — HANGRANKETTY. — MEDDA-WALLATENE'. — KOORNAGALLE.

The next excursion into the Interior which I shall describe, was one of considerable extent and of seven weeks' duration, which I commenced alone, and undertook with the sole design of seeing the country. From the nature of the roads, being soon obliged to send back my horse, the greater part of the journey was performed on foot, or in a chair tied to two poles and carried on men's shoulders.

On the 11th of March, 1819, I set out from Colombo and proceeded to Hanwellé where I slept. I am tempted to transcribe from my note-book, a very delightful scene, which I witnessed at dawn the following morning. When I rose at half past four, the full moon was still high in the west, and Jupiter in the east; the sky was of the purest blue, excepting over the grey Kandyan hills, where a just perceptible tint of yellow marked the approach of day: not a breath of air was stirring; the smooth river (the Kalany ganga) that ran by, reflected the light of the moon and the shadows of the groves of cocoa-nut trees on its banks; the air was most agreeably cool, of the temperature 70°; the grass and leaves were covered with dew; some doves answered each other in an adjoining wood, and the air was so still, that even the faint echo of their cooings was heard: — the whole was a tropical scene of solemn and tranquil beauty, that could hardly be surpassed.

From Hanwellé we went to Avisahavellé; and from thence across the south-west portion of Saffragam to Ratnapoora, through a part of the country little known to Europeans, lying at the foot of the frontier mountains, and generally low and uninteresting, and only very partially cultivated. Owing to a sudden change of weather, from long drought to heavy rains, this part of Saffragam appeared to great disadvantage, and travelling through it was attended with some difficulty. The path was frequently under water; the small streams were converted into torrents, and the larger streams, which were numerous, could only be crossed by the giddy and shaking Singalese bridges, consisting generally of a single plank or tree, and raised above the water, often twenty and thirty feet. Leeches abounded; and, excited into unusual activity by the kind of weather, they proved excessively annoying. Though the distance from Avisahavellé to Ratnapoora is only thirty miles, yet, owing to the many impediments in the way, we were nearly three whole days on the road. One night we passed at Palliagallé Wiharé, where my people found shelter from heavy rain under a small open shed; and I was hospitably received into the little room of a young Samaneroo, who resided there alone in charge of the temple. The lamp with which he lighted his apartment, and which is commonly used by the natives, may be worth noticing for its simplicity, utility, and resemblance to some of our lamps of modern invention. Its figure is represented in the wood-cut subjoined.

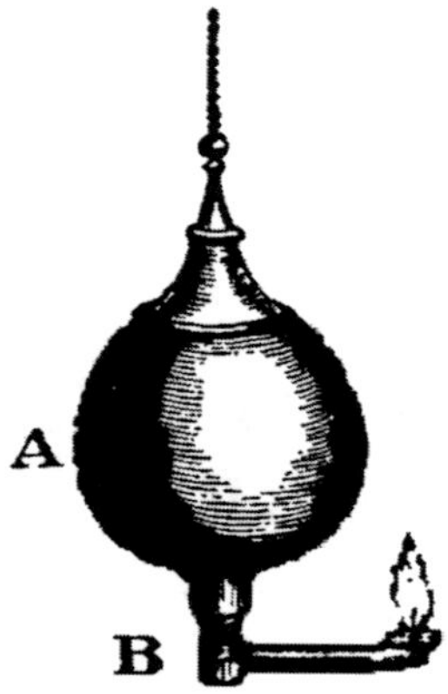

It was made of brass, and composed of a receiver (A) air-tight, and of a burner (B) which screwed together. The next night we passed at Korowitté, under a shed, which had been constructed during the rebellion, and which we found occupied by cattle. It may be remarked, that the country, within three or four miles of Ratnapoora, greatly improves in appearance, and affords a favourable example of Saffragram scenery: — flat green meadows occur in succession, bounded by low wooded hills, and skirted with a border of palms and fruit-trees, under which the scattered dwellings of the natives are here and there visible.

Between Ratnapoora and Balangoddé, a distance of twenty-nine miles, which we travelled in two days, there is considerable variety of country. The first part of the way is through charming meadows, such as have just been described, but more extensive, and bounded by lofty mountains; the chain of which Adam's Peak is the summit, towering magnificently on the left. The latter part of the way is hilly, and the immediate ascent to Balangoddé is steep and mountainous. The scenery, in general, is of a very exquisite character, gradually increasing in wildness with the elevation of the country. The vallies are very well watered, and appear to be populous and well cultivated. About two miles from Ratnapoora, we went through the little village of Baddegeddera, consisting of a single street of huts, inhabited chiefly by trading Moormen, from the low country, who supply the natives with salt, tobacco, and the finer cloths, bartering them generally for rice, at great profit. We passed by three different temples, all dedicated to Boodhoo; one of which, the Gonagammé Wiharé, is said to be five hundred years old. Neither of them exhibited any thing peculiar; each, as usual, was an establishment of itself, and consisted of a wiharé, a dagobah, and a pansol, in which the officiating priests reside. A bogah, by the road-side, walled round and surrounded by iron-trees, was not an unusual sight. To one of them an adjoining grove of cocoa-nut trees was dedicated. The people of the place, to whom we applied for a cocoa-nut to drink *, refused it, pretending fear of the demon (Yakshyayo) if they gave away the consecrated fruit. I mention this rather as a trait of the superstition of the natives than of their incivility, of which the one is as common as the other is rare.

At Balangoddé, during the rebellion, a military post was established, which is still occupied. The fort, containing rude barracks and officers' quarters, stands on the top of a commanding hill, and is defended by a parapet and ditch. Below the fort is a cantonment for native troops, a small bazar, and the house of the Dissave of the upper part of the province. The breast-work and ditch, with which this house is surrounded, mark the period at which it was built, and the apprehension of its proprietor of being taken by surprise, and carried off or put to death by his countrymen. Balangoddé stands pretty high, about 1742 feet above the level of the sea †; and, in consequence, enjoys a comparatively cool atmosphere, and a very agreeable climate. The country immediately round the fort is rather hilly, and covered with jungle, consisting chiefly of Guavo bushes, with forest-trees interspersed; it is very partially cultivated, and the fields being situ-

* The young cocoa-nut is lined with a soft gelatinous pulp, and full of an agreeably sweet and nearly transparent fluid. The pulp is good eating. Fresh from the tree, the water is always cool, and, to the hot and thirsty traveller, proves a most agreeable and wholesome beverage.

† At the Fort, at 4 P. M. when the thermometer was 80°, and at 6 A. M. the next morning, when the thermometer was 65°, the barometer of the same temperature was 28.35 inches.

ated in hollows are generally hid from view. The neighbouring scenery is wild and picturesque, especially towards the north, in which direction four distinct chains of mountains have a fine effect, rising one above the other ; and indeed, in the morning, early, when I saw them, their appearance was quite beautiful,— the nearest was green, the most distant, purple, and the intermediate two of different shades of blue.

The next stage beyond Balangoddè is Alutneura, about seven miles distant, and rather less elevated. * The country between the two places is very like that in the immediate neighbourhood of the former, but better cultivated. About a mile from Balangoddè, we came to the Weleway oya, already a pretty wide and deep stream, which we crossed on a raft made of bundles of bamboos, piled on one another and tied together. We found cover for the night in some huts, on the top of a little hill, that had been occupied during the rebellion as a military post. Having been since deserted and neglected, it afforded bad shelter from a storm, which commenced in the evening and lasted almost the whole of the night, accompanied with heavy rain and thunder and lightning. About half a mile from our halting-place, we passed by the Alutneura Dewalé, where there is a temple of some extent, said to be eight hundred years old, dedicated to the Katragam god, and a small wiharé and dagobah, within the same inclosure as the dewalé. The temple was undergoing repair: the men employed about the walls worked under the cover of a temporary roof; a precaution very necessary at a season when a good deal of rain falls, one shower of which would destroy the labour of many days. In the afternoon I was visited by a

* At 3 P. M. on the hill where we stopt, the barometer was 28.50, the air 70°, and the attached thermometer 72°.

Nilami*, who, though seventy-six years of age, were it not for his fine flowing white beard and white locks, might have passed for sixty, — he was so good-looking, stout, and hale. He gave a very unfavourable account of the upper part of Saffragam, which he described as suffering greatly from famine, the consequence of the rebellion, which extended thus far. A good many of the people, he said, had been obliged to migrate to the lower provinces in search of food; and, of those who remained, many subsisted on wild plants, and on a kind of sago prepared from the inner substance of different kinds of palm-trees. Whilst he was speaking, a wretched woman presented herself, as it were, to confirm his remarks. She was Famine personified: with uplifted hands and most imploring expression of countenance, she begged a little food; adding, she had ate nothing for three whole days.

Kalapahané, the next stage, is about fourteen miles from Aluneura. At the distance of half a mile from our resting place, we came to the Belhool oya, which is always a considerable stream, and now flooded by the late rains, it had a formidable appearance. We crossed it with some difficulty, fording it naked, and helping each other. Owing to the rapidity of the torrent and its depth, (reaching nearly to the middle,) and the slipperiness of its rocky bottom, there was danger of being carried off one's legs, and of being hurried down a rapid below, where destruction would have been inevitable. This river, and indeed all the numerous streams that we crossed in the course of the day, had completely the character of the mountain torrent descending rapidly from its source through a channel of primitive rock: their waters were in

* Nilami is a term of respect in Singalese, somewhat similar to that of country-gentleman in English.

every instance cold; the temperature of the Belhool oya was 67°, and though flooded, they were all clear as crystal. The country between this river and Kalapahané is a succession of steep rocky hills, that are occasionally bare, with the exception of a covering of long grass, but more generally wooded. Though it was dry over-head, it threatened rain; the bold mountains on our left and in front were almost constantly enveloped in clouds, and the low country which lay on our right, resembling a great plain or rather sea, was every now and then hid by the passing mist. All the way we did not see a single inhabited house, or any marks of very recent cultivation, nor did we meet a single native; — dwellings, here and there in ruins, paddy-fields neglected, and a human skull that lay by the road-side, under a tree, to which the fatal rope was still attached, gave us the history of what we saw, in language that could not be mistaken. Kalapahané was quite in character with the general appearance of the country. We found shelter for the night on the top of a steep hill, which had been occupied during the rebellion as a military post, and was now tenanted only by the Dissave of the Kandapala Korle with a few of his people, here on government duty, to expedite the transport of seed-paddy from the low country into Ouva, which was almost entirely destitute of it. Wrapped up in a blanket to defend himself from the damp cold air, he looked little like a Dissave, except indeed of such a district. His account of the country agreed with its desolate appearance; before the rebellion, he said, it had been pretty populous, but it was now quite deserted. This place, rising about 2400 feet above the level of the sea*, is situated at the foot of the great barrier ridge of Upper Ouva, and commands a very extensive

* On the top of the hill at 4 P.M., when the air was 70° and the attached thermometer 71°, the barometer was 27.67.

prospect of the low wooded country beneath the mountains to the eastward and the southward.

The next stage is to Velangahena, eight miles distant, across the Idalgashena, the summit of which is about 4700 feet above the level of the sea.* This is the principal pass from Saffragam into Upper Ouva. The weather being fine, the feeling of fatigue was lost in the enjoyment of the magnificent scenery of the mountains. From the Velé oya, a rapid torrent which is crossed about three-fourths of a mile from Kalapahané, and considerably below it, there is a continued ascent of about four miles to the head of the pass. It is worth remarking, that whilst the top and lower part of the Idalgashena are only covered with grass, its middle-region is occupied by noble forest. Nothing can be more striking than the difference of prospect on the opposite sides of the mountain. Ascending, the scenery is what one has been accustomed to, at least in kind, though of superior quality; but not so in descending. On that side the view is quite novel: on the top of the pass, the path makes a turn, and brings one suddenly in view of Upper Ouva, consisting of an extensive surface of green grassy hills, walled round by lofty blue mountains, laid out like a map at one's feet. The sight of such a country, free from jungle, was quite a treat, and the eye at liberty wandered with delight from hill to hill, and from mountain to mountain. Velangahena, in a straight line from the top of the pass, may be about two miles distant, and it is about 700 feet lower †;

* At the head of the pass, about two or three hundred feet below the summit of the mountain, a short mountain-barometer was stationary at 25.55. This was at 10 h. 25 m. A.M., when the air was 68° and the thermometer attached 71°.

† At Velangahena, on the 19th March, at 3 P.M., a long barometer was 26.10, the thermometer, attached and free, was 69°.

a deep valley intervenes, both sides of which are steep and covered with grass, excepting in hollows and sheltered places, where there are little patches of wood, amongst which the *rhododendron arboreum*, in flower, made a conspicuous figure. We occasionally met with this tree on the side of Idalgashena : the lowest situation where I have seen it, was at the foot of the hill of Velangahena, which cannot, I think, exceed 3000 feet above the level of the sea.

Velangahena is a small military post, which was established during the rebellion, and is still occupied. If Himbleatawellè be not an exception, it is the highest inhabited spot in Ceylon. Its climate is peculiar, verging rather on cold than hot, and, in consequence, it agrees much better with Europeans than with natives. On the morning of the 20th of March, just before sunrise, I observed the thermometer at 57°, and the air was not then considered unusually cold. The prospect of Upper Ouva, from the top of this hill, which is one of the highest within the mountain-wall, is still more impressive than from the summit of the Idalgashena. On looking round the country, it has the appearance of a magnificent amphitheatre sixty or eighty miles in circumference, formed of a succession of steep, smooth, green, conical hills, and of deep narrow glens remarkably free from wood, enclosed on every side by mountains varying in perpendicular height from four to six thousand feet. I shall have an opportunity hereafter to consider the causes of the peculiar features of this district: I particularly allude to the rounded forms of the hills, and the general absence of wood. Another peculiarity, and a painful blemish of the scenery, forces itself on one's notice, and produces a melancholy train of thought: it is the deserted appearance of the surrounding country ; — its cottages in ruins, its fields lying waste, its cattle destroyed, and its population fled, — all effects of the rebellion, of which this province was the principal theatre. Had the country never been inhabited, its desert appearance would be little thought of; the wild beauty and untamed majesty of nature, which displays itself around, would occupy the mind with delight, instead of associations of every kind of human misery that war and famine can inflict.

Himbleatawellé is fifteeen miles from Velangahena. The intermediate country is such as has just been described. The hills are covered with clumps of lemon-grass of a very agreeable smell ; and wood is to be seen in sheltered hollows only, though a solitary tree now and then appears in an exposed situation, but, with the exception of the bogah, always stunted and small. The bogah, where most exposed seems to flourish best ; it here appears to be self-planted and neglected ; it is not walled round, as in most other provinces ; and thus confirms what is commonly said of the mountaineers of Ouva, that they have little regard for their national religion, by which this tree has been consecrated. The whole way we saw very many neglected, but very few fields in actual cultivation. The first that occurred were some green paddy-fields, in a valley about six miles from Velangahena. The dwellings of their proprietors, three neat cottages, shaded by the luxuriant foliage of jack, jaggery, and shaddoc trees, were prettily situated on a little rising ground above them, and by the side of a clear stream by which they were watered. After having been travelling three days through an artificial desert, this sight did one's heart good ; it produced a degree of pleasure, even in my coolies, greater than can well be conceived, and which would appear affected if described, though easily

explained on the principle of the association of ideas, and the sympathies of our nature; the green crops and inhabited houses suggesting peace and quietness, domestic comfort, and human happiness.

Himbleatawellé is also a military post, of the same date as Velangahena, and still occupied. Owing to its great height and situation, the views from it are very extensive, including not only the greater part of Upper Ouva, but also a considerable portion of the mountainous district of Walapany, and extending, it is said, to Doombera and Bintenné, where the Mahawelle ganga may be seen for a short space in clear weather. A mist, that enveloped the hill almost the whole time I was there, shut out this extensive prospect. This post is particularly useful for purposes of communication, most of the other posts of Upper Ouva being visible from it. Its flag-staff, it is worth remarking, (and it is not a diminutive one,) is made of a cinnamon-tree.

From Himbleatawellé to Badulla, distant eight miles, there is almost one continued descent, which in many places is steep and difficult. Badulla is the principal station of Ouva; it is the residence of the Agent of Government, and the head-quarters of the officer commanding the district. It is situated on a gently rising ground, about 2100 feet above the level of the sea*, in an extensive valley, bounded by lofty mountains, and watered by the Badulla oya, a considerable stream that runs sluggishly and tortuously along, and almost surrounds the station. The valley of Badulla is in that part of Ouva called the Yattikinda, or lower portion, in contradistinction to the Oudakinda, the upper, and the Meddakinda, the middle division. The character

* At Badulla, on the 23d of March at ten A.M. the barometer was 28.05; the thermometer, attached and free, the same, viz. 73.

of this part of the country is different from that already described; its valleys are more expanded and prolonged; its hills, or rather mountains, run more in ridges, and there is not the same scarcity of wood. Badulla itself is an inconsiderable place; its only fortification is a small star-fort, in which the commandant resides, in an old Singalese house, which was formerly a royal palace. The buildings are few, and confined chiefly to officers' quarters of a very humble description, a barrack for European troops, a good hospital, a native cantonment, and a small bazar; there are, besides, a dewalé dedicated to the Kattragam god, and a wiharé, the dagobah attached to which is of large size. The chief ornaments of Badulla are its fine trees and its rich and extensive paddy-fields: here, for the first time since I had been in Ouva, I saw the cocoa-nut tree; it appeared to flourish, at least in the temple-grounds where it was protected; elsewhere it was emblematic of the state of the country, — without fruit, which had been prematurely plucked by the hungry people, and often without leaves, presenting a miserable appearance. The jack-fruit tree is abundant, and in many instances it has attained a gigantic size. The paddy-fields are the property of government; very many of them were in cultivation, and being covered with a young crop beautifully green, they were a most agreeable sight. As a station, little can be said in favour of Badulla; and, were it not for its rich valley, it would probably be deserted. It is said hardly to admit of defence, and being so centrically situated amongst the mountains, communication with it is difficult, and the transport of supplies to it tedious and expensive.

Namina-cooli-kandy, next to Adam's Peak perhaps the highest mountain in Ceylon, rises in massive grandeur above the valley of Badulla. On the 21st of March, the day I arrived. this mountain

was ascended by Mr. Moon, the first European who had ever been on its summit. On the evening of the 23d, in company with H. Wright, Esq., the Agent of Government, my friend Mr. Nicholson, and Lieut. Hay, I set out to attempt what Mr. Moon had accomplished. At two the next morning we started by torch-light from a small village about three miles from Badulla, and a little way up the mountain: we first passed through a tract of gentle ascent covered with guavo-jungle, and infested with leeches, which, though it was night, were on the alert, and proved very troublesome. We next ascended with some difficulty and considerable labour through a forest, over very irregular and steep ground, which in some places would have been inaccessible had it been bare, and which we surmounted by pulling ourselves up by the branches of the trees. Still higher, the side of the mountain was without wood, and covered with lemon-grass; and higher still, we ascended over immense masses of bare rock: above this rocky region, to its very summit, the mountain was covered with thick wood, through which we found our way with some difficulty, often bewildered and led astray by the tracks of wild animals. We had hoped to have been on the top of the mountain by sunrise, but notwithstanding much exertion we were disappointed, — it was half-past seven before we reached it.

The top is almost table-land, gently sloping on every side, and of the extent of many acres: it is without rock; its surface and soil consist almost entirely of friable and, as it were, disintegrating quartz, and of quartz-gravel, in some places discoloured by black mould, in others as white as snow, with pieces of iron-stone here and there intermixed. The vegetation is peculiar and very different from that in the forest below: it is composed of low trees and bushes, which grow in clumps, separated from each other by little open spaces either of white gravel or of dark soil covered with mosses and lichens. The plants, though apparently dwarfish and stunted as if they had struggled for life with the elements, looked fresh and healthy; many of them were in blossom and bore very handsome flowers. With one exception, they were all new to me: the exception was the rhododendron arboreum, which was here abundant, exceeding all the other plants in size and in rich blossom. The natives who were with us called it *diaratmala*, which translated literally, is god-red-flower. The shrub which attracted their attention most was not the diaratmala, but what they called the *kapooroowelle*, not unlike the laurustinus both in leaf and flower, and much prized for its leaves, which have an agreeable astringent and aromatic flavour. They are chewed with betel; and a large quantity of them was gathered and carried down for that purpose. Another shrub attracted attention by its flower, very like that of the *erica vagans*; its flower had a very pleasant acid taste; its leaf was also acid, but astringent too, and rather bitter.

To have a view of the surrounding country, one was under the necessity of climbing a rhododendron. The sun being high and the atmosphere not very clear, the prospect was not of much interest, and in point of beauty and effect not to be compared with that which we enjoyed under more favourable circumstances, from Adam's Peak. With a compass and map in my hand, I in vain searched for that mountain; and, as the air was pretty clear in its direction, I infer it was hid by the lofty mountains of Kotmalè. The valley of Badulla, in miniature, appeared at a great depth below, like a circular basin, formed by the expansion of several valleys at their place of junction, and flanked by a double row of hills of very unequal heights.

In a former part of the work, some notice was taken of the pits of water on the top of the mountain in relation to temperature. I recur to them to mention a superstitious practice to which they are applied. On the occasion of long drought, the Kappurales of the Katragam temple ascend the mountain, and with a leaf of a particular kind, throw water to the sound of tom-toms, from the deepest pit into the air, and scatter it over the people, as an offering to their god. This done, they descend, confident of having a fall of rain, before they are half-way down; and every native has a thorough conviction of the infallibility of the ceremony in producing the effect. It was last had recourse to eight years ago, and with the usual happy result. This, I hardly need remark, is only another instance of the fraud of the few, and of the credulity of the multitude. If rain invariably follow the performance of the ceremony as believed, of course the priests do not ascend the mountain till they have clear signs of change of weather approaching.

During the time that we remained on the summit, from half past seven till twelve, the thermometer varied from 57° to 68°. About 1000 feet lower, at break of day, it was only 53°. On our arrival we suffered from cold, and were glad to sit by a fire; but before we descended, though the air itself was cool, the sun was powerful and troublesome, and drove us in quest of shade. At 9 A. M. the short barometer, hung from a tree, was stationary at 24.32, when the attached thermometer was 63°, and the air 64°.*

From Badulla I had the pleasure of making an excursion into Lower Ouva and Welassey, in company with Mr. Wright and Mr.

* Making allowance for probable difference of temperature, the height of this mountain may be estimated at about 5900 feet above the level of the sea, instead of 5548, its approximate height, which is assigned in p. 4.

Moon. On the 28th of March we set out from Badulla, and proceeded over a very hilly and rugged road to Passera, distant eight miles and a half.

I noticed, in one place by the road-side, the trunks of trees deprived of their branches, fixed in the ground inverted. On enquiring the meaning of this unusual appearance, I was informed, that they were thus planted, at a time that small-pox raged, to appease the goddess Patiné, by whom in her wrath the disease was supposed to be sent. The trees for this superstitious ceremony are not cut down, but broken to the sound of tom-toms, by mere dint of pulling; and to the sound of the same instruments they are planted with their heads in the earth.

I have more pleasure in noticing another spot, just by the road-side, on a little rising ground that was pointed out to me as the scene of an act of heroism and feeling, of the most noble and disinterested kind, which was performed during the height of the rebellion. I shall quote the part of the general orders in which it was noticed at the time by the Governor, and in which its history and eulogium are happily combined: — "In concluding these orders, it is with feelings no less gratifying that the Commander of the Forces places on record a display of heroism most honourable to the individuals who achieved it, in the instance of Lance Corporal M'Laughlin, of the 72d, and a detachment of four rank and file of that regiment; six rank and file (Malays) of the 1st, and six rank and file (Caffries) of the 2d Ceylon; when on their march, on the 16th ult., from Passera to Badulla.

"This small party was beset about midway by a horde of rebels in a thick jungle, who fired on the detachment from their concealment, killing two soldiers of the light infantry of the 73d (James Sutherland and William Chandler) on the spot, and immediately showing themselves in numbers around this little band of brave soldiers, whom they no doubt considered a certain prey; but, regardless of their menaces, and faithful to their fallen comrades, ten of these gallant men encompassed the dead bodies of their brother-soldiers, while Corporal M'Laughlin with the remaining five, fought their way to Badulla at two miles' distance, through some hundred Kandyans, to report the situation of the detachment they left surrounded by so immense and disproportionate a force, in conflict with which they continued for two hours, when, being relieved by a party detached by Major M'Donald under the command of Lieutenant Burns, of the 83d regiment, from Badulla, they had the triumph of seeing the insurgents fly before them, and of bringing in the dead bodies of their comrades to be honourably interred."* — It is a singular circumstance, I may add, that after the generous determination was formed to hazard their lives in so perilous a manner to defend the dead bodies of their companions in arms, not another man was hit by the fire of the enemy, though exposed to it uncovered and stationary in one place for so long a time. Other actions equally praise-worthy, and almost as noble as this, might be related, performed by our men during the rebellion; and, it was to such I alluded, when I spoke of the redeeming circumstances of the manner in which hostilities were conducted, — a manner that seems inseparable from a war of the kind, in which the combat is personal, and the passions strongly excited.

Passera is situated in a deep valley, between Namina-cooli-kandy and Luna-gallé-kandy; the one generally wooded, the

* General Orders. — Head Quarters, Kandy, July 7. 1818.

other bare. Lunagallé, which may be 2000 feet lower than the former, is of a conical shape, and its summit is surrounded by a façade of quartz-rock; which, from below, has a columnar appearance, and reminds one of basalt. Owing probably to the abundance of friable quartz on this mountain, it has obtained its name, Lunagallé *salt-rock*. The small military post at Passera, established during the rebellion, and still occupied, stands on a steep hill, of no great elevation, above a torrent, and commands a view of the valley, which before the rebellion was well cultivated and pretty populous. It is about 1500 feet above the level of the sea. *

Alipoota, to which we proceeded the day following, is eight and a half miles distant from Passera, and about 700 feet lower.† The intermediate country is hilly and difficult. Many of the valleys that are now lying waste were before well cultivated; the hills, in exposed situations, are covered with grass; and, where sheltered, with wood. About two miles from Alipoota there is a very steep descent, which was formerly fortified by a strong kadavetté, now in ruins. At this pass a few resolute men might have made a successful stand against an invading army. On the road Mr. Wright was joined by the Dissave of the Kandookara Korle‡, with tom-toms, pipes, &c. according to custom. The people who accompanied him generally wore ear-rings. They

* At the post of Passera, at 4 P. M., the barometer was stationary at 27.65; the thermometer, attached and free, 77°.

† On the 28th of March, at 3 P. M., at the post of Alipoota, the barometer was 28.90, the thermometer, attached and free, 85°. The air at this time was parched; a thermometer, with its bulb enveloped in wet muslin, fell 15°.

‡ The whole of Ouva, which, before the rebellion, was under one native Dissave, has since been parcelled out into seven different dissavonies, under the general direction of the Agent of Government, whom the natives call the Maha Dissave.

were in better condition than any of the inhabitants of Ouva I had yet seen, and, judging from their appearance, seemed in no want of food. Some of the coolies who came with us from Badulla, declared that for two days they had tasted nothing, and certainly they had the looks of famished men.

Alipoota is the principal military station of Lower Ouva. The post is situated on a hill, in a pretty populous neighbourhood. On one side it has a view of the lofty mountain-chain of which Namina-cooli-kandy is the summit; and, on the other, of the wooded hills and flats of the low country. Its climate, like that of Nalandé, in its nature partakes more of the climate of the plains than of the mountains, both in point of comparative temperature and salubrity; — our own feelings forcibly told us the former, and the experience of the last twelve months has proved the latter.

On the 30th of March, we visited Battagammana *, about twelve miles distant, in the Mahawedderatté, a country in general overgrown with jungle. Our object was to examine the locality of corundum. The observations which I made on the spot, relative to this mineral, are stated in a former part of the work.

From Battagammana we went to Kotabowa, in Welassey, distant about twenty miles, and about twenty-two miles from Alipoota. We passed through two moor-villages, Buckinahgahavilla, and Madagamwellè, whose inhabitants, having been our friends during the rebellion, were in good circumstances. The country through which we came had, in general, an agreeable appearance, consisting of open grass plains, and pretty extensive

* At 2 P.M. at Battagammana, in the shade, the barometer was 29.50, the attached thermometer 89°, and the air 90°; the bulb moistened, it fell 19°.

paddy-fields, with jungle intermixed. Clumps of cocoa-nut trees were common, indicating a tolerably populous state of the district. The talipot-tree * was of frequent occurrence, and we saw one specimen of it in blossom. This noble palm has been the subject of a good deal of fabulous story. It has been called the giant of the forest: but, like the cocoa-nut tree, it is never found wild. Its blossom is said to burst forth suddenly, with a loud explosion; but it expands gradually and quietly. When its flower appears, its leaves are said to droop, hang down, and die; but they remain fresh, erect, and vigorous till the fruit is nearly ripe, and their drooping precedes only the death of the tree, which speedily takes place after the ripening of the fruit. Even the disagreeableness of the smell of the flower has been exaggerated greatly.

Kotabowa is a considerable moor-village, and it is our principal military station in Welassey. The post, surrounded by a low breast-work, with a ditch inside, is situated on a little plain skirting the village. The quarters of the officers and men are made of a frame-work of stakes, lined and covered over with paddy-straw.

Though the district of Welassey is not very low †, its climate is, like that of the plains, subject to long droughts, and to periodical sickness. The most unhealthy months are July, August, and September, when the wind is generally from the north-west, and the country parched with drought. Last year, the

* This palm, (*Licuala spinosa*) the largest of the order, has a circular fan-shape leaf, from twenty to thirty feet in circumference; its flower, which it bears once only in its life, is a conical spike, occasionally thirty feet high.

† At Kotabowa on the 1st of April, at 3 P. M., the barometer was 29.35 inches; the thermometer attached was 88.5, free 90°, and moist 72.5.

most unhealthy season ever known was experienced. Of two hundred and fifty Europeans in the district, between the 11th of July, 1818, and the 20th of October, only two escaped disease, and of those attacked by the endemic fever, about two hundred died, including five officers. The two who escaped disease, amidst this universal sickness, were, fortunately, the commanding officer, Captain Ritchie, and the medical officer, Mr. Hoatson, whom we had the pleasure to find still at the post, in the enjoyment of uninterrupted health.

For the purpose of having a view of the surrounding country, we ascended, at break of day, a very steep rocky hill*, about three quarters of a mile from Kotabowa. When we reached its summit, the low grounds were covered with a dense grey mist, resembling water, and the hills and mountains, rising above it, looked like islands. As the sun rose, the mist dispersed and afforded us a clear view. We could see a considerable part of Welassēy; it was all comparatively low ground, almost plain, bounded by hills, and, as already described, a mixture of clear open tracts and of jungle, the latter predominating. This kind of country stretched between the hills, in a north-west direction towards Bintenney, in an easterly towards Batticaloa, and in a southerly towards Alipoota. The hills and mountains visible were surprisingly numerous. The most remarkable that we noticed were Namina-cooli-kandy, in Upper Ouva, and Hoonis-giri-kandy, in Doombera. Very many hills, of a great size, presented themselves in a quarter where I least expected to have seen them, viz. in the direction of Batticaloa. Here I may suggest, that the circumstance of many remarkable points

* On the summit of this hill, at 7 A. M., the barometer was 28.50 inches. The thermometer, both attached and free, 78°.

being visible from one spot, elevated like a watch-tower above the adjoining plain, is worth keeping in mind, should a general trigonometrical survey of Ceylon be undertaken, as has been contemplated.

On the 3d of April we left Kotabowa and returned to Alipoota. Welassey abounds in game. On our way back we saw an elephant, a wild hog, and an elk, and very many peacocks. One of the prettiest sights I have ever witnessed was eight of these birds collected in a small tree.

On the 5th of April we continued our excursion into Lower Ouva, and proceeded to Katragam by way of Boutle and Talawa, a distance of forty miles, which we accomplished in three days.

The first three or four miles from Alipoota is hilly and rugged, and covered with jungle. After this there is little descent, and the remainder of the way is through a flat country *, which, with few exceptions, is covered with forest, and uninhabited.

The first night we slept at Boutle, ten miles distant from Alipoota, where there is a small military post occupied by Malays, and a considerable tract of country that was once well cultivated, and is still pretty populous.

Between Boutle and Talawa, where we slept the next night, we twice forded the Parapà oya, a fine sweeping stream, with banks nobly wooded. Talawa is a beautiful part of this desert

* At Boutle, at 7 h. 30 min. P. M., the barometer was 29.70 inches; the thermometer attached 80°, and free 76.

At Talawa, at 4 P. M. the barometer 29.75 inches; thermometer attached 82°. free 81.

At Katragam, at 3 P. M., the barometer 29.95 inches; thermometer attached 87 , free 89.

country. It is a plain of many miles in extent, covered with fine grass, and ornamented with clumps of trees resembling the wildest part of a nobleman's park in England. We found shelter in some huts on a rising ground, where, during the rebellion, an attempt was made to establish a post, which the extreme unhealthiness of the place rendered abortive. At sunrise the next morning, the prospect was delightful. The eye wandered over this rich plain to the long line of blue mountains of Upper Ouva *, that rose in the horizon under a sky brilliantly coloured by the rising sun.

Here we expected to have seen much game, the country abounding in wild animals; but we saw traces of them only. In the soft sand of the road, which had been wetted by the heavy rain of the preceding afternoon, we could distinguish with ease the footsteps of the leopard, elephant, and buffaloe, and of two or three different kinds of deer.

Two miles from our halting-place, and ten miles from Katragam, we came to an immense mass of rock † by the roadside, called Gallegay by some, and Kimègalle by others. It derives the former name, signifying *rock-house*, from several capacious caverns in its side, which afford good shelter to the traveller;—and the latter name, signifying *water-rock*, it has obtained from two deep cavities in its summit,—natural reservoirs that are never without water, an element that is often extremely scarce in this desert, and hardly any where else to be found.

* The distant view of Namina-cooli-kandy, forming the vignette to this chapter, was taken here.

† This rock is gneiss, containing much mica, and so large a proportion of carbonat of lime, that it effervesces with an acid.

Near Katragam the people of the village came out to meet us, and the only present they brought was quite characteristic of the nature of the country; it consisted of good river-water in large calibashes.

Katragam has been a place of considerable celebrity, on account of its dewalé, which attracted pilgrims not only from every part of Ceylon, but even from remote parts of the continent of India. Aware of its reputation, — approaching it through a desert country, by a wide sandy road that seems to have been kept bare by the footsteps of its votaries, — the expectation is raised in one's mind, of finding an edifice in magnitude and style somewhat commensurate with its fame; instead of which, every thing the eye rests on only serves to give the idea of poverty and decay.

The village, situated on the left bank of the Parapa oya, consists of a number of small huts, chiefly occupied by a detachment of Malays, stationed here under the command of a native officer.

Besides the temple of the Katragam god, there are many others, all of them small and mean buildings, within two adjoining enclosures. In the largest square are the Katragam dewalé and the dewalé of his brother Ganna; a wiharé dedicated to Boodhoo, in a state of great neglect, and a fine bogah; and six very small korillas, mere empty cells, which are dedicated to the goddess Patiné, and to five demons. In the smaller square are contained a little karandua sacred to Iswera, the Kalana-madima, a kovilla dedicated to the demon Bhyro, a rest-house for pilgrims, and some offices. Opposite the principal dewalé, both in front and rear, there are two avenues of considerable length, one terminated by a small dewalé, and the other by a very large dagobah of great antiquity, in a ruinous state. These objects are deserving of little notice excepting as illustrating the superstitious belief and feelings of the natives.

The Katragam dewalé consists of two apartments, of which the outer one only is accessible. Its walls are ornamented with figures of different gods, and with historical paintings executed in the usual style. Its ceiling is a mystically painted cloth, and the door of the inner apartment is hid by a similar cloth. On the left of the door there is a small foot-bath and basin, in which the officiating priest washes his feet and hands before he enters the sanctum. Though the idol was still in the jungle where it had been removed during the rebellion, the inner room appropriated to it was as jealously guarded as before ; and as we could not enter it without giving offence, we did not make the attempt. The only other objects that I think it necessary to notice, even in a slight manner, are the karandua of Iswera, and the Kalana-madima. The former standing on a platform in a small room, is somewhat in the shape of a common oven, and contains a little image of the god, and a diminutive pair of slippers, of which we were indulged with a sight through the door. The Kalana-madima is greatly respected, and it certainly is the chief curiosity at Katragam : it is a large seat made of clay, raised on a platform with high sides and a back, like an easy chair without legs ; it was covered with leopards' skins, and contained several instruments used in the performance of the temple rites ; and a large fire was burning by the side of it. The room in the middle of which it is erected, is the abode of the resident Brahmen. The Kalana-madima, this Brahmen said, belonged to Kalana-nata, the first priest of the temple, who, on account of great piety, passed immediately to heaven without experiencing death, and left the seat as a sacred inheritance to his successors in the priestly office; who have used it instead of a dying bed: and, it is his fervent hope, that, like them, he may have the happiness of occupying it once, and of breathing his last in it. He said this with an air of solemnity and enthusiasm that seemed to mark sincerity, and, combined with his peculiar appearance, was not a little impressive. He was a tall spare figure of a man, whom a painter would choose out of a thousand for such a vocation. His beard was long and white; but his large dark eyes, which animated a thin regular visage, were still full of fire, and he stood erect and firm, without any of the feebleness of old age. A yellow handkerchief girded his loins; a red robe was thrown over one shoulder; a string of large beads hung from his neck; and on his right arm he wore a bracelet of the sacred seeds that are believed to contain the figure of Lakshamé.

The Katragam god is not loved, but feared; and his worship is conducted on this principle. The situation of his temple, and the time fixed for attending it, in the hot, dry, and unwholesome months of June, July, and August, were craftily chosen. A merit was made of the hazard and difficulty of the journey through a wilderness, deserted by man, and infested with wild animals; and the fever which prevails at the season was referred to the god, and supposed to be inflicted by him on those who had the misfortune to incur his displeasure.

In the adjoining country, there are a few small villages, which belong to the temple, whose inhabitants are bound to perform service for the lands which they hold. The officers of the temple, besides the Brahmen priest, are, a Basnaike-rale, who has the superintendence of the temporal concerns of the establishment, under the controul of the Agent of Government.

and twelve Kappurales, who do duty in turns. On our arrival, they were all assembled. Their gloomy, discontented appearance, and unmannerly behaviour, corresponded well with their conduct during the rebellion, in which they took a most active part.

Before we had possession of the country, Katragam was greatly frequented. The number of pilgrims is now annually diminishing, and the buildings are going to decay. In a very few years, probably, they will be level with the ground, and the traveller will have difficulty in discovering their site. Such, we must hope, will be their fate, and the fate of every building consecrated to superstition of this very degrading and mischievous kind.

Early the next morning after our arrival, we set out from Katragam, to return to Upper Ouva, by the route of Weleway, with the design of visiting a large nitre-cave in the neighbourhood of that place.

The first day we travelled about twelve miles, to Yadalgammé, through a very thick jungle, by a narrow path, little frequented, and in many places overgrown with wood, rendering a passage difficult. Yadalgammé, where we spent the night, is a wretched little temple-village, on the bank of a branch of the Parapa oya, and in the midst of an immense wilderness of wood. The two or three families that constitute the village, have some cattle, and a little paddy-ground adjoining. Their huts are fortified, by an enclosure of strong pallisades, against the attacks of the wild animals, which are here exceedingly numerous, as we might infer from their traces, though we only saw a single buffaloe and an elephant, and two or three herds of deer. The latter made their appearance on a little marshy plain, which, if tradition be correct, was formerly the bed of a tank.

During the night at Yadalgammé, we heard the cries of the demon-bird, or Ulama, as it is also called by the natives. Perched in a neighbouring tree, it made loud and hideous screams, conveying the idea of extreme distress. Its harsh and horrid notes are supposed, like those of the screech-owl, to be of evil omen, and a prelude to death or misfortune. The bird (if it be a bird) is very rare, and I have not been able to get any tolerable account of it.

The next day we proceeded to Weleway, about twenty miles distant, through a country consisting partly of thick jungle, and partly of open grass-plains, like those of Talawa, with which, probably, they communicate. They commence close to Yadalgammé, and extend about five miles in the direction of the path we were pursuing. Their resemblance to a park was strengthened by the circumstance of their abounding in deer, of which we saw many herds, both of the small spotted, and larger red kind, resembling the red deer of Europe. Between Yadalgammé and Weleway, we crossed two streams, — one very small, about half-way, and the other of considerable size (the Kirindé oya), about two miles from the latter place.

We crossed the former stream just below a spot called Undagalla-walla, where it forms a deep pool, on the banks of which are some remains of masonry. According to tradition, there was formerly a large tank hereabout, by means of which a considerable part of the Megampattoo was formerly watered and rendered fertile. The level of the ground above the sea * is not

* At 1 P. M. on the bank of the stream, the barometer was 29.7 : thermometer attached 83°, free 82°.

incompatible with the accuracy of this tradition, which other circumstances render highly improbable. The few cut stones which occur are so neatly wrought, that it is more likely they belonged to a temple or palace, than to an embankment; particularly as there is the figure of the moon on a fragment of one stone, and that of the sun on another: had a great embankment ever existed here, it would still be visible; but I could observe no distinct traces of such a work: lastly, the ground itself is very unfavourable for the formation of a tank; on one side, indeed, a huge rock, or rocky hill, rises out of the plain, to the height of, perhaps, two or three hundred feet above its surface; but, on the other side, there is no corresponding elevation, that I could observe, for many miles. Taking into consideration these circumstances, I infer that the story of a tank in this place formerly, is either false or exaggerated; in other words, that it never existed, or was of very small dimensions.

From the top of the rocky hill, which I ascended, the prospect was extensive. With the exception of two or three similar rocks in the neighbourhood, and a few distant and gentle elevations of ground, the whole country to the southward, and to the eastward and westward of that point, was a dead flat covered with a wilderness of jungle. In the opposite direction hills and mountains made their appearance, but they were indistinct, from a covering of thin mist.

From this place to Weleway, we were deluged with rain, accompanied with loud thunder and vivid lightning. During the rain, I observed a phenomenon that deserves perhaps to be mentioned. The surface of some large low masses of rock over which we passed, had the appearance of smoking. I took it for granted that the appearance was owing to the heat the rocks had absorbed during the fine morning, acting on the rain with which they were wetted: so it proved; for though it had been raining an hour, the rock still felt warm. There were several large masses of rock on a gently rising ground at a little distance, and a cloud of vapour hung over each. Perhaps the cause concerned in this instance operates pretty generally; and to it, probably, may be referred much of the floating mist, with which hills, particularly in a hot climate, are often surrounded after showers.

Weleway is a little plain about a mile in circumference, on the confines of the level country, and, excepting to the southward, every way bounded by hills.* We were much pleased with its natural beauties, and not a little disappointed to find it desolate. We found a shed of green branches constructed for us, but though just made, the workmen had forsaken it, and not a native was to be seen. A field of natchiné was visible at a little distance, to which we sent a Lascoreen, who returned bringing by force two wretched men, whose looks told their tale of distress, and assured us that we must expect nothing from the country. This too was confirmed by the ruined state of the village of Weleway, a little farther on; not one of its many houses standing; its groves of fruit-trees looked as if they had suffered from a violent storm,—the cocoa-nut trees without fruit, the areka-nut trees cut or broken down, and the talipot-trees stripped of their leaves, and of a piece with this, the paddy-fields around lying waste.

This day's journey was the most harassing we had yet made. and most unfortunate in its consequences, as if confirming the popular notion alluded to, of the cries of the Ulama foreboding

* On the plain at 7 P. M. the barometer was 29.50 inches: the thermometer. both attached and free, 78.

evil. Here the seeds of disease, which were most likely received in passing through the low jungly country, began to burst forth, excited into action by the fatigue of the day, by exposure under it to heavy rain*, and by the want which our people experienced of every comfort at this place, and particularly by being obliged to sleep on the wet ground unsheltered from the night-air.

Before quitting the plains, I may remark, that the least reflecting observer must be struck with the analogy of the country in the northern part of the island, (for instance between Nalandé and Trincomalie,) and that which we had been travelling through during the last five days: both low and nearly flat; both in a great measure overgrown with wood, and uninhabited; both extremely unwholesome; and, to complete the similarity and mention its most important and interesting circumstances, both exhibiting strong marks of change, and of ancient cultivation and population. In the northern part of the island, the great tanks that remain, are the strongest proofs of the sad revolution that has taken place: here, the marks are of a more miscellaneous, but equally unequivocal nature; — as the tracts of cleared ground in

* The Singalese are strongly impressed with the idea, that travelling in rain is most unwholesome, and they avoid it in consequence as much as possible. Be this as it may, I have no doubt that exposure, particularly of the naked body, to rain after fatigue, amounting to a certain degree of exhaustion, is a powerful exciting cause of disease; and in extreme cases, immediately dangerous. In illustration of this might be mentioned the fatal effect occasionally resulting from plunging into cold water, after violent and long continued exertion, — an effect well ascertained, though not yet explained in a satisfactory manner. I believe it to be connected, not only with an exhaustion of strength and of the powers of life, but also with a low temperature of the body, and a rapid reduction of it still lower by immersion: in one instance that I tried the temperature of a man perspiring freely, exposed to a hot sun, and labouring hard (carrying a palanqueen), I found his heat under the tongue a degree lower than it was before he commenced his labour.

the midst of jungle in situations favourable to the growth of wood; the small tanks that occur here and there; and the ruins of buildings, particularly of immense dagobahs of superior construction, which have been discovered in the Megampattoo, similar to the dagobah at Katragam. Nor does the analogy, I suspect, fail in relation to causes. History informs us, that when the northern portion of the island was invaded by the Malabars, the native princes took refuge in this part of the country, established themselves here, built towns, and cultivated lands: and farther, it informs us, that when the successors of these princes accomplished the expulsion of the invaders and the recovery of their territory, they returned and re-occupied the old capital. Then, probably, (to pass from the fact to the inference,) the current of population flowed back, and an unwholesome and unpropitious climate, the first cause perhaps of the reflux, gradually gaining strength, completed the work of desolation, and rendered the country desert.

From Weleway we proceeded to Boulatwellegoddé *, distant about six miles, through a hilly, but not difficult country, that appeared charming to us in comparison with the monotonous jungle we had left. The only drawback on the pleasure derived from the natural beauties of the scenery, was the desolate air and ruinous aspect of the fields and villages. Before the rebellion, five contiguous and pretty considerable villages gave the name of Gampaha (the five) to the little district in which they are situated. Boulatwellegoddé was one of them, and, like the rest, it is ruined and deserted. The only person we found

* At 10 P. M., at Boulatwellegoddé, the barometer was 28.80; the thermometer, attached and free, both 71°.

on our arrival was a single man, sent to meet Mr. Wright by the Dissave of Kandapalla; and the only shelter prepared was a wretched shed, made of charred wood and green leaves, on the foundation of a burnt house.

With considerable difficulty we learned the situation of the nitre-cave we were in quest of, and that we had left it on our left hand, about half-way between Weleway and Boulatwelle-goddé, from both of which it is about five miles distant. We visited it the same day, guided by two or three of the half-starved natives, who made their appearance soon after our arrival.

Situated in a thick jungle, in the side of a hill, it is difficult of discovery and of access. Its mouth is comparatively small — hardly twelve feet wide, and, where highest, hardly high enough for a man to stand erect. The entrance is irregularly arched, and has the appearance of having been cut through the solid rock by which it is surrounded and overhung. Looking down into the cave, nothing can be more gloomy and dismal; the eye can penetrate but a very little way into its dark recesses, from which a loathsome smell issues, and a dull, confused noise, like that of a subterraneous torrent.

As soon as light could be procured *, we commenced the descent, each of us bearing a candle, and our people carrying either candles or torches. Having descended, through a steep, narrow, and slippery passage, about thirty feet, we found ourselves in a cave of vast size, and of such a very irregular form,

* It was struck by a native, by means of a bit of rock-crystal and a small piece of iron. He received the sparks on a piece of rotten cloth, and kindled a flame by whirling the tinder round, enveloped in dry leaves.

that it was impossible to have any accurate notion of it. The rugged bottom, which descended, perhaps, fifty feet, was covered with fragments of decomposing rock, and a thick stratum of black earth. The roof in general was too high to be visible. The walls consisted either of dolomite rock, or of granitic varieties, most of them in a state of decomposition, particularly those containing a portion of calc-spar. The noise and offensive smell which we perceived at the entrance, were here much increased; and they both proceeded from innumerable bats, that flitted round us like shadows, disturbed by the intrusion of such unusual visitors.

We returned to the open air, after having been under ground an hour. We walked, perhaps, a quarter of a mile without exploring the whole of the cave, which the natives, always fond of exaggeration, say is two miles long.

Relative to the saltpetre found in this place, impregnating the earth and decomposing rocks, I have already, in a former part of the work, offered the observations I collected.

Like the nitre-cave in Doombera, its excavation is, perhaps, more artificial than natural. It has been worked for very many years by the natives, a party of whom, whose express occupation and duty it was, came annually from the neighbourhood of Passera for the purpose. Their mode of extracting the salt was very similar to that employed at Memoora. What quantity they obtained, I have not been able to learn. Judging from the dimensions of the cave, and the proportion of saline impregnation, large quantities of nitre might be manufactured from it, and with profit to government, were such improved methods employed as modern science suggests.

At Boulatwellegoddé, we were so hard pressed for provisions

the stock that we had brought with us being nearly exhausted, that we were under the necessity of killing one of our baggage-bullocks.

The following day we went to Kirriwannagammé. Though the distance was only about six miles, owing to the sickness of many of the coolies, the fagged state of all, and the badness of the road, through an extremely hilly and rugged country, we were four hours accomplishing it. Almost all the way, the traces of war were too apparent in the ruined dwellings of the natives, the uncultivated paddy-fields, and the occasional obstructions on the road: in many places, trees were felled and thrown across it; and, in one place, a thorn-gate still remained erect.

At Kirriwannegammé we spent the day in a neat pansol of a small wiharé, finely situated on a little rocky platform, in the side of a steep hill *, overlooking a considerable extent of paddy-ground below, and several villages, — or, I should rather say, the spots where villages had once stood, now to be recognised only by ruins, and the groves of fruit-trees laid waste. This, I should remark, and the different scenes of the same kind which we had witnessed all the way from Weleway, were principally the work of the people of Saffragam, a large number of whom, led by Eknelligoddé Dissave, supported by a small party of our troops, over-ran the disaffected districts of Ouva, and carried ruin wherever they went; intent only on plunder, and on shewing their zeal by their depredations.

On the 12th of April we left Kirriwannagammé, and crossing

* At 10 h. 30 m. P. M., at the pansol, the barometer was 28.55; the thermometer, attached and free, 79

the mountain-ridge of Upper Ouva, by the Apotella pass, arrived at Velangahena. The distance over the mountain is only about eight miles. The ascent, though steep, is not difficult; and the height is certainly less than that of the Idalgashena. This conclusion is not drawn from barometrical observation, which an accident interfered with on the top of the pass; but from a comparison of the apparent heights of the two from Velangahena, from whence they are both visible.

On reaching Velangahena the effects of the journey in Lower Ouva were too visible on the whole party, and particularly on our servants and coolies, the majority of whom were indisposed, and more or less affected with fever of the intermittent kind.

After halting a day, and taking leave of Mr. Moon, who returned to Colombo, by way of Saffragam, Mr. Wright and myself proceeded to fort M'Donald, in hope of being able to cross the mountains, and pass into Kotmalè; a district into which very few Europeans had yet penetrated, and no one by the route that we meditated.

The distance of fort M'Donald from Valangahena is about seventeen miles. All the way the country is hilly, but not of the same character. The hills, the first part of the way, though rounded are exceedingly steep and abrupt; those which succeed them are less bold and lofty, of greater sweep, and rather undulating than of the abrupt conical form; whilst the hills, the latter part of the way, are more irregular than either, and bolder than the intermediate, though less so than the first.

About half way we stopt two or three hours at Dambawinnè, where we had the pleasure, greatly heightened by contrast, of finding every thing the reverse of what we had been accustomed to: — fields neatly cultivated, covered with green paddy, the large house of a Kandyan chief, in the nicest order, surrounded by fruit-trees, uninjured and in bearing; and the chief himself and his people all attention and civility. Dambawinè Dissave, to whom the place belongs, is a man of a good deal of influence in the country, and much respected. Though he engaged at first in the rebellion, he submitted early, and avoided the ruin which involved those who persisted in resistance. *

About half a mile from fort M'Donald we passed by the hill on which Lieut. Colonel M'Donald (from whom the adjoining post has its name) made a remarkable stand, during the rebellion, against the whole force of the country assembled under the command of Kappitipola. On this hill, of gentle ascent, with the advantage only of not being commanded, the gallant Colonel, with a party composed of sixty rank and file, for eight days in succession, stood and repelled the attacks of about seven or eight thousand Kandyans. And, it is very remarkable, that though half the enemy perhaps were armed with muskets, and our men were much exposed to their fire, particularly in the charges which they made to keep the Kandyans at a distance, not one of them was killed or wounded.

Fort M'Donald is about 3000 feet above the level of the † sea. It is situated on a low hill, in the fertile and extensive valley of Parnegamme, at the foot of the barrier-mountains of Upper Ouva, and immediately under the pass of the lofty Dodanatukappella

* If I recollect rightly, the attachment of this chief to his family was the cause of his submission; surrendering himself, immediately on the capture of his wife and children, whom he had concealed in a thick jungle, on a mountain of difficult access.

† On the Fort, at 3 P. M., the barometer was 26.70; the thermometer, attached and free, 73°. On my second visit, on the 29th of August, at 4 P. M., the barometer was 26.65, the thermometer 77°.

mountain. Thus situated, it is hardly necessary to add, that its scenery is of a very exquisite kind; it displays, most happily mixed, the grand and beautiful; and what adds to and enhances greatly the effect of the latter, is the appearance of cultivation and population in the surrounding country, which has suffered in a less degree than any other part of Ouva from the effects of the rebellion.

The heavy rains which attend the setting in of the south-west monsoon, and which extend over a great part of the island, now commenced and frustrated the plan which we had formed, of passing into Kotmalè. After waiting two entire days at Fort M'Donald, in expectation of a favourable change of weather, Mr. Wright and I parted; — he to return to Badulla, and I to continue my journey through some other parts of the country which I had not yet visited.

On the 17th of April I ascended the Dodanatukapella, and proceeded over the mountains to Maturatta, at the distance of sixteen miles, which we reached in eight hours, wet to the skin from heavy rain, to which we were exposed the latter part of the the way. The ascent of the pass commences immediately on quitting Fort M'Donald, and continues, with very little interruption, very steep up to its summit, about two miles distant, where there are the remains of a Kadavettè at the entrance of a forest. This is at the height of between four and five thousand feet above the level of the sea. * The views that present themselves from different points of the ascent of this lofty green mountain, thus far almost entirely free from jungle, are various

* A short barometer suspended here, at 7 h. 30 min. A. M. from a branch of a rhododendron in flower, was stationary at 25.2; thermometer attached 68°, free 63.5.

and magnificent, particularly of Upper Ouva, almost the whole of which is visible; and in the direction of Weyaloowa, the summits of whose mountains rising above a stratum of silver vapour, had a very singular and beautiful effect. Beyond the Kadavettè, for at least ten miles, there is a constant succession of ascents and descents, the general level of the road rather increasing than diminishing in altitude. The greatest elevation it attains is about seven miles from Fort M'Donald * About three or four miles from Maturatta a steep descent begins, and lasts without interruption to the bottom of the valley, which is nearly 1000 feet below the military post, where I stopped †, and probably little less than four thousand feet below the loftiest summit of its including mountains. This elevated mountain-tract bears some resemblance to Upper Ouva. Like it, it is generally enclosed by still higher mountains; and, like it, its surface is composed of hills of a conical or undulating form. Its scenery is of such a nature, that feeble description is inadequate to convey a tolerably correct idea of it. The most beautiful part of the way, and the most interesting, is between two mountains, about a mile and a half on each side of the Halgaran oya. Here the country is comparatively open. It is bounded on one side by a mountain-ridge covered with forest, and on the other by the blue summits of a few distant mountains, the loftiest and most conspicuous of which is Namina-cooli-kandy. The hills over

* At 10 h. 45 min. A. M. the barometer suspended from a rhododendron, on a green hill, the highest, perhaps, over which the path passes, was stationary at 24.85; thermometer attached 72°, free 67°.

† On my second visit to Maturatta, on the 1st of September, at 11 A. M. the barometer at the post was 27.14: both thermometers 80°. An hour and three quarters after, at the bridge in the bottom of the valley, the barometer was 28.1; both thermometers 83°.

which we passed, were of the liveliest verdure, ornamented with a profusion of rare flowers and flowering-shrubs; and the hollows between the hills, into which we looked down, were luxuriantly wooded, presenting surfaces of the richest foliage, of an astonishing variety of colour and tint, from admixture probably of different kinds of trees in different stages of vegetation. An interest was given to this wild and beautiful scenery by traces of ancient works on a hill to the right, not far from a remarkably bold façade of rock, projecting from the side of the mountain like a promontory, and by a new building to the left, situated on a green declivity skirted by forest. The ancient works consist of trenches and of low stone walls, both as if intended, not for fortifications, but as simple enclosures. They are attributed to a native prince, who, according to tradition, being banished here, stopped passing travellers, and compelled them to labour for him. The modern building is very recent. It consists of a large bungalow, with watch-houses at regular distances in front. It was constructed during the rebellion, and was occupied for some time by the Pretender, when he sought concealment in these wilds. The forests, between which the country just mentioned is situated, have a very peculiar character, especially that nearest Maturatta. It is the most gloomy one I ever entered; indeed, its gloom exceeds imagination. The trees, small but lofty, are crowded together in the most confused manner,—the young and old, the living and dead intermixed. But the melancholy appearance does not arise so much from this circumstance as from the density of the shade, and the extraordinary manner in which it is in great measure produced by an exuberance of mosses, with which the trunks and branches, and even delicate twigs, of the trees in general are covered. The moss, hanging in filaments, actually conceal the leaves, and, at the first glance, you suppose it to be natural foliage. Farther, the dismalness of the scene is increased by the closeness and chilling dampness of the air, and by the profound silence that prevails. The country beyond this forest, descending to Maturatta, is partly wooded and partly open, only covered with long lemon-grass and low shrubs. The prospects which open in the descent (and it was only occasionally that they did, through the mists and clouds in which we were enveloped) were very striking, and, without exaggeration, might be called sublime, especially the view of the deep valley, exhibiting at the time an extraordinary assemblage of clouds and torrents, rocky heights and wooded mountains, green fields and diminutive cottages, seen perhaps, for a moment, illuminated by a burst of sunshine, and then again veiled in mists.

The military post at Maturatta is remarkably situated on a little hill, a process as it were of the mountain, about 2700 feet above the level of the sea; and, as already remarked, nearly 1000 feet above the bottom of the valley, of which it commands very fine and extensive views. Though this post is of a very humble description and rude construction, — the work of a small detachment of troops, aided only by the natives, — it is not void of interest. The officer commanding it, in the short space of eight months, has made an excellent garden, (perhaps the most productive in the island,) where he found a jungle; and has collected such a stock of cows, pigs, and poultry, as to stand in little need of supplies from a distance: his garden has the advantage of a good soil, of being well watered by a stream that runs through it, and of having a mean annual temperature probably of about 68 It produces pease and beans, cabbages, and salad in abundance, and almost in constant succession; other vegetables that have been tried, as potatoes and onions, have also succeeded.* This is a very encouraging result. If our vegetables thrive so well here, may we not calculate with certainty on their coming to perfection 2000 feet higher;—on the fine elevated region, for instance, over which we had just passed, where the average temperature can hardly exceed 60°? May we not calculate, too, with tolerable certainty on wheat and other European grain, and on the vine and different European fruit-trees, flourishing on the same region? In confirmation, I may remark, that a little wheat sown at Himbleatawellé succeeded well, though a long drought was unfavourable to its growth; and further, that barley of good quality was nearly ripe when we passed in the garden at Fort M'Donald; and, what is a very encouraging circumstance, it sprung from native seed, brought from a royal garden in the neighbourhood, where it was introduced many years ago, and has not degenerated. And, still farther, I may observe, that grapes were amongst the fruit brought to us at Dambawinné, the produce of a vine of considerable size, growing just by the Dissave's house; the bunch was large, though from a neglected tree, and though not ripe the grapes were of good size. It occurred to me, in passing, that no part of the Kandyan country, that I had yet seen, is better adapted for an English settlement than the high region alluded to: it is the sole property of government; for during the king's time the road was prohibited, and it does not contain a single inhabitant. Were fifteen or twenty families settled here, and provided with tools and stock, they might station themselves on one of the green hills, surround it with a wall and ditch, enclose the ground in the neighbourhood, and, being cleared to their hand, they might

* At Kandy, Amanapoora, and at similar heights, they succeed almost as well.

turn it up and plough it at once; and in less than twelve months get a good return for their labours, — grain perhaps in plenty from their fields, and vegetables in abundance from their gardens. Their cattle would thrive on the fine grass-hills, and rapidly multiply; and their poultry, in all probability, would increase equally fast. The climate being cool, and there is good reason to believe, healthy, the people as well as their stock would soon spread over the country. From such a centre as this, European arts and sciences, our manners and virtues, might be diffused amongst the natives: the experiment is easy; the result most important: were it to fail, it would cost little; were it to succeed, the good, moral and political, produced, would be incalculable.

During the day that I spent at Maturatta, I saw a good deal of the grand and beautiful scenery of its valley, to which a particular charm and interest is given by successful and pretty extensive cultivation, in situations apparently most unfavourable for the attempt, in many of which you rather expect to see overhanging wood than green terraced fields, and the eagle's nest than the dwelling of man. The cause of this forced fertility need not be sought farther than the numerous streams which descend from the mountains and furnish an almost constant and abundant supply of water for the irrigation of crops. The only object requiring particular attention in the neighbourhood, is a cave about two miles from the post, and considerably lower, where a little nitre has been made, and a considerable quantity of native carbonat of magnesia has been found.* The cave is situated in the side of the mountain, and is surrounded by jungle: its

* Vide p. 27. for a description of this mineral, &c.

dimensions are comparatively small; where highest, its roof may be reached with the hand; and where widest, it hardly exceeds twenty-four feet. Its floor, though nearly horizontal in its general direction, is rugged and uneven, from masses of rock, and from pits dug in it during the rebellion, for the purpose of secreting grain. Its roof is much fissured; as you advance it becomes lower and lower, and the cave darkens: you can go a very little way without light, and a very little way walking erect. To reach the end, as I did, I was obliged to go on my hands and knees, and in some places lie down and creep forward. The distance from its mouth to its extremity may be about 150 feet, instead of three miles, which is the depth assigned to it by the natives, who speak merely from guess, being afraid to explore its recesses, (so they say,) believing them to be inhabited by demons.

From Maturatta I proceeded to Marasena, and from thence to Kandy, a total distance of twenty-six miles. The intermediate country, in general, is not particularly interesting. The ground is exceedingly hilly and difficult; a good deal of it is cultivated, but a still larger proportion is covered with low jungle. Few objects requiring particular notice present themselves by the way. Two, of several streams that are to be crossed, deserve to be mentioned: viz. the Bilhool oya, that descends through the valley of Maturatta, and the Maha oya, which flows by Hangranketty. Both are considerable torrents. The former is seldom fordable; and it is rather a nervous undertaking to cross it on its Singalese bridge of a single tree thrown from one bank to the other, at the height of twenty or thirty feet above the torrent. The latter, rushing over a wide, rocky bed, is more formidable in appearance than in reality: though swollen by the late rains, we forded it with little difficulty. Hangranketty, through which we passed (sixteen miles from Kandy), for a long period was a royal residence. When we entered the country in 1815, its palace was entire, and the temples attached to it in perfect preservation. Now, hardly the ruins of the former are to be traced; and, in two or three years more, the latter will be level with the ground; indeed, the Patiné Dewalé is already a ruin, and the Maha Visnu Dewalé is in the act to become one. Two years ago, when I first visited this place, we were hardly allowed to remain in the outer verandah of this temple; and now, I walked through its sanctum as through a thoroughfare; every door being broken, every room empty, and the buildings, in general, unroofed. The palace owed its destruction to the natives, who set fire to it when plundering it; and the temples owe their ruin to our troops, who took up their quarters in them during the rebellion, and, on more than one occasion, here stood the attack of the enemy, collected in great force. Maresena, where we spent the night, is ten miles from Kandy. Its neat wiharé, enclosed by a white wall, is a conspicuous object. We found it occupied by a detachment of Bengal Sepoys, who, in the figure of Boodhoo. recognise their Maha Deo, and worship it as such.

After halting at Kandy five days, chiefly on account of the indisposition of myself and of several of my people, one of whom died of cholera, and another had a very narrow escape from remittent fever, I set out on the 26th of April, on my return to Colombo, by the way of the Seven Korles.

My first day's journey was to Meddawallatené, in Toompané, distant from Kandy about twelve miles. The Hariseapattoo, which intervenes between Katisgastotté, the ferry of the Mahawellé ganga, which we crossed, and the Girriagamme pass, which we descended, is a beautiful little district, almost free from jungle; consisting of rounded hills, charmingly spotted with clumps of palms and other fruit-trees, and of narrow valleys, laid out in paddy-fields. Before the rebellion, it was the garden of the country, well cultivated, productive, and populous; now, it is merely the wreck of what it was, and one sees nothing that does not denote its wretchedness, and the example that was made of it on account of the resistance of its inhabitants.

The little military post of Meddawallatené * is situated on rising ground at the bottom of the Girriagamme pass, and at the head of the Galgedera pass. It is almost surrounded by paddy-fields, which are bounded by fine wooded and rocky heights, that reminded me of the Troshachs. The two passes which this post commands, are by nature very strong and difficult, being narrow, steep, and rocky, though not long; and being flanked by wooded hills, which, on the right, in many places present almost perpendicular walls. In addition, the Galgedera pass is rendered more difficult by a river that runs through it (the Deek oya), in the rocky bed of which one has to wade, perhaps, a hundred yards.

From Meddawallatené we proceeded to Koornagalle, in the Seven Korles, distant eighteen miles. Below the Galgedera pass, the road is almost level, through a wide valley, diversified with green hillocks and patches of jungle, with extensive paddy-fields and numerous groves of cocoa-nut trees, and skirted by

* At 3 P. M. at this place, the barometer was 29.20; the thermometer, attached and free, 84°.

wooded hills. The upper part of the valley is most picturesque, and best cultivated: towards Koornagalle, the scenery becomes tame, and jungle predominates.

Koornagalle, where I halted a day, is our principal station in the extensive and fertile district of the Seven Korles. It is situated on a gently rising ground at the base of a contiguous chain of rocky heights, from one of which Kooroovinia-galle (beetle rock) is said to derive its name.* The extent of cultivation in the neighbourhood is considerable. The paddy-fields, most of which are the property of government, are irrigated by a tank, the water of which is confined by a strong embankment. The outlet is not formed in the same artificial manner as at Kandellé and Mineré: it is at one extremity of the embankment where it joins a low rocky hill, and is like a natural passage. Formerly it was probably dammed up by wicker work, supported by upright posts, strengthened by oblique props. This may be inferred from two rows of cavities in the rocky bed of the channel, the one anterior being square, and the other posterior, angular, or wedge-shaped; thus, 

Each of the rocks of the remarkable chain in the neighbourhood has a name from a fancied resemblance to some animal. Thus, the first is called Atu-gallé, (elephant-rock,) and it certainly is very like an elephant; the next is called Kooroovinia-gallé; the next Ibba-galle, (tortoise-rock,) and the last Anda-galle, (eel-rock.) The loftiest and most remarkable of the four is Atu-gallé, which rises to the height of between five and six hundred feet above the

* At the cantonment, at 8 h. 30 m. A.M., the barometer was 29.35; the thermometer, attached and free, 80°

plain*, almost quite naked, and without crack or fissure. Besides these rocks there is another, more remote, though apparently belonging to the same chain, which rises boldly to the height of perhaps 1000 feet, and makes a very conspicuous appearance; it is called Yakdessa-gallé, (the demon-dancer,) from an imaginary resemblance to the performer whose name it bears.

Koornagalle is rather remarkable for what it once was, than for what it now is. It was formerly the residence of the princes of the Seven Korles, the remains of whose palace are still visible at the foot of the Elephant-rock. The most perfect part of them is the entrance, which is a handsome arched gate-way, formed by overlapping stones.

Besides these ruins, the tank and the chain of rocks, there is little else deserving of notice at this place. The village and bazar are small, and our cantonment is only a temporary erection. There is a little wiharé about a mile off, romantically situated on the side of the second rocky hill which is worth visiting, particularly as it contains a copy of the imaginary impression of the foot of Boodhoo on Adam's Peak.

From Koornagalle, we proceeded to Giriulla, twenty-two miles distant. The country between the two places is almost flat, — a succession of plains and of woods; many of the former cultivated, and many of the latter in the state of thick jungle. Forest prevails most towards Giriulla, and cultivated ground most towards Koornagallé. Little that is interesting occurs by the way. Dambadinia, about five miles from Giriulla, which, it is said, was formerly a royal residence, is now only remarkable for

* On the top of this rock, at 7 A.M., the barometer was 29.20; the thermometer attached 75°, free 73°.

a lofty naked and insulated rock, that rises perpendicularly out of the plain. Several small streams, requiring bridges, intersect the road, but the only river that is to be crossed, is the Maha oya, known at its mouth by the name of the Kaymelle. It is the same that flows by Fort King, and it is here a considerable stream. It is the boundary in this direction of the Kandyan and maritime provinces, and is navigable for large boats, as high up as Kotodinia, which is about three miles below Giriulla. It would be navigable still higher, were it not for rocks in the bed of the river, which probably may be removed. Giriulla is only a very few feet above the level of the sea*, and though the station of a temporary commissariat store, affords no accommodation to the traveller.

Colombo is thirty-eight miles distant from Giriulla. We reached it on the 1st of May. The intermediate country is in no respect remarkable, and it has been described already in Mr. Cordiner's work on Ceylon.

* At 8 P.M. the barometer at this place was 30.05, the thermometer, attached and free, 80.

CHAPTER IV.

EXCURSION THROUGH UPPER BOULATGAMME′ INTO KOTMALE′.—POUHALPITTYE′.—DIMBOLA.—ASCENT OF THE MOUNTAINS BETWEEN KOTMALE′ AND UPPER OUVA.—NEURAELLYIA-PATTAN.—DESCENT TO FORT M'DONALD.—EXPLANATION OF SOME PECULIARITIES OF UPPER OUVA.—APPEARANCE OF THE COUNTRY BETWEEN FORT M'DONALD AND MATURATTA.—EXCURSION FROM KANDY INTO MATELE′.—DESCRIPTION OF DAMBOOLOO WIHARE′.—TELDENIA.—RETURN TO COLOMBO THROUGH THE SEVEN KORLES.

In the next and the last excursion which I made into the Interior, I had the honour of accompanying the Governor and Lady Brownrigg on their way to Kandy, as far as Ruwenwellé, of joining their suite at Maturatta, and of attending them on their tour through Matelé and the Seven Korles. We left Colombo on the 21st. of August, 1819, and returned to it on the 27th of the following month. I shall confine my narrative and remarks chiefly to those parts of the country which were new to me, and which have not yet been described.

Provided with a travelling chair and four bearers, as on my former excursion, and with a sufficient number of baggage coolies to carry provisions, &c. I set out from Ruwenwellé on the 23d of August, and proceeded that day to Ganepali, in Lower Boulatgammé, distant about ten miles. The country in general through which we passed, was rather difficult, though only slightly hilly: it exhibited very little cultivation, and excepting near Ruwenwellé, was very thinly inhabited. Thick low jungle and forest succeeded each other the greater part of the way: where the ground was low and damp, the former prevailed; and where it was hilly and dry, the latter. The jungle consisted chiefly of a species of cane, which is the favourite cover of elephants, that greatly abound in these wilds: I was cautioned concerning them, and expected to have encountered some; but we only saw their traces, and noticed a precaution of the natives to aid escape when pursued by them. It was exceedingly simple and effectual; consisting merely in tying a strong pole or two across the narrow foot-path, at the height of five feet from the ground; under which, of course, a man might run at full speed, whilst the huge pursuing animal would be completely stopped. This circumstance, too, will serve to illustrate the thickness and imperviousness of the jungle in general hereabout, which can be penetrated only by the paths made by man, or by the tracts of its wilder inhabitants. Few parts of the island are so copiously watered as Lower Boulatgammé: besides a number of small streams, we passed two of considerable size, which when flooded are not fordable. viz. the Wahoya, about four miles from Ruwenwellé, and the Hické oya, that first appears about two miles further: both flow into the Kalany ganga. The Hické oya is a most troublesome stream to the traveller; we had to cross it no less than sixteen different times, and in several places our way lay through its bed. The Wahoya, which is much the larger of the two, is crossed only once. This river (for I believe it is the same, though called the Baliakudah ella) about a mile above its ferry, where the road passes a little way along its left bank, exhibits the character of a mountain-torrent: pent up in a narrow gloomy valley, its fine volume of transparent water rushes down a rapid over immense masses of rock, and forms, with the help of a variety of heightening circumstances, one of the wildest and most impressive scenes of the kind that I have ever witnessed.

Ganepali, where I spent the night, in a little amblam that had been unroofed a few days before by elephants, is prettily situated in a valley formed by lofty woody mountains, which rise apparently to the height of two or three thousand feet. The village is very small, containing only about twenty people, whose dwellings are situated in the midst of fruit-trees on the border of a large paddy-field, almost surrounded by the Hické oya. Belonging to this place is a boy, whom I saw, whose tongue from birth has been of a monstrous size: it is so large that it usually projects out of the mouth, and almost prevents the closing of the lips; the skin of the part most exposed is thickened and somewhat discoloured; though the frænum is connected with the tip of the tongue, and the organ is almost motionless, the boy speaks perfectly well.

The next day's journey brought us to Ambigammué, in Upper

Boulatgammé, said to be two gows and a half, or ten miles distant, but apparently much more. About two miles from Ganepali we crossed the Bibilé oya, and, about a mile farther, the Gerankitty oya, both considerable streams, and often impassable. At the distance of about four miles, we came to Kittoolgullé. The country, this first part of the way, is wild and hilly. Its scenery in many places, particularly where the path skirts the Kalany ganga, is of a magnificent kind.

Kittoolgullé, where we stopped to breakfast in an abandoned post, which was occupied during the rebellion, is prettily situated in a little cultivated plain, embosomed in woody mountains. Its elevation above the level of the sea * is very inconsiderable. Were one to judge of its elevation by the most fallacious of all methods, — the difficulty of the approach to it, and the apparent ascent, one would pronounce it to be many hundred feet higher than it really is. Did the barometrical result require confirmation, the circumstance would afford it, of the Kalany ganga being navigable within two miles of this place.

Beyond Kittoolgulle the country is exceedingly difficult, and perfectly mountainous. The beauty of the scenery amply compensates for the toil of the journey, which the cool air of the hills and the dense shade of the forests with which they are covered, render one better able to bear. From the highest mountain-ridge which we crossed, and which I conjecture was about 3000 feet above the level of the sea, the prospects in every direction were particularly fine. One way we looked down upon Ambigammué, in the midst of cultivated green paddy-fields,

* At 10 A.M. at this place, the barometer was 30.05 inches; both thermometers 80°.

surrounded by hills, many of them bare and green, like those of Upper Ouva: in another direction, looking towards Adam's Peak, which was concealed by clouds, we saw a succession of conical mountain-tops, luxuriantly wooded, here and there connected by a bare mountain-ridge: and, at the time when we were not two miles from the Mahawellé ganga, we were within hearing and sight of the Maskelli ganga, which uniting with the Kalugammua ganga forms the Kalany river. The sound and view of this fine fall of water, brought strongly to my recollection an unsuccessful attempt which I made last October to reach Adam's Peak, when I found this formidable river flooded, and should have lost a soldier of the 83d regiment, had it not been for the active intrepidity of two of the natives accustomed to struggle with the torrent, who pursued him when carried away by the strength of the stream, and dragged him out of a rapid, where an European could not have stood.

Ambigammué, though elevated between fifteen and sixteen hundred feet above the level of the sea *, is in every direction surrounded by mountains. The appearance of this place is greatly altered from what it was on my first visit to it, in October last: the natives, the majority of whom were then hiding themselves in the jungle, have returned, and have constructed huts in lieu of their old houses, which were destroyed; the fields, which were then lying waste, have been cultivated, and are now covered with green crops; and the military post, which was then occupied by a detachment of Europeans, has been converted into a farm-yard, and, with the exception of an old house, all the quarters of the soldiers have been levelled with the ground.

* At 9 h. 30 m. P.M., at this place, the barometer was 28.35; both thermometers 75°.

The Mahawellé ganga flows by the old post of Ambigammué. Having just issued from its parent mountains, it is here an inconsiderable stream, and, excepting when flooded, hardly knee-deep.

On the following morning, crossing this stream just where it is joined by the Kawataroo oya, which is very little inferior to it in size, we went to Passbagé, distant about eight miles. The country, all the way, is very agreeable along the course of the river, which steals quietly through a tolerably cultivated and open valley, watered by very many rills and bounded on one side by rocky, precipitous mountains, and, on the other, by green rounded hills.

During the rebellion Passbagé was a military station. Our post was on a hill, about fifty feet above the river, at the confluence of the Kotmalé ganga and the Mahawellé ganga.* I knew that it had been abandoned, but I expected to have found some of its quarters standing that would have afforded shelter. I was mistaken: not a vestige of the post remained; the ground where it had stood, and where, not quite twelve months before, I had passed a night amongst my countrymen, was now covered with natchiné, and not a soul was to be seen but a wretched old man, under a shed, just large enough to cover his body, guarding his little crop; none of the former inhabitants of the immediate neighbourhood, who had fled during the rebellion, having returned to cultivate their grounds. The weather being fine, want of shelter was of little consequence; and the sensation of cold,

* On the 13th of October 1818, at 8 P. M., on the hill, the barometer was 28.30 inches; both thermometers 72°.

This time, below the hill, just above the river, at 7 P. M., the barometer was 28.38; both thermometers 70°.

so very unusual, was the only unpleasant circumstance we experienced from sleeping at night in the open air.

Starting early the next morning, we crossed the Mahawellé ganga, in a canoe belonging to the ferry, and made the best of our way, without a guide, to Pouhalpittyé, our military post in Kotmalé, at the distance of about seven miles. From the river we ascended about three miles, to a considerable height, over a succession of steep rounded hills, the hollows of which were occupied with wood, and the tops and sides covered with luxuriant grass. We crossed several small, clear rills, and passed over many neglected paddy-fields, which, with the ruins of several little villages, indicated that, like Passbagé, this part of Kotmalé had been desolated during the rebellion. Where our ascent terminated, a prospect of a new kind, and quite unexpected, opened before us. We looked down into a deep extensive valley, which expanded as it ascended, formed by steep hills, tapering towards each other, and bounded by a chain of lofty mountains, the tops of which were hid in clouds. From the height commanding this view, — the minute beauties of which it would be idle to attempt to describe, particularly the glorious manner in which it was illuminated by the light streaming along its tract from east to west, — from this height, we descended a very steep hill, to the Kotmalé ganga, that flows through the valley; and, re-ascending a little, reached Pouhalpittyé, by a path winding along the rugged side of the hill, chiefly over paddy-fields partially cultivated, and through two or three villages exhibiting strong symptoms of the effects of the late rebellion.

The post of Pouhalpittiyé, where we halted and spent the night, is finely situated on a steep green hill, on the left bank of the river, and rather more than 2000 feet above the level of the sea.* The prospects from it vary in different directions. Grandeur is the characteristic of the view up the valley, where the scenery is wild, — consisting of green uncultivated hills, surmounted on one side by wooded mountains of great elevation, from which two torrents rush, fresh from the clouds, by which they are fed, and which at this season generally hide their summits. In the opposite direction, the features are less bold, and the landscape is more beautiful. The river, running over a rocky bed, is the conspicuous boundary of the two sides of the valley; one of which, the left, rises rapidly, and is abruptly terminated by a lofty façade of rock above the scattered village of Tispané; whilst the other ascending more gradually, ends in a lofty green ridge fringed with jungle. Both declivities are cultivated, and being cut into steps or terraces, the fields have a singular and pleasing appearance, which is much increased by the very many fruit-groves and neat houses that present themselves, rising one above another.

Leaving Pouhalpittyé, the following morning we proceeded on our way towards Ouva; a route hitherto unexplored by any European, and which the natives seemed very averse from my attempting. Ascending the valley, we soon entered another communicating with it, and nearly at right angles to it, in which is the fertile little district of Dimbola. About two miles from the fort, where we entered this district, the prospect of the country was beautiful and interesting, — general terms, it must be confessed, of vague import, when thus applied. The principal features of the scenery (barely to mention them) were, — a long,

* At 7 P.M. the barometer was 27.70; both thermometers 70°.

wide, and deep valley; the river, quite a mountain-torrent, hurrying through it, foaming over rocks, visible with little interruption for two or three miles; the sides of the valley to a considerable height most artfully cultivated, presenting a succession of steps or terraces covered with green paddy, admirably irrigated, and this, even where the ground was so steep and difficult, that the perpendicular side of many of the beds exceeded their horizontal surface, and required a facing of stone to support them; here and there in the paddy-fields, rude but permanent watch-houses; here and there, the dwellings of the natives surrounded by fruit-trees; and towering above all, and bounding this rural and artificial scene, green hills on one side, and lofty-wooded mountain on the other, and at each extremity apparently a mountain-barrier. This valley was the most perfect thing of the kind I ever saw, and it was in a very flourishing state, having escaped entirely the calamities of the recent rebellion, not owing to any peculiar merit of the inhabitants, but rather to its remote and secluded situation, and to their timely submission.

About three miles from the fort, we crossed the Kotmalé ganga at Haleltotté, where the river is narrow and deep, and not fordable. We were conveyed over in a canoe of the rudest construction, which, it might be inferred from its appearance, would hardly carry a single man, and yet it conveyed three or four with perfect safety. It consisted merely of the rough trunk of a jaggery-palm hollowed out and supported on each side by a plantain-stalk as outriggers. Here, about to quit the cultivated and inhabited part of the country, I took leave of the few natives who had accompanied me thus far, with the exception of a Satambi and one or two more, who were to act as guides.

The remainder of the journey, which lasted from six in the morning till a little after four in the afternoon, was very laborious and uninteresting. After clearing the lower part of the mountain, covered with lemon-grass, we entered thick jungle of the most monotonous, and often of a very gloomy description, shutting out all prospect, producing a dense shade, and varying only in its character according to the nature of the ground; — in marshy places consisting of rank succulent plants and shrubs, through which there was some difficulty in forcing one's way; in damp places, of trees overgrown with moss; and on the steep and dry sides of the mountain, either of thick underwood, or of forest-trees and underwood intermixed. At one o'clock we halted a little while above a fine fall of the Poondool oya, a considerable stream which we had to cross, and which joins the Kotmalé ganga a little below Dimbola. Here we had attained the height of at least three thousand feet above the level of the sea *, and, according to our guide, had come about seven miles, or about a mile an hour, travelling without stop; and, judging from the difficult nature of the path (sometimes so steep and rugged as almost to require climbing,) the distance assigned was not under-rated. The latter part of way, beyond this river, was not less difficult than the preceding, but it was drier, and less disagreeable. We passed the night at the elevation of rather more than four thousand feet above the level of the sea †, on a little clear spot of ground known to the natives by the name of Unapatpalassé, in the midst of forest, where I found prepared a small hut of green branches, lined with white cloth; but no

* The water of this stream was 63°; the air 72°; the barometer 26.55.

† At 5 A. M. at this place, the barometer was 25.65; both thermometers 53°.

shelter for the attendants, who slept in the open air by the side of large fires, which were well fed, both from apprehension of wild animals, and from the more pressing sensation of cold. The night was very fine; the air and sky perfectly calm and clear, and the latter of a very dark blue, in which the moon and stars shone with a lustre that I never saw exceeded. Just before sunset the thermometer was 62°; at eight o'clock at night it was 56°; and at five in the morning, 53°. The bright blazing fires, the clear star-light, and the frosty feel of the air, reminded me of a winter-night in England.

The journey of the next day, commenced at six o'clock in the morning and not concluded till five in the afternoon, was as laborious as that of the preceding, but far less monotonous. During the first three hours we walked over very irregular ground, covered with stunted jungle, in which the rhododendron began to appear, and intersected by two or three fine streams, as clear as crystal, and unpleasantly cold, the temperatureof the lowest being 55.5. Then we came to a steep hill, which our guides assured us (and, I believe, correctly) is the most elevated part of the way. Here the scenery began to be interesting, though the first object that met our attention was of a melancholy kind. It was the dead body of a native, in a fœtid state, reduced almost to a skeleton, lying by the side of the footpath; in which, probably, attempting to pass, as many did, from Ouva into Kotmalé to avoid starvation, he dropped down exhausted. In ascending the hill just alluded to, the country began to open around us, and we had occasional views of the wooded mountain tops, with which we appeared to be nearly on a level; and from one spot we had a view of the valley of Kotmalé; but, owing to the distance and height, we could distinguish nothing minutely; we could see only the great features of the country, which, with the effects of different lights and shades, and colour, constitute the beauty of alpine scenery, and were more than sufficient to afford us no inconsiderable delight, after having been so many hours in gloomy jungle. Where the road was highest, on the brow of the hill, the barometer was 24.75 inches, and both thermometers 62° ; this was at 9 h. 30 m. A. M.

Descending this hill on the other side, we arrived, at ten o'clock, at a spot of open ground, very little lower *, called Kicklemanè, of the extent of several acres, nearly circular, of very irregular surface, surrounded by forest consisting chiefly of rhododendrons, spotted here and there with solitary trees of the same kind, and watered by a purling stream that ran through the middle of it. Leaving this place, which is said to be the boundary of Kotmalé and Ouva, we entered a forest, in which we began to see traces of elephants, and proceeded over wooded hills gradually descending till we came to a great extent of open country, the aspect of which was no less novel than agreeable.

Our guides called it Neuraellyia-pattan. In point of elevation and extent, this tract, there is reason to believe, surpasses every other of the kind in the island; perhaps it is fifteen or twenty miles in circumference, and its average height may be about 5300 feet above the level of the sea. † Surrounded by the tops of mountains, which have the appearance of hills of moderate height, its character is that of table-land, elevated and depressed into numerous hillocks and hollows. The wood which covers

* Here the barometer was 24.80 ; thermometer 65°.

† About noon, in a spot sheltered by several large rhododendrons, two or three hundred yards on the plain, the barometer was 24.90 ; the thermometer attached 60°, and detached 64°.

the boundary mountains (and they are all, without exception, covered with wood,) is of a peculiar kind, quite alpine, and very similar to what we found on the summit of Namina-cooli-kandy. The same kind of wood ramifying into the table-land, and occuring scattered about in insulated clumps, with large solitary rhododendrons here and there, has a very picturesque effect, and helps to make a very charming landscape.

Beautiful as this region is, and cleared, and possessing, in all probability, a fine climate, (certainly a cool climate,) like the similar heights between Maturatta and fort M'Donald, it is quite deserted by man. It is the dominion, entirely, of wild animals; and, in an especial manner, of the elephant, of whom we saw innumerable traces; indeed, judging from the great quantity of the dung of this animal which was scattered over the ground, it must abound here more than in any other part of the island. Reasoning *à priori*, would have led to a different conclusion; and, at first, it appears not a little singular, that the most elevated and coldest tract of Ceylon, where the average temperature of the air is, probably, below 60°, should be the favourite haunt of an animal that is supposed to be particularly fond of warmth. He is probably attracted to this place by the charms of good pasture, and of a quiet peaceable life, out of the way of being annoyed by man. In respect to cold, I suspect he is much less delicate than is commonly imagined, and that he is capable of bearing with impunity considerable vicissitudes, and a pretty extensive range of temperature; and this seems to be established by the circumstance of elephants being numerous in some parts of Southern Africa, where ice occasionally forms, and where the climate is certainly colder than on the Neuraellyia-pattan. The importance which I attach to this fact is in its geological bearing. It tends apparently to diminish the marvel of the occurrence of the bones of elephants in the alluvial deposits of temperate climates, and seems to render it far from improbable that the animals to which they belonged lived in the countries where their remains are now found; and, the arctic species, of which one specimen has been discovered included and preserved in ice, in Siberia, may, perhaps, entitle the same explanation to be extended to the bones of elephants found in high latitudes.

Crossing the pattan, where it is about two or three miles wide, we soon came to the Kotmalé ganga, which here, almost at its source, is a little stream hardly knee-deep. It descends, forming a pretty water-fall, from a rocky height, and runs, as far as the eye can follow its meanderings, in a southerly direction. Beyond this we crossed another rivulet, very little smaller, descending from the same height, and pursuing the same course.

In crossing the Pattan, though it was about noon, the sun nearly vertical, and the sky quite unclouded, the thermometer, even exposed to the direct rays of the sun, did not rise above 62°.* The wind was blowing strongly from the mountains in our rear, and felt so cold and piercing, that it was really disagreeable; we spread our umbrellas to break its force, and, on quitting the open plain and entering a wood through which the path led, we found the shelter it afforded exceedingly comfortable.

Before I entirely quit this region, I may remark, that I could obtain very little information respecting it from my guides. The probability is, though I am not aware, it is supported by tradition, that it was once inhabited and cultivated, or, at least, cleared by man; and, for a reason assigned already, that in a

* The thermometer used had a very small projecting bulb, and, in the shade, would have been about two degrees lower.

state of nature the local circumstances are such as would favour rather than prevent the growth of wood. All I could collect from the natives with me amounted to this, — that the Pattan was never inhabited, and that, except by the passing traveller, it is visited only by two descriptions of men — by the blacksmiths of Kotmalé, who come in the dry season to make iron, and by the gem-renter and his people in quest of precious stones. I could not learn, with any precision, either the spot where the ores of iron occur, or where the gems are found. When at Badulla I saw some specimens, said to have been collected on the Neura-ellyia; they were chiefly cat's-eye, and adularia, and different varieties of sapphire, all very similar to the minerals of the same kind from Matura and Saffragam.

In the wood, in which we found shelter from the piercing wind, and indeed the greater part of the remainder of the way, we were in constant expectation of encountering elephants, of whom the marks were numerous, — as the impression of their feet, their fresh dung, &c.; but none made their appearance, owing, probably, to the clear, bright weather, in which, in the middle of the day, they generally seek the shade of the thickest part of the jungle.

Descending through this wood, we soon came to an open spot of no great extent, through which a considerable rivulet, called the Hawellé oya, flows on its way to Ouva. On the Neuraellyia-pattan, where the ground was swampy, and the vegetation of mosses luxuriant, the soil resembled peat; and the same appearance, in still greater perfection, was observable on the moist banks of this stream.

Again entering thick forest, we forded, a second time, the Hawellé oya, where its course is very rapid, and its bed rocky.

Our experienced guides led us with some difficulty through the jungle, which became thicker as we descended; and, though they had their private marks,—as notches on trees, they occasionally went astray, misled by the tracts of wild animals.

About three o'clock in the afternoon, we emerged entirely from the forest, and had immediately, from our commanding height, a most extensive view of Upper Ouva, which appeared laid out before us like a magnificent map. The first object in the prospect that arrested attention, was Namina-cooli-kandy, rising in the eastern horizon, of a light-blue colour, and surpassing every other mountain in the circle that surrounds Upper Ouva, as much in its massive form as its apparent height. With the general appearance of the country I was disappointed: its surface was not fresh and green, as when I viewed it the first time from the Idalgashena, reminding me of the hills of England in spring; but of a light yellowish-green colour, as if parched and withered: nor were its mountains of the intense blue which I then so much admired; but of a light, dazzling, aerial hue. This appearance of the country having suffered from a long drought, was greatly heightened by the clouds of smoke in which many parts of it were enveloped, and which, driven before the wind, had a singularly wild effect, giving the idea that the ground was not only parched, but in a state of conflagration.

Descending the bare side of the mountain, we now and then passed through narrow slips of jungle in sheltered hollows. In these situations, the remains were visible of several rude huts, constructed by the natives during the rebellion, when they deserted the inhabited part of the country, and fled to these heights for concealment. We found the wind so hard and troublesome, and so parching and cold, that we were obliged to walk with caution in steep places, to avoid being blown over; and we felt no inclination to halt to rest, excepting where we were sheltered from its chilling effects. Below a very rocky height, the path led us very near the fine fall of the Dugullé oya, which is a striking object in the prospect in this direction from the neighbourhood of Fort M'Donald. As we passed, it appeared under peculiar circumstances, and the scene, as it were, of war between two elements: a fire that had been kindled below, had spread up the mountain, and was raging in a ravine, and consuming a narrow strip of jungle close to the water's edge.

At five o'clock in the afternoon, we arrived at an inhabited spot, about 3700 feet above the level of the sea*, and nearly at the bottom of the descent, called Perowellé; where, though the shelter was wretched, fatigued and hungry as we were, we gladly halted and took up our quarters for the night.

The next morning we proceeded to Fort M'Donald, about four miles distant. The walk was far from pleasant, both from the hardness and parching dryness of the wind, and the miserable aspect of the country, — the paddy being cut, and the fields covered with dry stubble, and the grass on the hills either withered by a long drought, which I learned had now lasted nearly four months, or burnt by the natives to ensure a better crop in the approaching wet season.

Visiting Upper Ouva at this dry season of the year, the causes of its peculiar condition, viz. the bareness of its hills, and the absence of wood, excepting in a few and particular situations,

* At 5 A. M., at this place, the barometer was 26.40; both thermometers 65°.

court observation, and thrust themselves on one's notice: they appear to be principally, a long, dry season; the strong winds which are prevalent at all times, but particularly during this season; and the practice, general amongst the natives of Ouva, of setting fire annually to the dry grass for the purpose of improving the pasture, and occasionally to the upland jungle, for the purpose of cultivating grains that do not require irrigation. These three circumstances combined appear quite adequate to account for the effect; and each of them appears to be essential to its production, as is well illustrated in other parts of the country, where they occur separately. Thus, in all situations where the ground is moist, whether it be from frequent showers or natural irrigation, burning has only temporary effect; the branches and trunks are indeed consumed, but the roots appear to be uninjured; and, in less than twelve months, the jungle re-appears in a state of most luxuriant growth. Thus, again, where the winds are not generally powerful, though there is a dry season, and burning is practised, the face of the country remains covered with wood, with the exception of the few localities where the operation of burning has been performed. In further confirmation of the joint influence of these three causes being requisite, I hardly need remark, that where the application of fire is never made, as in the uninhabited parts of the country, though subject, in a remarkable manner, to long drought and hard winds, wood is most abundant.

This explanation of the peculiar openness and want of wood of Upper Ouva, is applicable to other parts of the country, that in this respect at all resemble it; for instance, Upper Boulatgammé, the adjoining hills of Kotmalé, and a considerable portion of farther Doombera, where the climate is similar, and the practice of burning grass and jungle the same.

There is another and striking peculiarity of Upper Ouva, that deserves notice, and requires explanation; I mean, its undulating surface of hills and valleys, rounded and smoothed as equably as if, instead of primitive rock, they consisted of chalk or clay. This peculiarity of appearance, I believe, is owing entirely to the rock in general being nearly of the same quality, and of such a nature, that it undergoes rapid decomposition and disintegration from the action of air and water.

To renew the journey: early the following morning we quitted Fort M'Donald, ascended the Dodanatukapella pass, and spent the day and the night on the elevated ground above the Halgaran oya, where a couple of tents had been pitched for the reception of Major-general Sir Edward Barnes and his party, who were to pass this way the next day.

Owing to the long drought which prevailed here, as well as in Ouva, the aspect of this elevated region was not nearly so beautiful as when I last passed, in the month of April. Most of the small streams were dried up; the trees and shrubs exhibited little variety of foliage; none of them were in flower, and hardly a flower of any kind was to be seen. An additional gloom, through the day, was imparted to the scenery by a wild cloudy sky, and by the distant atmosphere over Walapany and Ouva being obscured by immense volumes of smoke, rising from a great extent of burning grass and jungle, the fire of which, in two or three places, was so large and fierce as to be distinguishable by broad day-light. The evening here, and night, amply compensated for the day; the evening was quite delightful, like an evening in England in autumn, after a sultry day; the air was fresh and cool; the thermometer, at sunset, at 60°; and many birds, whose notes resembled those of the robin, sung sweetly in an adjoining wood. The scenery, by the soft light of evening, under the influence of a perfectly clear sky, was charming in its appearance, particularly its distant features; as the lofty chain of Walapany mountains in the east, and the loftier Namina-cooli-kandy a little to the south of east, both of the finest tint of blue. I do not recollect having ever more enjoyed a solitary walk than I did this evening, refreshed by the cool air, and delighted by the beautiful prospect. Often since, when suffering from the heat, and tired of the monotony of a lowland district, I have thought of this region, — of its beauties "wasted on the desert air," — and of the benefit and pleasure we might derive from it as a place of temporary residence and retirement.

Having already described Maturatta and Kandy, and the country between Kandy and Nalandé, it is unnecessary to enter into any minute particulars of the journey along this line of road. It will be sufficient to notice such circumstances only as have novelty to recommend them.

At Kandy, where we arrived on the 3d of September, we found a climate very different from that which we had experienced in Ouva and at Maturatta, and even at Marasena, only ten miles distant. Here, there were no symptoms of drought; on the contrary, the air was humid and showers were frequent. In all probability, this striking difference of climate depends solely on the circumstance of the preceding places being skreened from the direct impulse and effects of the south-west monsoon by the lofty intervening mountains of Saffragam and Kotmalé, which rob it of moisture by precipitation in passing, and in relation to humidity completely alter its character.

Between Kandy and Nalandé a remarkable change was visible since we were last this way, on the Governor's return from Trincomalie, at the period of the commencement of the rebellion. Now, every attention and mark of respect was paid to His Excellency. The roads had been put in good order, and were handsomely decorated in the Singalese fashion, and, as a distinction of the highest kind, due only to royalty, they were here and there sprinkled with quicklime. The headmen, with the Dissave of the province, were in attendance, and the people of the country of both sexes, looking well and contented, having suffered very little during the rebellion, made their appearance in great numbers, to pay their respects and gratify their curiosity.

Again at Nalandé we experienced another sudden and great alteration of climate. The wind was strong, and disagreeably dry; the grass was turned yellow, and the leaves of the trees, with the exception of those least succulent, were either drooping or withered. The aspect of the sky, at the time of our arrival, was in harmony with the wretched appearance of the country; it was troubled and fiery, and the effect of the whole was heightened by the ruined state of our old military post and the desolate air of the new one, which, before its works were half finished, was deserted on account of its extreme unwholesomeness.

From Nalandé we proceed to Dambooloo, about fifteen miles distant, through a country parched up by drought, nearly level, overgrown with jungle and forest, and almost entirely deserted by man.

Dambooloo, where we arrived late in the afternoon, is a scene of peculiar interest. Its rock-temples are the most extensive in the island, the most perfect of their kind and the most ancient, and in the highest state of preservation and order.

Dambooloo-gallé, the rock in which these temples are situated, is almost insulated and of a vast size. Its perpendicular height above the plain is about six hundred feet.* Very few parts of it are covered with wood, and in general its surface is bare and black. The following outlines, intended to represent longitudinal and transverse sections, will give a more tolerably correct idea of its form than verbal description perhaps can convey.

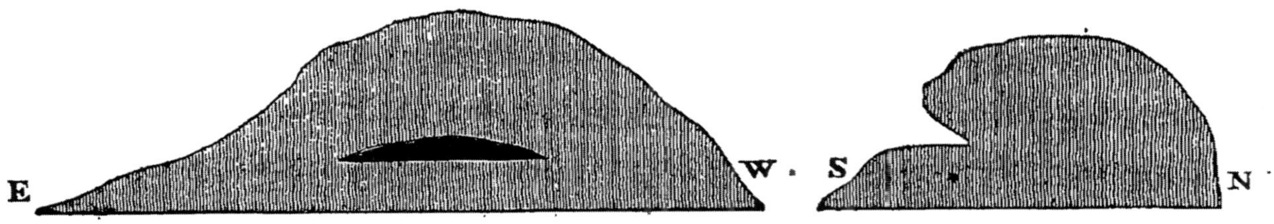

The temples, which give this place celebrity, are parts of a vast cavern in the south side of the rock, at the height of about three hundred and fifty feet above the plain.† The approach to them is up the eastern shelving extremity of the rock, and through an archway of masonry of apparently modern construction, and along a narrow platform of solid rock open to the south, enclosed by a low wall, shaded by trees, and containing in its area a cistern holding rain water, a very small temple and a bogah. The interior of the temples is hid externally by a wall rather more than four hundred feet long, perforated with a number of doors and windows, and sheltered and defended not only by the overhang-

* On the top of the rock, at 4 P.M., the barometer was 29.0; both thermometers 79°. On the plain below, at 6 P.M., the barometer was 29.69; thermometers 80°.

† At 4 h. 30 m. P.M., the barometer on the platform before the wiharés was 29.29; thermometers 79°.

ing concave surface of rock, but likewise artificially, by a rude verandah, consisting of a thatched roof supported by wooden posts.

This approach, platform, and front raised our expectations very little, and did not at all prepare us for what we discovered on entering the temples. The wiharé we first explored is the last in order from the entrance. It is about fifty-four feet long and twenty-seven wide; and its shelving roof, which dips rapidly inwards, where most lofty, is about twenty-seven feet high. It contains ten figures of Boodhoo, and a neat dagobah about twelve feet high. The figures are well executed and brilliantly painted, and most of them are as large or larger than the ordinary size of man. The roof and sides of the rock and the front wall are painted of the brightest colours, and illuminated with a number of figures, chiefly of Boodhoo. The general effect of the whole is exceedingly striking and pretty.

The next wiharé, called the Alut Wiharé, is separated from the preceding, partly by abutting rock, and partly by a wall of masonry, in which there is a door of communication. Its principal entrance is by a door in front. We were taken by surprise on entering this temple; we were astonished by its great size, the brilliant effect of an immense surface of rock painted of the richest colours, and by the numerous figures of Boodhoo, which it contains in different attitudes and groupes, all coloured in the most lively manner. It is about ninety feet long, eighty-one wide, and its shelving roof where highest, is about thirty-six feet high. The figures which it contains are fifty in number. One statue of Boodhoo, in the recumbent posture, its head on a pillow resting on its right hand, is of gigantic size, about thirty feet long and well proportioned; its face is handsome, and its expression of countenance remarkably placid and benignant. Seven other statues of Boodhoo in the standing attitude, are about ten feet high, and all the rest are as large as life, or very little less. Most of them are coloured bright yellow; two or three have red robes, and reminded me of the two classes of Lamas in Tibet, described by Captain Turner, who are distinguished from each other, by one wearing red and the other yellow garments. Towards the western end of the temple there is a well executed figure of King Kirtissiré, the last great benefactor of Dambooloo, in his robes of state, which very much resemble those worn by the late king.

Between this temple and the next there is no direct communication; I believe they are separated from each other by a stone wall. The portal by which you enter is in front; it is a lofty archway, guarded on each side by figures in stone, intended to represent Janitors. This temple, called the Maha-rajah wiharé, almost as much surpasses in size and effect the last, as that does the first described. It is about one hundred and ninety feet long, about ninety feet wide, and forty-five feet high where highest; nor does obscurity add to its grandeur; for it is perfectly well lighted through numerous windows, and several doors in front. It contains altogether fifty-three images, and a handsome dagobah, about fourteen or eighteen feet high, the broad circular pedestal of which is ornamented with four figures of Boodhoo, each facing a different quarter, each seated on the coil of a Cobra de Capello, and shaded by its expanded hood. As in the two preceding temples, so in this the images are arranged in a row at a little distance from the sides and inner walls of the room, but not grouped; and as in the last, none are placed near the outer wall with the exception of the statues of two kings: at the western end of the temple the figures are arranged in a double row. The majority of the statues are Boodhoos of different dimensions, and in different attitudes; many of them larger, but none of them much, if at all, smaller than life. Besides forty-six figures of Boodhoo, there is, in company with them, one of Mitré-Deo rajooroowo, who, it is imagined, will be the next Boodhoo, the successor of Goutama; and one of each of the three gods,—Visnu, Samen, and Nata; the first in blue robes, the second in yellow, and the third in robes of white. The statues of the two kings alluded to above, as standing apart against the outer wall, are those of Wallagam-bahoo and Nisankai, at opposite ends of the temple: the first, representing the earliest benefactor of Dambooloo, is the rudest figure in every respect, and its dress is the simplest and least ornamented; the ears are long, and drawn down in the Malabar fashion; there is a double-headed snake about the neck, the body of which serves as a necklace, and the heads as ear-pendants. At the eastern extremity of the temple there is a little recess formed by a high projecting rock, the walls of which are covered with paintings illustrating the history of Ceylon, beginning with the earliest and most fabulous period, and continued down to the introduction of the bo-tree and the sacred relic. The exploits of Wijeya, the first king, make a conspicuous figure, and cover a great deal of space; more especially the voyage of this hero, which is represented by a boat surrounded by sea-monsters. The dedication of the island to Boodhoo after the arrival of the relic, is figured by a king guiding a plough drawn by a pair of elephants, attended by priests, &c. Towards the eastern end of the temple there is a perpetual dripping of water that filters through the roof from hollows on the top of the rock, which are supplied by rain. The water as it drops is caught in a chatty for the purpose, placed in a small square inclosure sunk in the floor. Though the water is particularly good, no native, through superstitious dread, which restrains them, ventures to use it; — and, when I told a priest that I had tasted it, he replied, that though we might drink it, perhaps, with impunity, it would certainly prove fatal to them were they to indulge in it.

Before quitting this temple, in which there was a pleasure in remaining on account of its cool and fresh air, so different from the close and hot atmosphere of small wiharés in general, we had an opportunity to witness the manner in which Boodhists worship their divinity. The service was performed at the Governor's desire, and without the least hesitation, under the direction of the chief priest, who intimated the wish to the people, and supplied them with flowers. Each person, on receiving his flowers, went and laid them before an image of Boodhoo, and accompanied the offering with a pious exclamation. The offerings being all made, and all the people arranged in a line before the images, and kneeling, the priest stood in the middle, and with a clear voice, sentence by sentence, recited the common obligations of their religion, the congregation repeating each sentence after him. The united voices of at least one hundred men in the highest key of recitative, or rather of the loudest exclamation, made the cavern resound, and had a fine awful effect, producing a thrill through the system, and a feeling and sentiment not to be described.

The next and last temple, called the Dewaa-rajah wiharé, because the god Visnu is supposed to have aided in the construction of its principal image, is very inferior in every respect to either of the preceding, especially the two last. It is about seventy-five feet long, twenty-one wide, and twenty-seven high; and so dark, that I had only a very imperfect view of it, even with the aid of a lamp. It contains six images of Boodhoo, and one of Visnu, all of them of ordinary size, with the exception of that just alluded to as the principal figure, which is a gigantic recumbent Boodhoo, about thirty feet long.

Whether the cavern in which these temples have been formed, is altogether natural, or partly natural and partly artificial, it is not now easy to determine. The probability is, that it is principally natural, and that man has had very little to do in excavating it. I am not aware that history throws any light upon this point; and, indeed, it can hardly be expected that it should. All I have been able to collect amounts to this,—that the Maha-rajah wiharé was commenced 1924 years ago by Walagam-bahoo, during his retirement in this part of Matelé, between the period of his defeat by the Malabars and the recovery of his capital; that it was repaired and embellished two hundred and twenty-seven years ago by King Nisankai, who is said to have laid out in ornamenting it six hundred thousand pieces of gold, but of what value is not known; and lastly, that the Alut wiharè was formed sixty-four years ago by King Kirtissrie, by whom also the great wiharé was again repaired.

These temples are attached to the Asgirie wiharé, and are under the care of seven resident priests. It is pretended, that all the country round, as far as the eye can reach from the summit of the rock, is temple-property, and a priest offered to produce a sanus to prove it. At present the priests can command, or rather I should say demand the services of about forty people only, the inhabitants of twelve villages that belong to their establishment.

For want of time, we were not able to visit the dwellings of the priests, which are situated somewhere on the southern side of the rock, below the wiharè, and are said to be of a very superior kind. We preferred ascending the rock for the sake of the view which its summit commands. This view is very extensive, comprehending, when the atmosphere is unclouded, a large portion of Matelé, of the Seven Korles, and of Nuarakalawea. In the direction of the Seven Korles and the eastern part of Matelé, the prospect was hid from us by mist, and we could see but a very little way. Over Nuarakalawea and the northern portion of Matelé, the air was pretty clear, and the view was terminated only by the horizon. The former district commences about two or three miles from Dambooloo: as far as the eye could reach, it appears to be low and level, and covered with wood. In respect to wood, the character of the northern part of Matelé appeared very similar to that of Nuarakalawea, and seemed to differ only in its surface being rather more irregular and hilly.

On the morrow early we left Dambooloo, and proceeded by way of Nalandé to Taldenia, about eight miles distant from it. Taldenia is the property of Eheylapola, and was his favourite country-residence. His house is the most spacious one I have seen in any part of the country, and it is amply provided with granaries. It is about 1200 feet above the level of the *sea, situated on a gentle green declivity in the midst of a grove of young cocoa-nut trees; and for security against elephants, which are here very numerous and troublesome, both it and the adjoining ground is surrounded by a ditch and breast-work. The climate of this place, it is remarkable, is totally different from that of Nalandé, though the distance between them is so short.

* At 7 A.M. barometer 28.85; thermometers 72°.

The Asgirie Korle to which Taldenia belongs, commences about a mile or two from Nalandé, and immediately where it begins, the difference of climate and scenery is perceptible. On entering it, we could see no marks of drought; the air was moist, the grass green, vegetation luxuriant, the paddy-fields were covered with green crops; and what was most decisive of all, leeches were abundant. Nor, does it differ less in point of salubrity: whilst Nalandé and the adjoining country is notoriously unwholesome, this korle is remarkably healthful. The country is hilly and is separated from the Seven Korles by a narrow mountain-ridge of considerable height. Its peculiarities of climate, no doubt, are connected with this circumstance. The mountain in question acting as a refrigeratory on the passing air, is the chief cause, probably, of the frequent showers with which this favoured little district is refreshed during the south-west monsoon.

The following day we crossed the Yattéwatté pass, over the lowest part of the mountain-ridge already alluded to, entered the Seven Korles, and proceeded by the way of Kandeloya to Koornegalle twenty-eight miles distant. The Yattéwatté pass is not very steep, and though much neglected, the road over it is not very difficult. Between the pass and Kandeloya the country is hilly, and often picturesque, but little cultivated. Between Kandeloya and Koornegalle, the road is through narrow plains abounding in paddy-fields and skirted by woody hills. The Didroo oya which we forded about eight miles from the latter place, is a pretty wide and rapid stream, but seldom more than knee-deep. I have already suggested the idea of conveying the water of this river, at present useless, by a canal, into the Maha oya, above Giriullé. Judging roughly from the difference of levels and the nature of the intervening surface, it is not improbable that it may be practicable. Could it be accomplished, its advantages would be incalculable; a fine navigable river would be formed, communicating with the sea; and an inland navigation would be established through the most fertile part of the Kandyan provinces. I have now brought to a conclusion my account of this excursion, having nothing new to offer respecting either Koornagalle, or the country between it and Colombo.

PART III.

OBSERVATIONS ON THE EFFECTS OF THE CLIMATE AND ON THE DISEASES OF CEYLON.

IN this last part of my work I shall, as much as possible, studiously avoid professional disquisition, and confine myself chiefly to such views and observations as are likely to be useful to those who may visit Ceylon, or promise to be interesting to the philosophical reader.

The effects of a climate such as that of Ceylon on the constitution, may be conveniently considered under three different heads: 1. those which occur immediately; 2. those which are produced slowly and gradually; and, 3. those which arise occasionally and unexpectedly from the agency of peculiar causes.

In passing suddenly from a cold or temperate climate into a tropical one, the temperature of the body is raised one or two and sometimes even three degrees of Fahrenheit, above 98°, which may be considered as the standard of health in England; and a disagreeable sensation of heat is experienced, with acceleration of the heart's action, increased perspiration, languor, restlessness and thirst, diminished appetite, and slight general indisposition, which rarely amounts to actual illness.*

---

* In proof and illustration of the temperature of the body being raised from the transition stated in the text, I may mention the result of the observations which I made during my voyage to India in relation to this point.

In the month of February we set sail from England: on the 10th of March, when we were in latitude 9° 42′ N., the thermometer 78°, under an awning on deck, and we had begun to experience the disagreeable effect of a tropical climate, I tried the temperature of seven individuals, in good health, perspiring gently, about three hours after breakfast, and in a state of rest. A delicate thermometer placed under the tongue, as far back as possible, and the lips closed, rose in each instance as follows:

No. 1.	aged 24	years, to 99°
2.	28	99.5
3.	25	98.75
4.	17	99
5.	25	99
6.	20	98
7.	28	98.75

Again, on the 4th of April, in latitude 23° 44′ S., the thermometer 80°, after having been exposed to a tropical heat for nearly a month, I made some further trials of the temperature of the same individuals, and of some others. The temperature under the tongue of

No. 1.		was 99.5
2.		99.5
3.		99.75
4.		100
5.		99.5
6.		100
7.		99.5
8.	aged 25 years,	101
9.	40	99.75
10.	43	99

On landing in a tropical country, where the heat is generally greater than at sea, and the unavoidable causes of excitement are more numerous and active, the effects are more strongly marked and more troublesome, though still seldom so severe as to constitute actual disease and require medical treatment, unless aggravated by excess and acts of imprudence.

To counteract these primary effects of heat, especially on first landing, temperance, in the strictest and most general sense of the term, cannot be too strongly inculcated. Gentle aperient medicine may be advantageously used; all high excitement, all powerful stimuli, much exposure to the sun, violent exercise, should be carefully avoided: nor should the contrary extremes be shunned more industriously, were it only for the sake of escaping habits of indolency and effeminacy which too often insensibly creep on Europeans in India, and deprive them of their native strength,

---

No. 11. aged	40 years,	99.5
12.	13	100
15.	4	99.5

Lastly, on the 5th of May, in latitude 35° 22′ S., after having been three weeks between this latitude and that of 30°, and experienced damp aud cool weather, I repeated my observations on a few of the same gentlemen as before, now that the thermometer was at 60°, and we felt cool, almost cold. The temperature of

No. 1.	was	98.5
3.		98.25
5.		98
6.		98.75
7.		98.25
8.		98

It is hardly necessary to observe, that with this reduction of external and internal temperature, all the disagreeable effects enumerated in the text, disappeared.

energy both of body and mind. Wine and spirits, which the legislators of hot climates have wisely prohibited, should be used, if at all, very sparingly; and young men might abstain from them altogether with infinite advantage. Relative to diet and regimen, it is useless to lay down strict rules, which cannot be followed, and which, fortunately, are not required. Man is a hardy animal, and is suited by nature for a wide range of climate and circumstances, and is possessed of a constitution that, if not abused, is in most instances capable of bearing them with impunity. It is sufficient to remark that less animal food in general is required than in a cold climate; and, invariably, the simpler the diet, the better. Respecting dress and change of linen, and the use of the bath, and many other particulars which are insisted on by some writers, they are comparatively of so trivial a nature as hardly to require being mentioned. When the heat is at all oppressive, the dress of course must be of the lightest kind; the only part of the body that requires to be guarded in a particular manner, is the abdomen or belly, which is as much the prevailing seat of disease in a hot climate, as the chest is in a cold one. In consequence, a flannel roller, or one of coarse linen, or even of muslin, may be advantageously worn about the loins, wrapped round several times, moderately tight. Cleanliness and comfort cannot be indulged in without frequent changes of linen and the daily use of the bath; and there is little danger of either being abused, though some medical men have sounded an alarm respecting excess of clean linen, on the score of endangering health. Perhaps rubbing the skin with a wet rough towel is generally preferable to immersion in water; and if soap be used once in the day, and the body washed all over with it, and afterwards rubbed with a little sweet or scented oil, it may have a very salutary effect.

Judging from experience, in Ceylon, the diseases which are apt to occur, immediately on landing in a hot climate, the atmosphere of which is not vitiated with miasmata, are few in number. The prickly heat, (lichen tropicus,) which few are exempted from on their first arrival, though a very troublesome affection of the skin; is generally the companion of good health. The best mode of allaying its irritation, when severe, is by taking mild aperient medicine, abstaining from acidulated drinks, and using a light diet, from which such vegetables as are liable to become acid should be excluded. Fever is the most common disease, of any severity, to which the newly arrived are subject. It commonly arises from imprudent exposure to the sun, or from some act of intemperance. It is frequently quite ephemeral, and always of an inflammatory kind, that requires an active depleting treatment.

It is not easy to trace all the effects of the slow and gradual operation of a hot climate on the constitution. When the temperature of the air does not exceed 80°, the disagreeable sensation of heat first experienced, and many of the uneasy feelings connected with it, soon disappear. The temperature * of the body in

* In proof of this, I might adduce a number of observations on the temperature of man, made, not only in different parts of Ceylon, but likewise at the Cape of Good Hope, and at the Mauritius, on natives as well as on Europeans. As the general results are similar, it will be sufficient to give a very few of them. In the month of September, 1816, between six and seven o'clock in the morning, when the air was 79°, I found the temperature of six Singalese, in the neighbourhood of Colombo, as follows: —

Sex.		Age.		Temperature under the tongue.
Female	-	50 years	-	101°
Do.	-	4 —	-	101.5
Male	-	20 —	-	101
Do.	-	8 —	-	101.5
Do.	-	40 —	-	100
Do.	-	25 —	-	100

They were all in good health, and fasting.

general, and especially of the extremities, continues permanently high. The pulse, I believe, commonly does not increase in frequency, but rather diminishes, and, at the same time, becomes more full. The respiration, too, perhaps diminishes a little in frequency. The quantity of cuticular perspiration continues augmented. The urine appears to be secreted in rather less quantity, and to contain more urea, and less uric acid, and to be of higher specific gravity. The bowels become less active, and more disposed to constipation.

Connected with this state of the functions, as effects, perhaps with their causes, other changes are observable. The skin loses its fresh ruddy hue, and, if not tanned by exposure to the sun,

---

In the next month I made the following observations, under similar circumstances, on a number of boys and girls, in the orphan-school in the neighbourhood of Colombo: —

Sex.	Age.	Temperature under the tongue.	Temperature under the axilla.
	Half-Caste.		
Female	12 years	100.5	98.5
Do.	14 —	101	——
Do.	17 —	100	——
Male	14 —	102	100
Do.	10 —	101.5	99.5
Do.	14 —	100	99
Do.	10 —	100	99
	White.		
Female	9 —	101	99.5
Do.	6 —	101	98
Do.	9 —	101	98.5
Do.	12 —	102	100
Male	8 —	102	100

It has been asserted by Dr. Chalmers, in his History of South Carolina, that the temperature of man in a hot climate is rather lower than in a cold one. It is chiefly with a view to disprove this assertion, which for many years has been taken for granted as correct, and made, in more than one instance, the foundation of ingenious speculation, that I have thought it necessary to enter into any detail on the subject.

becomes exceedingly pale, or of a sickly yellowish tinge. Both body and mind seem to diminish in activity; there is less disposition to exercise either, and both become less fitted for action. It has been stated, and by high authority *, that irritability is increased in a hot climate, and frequently in a very high degree. The term is rather vague; but, in whatever sense taken, the experience which I had in Ceylon is not favourable to the accuracy of the remark. Instead of increased irritability, both nervous and muscular irritability appeared to me to be diminished in a hot climate; and that this is the fact in Ceylon seems to be confirmed by the rareness of spasmodic complaints. It is also said, and generally believed, that a hot climate disposes to voluptuousness. I very much doubt the correctness of the assertion. The behaviour of the natives does not shew it. If the propensity be felt by some Europeans in an increased degree, I would attribute it to collateral circumstances, — to idleness and facility of indulgence, rather than to the mere effect of climate.

The diseases which arise in consequence of the long-continued action of a hot climate, are most generally seated either in the skin, abdominal viscera, or the brain.

The only severe cutaneous affections to which Europeans are much subject in Ceylon, are boils; and another disease, which requires particular notice.

Few Europeans have been in the country long without suffering severely from the former. They seem, in general, to have a salutary operation, and to tend to prevent more formidable complaints. It is remarkable that erysipelatous inflammation of the skin is as rare as the phlegmenous is common.

* Nosographie Philosoph. tom iii. p. 159. edit. 6.

The other disease alluded to has not, that I am aware of, been described by authors. Its seat is the cutis, or true skin. It consists in a peculiarly inflamed state of the texture, indicated by redness, slight swelling, and severe itching, and, in most instances, by a serous discharge. Desquamation of the cuticle constantly attends it, and is the more abundant according to the severity of the disease. Neither pustules, papulæ, nor any other form of eruption, appears to be essential to it, though it is sometimes accompanied with minute irritable pimples, and sometimes, but still more rarely, with minute pustules, which give rise to small superficial ulcers, which in general heal readily, if not neglected. In its character, this disease most resembles the prurigo senilis of Dr. Willan. It differs, however, in many particulars, and in one point essentially,—in most frequently attacking men in the vigour of life. The diseased action commonly begins between the toes, and in the soles of the feet, and the palms of the hands. It often spreads from one part to another. Whilst it spreads from old parts to new, the former frequently heal, or become less severely affected. From the feet, the most common seat of the disease, it has occasionally extended to the legs, and even to the thighs. The exciting causes of it are obscure: the individuals attacked can in general assign no reason for it. It appears to be intimately connected with the high temperature of the extremities, and to be quite independent of mechanical irritation, or derangement of the general health. I believe it has a tendency to wear itself out: I have heard of instances of its healing spontaneously, after a duration of a considerable time, often amounting to many months. Exercise has a considerable effect on it; and, contrary to what might be expected, a very beneficial effect: indeed, in most instances, severe exercise on foot, I believe, would be sufficient to cure the disease. In accordance with this fact, rest, and a horizontal posture, aggravate the complaint. The mode of treating the disease is still but imperfectly understood: a great variety of local applications that I tried seemed to have little or no effect. The itching, which is often intense, and always the most troublesome symptom, is more allayed by covering the parts affected with simple dressing, after washing in lukewarm water, than by any other plan I am acquainted with. I believe, the cure of the complaint can be accomplished only by the use of internal medicine. Calomel, as an alterative, is deserving of a fair trial: in one instance, a grain of it given daily speedily removed the complaint; and, in another instance, it afforded considerable relief, though it did not accomplish a cure.

The natives are much more disposed to cutaneous diseases than Europeans residing in the island. The Cochin leg, or elephas, is not uncommon amongst them: it seems to be confined chiefly to the south-west shore of Ceylon, between Negombo and Matura, where the temperature, throughout the year, is uniformly high, and the air, the greater part of the year, loaded with moisture. Both species of elephantiasis, so well described by Mr. Robinson, in the 10th volume of the Medico-Chirurgical Transactions, are far from rare, especially in the same district in which elephas occurs. Having paid considerable attention to these diseases at the Lepur-Hospital, in the neighbourhood of Colombo, humanely established by Government as an asylum for the wretched beings afflicted with these cruel maladies, I can bear witness to the accuracy with which this gentleman's descriptions are given. In a very few instances,

I have seen the two kinds of elephantiasis, viz. "the leprosy of the joints," and the tuberculated species, combined.* For very valuable observations respecting the treatment of these two

* I may mention one case in particular of this combination, as I had an opportunity, on its fatal termination, of examining the diseased appearances. The individual affected was a Singalese, sixty years old. The disease had been increasing on him fourteen years when I first saw him, in September 1816. The symptoms were then nearly as follows: — The face and ears were puffy, and deformed with tubercles; and the latter, as well as the alæ nasi and lips, were enlarged. The eyebrows were without hair; the skin of most parts of the body was thickened and tuberculated; both feet were much swollen, and in many places ulcerated; the outer surface of the left foot was covered with a foul ulcer; the fingers and toes were greatly disfigured, and several joints of the former were wanting, having dropped off in the course of the disease. The glands of the groin were only very slightly enlarged. He was in a very debilitated state, and his general health was deranged greatly. On the 26th of November, when I saw him again, he was moribund. The surface of the body was fissured and excoriated in a hundred different places. The excoriated patches were slightly red, and merely moist. The left foot was in a state of gangrene. He expired the day following. I examined the body about twelve hours after death: the heart was rather small and flaccid, and its parieties were thin; a thick layer of fat covered its outer surface. The liver was larger than usual; of a pale colour, and marked with white spots. Near the lobulus quadratus an appearance was noticed, as it were, of an old cicatrix. The gall-bladder was distended with greenish bile. Much fat was accumulated about the mesentery. A few red spots appeared on the mucous membrane of the intestines. A section of the slightly enlarged glands of the groin exhibited no decidedly-marked diseased structure. The tuberculated parts of the skin were thickened, and each tubercle seemed to be produced chiefly by a thickening of the cutis. The integuments of the lower extremities, and especially of the knees, legs, and feet, were generally thickened; in most places, the true skin was not less than a quarter of an inch thick. Under the thickened skin, a thick layer of fat presented itself, which was also diffused through the cellular membrane, between the muscles. Most of the muscles of the legs appeared to be converted into a species of adipose matter, so that very little muscular fibre remained. At both knee-joints, the capsular membranes and bursæ were distended with an oily or fatty matter, which was yellow, semi-fluid, and granular, and, in appearance, very like honey. No serous effusion was observed in any part of the body.

diseases, I must refer the medical reader to Mr. Robinson's paper. It is ardently to be hoped, that farther experience will confirm the very favourable account which he has given of the curative power of the bark of the root of the asclepia gigantea in elephantiasis tuberculata, and that some more effectual remedy than arsenic may be discovered for elephantiasis anaisthetos. Besides these formidable diseases, the natives are liable to a great variety of other complaints of the skin; so much so, indeed, that there is hardly a species in Dr. Bateman's Synopsis, of which I have not seen an instance amongst them.

The abdominal viscera most subject to disease in Ceylon, are the large intestines and the liver. I mention the former first, because they are much more frequently affected than the latter; though, according to popular opinion, the liver is the grand seat of Indian maladies.

Acute inflammation of the intestines is not of common occurrence; diarrhœa and dysentery are infinitely more frequent. There is a species of the former, not unusual, in which the dejections are white; the debility and emaciation of the body considerable, accompanied with a state of feverishness. In these cases, in which the liver, probably, is affected, as well as the large intestines, I have seen very great advantage derived from the use of the blue-pill combined with opium, and a cure speedily effected, when other medicines, as tonics, astringents, &c. have done harm. The dysentery of Ceylon is a terrible disease, from the severity of its symptoms, the rapidity with which it runs its course, the difficulty of checking it, and its frequently fatal termination. Even at its very commencement, it appears to be attended with ulceration; and in most instances, before death, the whole tract of the large intestines is more or less covered with ulcers. I cannot here enter into details of this formidable complaint. In the Interior, during the period of the late rebellion, when it prevailed greatly, it in general proved fatal to about one in four of those whom it attacked. It is greatly to be regretted, that the mode of treatment of this disease is still far from settled. The treatment which appeared to me most successful,—certainly that by which I accomplished most cures,—consisted in the use of opium immediately, in large and frequently repeated doses,—as a grain every hour through the twenty-four. It often acted in the most favourable manner, relieving the symptoms, and restoring health, without producing any of its narcotic effects; and the experience of two or three of my medical friends, who at my suggestion tried it in large doses, was confirmatory of mine. I was led to make trial of this practice, from the high manner in which it is recommended in a valuable article on dysentery in "Le Dictionnaire Medical." Of the effect of blood-letting in the dysentery of Ceylon, I am in great doubt. Judging from the experience which we had of it in Kandy, I would say, it does harm rather than good, exhausting strength without arresting the inflammatory and ulcerative process. But others have reported favourably upon it, and even highly; and have trusted to it chiefly for the cure of the disease. I can only account for this difference of result, on the supposition that the dysentery of the Interior, in which venæsection seemed to have had a bad effect, is somewhat different in its character from the dysentery of Trincomalie and Colombo, where the lancet is said to have been used advantageously. Calomel, in large doses, has been strongly recommended in the dysentery of India. From numerous dissections, I infer, that the disease is not commonly and essentially, but only rarely and accidentally, complicated with disease of the liver. But, laying aside all theoretical views, I may briefly state, that in a few instances, in which I have seen calomel administered in large doses, it appeared to aggravate the complaint. The causes of dysentery in Ceylon are exceedingly obscure: perhaps they belong rather to those which act only occasionally than constantly, and consist in some condition of the atmosphere, of the exact nature of which we are at present ignorant. It has been asserted, that Indians are exempted from this complaint; which is far from correct. It would be more correct to state, that they are less liable to it than Europeans. M. Penel, who has admitted the assertion, attempts to account for the imaginary exemption, by referring it to the use of betel, so general amongst Indians.* Were it a fact, it could hardly be accounted for in this way. Did the natives swallow their saliva in the act of chewing betel, then it might have some effect on their intestines; but this is rarely done: indeed, I believe, never, excepting by the indigent and hungry, when they have no other means of allaying a craving appetite, which it is said to do in a remarkable manner. The fact, that Indians are even less liable to dysentery, I would not attribute to any one cause alone, but to several circumstances, most of which Europeans in India would do well to keep in mind:—as their habits of temperance; abstinence from intoxicating liquors; the use of a large proportion of farinaceous food, highly seasoned with red pepper; their dress, so well adapted to keep the abdomen warm; and their custom of avoiding the night-air. By way of prevention, wearing a flannel or calico bandage or band about the loins; washing

* Nosographie Philosoph. tom. ii. p. 321.

the surface with a rough towel, with soap and water, daily, and carefully avoiding constipation, by attention to diet, rather than by the use of medicine, cannot be too highly recommended.

Disease of the liver is not so common in Ceylon as is generally imagined. Other complaints of the abdominal viscera, especially of the larger intestines, are often mistaken for it, the diagnosis being exceedingly difficult. * Abscess of the liver and chronic inflammation are of more frequent occurrence than acute inflammation. Though a high temperature does dispose to hepatic derangement, I suspect, in most instances it would have little effect, were it not aided by intemperance and inactivity, and especially by the abuse of ardent spirits. In confirmation of the effect of ardent spirits, it may be remarked, that amongst our troops in Ceylon no class of men suffer so much from this disease as artificers, who, being much better paid, and having more liberty than soldiers in general, invariably indulge in drinking. The majority of them, sooner or later, are carried off by abscess or inflammation of the liver. Confirmatory of the good effects of exercise in preventing this disease, it is worthy of notice, that during the rebellion, when our troops were actively employed in the field, and making extraordinary exertions, other diseases increased in frequency and fatality in a very high degree, whilst abscess and inflammation of the liver actually diminished. This important fact was established in the most satisfactory manner by the result of dissections.

Dyspepsia is not an uncommon complaint in Ceylon, particularly amongst Europeans who indulge in the luxuries of the table.

* In forming the diagnosis, the composition of the urine is of comparatively little assistance. In several instances in which abscess of the liver was discovered after death, there was no deficiency of urea in the urine.

It is seldom connected with organic disease of the stomach, and is best remedied by attention to diet and exercise.

Diseases of the urinary organs appear in general to be much more rare in a hot climate than in a temperate one. During the whole time I was at Ceylon, I met with three cases only of gravel, and these were in English officers. The complaint was connected with dyspepsia, and in two instances the gravel was the ammoniaco-magnesian phosphat. Diabetes mellitus is not very uncommon amongst the natives, who, from time immemorial, have been acquainted with the disease, and with the peculiar property of the urine characteristic of it. Perhaps its origin is connected with the circumstance of their food being chiefly vegetable.

Though I believe that spasmodic, and what are commonly called nervous complaints, are less prevalent in Ceylon than in a cool climate, I am disposed to think that the brain is more liable to disease in the former than in the latter. Cases of tetanus, of corea, and hysteria, are very rare; but those of palsy are pretty numerous amongst the natives, and instances of insanity both amongst them and Europeans residing in the island, are of frequent occurrence. The latter disease most frequently appears amongst Europeans of the higher ranks in society, who either lead debauched lives or sedentary ones, engaged in business or pursuits that require considerable application and mental exertion.

Diseases of the lungs are exceedingly uncommon in Ceylon, both amongst Europeans and natives. Asthma and pneumonia now and then occur; consumption rarely appears, excepting amongst the descendants of the Dutch or Portuguese, who, in very many instances, have weak frames and ill-formed chests, and appear to be particularly liable to this disease. As they are generally attended by their own medical men, and never permit a body to be examined, I have no correct information to offer respecting the complaint; nor can I venture to attempt to determine its exact species.

Colds and sore-throats, of the mildest kind, are far from unfrequent, particularly in the hot damp atmosphere of the south-west part of the island.

Gout is entirely unknown to the natives, and I have not heard of any European acquiring the disease in Ceylon. Rheumatism, on the contrary, of a sub-acute kind, is not uncommon, and it attacks equally natives and Europeans. Its cause is pretty obviously the partial exposure of the body, when heated, to currents of cool air, which it is very difficult to avoid in rooms, the doors and windows of which are seldom closed.

It is a striking feature of the medical history of Ceylon, in common with that of India in general, that its climate does not breed or tolerate any infectious fever. Typhus and the plague are both equally unknown to the eastward of the Indus.

Unfortunately, that river does not present the same barrier to the two most formidable of the exanthemata, viz. small-pox and measles, the former of which, when it appears, is exceedingly destructive. For several years, Ceylon seemed to have been effectually guarded from small-pox by vaccination. Last year it again intruded itself, imported from the coast; it raged with violence little less than formerly, and proved very fatal both to those who were and those who were not vaccinated, but more especially to the latter.* Measles, in general, is a mild

* This result does not invalidate the preventive effect of Vacciola. From the manner in which vaccination was performed amongst the Singalese usually by native vaccinators, there is reason to believe that in very many instances it did not take effect.

disease in Ceylon, and rarely proves fatal. The same circumstances of temperature and climate which aggravate small-pox, and render it confluent and so destructive, appears on this disease to have an opposite effect, as might be expected: on a similar account, perhaps, whooping-cough, which now and then occurs, is commonly much less severe than in a colder climate. According to the best information I could collect, scarlatina has never made its appearance in Ceylon.

The third and last division of the effects of climate which I have to mention, are certain diseases, few in number, but formidable in kind, which burst out suddenly without warning, commit their ravages for a season, and vanish often in the same sudden and unaccountable manner as that in which they first appeared. The endemic fever of the country, in its different modifications, cholera-morbus and beri-beria, are the diseases of this description to which Ceylon has been more or less subject.

Intermittent and remittent fever are commonly, and there is reason to believe, justly, considered as varieties only of the same disease. The former most frequently attacks the natives; the latter, Europeans. It is worthy of remark, that though remittent fever rarely terminates in ague, in case of relapse ague mostly succeeds it; so that it is not usual for the same individual to experience two attacks of the disease, excepting after an interval of several years. It is astonishing how both the intermittent and remittent fever is modified and diversified by circumstances: the fever of almost every year, and season, and place, has something peculiar to mark it; in the endemic of one place or season there may be a strong tendency to delirium; in that of another to intermission and relapse, and disease of the spleen; in that of a third, to change of disease from fever to dysentery. As the diseases vary in different instances, so must the mode of treatment required vary; and till the peculiarities of the endemic are ascertained, the medical practitioner cannot prescribe with too much caution. Generally, I saw great advantage derived from blood-letting in remittent fever; and the beneficial effect of a large dose of opium combined with aperient medicine *immediately* after blood-letting, was often very remarkable. To venæsection, purgatives, opium *, and in the convalescent stage to bark, I trusted chiefly for the cure of the disease. The remedies which appeared to me most effectual in the cure of intermittent fever were aperients, opium, blue-pill, and bark, either given separately or in combination, according to circumstances. Arsenic may be sometimes used with advantage, when there is not a tendency to visceral disease, particularly to dysentery. In a former part of the work, I have offered the general results of my experience relative to the cause of endemic fever, than which nothing scarcely can be more obscure and mysterious. To escape the disease, the best advice that can be given is to quit for a season the place where it is prevailing; or, if this be not practicable, the next best plan is to take all possible care of the general health, attend to the state of the bowels, be exposed as little as possible to the wind, and avoid the night-air.

The spasmodic cholera morbus of India, which commenced nearly four years ago, and, according to the latest accounts, has

* The use of opium in remittent fever may startle some practitioners: I shall not speculate on the subject, but merely remark that in many instances I have observed the very best effects from it, and in no one instance any evil consequence.

not yet terminated, which has spread over a great part of that extensive continent, and visited Ceylon, and even the Isle of France, is a still more remarkable instance of disease arising from some peculiar and mysterious cause, of the nature of which we are at present completely ignorant. It has been supposed by some to be contagious. In Ceylon I am not aware of the occurrence of any facts in favour of this opinion. At one time, the disease broke out in several parts of the island, very remote from each other; it did not spread regularly and progressively, like a contagious disease, nor am I acquainted with a single instance of a medical officer or attendant on the sick contracting it. For a good deal of curious and useful information on this extraordinary and fatal epidemic, I beg leave to refer the medical reader to Sir Gilbert Blane's valuable paper on the subject, published in the eleventh volume of the Transactions of the Medico-chirurgical Society of London.

Beri-beria, a disease almost peculiar to Ceylon, has been supposed to be owing to ordinary causes, as a moist atmosphere, great vicissitudes of temperature, bad food, intemperance, &c. But I am more disposed to refer it, like remittent fever and the cholera morbus, to some unusual state or condition of the atmosphere; or, to be more correct, to confess ignorance of its exciting cause. I am forced into this conclusion, because the disease is of occasional occurrence only, and does not uniformly present itself with the circumstances to which it has been attributed. During the period of the late rebellion, the circumstances in question were of the most favourable kind for its production; and yet not a single case of it, that I am aware of, appeared; nor did I see a single instance of it during the whole of the time I was in Ceylon. A pretty good account will be found of this disease, as it occurred in 1803, in the Inaugural Dissertation of Dr. C. Rogers, printed at Edinburgh, in 1808. *

* The nosological name which he gives it is *hydrops asthmaticus*. He thus describes it: — "Debilitate prægressâ, dyspnœa, torpore, paralysi extremitatum stipata, œdemate, signis hydropis aliis eodem tempore instantibus, cursumque suum sæpius celerrime absolventibus; sæpius etiam anxietate, cordis palpitatione, vomitu, spasmisque sese comites præbentibus." He states that, in the fatal cases examined, more or less serum was found effused in all the cavities, and in the pericardium in particular. The treatment that he recommends, as most successful, was founded on the indications of producing absorption by diuretic medicine, as calomel and squills; of allaying spasm, by the external use of opium; and of gently stimulating and invigorating the system by gin-punch, and a nourishing diet.

APPENDIX.

No. I.

OFFICIAL BULLETIN.

British Head-Quarters, Kandy.
2d March, 1815.

THIS day a solemn conference was held in the Audience Hall of the Palace of Kandy, between His Excellency the Governor and Commander of the Forces, on behalf of His Majesty and of His Royal Highness the Prince Regent, on the one part, and the Adikars, Dessaves, and other principal chiefs of the Kandyan provinces, on the other part, on behalf of the people, and in presence of the Mohottales, Coraals, Vidaans, and other subordinate headmen from the different provinces, and a great concourse of inhabitants.

A public instrument of treaty, prepared in conformity to conditions previously agreed on, for establishing His Majesty's government in the Kandyan provinces, was produced and publicly read in English and Cingalese, and unanimously assented to.

The British flag was then for the first time hoisted, and the establishment of the British dominion in the Interior was announced by a royal salute from the cannon of the city.

All the troops present in this garrison were under arms on the occasion of this important event.

By His Excellency's command.
(Signed) JAS. SUTHERLAND,
Deputy Secretary.

OFFICIAL DECLARATION OF THE SETTLEMENT OF THE KANDYAN PROVINCES.

LED by the invitation of the chiefs, and welcomed by the acclamations of the people, the forces of His Britannic Majesty have entered the Kandyan territory, and penetrated to the capital: Divine Providence has blessed their efforts with uniform and complete success. The ruler of the interior provinces has fallen into their hands, and the government remains at the disposal of His Majesty's representative.

In this sacred charge it is his earnest prayer, that the Power which has vouchsafed thus far to favour the undertaking, may guide his councils to a happy issue in the welfare and prosperity of the people, and the honour of the British empire.

Under circumstances far different from any which exist in the present case, it would be a duty, and a pleasing one, to favour the re-establishment of a fallen prince. if his dominion could be fixed on any principles of external relation compatible with the rights of the neighbouring Government, or his internal rule in any reasonable degree reconciled to the safety of his subjects.

But the horrible transactions of the fatal year 1803, forced upon the recollection by many local circumstances, and by details unknown before, — the massacre of one hundred and fifty sick soldiers lying helpless in the hospital of Kandy, left under the pledge of public faith, and the no less treacherous murder of the whole British garrison commanded by Major Davie, which had surrendered on a promise of safety, — impress upon the Governor's mind an act of perfidy unparalleled in civilized warfare, and an awful lesson, recorded in characters of blood, against the momentary admission of future confidence; while the obstinate rejection of all friendly overtures, repeatedly made during the intermission of hostilities, has served to evince an implacable animosity, destructive of the hope of a sincere reconciliation.

Of this animosity a daring instance was exhibited in the unprovoked and barbarous mutilation of ten innocent subjects of the British Government, by which seven of the number lost their lives; a measure of defiance, calculated, and apparently intended, to put a final negative to every probability of friendly intercourse.

If, therefore, in the present reverse of his fortunes and condition, it may be presumed the king would be found more accessible to negotiation than in former times, what value could be set on a consent at variance with the known principles of his reign? or what dependence placed on his observance of conditions which he has hitherto so perseveringly repelled?

Still less could the hope for a moment be entertained, that any conditions of safety were capable of being established on behalf of the inhabitants who had appealed to His Majesty's Government for protection; and yet more hopeless the attempt to obtain pardon or safeguard for the chiefs who had deemed it a duty, paramount to every other obligation, to become the medium of that appeal.

How far their complaints have been groundless, and their opposition licentious, or, on the contrary, their grievances bitterly and intolerably real, may now be judged by facts of unquestionable authenticity.

The wanton destruction of human life comprises or implies the existence of general oppression: in conjunction with that, no other proofs of the exercise of tyranny require to be specified; and one single instance, of no distant date, will be acknowledged to include every thing which is barbarous and unprincipled in public rule, and to pourtray the last stage of individual depravity and wickedness, the obliteration of every trace of conscience, and the complete extinction of human feeling.

In the deplorable fate of the wife and children of Eheylapola Adikar, these assertions are fully substantiated; in which was exhibited the savage scene of four infant children, the youngest torn from the mother's breast, cruelly butchered, and their heads bruised in a mortar by the hands of their parent, succeeded by the execution of the woman herself, and three females more; whose limbs being bound, and a heavy stone tied round the neck of each, they were thrown into a lake and drowned.

It is not, however, that, under an absolute government, unproved suspicion must usurp the place of fair trial, and the fiat of the ruler stand instead of the decision of justice; it is not that a rash, violent, or unjust decree, or a revolting mode of execution, is here brought to view; nor the innocent suffering under the groundless imputation of guilt: but a bold contempt of every principle of justice; setting at nought all known grounds of punishment; dispensing with the necessity of accusation; and choosing for its victims, helpless females uncharged with any offence, and infants incapable of a crime.

Contemplating these atrocities, the impossibility of establishing with such a man any civilized relations, either of peace or war, ceases to be a subject of regret; since His Majesty's arms, hitherto employed in the generous purpose of relieving the oppressed, would be tarnished and disgraced by being instrumental to the restoration of a dominion, exercised in a perpetual outrage to every thing which is sacred in the constitution or functions of a legitimate government.

On these grounds, His Excellency the Governor has acceded to the wishes of the chiefs and people of the Kandyan provinces; and a convention has in consequence been held, the result of which the following public act is destined to record and proclaim.

Proclamation.

At a convention held on the 2d day of March, in the year of Christ 1815, and the Cingalese year 1736, at the palace in the city of Kandy, between His Excellency Lieutenant-general Robert Brownrigg, Governor and Commander-in-Chief in and over the British Settlements and Territories in the Island of Ceylon, acting in the name and on behalf of His Majesty

George the Third, King, and His Royal Highness George Prince of Wales, Regent of the United Kingdom of Great Britain and Ireland, on the one part; and the Adigars, Dessaves, and other principal chiefs of the Kandyan provinces, on behalf of the inhabitants, and in presence of the Mohottales, Coraals, Vidaans, and other subordinate headmen from the several provinces, and of the people then and there assembled, on the other part; it is agreed and established as follows:

1. That the cruelties and oppressions of the Malabar ruler, in the arbitrary and unjust infliction of bodily tortures and the pains of death without trial, and sometimes without an accusation or the possibility of a crime, and in the general contempt and contravention of all civil rights, have become flagrant, enormous, and intolerable; the acts and maxims of his government being equally and entirely devoid of that justice which should secure the safety of his subjects, and of that good faith which might obtain a beneficial intercourse with the neighbouring settlements.

2. That the Rajah Sri Wikreme Rajah Sinha, by the habitual violation of the chief and most sacred duties of a sovereign, has forfeited all claims to that title, or the powers annexed to the same; and is declared fallen and deposed from the office of king; his family and relatives, whether in the ascending, descending, or collateral line, and whether by affinity or blood, are also for ever excluded from the throne; and all claim or title of the Malabar race to the dominion of the Kandyan provinces is abolished and extinguished.

3. That all male persons, being or pretending to be relations of the late Rajah Sri Wikreme Rajah Sinha, either by affinity or blood, and whether in the ascending, descending, or collateral line, are hereby declared enemies to the Government of the Kandyan provinces, and excluded and prohibited from entering those provinces on any pretence whatever, without a written permission for that purpose by the authority of the British Government, under the pains and penalties of martial law, which is hereby declared to be in force for that purpose; and all male persons of the Malabar caste, now expelled from the said provinces, are, under the same penalties, prohibited from returning, except with the permission beforementioned.

4. The dominion of the Kandyan provinces is vested in the Sovereign of the British Empire, and to be exercised through the governors or lieutenant-governors of Ceylon for the time being, and their accredited agents; saving to the Adigars, Dessaves, Mohottales, Coraals, Vidaans, and all other chief and subordinate native headmen lawfully appointed by authority of the British Government, the rights, privileges, and powers of their respective offices; and to all classes of the people the safety of their persons and property, with their civil rights and immunities, according to the laws, institutions, and customs established and in force amongst them.

5. The religion of Budhoo, professed by the chiefs and inhabitants of these pro-

vinces, is declared inviolable, and its rights, ministers, and places of worship are to be maintained and protected.

6. Every specics of bodily torture, and all mutilation of limb, member, or organ, are prohibited and abolished.

7. No sentence of death can be carried into execution against any inhabitant, except by the written warrant of the British Governor or Lieutenant-governor for the time being, founded on a report of the case made to him through the accredited agent or agents of the Government resident in the Interior, in whose presence all trials for capital offences are to take place.

8. Subject to these conditions, the administration of civil and criminal justice and police over the Kandyan inhabitants of the said provinces, is to be exercised according to established forms, and by the ordinary authorities; saving always the inherent right of Government to redress grievances and reform abuses in all instances whatever, particular or general, where such interposition shall become necessary.

9. Over all other persons, civil or military, residing in or resorting to these provinces, not being Kandyans, civil and criminal justice, together with police, shall, until the pleasure of His Majesty's Government in England may be otherwise declared, be administered in manner following:

First, All persons, not being commissioned or non-commissioned military officers, soldiers, or followers of the army, usually held liable to military discipline, shall be subject to the magistracy of the accredited agent or agents of the British Government in all cases, except charges of murder, which shall be tried by special commissions to be issued from time to time by the Governor for that purpose: provided always, as to such charges of murder wherein any British subject may be defendant, who might be tried for the same by the laws of the United Kingdom of Great Britain and Ireland, in force for the trial of offences committed by British subjects in foreign parts, no such British subject shall be tried on any charge of murder alleged to have been perpetrated in the Kandyan provinces, otherwise than by virtue of such laws of the United Kingdom.

Secondly, Commissioned or non-commissioned military officers, soldiers, or followers of the army, usually held amenable to military discipline, shall, in all civil and criminal cases wherein they be defendants, be liable to the laws, regulations, and customs of war; reserving to the Governor and Commander-in-chief, in all cases falling under this ninth article, an unlimited right of review over every proceeding, civil or military, had by virtue thereof; and reserving also full power to make such particular provisions, conformably to the general spirit of the said article, as may be found necessary to carry its principle into full effect.

10. Provided always, that the operation of the several preceding clauses shall not be contravened by the provisions of any temporary or partial proclamation published during the advance of the army; which provisions, in so far as incompatible with the said preceding articles, are hereby repealed.

11. The royal dues and revenues of the Kandyan provinces are to be managed and collected for His Majesty's use, and the support of the provincial establishment, according to lawful custom, and under the direction and superintendence of the accredited agent or agents of the British Government.

12. His Excellency the Governor will adopt provisionally, and recommend to the confirmation of His Royal Highness the Prince Regent, in the name and on behalf of His Majesty, such dispositions in favour of the trade of these provinces as may facilitate the export of their products and improve the returns, whether in money or in salt, cloths, or other commodities useful and desirable to the inhabitants of the Kandyan country.

God save the King.

By His Excellency's command.
(Signed) JAS. SUTHERLAND,
Deputy Secretary.

In addition to the official document which we have this day to make public, from the head-quarters in Kandy, we persuade ourselves that a few further particulars, with which we have been favoured from good authority, will not be unacceptable to our readers.

We shall present the communication in its own words.

"The political and civil arrangements consequent on the great change which has been effected here, were interrupted for eight days by the absence of Mr. D'Oyley, in attendance on the king, during which period no conference of any moment took place. On his return the communications with the chiefs were renewed, and yesterday was at length appointed for a convention of the contracting parties.

"Of the treaty you will be enabled to judge, as it will be published. It comprises, though in a very summary way, the heads of a constitution carefully adapted to the wishes of the chiefs and people, and with a more particular degree of attention to some prejudices, the indulgence of which was plainly understood to be a *sine quâ non* of their voluntary submission to an European Power.

"The preservation of the religion of Boodho was the first; the other (hardly inferior in their estimation) was the recognition and continuance of their local institutions. I say nothing of their laws, because I should find it hard to point out what they are. Customs, however, they have, and established gradations of authority, and even known forms of justice; though the latter, for a long period, have been out of use. A general re-establishment of all these is the basis of the civil and judicial articles of the treaty.

"Early in the afternoon preparations were made for holding the conference in the great Hall of Audience in the palace; but the Governor declined using the adjoining room, where the king usually sat on occasions of ceremony, and chose to be placed within the hall, at the upper end, with his back to the door of that room, which was divided off by a screen.

" The troops composing the garrison of Kandy, with the corps of Ceylon Light Dragoons, and the addition of Major Kelly's division, now here on its march to Colombo, returning to Point de Galle, were drawn up at three o'clock in the great square before the palace, where they remained while the Adigars and principal chiefs passed, and a part formed a lane to the door of the hall.

" Eheylepola, late Adigar, who has declined official employ, preferring to remain in retirement, and soliciting only the title of *The Friend of the British Government*, entered first and alone. He was received with particular marks of favour and kindness by His Excellency, and seated in a chair on his right hand.

" Molligodde, acting on the occasion as First Adigar, then came forward, leading in the Dessaves of provinces and other principal chiefs, about twenty in number. The Governor rose up to receive them, and (with Eheylepola) continued standing throughout the conference.

" A scene no less novel than interesting was here presented in the state and costume of the Kandyan court, with an English Governor presiding, and the hall lined on both sides with British officers.

" The conference began with complimentary enquiries on the part of the chiefs, which were graciously answered by the Governor, and mutual enquiries made. His Excellency then thanked the Dessaves for the attention shown to the troops in their various routes through the country towards the capital; which gave occasion to the chiefs to observe, that they considered them as protectors, and that, by the arrival of His Excellency and the army, they had been rescued from tyranny and oppression.

" The Governor observed, he was gratified in having been the means of their deliverance: he assured them of full protection in their persons, their property, and all their rights; and added, that while he had the honour of holding the administration in the island, it would be his study to make them experience the blessings of His Majesty's benign government.

" It was then intimated to the chiefs, that a paper had been prepared, expressive of the principles on which the participation of His Majesty's government was offered to their acceptance, and that it was about to be read, which they requested might be done.

" The treaty was then read in English by Mr. Sutherland, deputy secretary to Government, and afterwards in Cingalese by the Modeliar of His Excellency's gate, Abraham De Saram. This important document was listened to with profound and respectful attention by the chiefs; and it was pleasing to observe in their looks a marked expression of cordial assent, which was immediately declared with great earnestness.

" His Excellency's part of the conference was communicated to Mr. D'Oyley, and by him to Molligodde Adigar, who declared it aloud to the audience. A chief of venerable and commanding aspect was the organ of the assembly, whose person and countenance were equally striking. His figure, the tallest present, was erect and portly; a high and prominent forehead, a full eye, and a strong expression of natural vivacity, tempered with the gravity of advanced age, marked by a long, full, and graceful white beard; and the whole, combined with his rich state dress, formed a subject for a portrait truly worthy of an able hand. His name was Millaawa, Dessave of Godapola. He was a great favourite of the king, and remained with him till a late period. This chief collected the sentiments of the assembly generally in silence, but with occasional explanations, and delivered them to the Adigar with the concurrence of the rest.

" Eheylepola, though not ostensibly engaged in the conference, took a marked interest in every part of it. His carriage was distinguished by a courtly address, politeness, and ease; and he was evidently regarded by the assembled chiefs with a high degree of deference and respect.

" After the treaty was read in Cingalese, the Adigar Molligodde, and the other chiefs, proceeded to the great door of the hall, where the Mohottales, Coraals, Vidaans, and other subordinate headmen from the different provinces, were attending, with a great concourse of the inhabitants; and the headmen being called on by the Adigar to range themselves in order according to their respective districts, the treaty was again read by the Modeliar in Cingalese; at the conclusion of which the British flag was hoisted for the first time, and a royal salute from the cannon of the city announced His Majesty George the Third Sovereign of the whole island of Ceylon."

Dated Kandy, 3d March, 1815."

No. II.

PROCLAMATION.

By His Excellency Lieutenant-general Sir Robert Brownrigg, Baronet, and Knight Grand Cross of the Most Honourable Military Order of the Bath; Governor and Commander-in-Chief in and over the British Settlements and Territories in the Island of Ceylon, with the Dependencies thereof.

ROBERT BROWNRIGG.

Preamble. Recital of cession of Kandyan provinces to Great Britain.

1. The chiefs and people of the Kandyan nation, no longer able to endure the cruelties and oppressions which the late king, Sri Wikreme Rajah Singha, tyrannically practised towards them, prayed the assistance of the British Government for their relief, and by a solemn act declared the late king deposed, and himself and all persons descending from, or in any manner related to his family, incapable of claiming or exercising royal authority within the Kandyan provinces; which were by the same solemn act ceded to the dominion of the British Sovereign.

Moderate exercise of power by the British Government.

2. The exercise of power by the representatives of His Britannic Majesty, from the date of that convention (the 2d March, 1815) till the hour that insurrection broke out, in the month of October, 1817, was marked with the greatest mildness and forbearance towards all classes; the strictest attention to the protection and maintenance of the rites, ministers, and places of worship of the religion of Budhoo; and a general deference to the opinions of the chiefs, who were considered as the persons best able, from their rank and knowledge, to aid the Government in ensuring the happiness of the mass of its new subjects. In exacting either taxes or services for the state, an extraordinary and unprecedented laxity was allowed to take place, in order that the country might with more ease recover from any evil effects sustained by the contrary

practice of the late king. In assessing punishments for offences, even where a plot to subvert the government was proved, the spirit which always characterises the British rule was strongly to be contrasted with the ancient and frequent recurrence of capital executions, preceded by the most cruel and barbarous tortures.

Flourishing state of the country.

3. Under this mild administration on the part of the British Government, the country appeared to rest in peace: cultivation was increased, and Divine Providence blessed the exertions of the labourers, and rewarded them by plenteous crops; yet all this time there were factious and intriguing spirits at work, seeking for an opportunity to subvert the government, for no purpose but to assume to themselves absolute power over the lives and properties of the general mass of subjects, which, by the equal justice of British authority, were protected from their avarice or malicious cruelty.

Notwithstanding these benefits, plots have been formed against the state. Motives of the factious.

Time and manner of executing the plot.

4. These plotters against the state were found among the very persons who had been restored to honours and security by the sole intervention of British power; and the opportunity of raising disturbance was chosen when, relying on the merited gratitude of all orders of the Kandyan nation, the Government had diminished the number of troops; and the insurgent leaders, unconscious or forgetful of the extensive resources of the British empire, thought, in setting up the standard of rebellion, as easily to effect their purpose of expelling the English from the country, as the people had been deluded to prostrate before the phantom, whose pretensions they espoused merely to cover their own ambitious views of subjecting the nation to their arbitrary will.

Manifestation of the power of the British Government.

5. After more than a year of conflict, which has created misery and brought destruction on many, the efforts of the British Government, and the bravery of His Majesty's troops, have made manifest to the Kandyans the folly of resistance, and that in the Government alone resides the power of protecting them in the enjoyment of happiness. The flimsy veil which the rebel chiefs threw over their ambitious designs was torn aside by themselves, and the pageant whom the people were called to recognise as the descendant of the gods, exposed as the offspring of a poor Cingalese empyric.

Detection of the imposition practised in the person of the Pretender.

Reasonable to expect delusion, in future, would be more difficult.

6. After such a display to the public of depraved artifice and injurious and unfeeling deception, the Government might reasonably hope, that a sense of the misery brought on them by delusion should prevent the great body of the people from listening to any one who should attempt in future to seduce them into rebellion against its beneficent rule. But it is also incumbent on it, from a consideration of the circumstances which have past, and the evil consequences which have ensued on the blind obedience which the people have thought due to their chiefs, instead of to the Sovereign of the country, to reform, by its inherent right, such parts of the practice of administration, as, by occasioning

Expedient to guard against a recurrence of the evil consequences, and to demonstrate to the people, that the Government is entitled to their obedience in superiority to the chiefs.

the subject to lose sight of the majesty of the royal government, made him feel wholly dependent on the power of the various chiefs, which, to be legal, could only be derived to them by delegation from the sovereign authority of the country.

Declaration of the supremacy of the British Crown, exercised through the Governor and his agents.

7. His Excellency the Governor, therefore, now calls to the mind of every person and of every class within these settlements, that the sovereign majesty of the King of Great Britain and Ireland, exercised by his representative the Governor of Ceylon and his agents in the Kandyan provinces, is the source alone from which all power emanates, and to which obedience is due: that no chief, who is not vested with authority or rank from this sovereign source, is entitled to obedience or respect; and that, without powers derived from Government, no one can exercise jurisdiction of any kind, or inflict the slightest punishment: and, finally, that every Kandyan, be he of the highest or lowest class, is secured in his life, liberty, and property, from encroachment of any kind, or by any person, and is only subject to the laws, which will be administered according to the ancient and established usages of the country, and in such manner, and by such authorities and persons, as in the name and on the behalf of His Majesty is herein declared.

No chief entitled to obedience or power, but when vested with authority by Government.

Equal rights of every Kandyan subject.

Delegation of the Governor's authority to the Board of Commissioners, and to resident agents in certain Dessavonies.

8. The general, executive, and judicial authority in the Kandyan provinces is delegated by His Excellency to the Board of Commissioners, and, under their general superintendence, to resident agents of Government in such Dessavonies of the said provinces in which it may please His Excellency to place such agents, with more or less authority or jurisdiction, as by their several instructions may be vested in them, and of which the present disposition and arrangement is hereinafter contained.

All chiefs to perform duty under the orders of the Board or other British Agents.

9. The Adigars, Dessaves, and all other chiefs and inferior headmen, shall perform duty to Government under the orders of the said Board of Commissioners and British Agents, and not otherwise.

No person to execute office, but under written appointments, signed by the Governor for superior chiefs, and by the Resident for inferior headmen; or provisionally, by agents in the Dessavonies; except in villages allotted to personal service of Dessaves.

10. No person shall be considered entitled to execute office, either of the higher or lower class of headmen, unless thereto appointed by a written instrument, signed, in respect to superior chiefs, by His Excellency the Governor, and for inferior headmen, by the Honourable the Resident, or provisionally, by any agent of Government thereto duly authorised, excepting in certain villages or departments which will be allotted for personal services to the Dessaves, in which the Dessave shall, as before, have the sole privilege of making appointments.

Honours to be paid to chiefs as before, except as under:

11. Honours shall be paid to all classes of chiefs entitled to the same under the former government, in so far as the same is consistent with the abolition which the British Government is resolved to effect, of all degrading forms whereto both chiefs and people were subjected under the ancient tyranny, and

Prostrations abolished.

which a liberal administration abhors. All prostrations, therefore, from or to any person, including the Governor, are henceforth positively, as they were before virtually, and in fact, abolished; and the necessity which existed that chiefs or others, coming into the presence of the Sovereign Authority, should remain on their knees, is also abrogated. But all chiefs and other persons coming before, meeting, or passing any British officer, civil or military, of rank and authority in the island of Ceylon, shall give up the middle of the road, and, if sitting, rise and make a suitable obeisance, which will be always duly acknowledged and returned.

Kneeling in presence of the sovereign authority abrogated.

Respect to be paid to British officers of rank by chiefs and others.

Respect to His Majesty's portrait in the Hall of Audience; and to authority presiding in courts of justice.

Attendance on the Governor in travelling.

12. It is also in this respect directed, that on entering the Hall of Audience, every person shall make obeisance to the portrait of His Majesty there suspended; and as well there, as in any other court of justice, to the presiding authority: and it is further directed, that when His Excellency the Governor, as His Britannic Majesty's representative, travels, he shall be attended by all the persons in office belonging to each province, in manner as they attended the former kings of Kandy; except that the Dessaves may always use palanquins beyond the river Mahavillaganga, within which limit the Adigars only have this privilege: and that when any of the members of His Majesty's Council, or the Commissioners for the Kandyan provinces, or the Commanding Officer of the troops in the Kandyan provinces, travel into any province on duty, they be met and attended in such province, in the same manner as the great Dessaves were and are to be attended in their provinces; likewise, the Resident Agents, and the officers commanding the troops in each province, are, in their provinces, to be similarly attended, and receive like honours.

Attendance on other officers of Government travelling on duty.

Salute by sentries to the First and Second Adigars.

Respect by Europeans;

By natives.

Respect to other chiefs.

13. The chiefs holding the high offices of First and Second Adigar will be received by all sentries whom they may pass in the day, with carried arms; and by all soldiers off duty, or other Europeans, or persons of European extraction, by touching their caps or taking off their hats; and by all natives, whether Kandyans or not, by rising from their seats, leaving the middle of the street clear, and bowing to the Adigars as they pass: and to all other Dessaves and other chiefs, all natives coming into their presence, meeting, or passing them, are to make a proper inclination of the body, in acknowledgment of their rank.

Attendance on Adigars, &c.

14. The Adigars, Dessaves, and other chiefs, shall further be entitled to proper attendance of persons of the different departments, in such numbers as shall be determined by His Excellency on the report of the Board of Commissioners; provided that where such persons are not belonging to the villages or departments allotted to the Adigar or Dessaves, the application for their attendance, when required, must be made to the Resident in Kandy, or to

the Agents of Government, in the provinces in which such Agents may be stationed.

Persons entitled to sit in Hall of Audience, or in presence of British Agents.

15. The persons entitled to sit in the Hall of Audience, or in the presence of the Agents of Government, are those chiefs only who bear commissions signed by the Governor, or to whom special licence may by the same authority be given to that effect. Of these, only the two Adigars or persons having the Governor's letter of licence, can sit on chairs; the others on benches covered with mats, of different heights, according to their relative ranks, in the courts hereinafter-mentioned of the Agents of Government: when the assessors are Mohattales or Corales, they may sit on mats on the ground.

Respect to priests, and processions of Budhoo religion.

General protection to all other religions.

Erection of places of worship under the Governor's licence.

16. As well the priests as all the ceremonies and processions of the Budhoo religion, shall receive the respect which in former times was shown them: at the same time, it is in no wise to be understood, that the protection of Government is to be denied to the peaceable exercise, by all other persons, of the religion which they respectively profess, or to the erection, under due licence from His Excellency, of places of worship in proper situations.

Fees on appointments abolished; except in temple-villages.

All taxes and duties abolished;

except a general tax on paddy-land, of a portion of the produce.

17. The Governor abolishes all fees payable for appointments, either to Government or to any chief, excepting for appointments in the temple-villages, which will be made by the Resident, on the recommendation of the Dewe nileme or Basnaike nilemes appointed by the Governor; the Dewe nileme or the Basnaike nileme receiving the usual fee. Also, all duties payable heretofore to the Gabbedawas aramudale awudege, and all other duties or taxes whatsoever, are abolished, save and except that now declared and enacted, being a tax on all paddy-lands of a portion of the annual produce, under the following modifications and exceptions, and according to the following rates.

General rate of tax fixed at one-tenth of the annual produce.

18. The general assessment of tax on the entire paddy-lands of the Kandyan provinces, is fixed at one-tenth of the annual produce, to be delivered by the proprietor or cultivator, at such convenient storehouse in every province or subdivision of a province, as shall be, with due regard to the interests of the subject, appointed by or under the instructions of the Revenue Agent.

In certain districts, which have stood firm in loyalty, the tax reduced to 1-14th.

19. To mark the just sense which His Excellency has of the loyalty and good conduct of the chiefs and people of Oodanoora, the Four Korles, the Three Korles, and the following Korles of Suffragam; to wit, Kooroowiti Korle, Nawadoon Korle, Colonna Korle, Kukula Korle, Atakalau Korle, the Uduwak Gampaha of Kadewatte Korle, the Medde Korle, except the villages Udagamme, Gonilande, Kolutotte, Golettetotte, Mollemore, Piengiria, and Mulgamma; and the following korles of the Seven Korles; viz. Tirigandahaye, excepting the villages Hewapolla, Katoopittiye, and Zorrewatere; Oodapola Korle, Kattugampaha Korle, Oodookaka, Kattugampola Korle, Medapattoo, Petigal Korle, Yagame Korle, Rakawah Pattoo Korle, Anganme

Korle; Yatekuha Korle, and of the villages Pubilia, Kougahawelle, and Nikawelle, lying in the Oodoogodde Korle of Matele: the Governor declares that the rate of taxation in these provinces or korles shall only be one-fourteenth part of the annual produce.

All lands forfeited in rebellion, and which may be restored to the former owners, to pay one-fifth.

20. But, on the contrary, that it may be known that persons who are leaders in revolt or disobedience shall meet punishment, all lands which may have been declared forfeited by the misconduct of the proprietors, shall, if by the mercy of Government restored to the former owners, pay a tax of one-fifth of the annual produce.

Temple-lands exempted from taxation.

Reservation of gratuitous service from certain inhabitants of temple-villages.

21. The Governor, desirous of showing the adherence of Government to its stipulations in favour of the religion of the people, exempts all lands which now are the property of temples, from all taxation whatever; but, as certain inhabitants of those villages are liable to perform fixed gratuitous services also to the Crown, this obligation is to continue unaffected.

Lands belonging to certain loyal chiefs exempted from tax.

22. All lands, also, now belonging to the following chiefs, whose loyalty and adherence to the lawful government merits favour; viz.

Mollegodde maha nileme;
Mollegodde nileme;
Ratwatte nileme;
Kadoogamoone nileme;
Dehigamme nileme;
Mulligamme nileme, lately Dessave of Welasse;
Eknilligodde nileme;
Mahawalletene nileme;
Doloswalle nileme;
Eheyleyagodde nileme;
Katugaha the elder;
Katugaha the younger;
Damboolane nileme;
Godeagedere nileme;
Gonegodde nileme, formerly Adikaran of Bintenne;

shall be free of duty during their lives; and that their heirs shall enjoy the same free of duty, excepting with regard to such as paid pingo-duty, which shall now and hereafter pay one-tenth to the Government of the annual produce, unless when exempted under the next clause.

Lands of chiefs holding office, exempted during their continuance in office.

23. All lands belonging to chiefs holding offices, either of the superior or inferior class, and of inferior headmen, shall, during the time they are in office, be free of duty.

Lands of cinnamon-peelers exempted from taxation:

24. All lands belonging to persons of the castes or departments allotted to the cutting of cinnamon, shall be free of duty: also lands held by persons, for

which they are bound to cultivate or aid in the culture of the royal lands: and also the lands of such persons who may be allotted to the performance of personal service to the Dessaves by the Board of Commissioners; and of those who perform Katepurüle or Attepattoo service gratuitously; it being well understood, that the persons last-mentioned have no right or authority whatever to exact or receive fees or fines of any kind when sent on public duty, which they are required to perform expeditiously and impartially.

Also of cultivators of royal lands: Also of attendants allotted to Dessaves; Katepurule and Attepattoo people.

25. The Veddas who possess no paddy-lands shall continue to deliver to Government the usual tribute in wax.

Veddas to continue tribute of wax.

26. All presents to the Governor, or other British authorities, are strictly prohibited. In travelling, every officer, civil or military, chiefs, detachments of troops, or other servants of Government, on notice being given of their intended march or movement, are to be supplied with the provisions of the country in reasonable quantity, and on payment being made for the same at the current price.

All presents prohibited. Provisions to British officers, chiefs, troops, or other servants of Government travelling, to be furnished for payment.

27. All fees on hearing of cases, to Dessaves or others, except as hereafter mentioned, which are for the benefit of Government, shall be and are abolished.

Fees on hearing cases abolished.

28. The services of the Adigars, Dessaves, and other superior chiefs, to Government, shall be compensated by fixed monthly salaries, in addition to the exemption of their lands from taxation.

Remuneration for service of superior chiefs.

29. The services of the inferior chiefs shall be compensated as above, by exemption from taxation, and that they also receive one-twentieth part of the revenue-paddy which they shall collect from the people under them, to be allotted in such portion as the Board of Commissioners shall, under the authority of Government, regulate.

Remuneration to inferior chiefs.

30. All persons shall be liable to service for Government on the requisition of the Board of Commissioners and Agents of Government, according to their former customs and families, or tenure of their lands, on payment being made for their labour; it being well understood, that the Board of Commissioners, under His Excellency's authority, may commute such description of service as, under present circumstances, is not usefully applicable to the public good, to such other as may be beneficial: and provided further, that the holding of lands duty-free shall be considered the payment for the service of the Katepurule and Attepattoo departments, and persons allotted to the Dessave's service; and also for the service to Government of certain persons of the temple-villages, and in part for those which cut cinnamon; and also that the duty of clearing and making roads, and putting up and repairing bridges, be considered a general gratuitous service falling on the districts through which the roads pass, or wherein the bridges lie; and that the attendance on

All persons liable to general service for payment.

the Great Feast, which certain persons were bound to give, be continued to be given punctually and gratuitously. The Washermen, also, shall continue to put up white cloths in the temples and for the chiefs, gratuitously.

Kadawettes, and services attendant, abolished.

31. All Kadawettes and ancient barriers throughout the country shall be from henceforward discontinued and removed, and the establishments belonging to them for their maintenance and defence abolished; the services of the persons usually employed therein being applied to such other more beneficial purpose as the Board of Commissioners shall determine.

Rules for service of Kunamaduwe, Talpataweduna Karias, and Pandan Karias.

32. And it being necessary to provide rules for the service of certain persons who were to perform duty to the person of the King of Kandy; viz. the Kunamaduwe or palanquin bearers, the Talepataweduna-karia, or talpat-bearers, and Pandan-karias, or torch-bearers; it is ordered by the Governor, that such persons, being paid for the same, shall be bound to serve, in their respective capacities, the Governor, the members of His Majesty's Council, any General-officer on the staff of this army, the Commissioners for Kandyan Affairs, the Secretary for the Kandyan Provinces, and the officer commanding the troops in the Interior.

Powers of Agents of Government to punish neglect of duty.

33. And for ensuring the due execution of all the above ordinances relative to the collection of the revenue, and performance of public duty, by all chiefs and others, His Excellency empowers and directs, that the Board of Commissioners in Kandy, collectively or in their several departments, and the Agents of Government in the provinces, shall punish all disobedience and neglect, by suspension or dismissal from office, fine, or imprisonment, as particular cases may require and deserve; provided, that no person holding the Governor's commission may be absolutely dismissed, but by the same authority; and no other chief, but by the authority of the Honourable the Resident; but as well the Commissioners as other agents, duly authorised by instructions from the Governor, may suspend chiefs of the superior or inferior order, on their responsibility, for disobedience or neglect of the orders or interest of Government; reporting immediately, as the case may require to the Governor or the Resident, their proceedings for approval or reversal.

Details of judicial administrations in cases wherein Kandyans are defendants.

34. And in order that justice may be duly, promptly, and impartially administered throughout the Kandyan provinces to all classes, His Excellency the Governor is pleased to declare his pleasure to be touching the same, and to delegate and assign the following jurisdiction to the public officers of Government, for hearing and determining cases wherein Kandyans are concerned as defendants, either civil or criminal.

Powers of Agents of Government sitting alone: in civil cases; in criminal cases.

35. Every Agent of Government shall have power and jurisdiction to hear and determine, alone, civil cases wherein the object of dispute shall not be land, and shall not exceed in value fifty rix-dollars; and also criminal cases of

inferior description, such as common assaults, petty thefts, and breaches of the peace; with power of awarding punishment, not exceeding a fine of rix-dollars twenty-five, corporal punishment with a cat-and-nine-tails or rattan, not exceeding thirty lashes, and imprisonment, with or without labour, not exceeding two months; to which terms of imprisonment and fine, such agents are also limited in punishing neglects or disobedience of orders, according to the provisions above detailed.

Powers of Judicial Commissioners, sitting alone.

36. The Second, or Judicial Commissioner, shall, sitting alone, have power to hear and determine civil cases wherein the object in dispute shall not be land, and shall not exceed rix-dollars one hundred in value; and also criminal cases of inferior description, with powers of punishment as in the last clause conferred on Agents of Government.

Courts to be held by Judicial Commissioners and Agents duly authorized, to consist of themselves and two Kandyan assessors, to try all civil cases and all criminal cases, except treason, murder, and homicide.

37. The Second, or Judicial Commissioner, and such Agents of Government in the provinces to whom the Governor shall delegate the same by his instructions, shall hold at Kandy and in the provinces, a court for the trial of all other civil cases, and of criminal cases, excepting treason, murder, or homicide; with powers in criminal matters to assess any punishment short of death or mutilation of limbs or member: which court shall consist, in K ndy, of the Second Commissioner, and two or more chiefs; and in the provinces, of the Agent of Government, and one or more Dessaves of the province, and one or more Mohottales or principal Korales, so as there shall be at least two Kandyan assessors, or two Mohottales or Korales where no Dessave can attend.

Mode of decision in courts of Agent of Government.

Reference in certain cases to court of Judicial Commissioner.

38. The decisions of the courts in the provinces shall be by the Agent of Government, the Kandyan assessors giving their advice; and where the opinion of the majority of such assessors differs from the opinion of the Agent of Government, there shall be no immediate decision; but the proceedings shall be transferred to the court of the Second Commissioner, who may either decide on the proceedings had in the original court, or send for the parties and witnesses, and re-hear the case, or take or order the agent to take further evidence, and shall decide the same.

Appeals to Judicial Commissioner.

39. Appeals also shall lie from the decisions of such Agents to the court aforesaid of the Second Commissioner, in civil cases, if the appeal is entered before the Agent in ten days from his decree, and the object in dispute be either land or personal property, exceeding rix-dollars one hundred and fifty in value; in which case execution shall stay, and the proceedings be transmitted to the said Commissioner's court, which shall and may proceed in the same as in the cases mentioned in the former article. That appeals also may be allowed upon order of the Governor or the Board of Commissioners, although not entered in ten days, if application is made in a year.

Mode of decision in court of Judicial Commissioner.

Reference in certain cases through the Board of Commissioners to the Governor.

Appeals, to the Governor.

40. The decisions in the court of the Second Commissioner shall be by the said Commissioner, the Kandyan assessors giving their advice; and if the opinion of the majority of such assessors shall be different from that of the Second Commissioner, the case, whether originally instituted, or in appeal or reference from the Agent of Government, shall be transferred to the Collective Board, and by them reported on to His Excellency the Governor, whose decision thereon shall be conclusive and without appeal; but that in civil cases decided by the Second Commissioner, either in original or brought before him by appeal or reference, appeal shall lie to the Governor, if entered before the Second Commissioner in ten days from his decree; and if the object in dispute be either land or personal property, exceeding in value one hundred and fifty rix-dollars; in which case execution of the decree shall be stayed, and the proceedings be transmitted to the Governor. But appeal may be allowed by order of the Governor, on application within one year from the date of the decree.

Disposal of appeals by the Governor.

41. Appeals to the Governor will be disposed of by His Excellency in correspondence with the Board of Commissioners, according to justice.

Limitation as to execution of sentences in criminal cases.

42. In criminal cases, no sentence, either by the Second Commissioner or the Agents of Government, shall be carried into effect, if it awards corporal punishment exceeding one hundred lashes, imprisonment, with or without chains or labour, exceeding four months, or fine exceeding fifty rix-dollars; unless after reference to the Governor through the Board of Commissioners, which will report on the case and sentence, and after His Excellency's confirmation of such sentence.

The Resident may preside in court of Judicial Commissioner, or hold a separate court.

43. The Honourable the Resident may, when he thinks needful, assist and preside in the court of the Judicial Commissioner; and that the Resident may also hold a court for hearing cases, to consist of himself and two Kandyan chiefs or assessors, under the provisions respecting references and appeals, and limitation of execution of sentences in criminal cases, prescribed to the Judicial Commissioner; and to preserve regularity, the records of such the Resident's judicial proceedings in each case shall be deposited with the Judicial Commissioner on the conclusion of the same.

Mode of proceeding in cases of treason, murder, or homicide.

44. In all cases of treason, murder, or homicide, the trial shall be before the courts of the Resident or of the Second Commissioner and his Kandyan assessors, whose opinion as to the guilt of the defendant, and the sentence to be passed on any one convicted, is to be reported, through the Board of Commissioners, with their opinion also, to His Excellency the Governor, for his determination.

Jurisdiction where superior chiefs are defendants, reserved to Second Commissioner.

45. All cases criminal or civil, in which a superior chief is defendant, shall be originally instituted and heard before the Resident or the Second Commis-

sioner: that all other cases shall be instituted before the jurisdiction in which the defendant resides. Provided, that in civil cases the plaintiff may appoint an attorney to prosecute in his behalf: as may the defendant to defend his case.

Jurisdiction in other cases.

46. In civil cases the losing party may be, by the Second Commissioner or Agent of Government, discretionally ordered to pay a sum to Government of one-twentieth part of the value of the object in dispute, not exceeding in any case rix-dollars fifty.

Assessment of fines in civil suits.

47. The First and Second Adigar shall and may execute civil jurisdiction over all Katepurules and their property, subject to appeal to the Second Commissioner; and also over such other persons and property as the Governor may, by special warrant, assign to the jurisdiction of either of these two great officers, subject to appeal as aforementioned; and that the Second Commissioner, or any Agent of Government, may refer cases for hearing, and report to him in his court, to the Adigars, Dessaves, or Mohottales.

Civil jurisdiction of First and Second Adigars.

48. The Adigars shall have jurisdiction to punish disobedience of their orders, and petty offences, by inflicting corporal punishment not exceeding fifty strokes with the open hand, or twenty-five with a rattan, on the back, or by awarding imprisonment for a term not exceeding fourteen days.

Criminal jurisdiction of Adigars;

49. The Dessaves or chiefs holding the Governor's Commission may also punish offences by corporal punishment, not exceeding twenty-five strokes with the open hand, and of imprisonment for a term not exceeding seven days; and similarly the principal Mohottales, Lieunerales, and Korales, being in office, may inflict corporal punishment for offences on persons over whom they might have exercised such jurisdiction under the former government, not exceeding ten strokes with the open hand, and may imprison such persons for a term not exceeding three days; provided that the several persons on whom the above power is exercised, shall be duly and lawfully subject to the orders of such Adigar, Dessave, Chief, Mohottale, Lieunerale, or Korale; and that no such power shall be exercised on persons holding office, or on persons of the Low Country, foreigners, or on moormen of the Kandyan provinces; and provided that in all cases where imprisonment is awarded for a term exceeding three days, the prisoner be sent, with a note of the sentence, to the Second Commissioner or the nearest Agent of Government, to be confined.

of Dessaves;

of Mohottales and Korales.

50. To ensure a due and uniform administration of justice, it is declared and enacted by His Excellency, that all evidence before the Resident, the Second Commissioner, or other Agent of Government, in a civil or criminal case, shall be taken on oath; which oath, in the case of Kandyan or Hindoo witnesses, shall be administered after the evidence is taken, (the witness being previously warned that such will be the case,) at the nearest dewale, before a

Mode of receiving evidence, and administering oath to Pagans.

commissioner or commissioners ordered by the court to see that the witness declares solemnly that the evidence he has given is the truth, the whole truth, and nothing but the truth; that no exemption can lie to this mode of giving evidence, except where Budhist priests are examined; and that every person, except a priest, giving evidence, must stand while he delivers it.

Jurisdiction over foreigners,

51. The people of the Low Country, and foreigners coming into the Kandyan provinces, shall continue subject to the civil and criminal jurisdiction of the Agents of Government alone, with such extension as His Excellency may, by special additional instructions, vest in such Agents, and under the limitation as to execution of sentences in criminal cases hereinbefore provided, as to Kandyans, in the 42d clause, until reference to the Governor through the Board of Commissioners, excepting in cases of treason, murder, and homicide, in which such persons shall be subject to the same jurisdiction now provided for Kandyans; and that the same line shall be pursued in cases wherein a Kandyan moorman shall be defendant.

and over Kandyan moormen.

Confirmation of privileges of moormen.

52. And His Excellency the Governor takes this occasion to confirm the provisions of his Proclamation of the 2d March, 1818, respecting the moormen; but to explain that they are nevertheless, when living in the villages wherein also Kandyans reside, to obey the orders of the Kandyan chief or headman of the village, on pain of punishment by the Agent of Government for disobedience, notwithstanding any thing in the said proclamation contained.

Exclusive local jurisdiction of Board of Commissioners.

53. According to such known rules, justice will be accessible to every man, high or low, rich or poor, with all practicable convenience, and the confident knowledge of impartiality of decision. And to give effect to this plan for the administration of justice, and to collect the public revenue, and ensure the execution of public duties, His Excellency is pleased to assign to the immediate controul and exercise of jurisdiction of the Board of Commissioners the following provinces: the Four Korles; Matele; Oodapalata, including Upper Bulatgamme; Oodanoora; Yatenoora; Tumpanne; Harissiapattoo; Doombera; Hewahette; Kotmale; the part of Walapana lying west of the Kuda and Ooma oya; and the Hooroole, Tamirawane, Maminiya, and Ollagalla pattoos of Nuwera Kalawiye; in all which the higher judicial duties, and the collection of revenues, will be made by the Commissioners of the Board; but in those limits there will be besides, two Agents of Government to hear minor cases; at Attapittia in the Four Korles, and at Nalende in Matele.

Agents of Government to hear minor cases in Four Korles and Matele.

Powers of Agent of Government in Ouva.

54. There will be an Agent of Government resident in Ouva, to whose immediate jurisdiction are assigned the provinces of Ouva, Welasse, Bentenne, Weyeloowa, and the royal village of Madulla: all civil and criminal cases will be heard by him, with the exceptions mentioned, and under the rules detailed above. He will give orders to collect revenue, perform public service, suspend

and punish headmen for disobedience, and exercise general powers of government in those limits, subject to the superintendence of the Board of Commissioners.

55. Similarly, an Agent of Government in the Seven Korles will exercise jurisdiction over that province and the northern part of Nuwere Kalawiye. An Agent of Government in Saffragam will perform like duties in that province. An Agent of Government will reside in the Three Korles with like powers; and the Collector of Trincomalee will hear all cases, and collect the revenue, and cause public service to be performed in the same manner in Tamaukadewe.

Similar in the Seven Korles;

Three Korles;

of Collector of Trincomalee in Tamaukadewe.

56. In all matters not provided for by this Proclamation, or other Proclamations heretofore promulgated by the authority of the British Government, His Excellency reserves to himself and his successors the power of reforming abuses, and making such provision as is necessary, beneficial, or desirable. He also reserves full power to alter the present provisions as may appear hereafter necessary and expedient; and he requires, in His Majesty's name, all officers civil and military, all Adigars, Dessaves, and other chiefs, and all other His Majesty's subjects, to be obedient, aiding, and assisting in the execution of these or other his orders, as they shall answer the contrary at their peril.

Reservation of powers of making further provisions and alterations.

Enjoining general obedience.

Given at Kandy, in the said island of Ceylon, this twenty-first day of November, one thousand eight hundred and eighteen.

By His Excellency's command,

(Signed) GEO. LUSIGNAN,
Secretary for Kandyan Provinces.

GOD SAVE THE KING.

GENERAL INDEX

OF

NAMES AND SUBJECTS;

COMPRISING ALSO,

UNDER THE WORD "CEYLON," A COMPLETE

TABLE OF CONTENTS.

A.

I.

K.

L.

M.

P.

Q.

R.

W

Y.

Z.

CONTENTS OF THE APPENDIX.

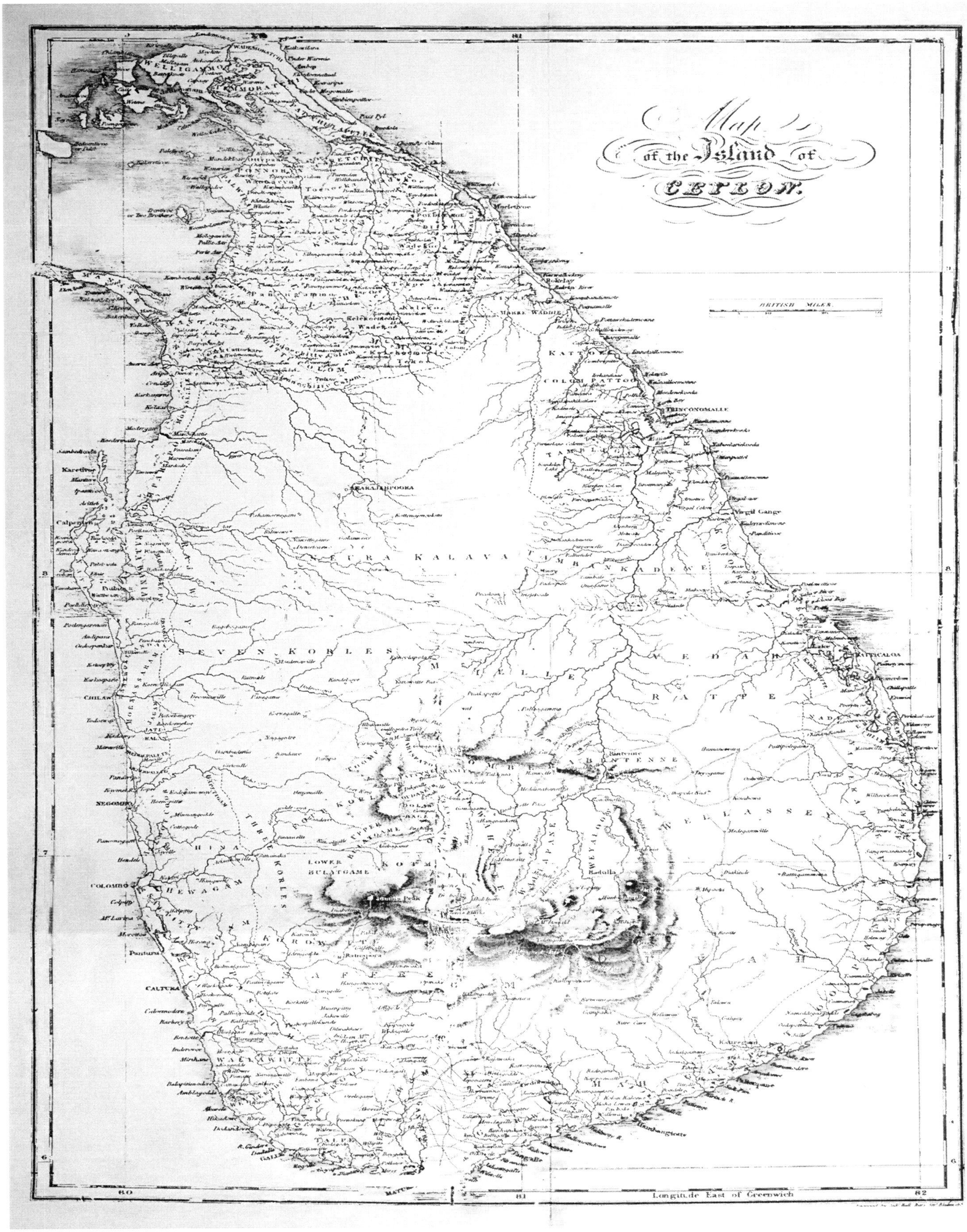
Map of the Island of CEYLON.
BRITISH MILES
TRINCONOMALLE
BATTICALOA
COLOMBO
NEGOMBO
CHILAW
CALTURA
Badulla
SEVEN KORLES
WELLASSEY
Longitude East of Greenwich
80
81
82